THE VISUAL J++ HANDBOOK

THE VISUAL J++ HANDBOOK

Chris H. Pappas
William H. Murray

AP Professional

AP Professional is a Division of Academic Press

Boston San Diego New York
London Sydney Tokyo Toronto

AP PROFESSIONAL

An Imprint of ACADEMIC PRESS, INC.
A Division of HARCOURT BRACE & COMPANY

ORDERS (USA and Canada): 1-800-3131-APP or APP@ACAD.COM
AP Professional Orders: 6277 Sea Harbor Dr., Orlando, FL 32821-9816

Europe/Middle East/Africa: 0-11-44 (0) 181-300-3322
Orders: AP Professional 24-28 Oval Rd., London NW1 7DX

Japan/Korea: 03-3234-3911-5
Orders: Harcourt Brace Japan, Inc., Ichibancho Central Building 22-1, Ichibancho Chiyoda-Ku, Tokyo 102

Australia: 02-517-8999
Orders: Harcourt Brace & Co. Australia, Locked Bag 16, Marrickville, NSW 2204 Australia

Other International: (407) 345-3800
AP Professional Orders: 6277 Sea Harbor Dr., Orlando FL 32821-9816

Editorial: 1300 Boylston St., Chestnut Hill, MA 02167 (617)232-0500

Web: http://www.apnet.com/approfessional

This book is printed on acid-free paper. ∞

United Kingdom Edition published by
ACADEMIC PRESS LIMITED
24–28 Oval Road, London NW1 7DX

ISBN 0-12-511915-1

Printed in the United States of America
96 97 98 99 IP 9 8 7 6 5 4 3 2 1

To Dr. Joseph M. Newmark

—Chris H. Pappas

To Dr. Frank X. Sutman

—William H. Murray

Contents

Chapter 3: Basic Language Features 65

Chapter 4: JAVA Programming Fundamentals 105

Chapter 1

JAVA—A HISTORY AND INTRODUCTION

If you have picked this book off the shelf, you already know the latest buzz word, *Java*. Unless you work at Sun Microsystems, Inc. (birthplace of the Java language), the only association you probably have with the word Java is a steaming cup of dark brown liquid that helps you meet your deadlines. In a way, this is the perfect metaphor for the Java language—a tool given to programmers, designed to help you meet your programming deadlines!

WHO INVENTED JAVA?

Knowing *who* invented a programming language is pivotal to understanding the capabilities of that language. Successful *new* languages solve problems left unresolved by older technologies. With today's accelerated rate of software and hardware development, there are now many programming problems that older languages, such as C and C++, are incapable of solving. These languages were originally developed by Dennis Ritchie and Bjarne Stroustrup to design operating systems (on the DEC PDP-11 with UNIX) and to provide the modular, portable, reusable, and up-to-speed implementations generated by object-oriented technologies. In many ways C and C++ are inappropriate for today's state-of-the-art development environment—the Internet.

Java was developed by a small programming team headed by James Gosling at Sun Microsystems, Inc., in Mountain View, California. The team's goal was to solve the problem of designing a language for programming consumer products. This new language did not necessarily have to be break-neck fast at run-time, but it did need to work on a diverse set of devices and require minimal hardware overhead.

For example, a microprocessor-controlled VCR does not need a Pentium or PowerPC microprocessor to calculate recording start and stop times. However, with today's burgeoning interconnections, you will soon be able to dial your home phone and instruct your telephone-connected VCR to catch a late-breaking story. This capability, in contrast to recording start and stop times, requires a sophisticated computer algorithm. Consumers will want this feature but will not want to pay hundreds of dollars more for it.

Many of today's computer languages are not well suited to programming consumer products. The biggest problem with these languages is that they all have to be compiled for a particular computer chip. Not only does the original source file need compiling to a specific platform; but with new chip designs constantly being developed, existing software must be recompiled in order to take full advantage of new hardware advancements.

There is another reason why you may have to recompile, or worse, rewrite source code. What if the compiler itself is updated? For example, once a C/C++ program is compiled, it is not easily adapted to use new software libraries. Often programs have to be rewritten and recompiled from scratch when the libraries change. This requirement would make it difficult for a manufacturer to patch or update the program in your microprocessor-controlled lawn-mower. One of today's solutions to this scenario is Java.

As tradition has it, the name for this new language was the direct result of the development team's frustrating, afternoon-long, name-the-language brainstorming session. James Gosling had originally called this new language Oak because of the tree outside his office window, but the name was already a registered programming language. The ensuing coffee break at the local coffee shop led to the new name—Java! The official announcement of the Java technology was made in May 1995 at the SunWorld conference in San Francisco.

WHY DO YOU NEED JAVA?

Do you want to *get* a job? Do you want to *keep* your job? Do you want to have *fun* programming for a change? Do you want to use a language that's *easy to learn*? Do you want a *state-of-the-art Internet presence*? Then YOU need Java!

While Java was originally designed to program consumer devices, its real horsepower breaks the gate when you use it to program for the Internet. Whether you are working for IBM, Microsoft, Apple, or a local distributor, or whether you are one of hundreds of thousands of individuals with a home page on the World Wide Web, you will quickly become addicted to the fun and useful features Java can add to your Internet presence.

What Is HotJava?

In early 1993 the Internet started transitioning from a text-based to a graphical interface. The Java development team immediately realized that a hardware-neutral language, such as Java, would be ideal for programming on the World Wide Web. Java code runs on the many types of computers hooked into the Internet, from PCs to Macs, running Windows, OS/2 Warp, or UNIX. This realization led to the development of a Web browser called *HotJava*, which was the first Web browser capable of supporting Java. When most people refer to HotJava, they actually mean Java applets, which are programs written in Java and included in HTML pages. The HotJava browser is similar to other popular browsers in the way it displays pages and allows you to navigate the Web.

What Are Java's Strengths?

Java's major strengths are that it is a relatively fast, small, and reliable language that is hardware-neutral. This means that you can write a single Java source file that is compiled and shipped "as is" to any Java-supported architecture. Java is similar to C, C++, Ada, and Pascal. Java's small size makes it easy to learn from scratch, and especially easy for those programmers already familiar with the C and C++ languages.

Java even goes one step further in that it solves, or actually prevents, many of the most nefarious sources of bugs found in C and C++ applications, namely memory leaks. Finally, not only is Java simple to use, but it is object-oriented, statically typed, multithreaded, robust, secure, extensible, and fun!

What Are Java's Weaknesses?

Look out any time you meet a programmer who tells you language *XYZ* is *the* de-facto standard, *the* language that solves all your programming needs, and *the* language for today and into the next millennium. The gurus at Sun Microsystems would have us believe that Java fits this description. However, no such language has ever been invented, nor, with the pace of techno-evolution, will it *ever* be invented. Java is not for everyone or for every application. It will not replace *any* language used today. There are four major weaknesses to the Java language:

1. In most cases, Java will be used only to enhance a World Wide Web presence. You can use Java to design standalone applications, but why learn a new language when you are probably already well versed in an existing language that serves this purpose?
2. Java does not run on *all* microprocessors. As of this writing, it runs on IBM PCs and IBM compatibles, Macintoshes, and UNIX machines, which are the microprocessors for which Sun Microsystems has translated the Java language.
3. The more complex your Java application (in the sense of multimedia, multithreaded applets) is, the slower its run-time performance will be.
4. Because it is *similar* to other languages such as C/C++, Ada, and Pascal, yet *different,* Java throws a curve to any programmer experienced in these other languages. A Java feature may not necessarily behave the same as its predecessor in a language you know.

What Can I Use Java For?

You can use Java for just about anything, from standalone Java applications to multimedia World Wide Web Java applets. For example, publishing companies are now looking seriously at publishing material via the Internet. In the past, you read magazines you held in your hand; in the future, this same material will be displayed on-line. The catalogs you currently receive in the mail may also soon be published on-line.

Other companies, such as National Semiconductor Corporation, have found that making real-time updates of technical information for their 30,000 products available on-line has dramatically improved sales. Companies such as Market Vision Corporation (security trading) haven't missed a beat in this fast-paced arena of Internet opportunities. This company has incorporated a Java applet front-end that communicates directly with its Link product, which provides up-to-the-minute stock information. Because of this platform-independent solution, any user with an Internet browser can access this information.

Though Java is capable of far more, its primary use will be to quickly add punch and pizzazz to World Wide Web home pages. This book will show you just how easily and enjoyably this can be accomplished.

JAVA AND COM

Microsoft is committed to delivering top-of-the-line Java development tools as well as reference implementation of the Java Virtual Machine for Windows platforms. Microsoft's COM (Component Object Model) is the cornerstone of the ActiveX™ platform, providing tight integration between Java and COM.

Tip: ActiveX™ controls is just a new name for OLE controls. Any Java applet can now be plugged into any application that supports ActiveX™ controls, including Visual Basic, Access, Delphi, and Power Builder.

While developed completely independently of one another, Java integrates extremely well with COM. This is unusual: often in computing, two diametrically opposed technologies are forced to coexist, usually by brute force. COM and Java, however, appear to be completely independent on the surface but in fact are complementary to one another. With this coactive relationship, Microsoft is helping customers and developers leverage hundreds of person-years of effort put into development tools, training, applications, and other infrastructure while still being able to take advantage of new and exciting technologies such as Java.

Because the Microsoft Java VM (Virtual Machine) exposes Java applets as ActiveX™ controls and controls are scriptable, all Java applets running in a browser that supports the Java VM are scriptable as well. Java supports the creation of "thread-safe" objects and COM allows these objects to be executed remotely in an efficient manner; as a result, Java is an awesome tool for creating server applications.

COM Development with Java

Java is a state-of-the-art programming language that takes the run-of-the-mill and error-prone aspects of COM development and makes them easy to implement. Enabling Java to create and use COM objects makes it a great programming language for COM.

All Java-class COM objects are **public** and can be called remotely just like any other COM object. COM and DCOM are really the same thing. The main difference between COM and DCOM is the length of the wire between the two software components. Any COM object can be used remotely or locally—a characteristic called location independence. Thus, any COM object developed in Java can be executed on a remote server as well as on the client machine.

All COM objects, regardless of the point of origin, appear to a Java program as standard Java class objects. As a result, Java COM objects do not need large class libraries that wrap existing objects. Also, there is no need for machine-generated "stubs." Instead, existing objects can simply be called directly.

Integrating COM with Java

The integration of Java and COM can be achieved by making changes to the Java VM (Virtual Machine); you do not need to add new keywords or constructs to the Java language itself. The pivotal capability that makes this possible is Java's multiple object interfaces. By integrating Java and COM technology, investments are preserved while new technologies are applied.

Integration of COM and Java does not interfere or conflict with the "spirit" of Java or COM in any way. For this reason, Java programs can call into any ActiveX™ component, whether it is a control, Microsoft Visual Basic, or Excel. Likewise, any ActiveX™ component can call into a Java component. There is no need for new programming models and additional layers that technologies such as CORBA bring to the table.

Note: The examples of Java-driven COM that are included in later chapters use compiler features of Microsoft's Java compiler, Visual J++. The details of the language integration are completely up to the compiler manufacturer. Other Java compiler vendors may expose Java/COM integration differently. However, the way that the compilers produce Java .class *files is standardized.*

Java, COM, and C/C++

Because Sun Microsystems has incorporated a design philosophy into Java product, which is respected by Microsoft, there are certain actions that Java-driven COM cannot do that C/C++-driven COM can. For example, Java-driven COM cannot restrict aggregation to a single aggregate object or restrict a set of types that can be used in a COM interface definition.

Java/COM Libraries

Microsoft J++ is shipped with a set of class libraries that provide the equivalent COM library API functionality, but the libraries are packaged and defined in such a way as to be natural for Java programmers to use. Visual J++ classes are provided for each of the following major COM technologies:

- Core COM library that maps to the API with names that are prefixed with Co.
- Monikers
- Standard utilities, such as StringFromGUID()
- Structured storage

The following list highlights those extensions provided by Visual J++ for implementing various ActiveX™ components as easily as inheriting from a particular base class:

- ActiveX™ controls and containers
- ActiveX™ DocObjs (Document Objects) and containers

Java/COM Security

For security purposes, Java applets running inside a Web browser such as HotJava are restricted from executing certain types of behaviors. For example, a Java applet cannot make a call into native code or call Java classes that are not verified by the Java byte code verifier. This is known as *sand boxing*. However, a call into arbitrary COM objects, whether locally or remotely from a Java applet, *is* calling native code. Therefore, this feature is disabled for applets.

The workaround involves secure digital signatures, which allow applets to recognize the COM as coming from a trusted source. If a Java applet is digitally signed, it *can* make COM calls. Notice that these concerns only exist for Java applets, not Java applications (see the following section, "Distinguishing Between Applications and Applets") or any other non-downloadable Java component.

Java/COM and Third-Party Developers

With Java/COM integration such a seamless part of the Microsoft VM, there is a potential bonanza for third-party object and tool libraries. Software layers on top of native Java code will enable developers to use more sophisticated tools to create Java programs as well as users to more easily build and incorporate Java applets into their Web pages.

Distinguishing Between Applications and Applets

Java *applications* are standalone Java programs that are run by using the Java interpreter, for example, from the command line:

```
c:\java\java myclass.class
```

The first few sample programs you write fall in this category.

Java *applets*, however, are run from inside a World Wide Web browser. A reference to an applet is embedded in a Web page using a special HTML (Hyper Text Markup Language) tag. You can think of HTML as being a visually static page of information that can include text, graphics, sounds, and video. The hypertext page also has "depth" if it contains hyperlinks connecting to other documents or resources. Java takes HTML one step further: the information on a Java page on the Web does not have to be visually static or limited to a predefined set of ways to interact with users. A Java-interpreted Web page transforms the user from being a passive viewer to being an active participant, with the ability to change what happens and then react to the information provided by the Web connection.

When a reader, using a Java-aware browser, loads a Web page with an applet in it, the browser downloads that applet from a Web server and executes it on the local system (the one running the browser).

Because Java applets run inside the Java browser, they have access to the same capabilities that the browser has; including sophisticated graphics, drawing, image processing, networking, and event handling. Java applications can also take advantage of these features, but they do not require them.

MAIN FEATURES OF THE JAVA LANGUAGE

You may have heard the phrase "something old, something new, something borrowed, something...." In a way, this describes Java. Java incorporates many of the programming fundamentals found in older programming languages such as Pascal and C. Java adds its own unique blend of new characteristics, such as firewall protection (determining resource access privileges for Java applets), and completes its formal definition by borrowing from object-oriented programming (OOP) philosophy. This section describes Java in greater detail.

Ease of Learning

Some things never change. While we all know that exercise is good for us, for example, most of us have trouble sticking to a regimented exercise routine. Likewise, while we all know that multi-tasking, object-oriented, GUI (Graphical User Interface) Window applications are state-of-the-art, their development demands the mastery of many new things, from OOP design philosophy to learning C++.

Many companies, relying on the human trait to resist anything new and/or difficult, have come to the programmer's rescue. Take, for instance, Borland's Delphi or Microsoft's Visual C++. These development tools take away some of the burden of Windows application development by presenting the programmer with a point-and-click environment in which the required code is automatically generated. From the programmer's perspective, these products replace the tedious Windows development phase with a product that is *fun* to use! The same holds true for Java.

Java is an easy-to-learn synthesis of many existing and successful languages, such as Pascal, Ada, C, and C++. For many programmers, this means that Java source code will already have a familiar look to it. From day one, Sun Microsystem's design goals were to keep Java small, simple, easy to write, easy to compile, easy to debug, and easy to learn. Keeping the language small also makes it more robust because there are fewer chances for programmers to make difficult-to-find mistakes. However, despite its size and simple design, Java still has a great deal of power and flexibility. Although Java looks similar to C and C++, most of the more complex parts of those languages have been excluded from Java, making the language simpler without sacrificing much of its bite.

Specifically, Java is missing C++'s pointers and the related topic of pointer arithmetic. Strings and arrays are real objects in Java. Memory management is automatic. To an experienced C/C++ programmer, these omissions may be difficult to accept; but to beginners or programmers who have worked in other languages, they make the Java language far easier to master.

A Language That Is Compiled and Interpreted

In the world of computer languages, at least until Java, there have been interpreted languages, such as BASIC, and many more languages that are compiled. (Technically, that Assembly Language source code is *assembled*.) You have probably never heard of a language that is both compiled and interpreted! Welcome to Java. You *compile* a Java source file into a platform-independent binary form, officially called *bytecode*. It is this bytecode file that is then *interpreted* by a platform-specific Java run-time environment.

This two-step process lets you develop and maintain a single source of Java code, generating the hardware-neutral compiled bytecode, which in turn runs on many platform-specific Java environments. For example, you develop a single Java application and compile it. You can then run the same application on a PC, UNIX, or Macintosh, as long as each has a platform-specific Java environment—one Java source file and many architectures.

Technically speaking, the compiled, binary bytecode file contains more compile-time data than is usually found in noninterpreted languages. This extra information is carried over and made available at run-time, providing checks for security, robustness, and even debugging. Most importantly, the interpretation phase of the binary bytecode frees developers from having to worry about the version mismatch problems that are so common to development environments. Java uses something similar to the UNIX make tool to resolve inconsistent definitions for module interfaces, thereby allowing developers to maintain a single source collection of Java code that easily moves to multiple targets. During interpolation, Java even provides dynamic behavior by allowing information to be included from the run-time environment.

Hardware Neutrality

One of the key advantages Java programs have over other programming languages, particularly in terms of systems that need to work on many different platforms, is *hardware neutrality*. Java is platform independent at both the source and binary levels. At the source level, Java's primitive data types have consistent sizes across all architectures. Java's standardized class libraries make it easy to write code that can be moved from machine to machine without the need to generate machine-specific versions.

Beyond source-level independence is Java's hardware neutral binary files, called bytecode, which run on multiple platforms without the need to recompile the source. You can use the compiled bytecode with the Java interpreter by itself (for Java applications), use the bytecode interpreter incorporated into HotJava, or use any other Java-capable browser (for Java applets), such as Netscape.

Portability

Java's hardware neutrality is one of the primary reasons why a Java program is so portable. However, another aspect of portability deals with Java's formal use of data structures or types in the language, such as integer, string, and floating point. This is possible because Java takes advantage of the IEEE standards for common data types of many computers.

For example, a Java float always complies with the IEEE 754 standard for floating-point numbers, with integers always being a 32-bit, signed twos complement value. Java's hardware-neutral bytecode also takes care of the memory mapping of low-byte at low-address, high-byte at high address, and vice-versa issues, presented by different types of architectures. For example, Intel-based PCs use low-byte-at-low-address/high-byte-at-high-address ordering, but Motorola-based PCs use the reverse.

Besides being internally portable, it is also run-time environment portable. The Java compiler is written in Java itself, while the run-time environment is written in ANSI C and sports a well-defined and succinct portability interface. The POSIX standardization effort was a huge influence on Java's portability interface. The result? Implementing an abstract Java Window class object with its associated methods that will run on a PC, UNIX, or Macintosh computer goes straight to the bottom line because it eliminates redundant implementation, testing, and maintenance efforts.

Robustness

The term *robust* usually refers to the degree to which an application can handle all circumstances, expected and unexpected. The more robust, the better the application is at withstanding all types of assaults. Less robust applications are typically plagued by one very annoying characteristic: they crash! The great news is that Java applications cannot cause a computer to crash. The Java system carefully checks each memory access to make sure that it is legal and won't cause any fatal errors.

Of course things can go wrong; and when they do, rather than crashing, a Java program throws an *exception*. Java traps these detected error conditions and allows the program to successfully recover. Finally, some of Java's robustness is a direct result of a Java program's inability to change those portions of a computer's memory critical to system performance.

Dynamic Linking

Dynamic linking, sometimes referred to as *delayed binding*, provides the utmost in programmer flexibility by not incorporating compiled subroutine code into the application's EXE file. Instead, at run-time, any called subroutines are brought into the processor as needed. This approach has many advantages, from minimizing the size of the executable to not overloading system resources with subroutines that may never be invoked. Dynamic linking also allows Java programs to adapt to changing computing environments.

Experienced object-oriented C++ programmers know that typical programs rely heavily on class libraries supplied by third-party vendors. Sometimes these libraries ship with the operating system. Should the vendor upgrade these libraries, existing applications cannot take advantage of the code changes until the application's source code is recompiled. This takes time and money and assumes you have access to the original code.

Java programs circumvent this bottleneck by delaying the binding of modules. You can take full advantage of object-oriented programming concepts, because new *methods* (which are functions bound exclusively to a particular object) and *instances* (an OOP term for variable) for an existing class in a library can be added without crashing the current application.

Technically speaking, this capability is possible because Java uses interfaces that specify inter-object interaction and excludes any instance variables or implementation methods. Each Java class (or object), has a run-time representation that allows programmers to query the class' type. The application can then decide whether to dynamically link the necessary class. These run-time representations also allow the run-time environment to check data structure casts at compile time as well as at run-time, providing yet another layer of error detection. This feature, known as RTTI (Runtime Type Identification), is not specifically available to C++ application developers.

Verifiability

Because there are many good programming languages available for writing standalone applications, you are most likely to use Java to enhance your World Wide Web presence. Because Java applets are downloaded to your computer and executed automatically, you may be concerned that your machine can be infected with a virus. However, this is not the case. Java applets cannot extract information or damage your computer. (Users can set how they want Java to enforce security by selecting from one of four *firewalls*: no access, Applet Host, Firewall, and Unrestricted; these topics are discussed thoroughly in later chapters.)

Java's security comes from its two-phase compile/interpret process. Phase one compiles the Java source code into easily verified bytecode instructions. Bytecode is similar to other instruction sets used by computers, yet hardware neutral; it can be easily checked for potential security violations. Technically, this is possible because bytecode contains additional type information that is used to double check that the program is legal.

Phase two security follows from the way Java interprets the bytecode. While most programming languages access functions by memory address, Java uses a totally different approach. Java methods and variables are always accessed by name, thus making it easy to determine what methods and functions are used. This process is called *verification*. Only after the bytecode is verified does the Java interpreter convert function names into addresses.

Even after the bytecode is verified, it must still behave itself by executing in a restricted environment. Java applets are prohibited from calling certain critical functions of the operating system unless given specific permission to do so. This set of checks and balances prevents the applet from breaking out of the restricted environment.

Object-Oriented Design

Java is exclusively object-oriented. Although C++ is also considered object-oriented, C++ lets programmers solve problems using a procedural approach. Java however, forces you to accept object orientation from the beginning, thus eliminating the problem of combining two dissimilar design philosophies.

It is easy to look at Java in terms of what it does and does not have in common with C++. In many cases, Java eliminates redundancies from C to C++, particularly any links to procedural design concepts. Java adds automatic boundary checking by eliminating the use of pointers and encapsulating arrays within a class structure as well as automatic garbage collection. Java also does not have many other features that made developing a C++ application so difficult.

Multithreading

Depending on your experience with operating systems and with environments within those systems, you may not have encountered the concept of threads. For example, when a program runs, it starts executing, runs its initialization code, calls subroutines (or object-oriented methods), and continues running and processing until it's done performing all required tasks. This is an example of a single-threaded program.

Multithreading enables several different execution threads to run at the same time, inside the same program, without interfering with each other. For example, a program may have to calculate a value using a time-consuming equation. However, the result of the equation is not needed instantaneously. A multithreaded program begins to solve the equation, while simultaneously performing some other task.

Using threads in Java, you can create an applet that runs by itself without interfering with any other part of the system. You can also have lots of applets running at once on the same page. The general rule is for an applet to use a thread for each process that is likely to continue for a long period of time—for example, an animation loop.

Prevention of Memory Leaks

Java incorporates automatic garbage collection. This built-in memory management, in addition to the built-in multithreading features, make it an ideal language for programmers. C++, in contrast, lets you write code at a very low level so that the resulting programs access hardware and calculate specific memory addresses and thus are platform-specific. Java eschewed this philosophy by ensuring that portability could be maintained by providing for all bounds checking and memory management. At the same time, Java maintained its respectable performance by adding built-in threading that could perform much of the garbage collection in a background process, simultaneously guaranteeing a robust and efficient algorithm.

Client-Server Readiness

At the heart of client-server applications is the distribution and sharing of information and workload. This client-server characteristic describes relationships between system objects that may be on a local or host system. In the case of the World Wide Web, this client-server relationship takes advantage of both information sharing and workload distribution. Java incorporates TCP/IP procedures in both the Java source and binary distribution code. This makes it easy for programmers to access remote information using protocols such as HTTP and FTP. Other protocols, such as gopher, news, and mailto, are well understood in the World Wide Web world, but have not yet been implemented in the Java language.

Speed

Java is a lot more efficient than typical scripting languages; but currently, it is about twenty times slower than C. However, for most applications, Java performance is acceptable. Even as you read this,

Sun Microsystems is working on code generators that will make Java programs execute as fast as programs written in C and C++.

JAVA AND THE WEB

Java-enabled Web browsers are capable of downloading *executable content*. This is one of the main differences between these browsers and those that are not Java-aware. Browsers that are not Java-aware download content using MIME (Multipurpose Internet Mail Extensions). This specification includes a variety of multimedia document formats. Once the content is downloaded, these browsers display the information, sometimes using other applications, such as paint, wave, and video programs, to accomplish the display.

Java-aware Web browsers, such as HotJava, initially follow the same scenario, but they go one step further by recognizing the special HTML tag **applet**. When downloading a Web page including this tag, Java-aware browsers recognize a link to a Java applet. At this point, a Java-aware browser downloads another file of information, as named in an attribute of the tag. Moreover, this executable content can include instructions for handling yet-undeveloped forms of media and information protocol.

Applets are written in hardware-independent Java bytecode format. The particular implementation of the Java-aware browser you purchased then takes this bytecode and interprets and runs the applet in a hardware-specific manner. This is the critical phase that takes machine-independent bytecode and enables it for a specific architecture.

THE FUTURE OF JAVA

With the growing acceptance and appreciation for all that Java can do, more and more programming solutions are being coded in Java. This exponential growth is driving the continual evolution of the Java language. While you are reading this, Sun Microsystems is furiously working on tweaking Java's performance characteristics, while third-party vendors continue inventing new uses and assumable characteristics. Two such evolving capabilities are persistence and virtual reality.

Persistence

Persistence, as it applies to Internet-based executable code, implies that your computer can permanently host that code (usually via download to your hard drive). Internet-based executable code will be available, thanks to new features being added to the Java language. Currently, in the partnership of Sun Microsystems and Netscape, Internet-based executable code is downloaded to the browser's Virtual Machine for interpretation, but not to the machine itself or its local storage. This lack of persistence is one of Java's most redeeming qualities. Because Java applets have no access to the local system or any of its resources, Java applications pose no security threat to the user.

However, persistence has its good side, too. Persistent code is downloaded only once. With the majority of users now accessing the Internet over 28.8K-bps modem links, Sun Microsystems is aware of this bandwidth bottleneck and is now working on a Java persistence.

Virtual Reality

The move toward interactive, three-dimensional World Wide Web sites took a major step forward with the official proposals for the upgrade to the "Moving Worlds" VRML specification. This specification, originally created by Silicon Graphics Inc., is being proposed for the next version of the Virtual Reality Markup Language (VRML) standard, Release 2.0., and is backed by nearly 50 vendors, including Microsoft, Netscape Communications, IBM, Adobe Systems, and Apple Computer.

Moving Worlds would allow Web site authors to create virtual worlds that support interactivity, motions, and "behaviors." VRML 1.0 provides only an open specification for creating three-dimensional sites through which users can navigate. Right now, the Web is noninteractive, and behaviors add a human element to a nonhuman world. The interactive environments as a class will enable better information sharing, such as teleconferencing or shared whiteboards over the Internet. This new interactivity is based on the Java programming language, which will eventually be incorporated into the Java language itself, thus enabling users to view VRML sites as well as add three-dimensional extensions to Java.

MICROSOFT AND JAVA

Microsoft has been known for providing one of the best, if not *the* best, programming development environments for over a decade. Microsoft products are known as the standard by which all user-friendly, programming development environments are compared. From BASIC to Visual C++, Microsoft's Development Studio has had enormous impact.

Designed to anticipate, streamline, and automate many of the mundane tasks required of programmers, the Development Studio makes programming as painless as a trip to a dentist using nitrous oxide. That is why Microsoft's association with Sun Microsystems is so exciting. Not only is the Java language fun and easy to learn, but it has now been combined with the best development environment ever invented—Microsoft's Development Studio!

As you will see in other chapters of this book, the Development Studio makes it easy for you to write, compile, debug, and test your Java programs. And as an added bonus, if you are already familiar with any of Microsoft's other programming development environments, such as Microsoft BASIC, FORTRAN, or Microsoft Visual C++, you will know most of the Development Studio commands needed to develop and use Java. The commands are identical.

HOT SPOTS ON THE INTERNET

The following list contains http:// World Wide Web sites to help get you routed to some up-to-the-minute locations specific to Java and HotJava. To access links to companies, contests, Java events, guides, tutorials, mailing lists, utilities, user groups, and more, point to http://www.yahoo.com/Computers_and_Internet/Languages/Java/.

Your first stop for the latest-breaking Visual J++ news should be http://www.microsoft.com. Here you will gain access to the very latest Help files, examples, future directions, as well as known bugs/fixes files.

Want a Java reality check? The Making Sense of Java site (http://reality.sgi.com/employees/shiffman_engr/Java-QA.html) addresses some common claims and beliefs about Java, and describes how accurate the claims are and where they go astray.

And, of course, be sure to check out some of the Java discussion groups. Developers of full-blown, industrial-strength Java applications (as opposed to applets) should try the STRONGJAVA mailing list. To subscribe, point to http://www.entmp.org/cgi-bin/lwgate/STRONG-JAVA/.

For just a little support, the Mid-Atlantic Java User Group (http://www.rssi.com/info/majug.html) or the Sacramento Java Users Group (http://www.calweb.com/~statenet/sacjug/) could be for you.

If you are concerned about security issues, try pointing your Web browser to http://www.cs.princeton.edu/~ddean/java/ for information on Java applets that can be used to attack networks behind firewalls.

WHAT YOU NEED TO WRITE JAVA CODE

The following configuration is recommended for writing Java code:

- Pentium processor—90 MHz or better
- Windows 95
- 16 MB RAM
- 1 gigabyte hard drive
- CD-ROM drive
- 28.8K-bps modem
- Internet access account (via America Online, Microsoft Network, CompuServe)
- Microsoft Visual J++

COMING TO TERMS: A DICTIONARY

The following section reviews the new terms discussed in this chapter. Take a moment to review the list so that you will become more Java-literate.

ActiveXTM—ActiveX™ controls is just a new name for OLE controls. Any Java applet can be plugged into any application that supports ActiveX™ controls, including Visual Basic, Access, Delphi, and Power Builder.

applet—Java applets are dynamic, interactive programs that can run inside a World Wide Web page. Java applets are Java programs that are downloaded over the World Wide Web and executed by a Web browser on the reader's machine. Running Java applets requires a Java-capable browser such as HotJava (which is an example of a stand-alone Java application, written in Java), or Netscape 2.0. The Microsoft J++ compiler ships with an AppletViewer for reader system viewing of Java applets. Note that a single Java source file may be written to be both an applet or application.

application—Java applications are more general programs written in the Java language. Java applications don't need a Web browser to run. In fact, Java can be used to create most types of applications that are currently written in more conventional programming languages such as Pascal, C, and C++.

bytecode—Java source code is first compiled into a hardware-neutral form called bytecode. Bytecode is almost native machine code, but not quite. The "not quite" part allows it to be hardware neutral. At run-time, this bytecode is executed by a Java interpreter, making Java both a compiled and interpreted language.

class—Class is an object-oriented concept. Simply stated, a class is a higher order of record or structure. Many languages have a record or structure syntax that allows programmers to combine standard data types into new application-specific types. However, any procedures or functions working on the fields or members of a record or structure, remain physically outside of the record or structure definition. This makes it difficult to re-use these new type definitions and their associated behaviors, because they are spread throughout your source code. Classes have a syntax that physically bundles a record or structure's data members with their associated function members. With this new syntax, a class behaves more like a complete miniprogram.

COM—Microsoft's COM (Component Object Model) is the cornerstone of the ActiveX™ platform and provides tight integration between Java and COM.

distributed—Java has an extensive library of routines for coping easily with TCP/IP protocols like HTTP and FTP. Java applications can open and access objects across the Internet via URLs with the same ease that programmers expect when accessing a local file system. Java even makes common gateway interface (CGI) scripting easier.

firewall—A firewall delimits which host system resources are available to a Java applet. Users can set how they want Java to enforce security by selecting from one of four firewalls: no access, Applet Host, Firewall, and Unrestricted.

hardware neutral—A Java application or applet can run on PowerPCs, as well as PCs with Intel and MIPS microprocessors. In other words, the Java source code is hardware independent. As a result, you do not need to re-invent an application for IBM-compatible, Macintosh, and UNIX-based machines.

inheritance—Many older high-level languages allow one record or structure definition to include, as one of its fields or members, a previously defined record or structure. This concept is known as nesting. This is the exact same concept involved in inheritance, only inheritance is an object-oriented concept. When one class is used to create another class, called a subclass, the subclass is said to inherit its parent's data members and function members. Java supports single-parent inheritance. Other languages such as C++ allow a subclass to inherit more than one parent's characteristics. This subtle difference isn't a problem if you have never programmed in an object-oriented language, but does require some logical and syntactical restructuring for experienced OOP programmers.

instance—Simply stated, creating variables in a procedure-oriented language is equivalent to *instantiating* an object in object-oriented terms. The instantiated object is referred to as the instance.

instance variable—Instance variables are class data members that are specific to a particular object instance.

interface—Many object-oriented languages allow a subclass to inherit the characteristics of more than one parent class. This is not possible in Java, which allows only single-parent inheritance. However, when two separate classes need to perform some subset of common behaviors, they both define the same interface. An interface, therefore, is a syntactic way of collecting what would normally be disparate member functions.

methods or *member functions*—Although Java does not allow any function to be unassociated with a particular class, other high-level languages do (C++, for example). Programmers can verbally distinguish between functions that are not associated with a particular class and those that are by using two new terms: method and member function. When a subroutine only works on a specific class, it is called a method or member function. In this context, simply using the term function tells another programmer that the subroutine is standalone.

MIME—Java-enabled Web browsers are capable of downloading executable content. This is one of the main differences between Java-enabled browsers and those that are not Java-aware. The latter download content using MIME (Multipurpose Internet Mail Extensions). This specification includes a variety of multimedia document formats. Once downloaded, these browsers display the information.

overloading—Subclasses are, by definition, children of some parent class definition. Because the subclass inherits both the member data and member functions of the parent class, there may come a time when the subclass will want the inherited member functions to do something different from the way they were originally written. With the proper syntax, you can override the parent class definition with an overloaded subclass member function. This process is called overloading.

package—All languages have some syntactic way for dealing with scope or visibility issues. Java solves the problem of visibility in one of two ways—either the scope protection provided by the class syntax or by using packages. Whenever a Java class has externally visible identifiers similar to some other previously defined Java class, collisions occur. The solution is to logically relate all noninterfering class definitions into a package. Now, any reused, duplicate identifier names are protected within each separate package and no collisions occur.

persistence—This term refers to a downloaded program's ability to run exclusively on the host computer. As of this writing, Java applets have no persistence. However, Sun Microsystems is updating the Java language to include this feature.

robust—Java is intended for writing programs that are reliable. A great deal of emphasis is placed on early checking for possible problems, later dynamic (run-time) checking, and eliminating situations that are error prone. The single biggest difference between Java and C/C++ is that Java has a pointer model that eliminates the possibility of overwriting memory and corrupting data.

subclass—A new class definition that is based on some previously defined class. The process of subclassing involves Java's object inheritance capabilities.

Chapter 2

THE MICROSOFT AND JAVA CONNECTION

This chapter covers the fundamental constructs of the Java language, its similarities to existing languages such as C and C++, and how its differences from these languages make Java the ideal development environment for today's programming needs. In addition, the chapter describes how to install Microsoft Visual J++ and lists the components that come with Microsoft Visual J++. With this background, you can begin using Visual J++ for Java, and writing understandable, introductory Java applications and applets.

MICROSOFT'S CONNECTION WITH JAVA

Microsoft's Visual J++ provides Java language development tools within the J++ Development Studio. With Microsoft Visual J++, you can write, compile, debug, and view Java applications and applets from within the Microsoft J++ (Integrated Development Environment).

Microsoft, Sun Microsystems, and Virtual Machine

The previous chapter explained how Java programs are compiled into special Java bytecodes, which are then interpreted at run-time by the Virtual Machine. To support Java on any particular operating system, someone writes a Virtual Machine for that operating system. The

Virtual Machine executes the program by reading and interpreting the compiled bytecodes.

Visual J++ provides its own run-time implementation of Java, which has the creative and original name "theWindows Virtual Machine for Java." As part of its reciprocal licensing agreement with Sun Microsystems, Microsoft licenses this Virtual Machine back to Sun as the *reference implementation* of Java for Windows.

This marketing arrangement liberates the Virtual Machine so that Microsoft can make Java for Windows available to all applications on the system, not just browsers. Word processors, spreadsheets, databases, and other traditional desktop applications can all use Java. For example, you can run a Java applet from within your desktop application, or even write the applet itself in Java. With Java Virtual Machine a part of Windows, Microsoft elevates Java to a full-blown application development language, on a par with languages such as C++ and Visual Basic.

Shortening Run-time Performance with JIT

The most common complaint about interpreted languages is that they are slower than native-compiled languages such as C/C++. One way to address this problem is to compile the bytecodes on the fly, as they execute. You may think that compilation must be a slow and tedious process. Maybe this is true for some languages, but here is where Java really shines. Because Java is so simple, and because the bytecodes are designed with machine language in mind, compiling is extremely fast! In fact, Microsoft claims that Visual J++ can compile almost a million lines of code per minute.

Java's slick run-time performance is enhanced by Microsoft's JIT (Just-In-Time) compiler, using an innovative compile-on-the-fly strategy. Instead of interpreting bytecodes one at a time, the JIT compiler translates bytecodes into native machine instructions and executes them on the host computer. Each bytecode is compiled just once, and then invoked repeatedly for each of the possible millions of times it may be used within the program.

Technically, JIT accomplishes this Herculean task by analyzing each bytecode, and then storing a link to the corresponding compiled code. When the bytecode comes up again, the link is activated and the native code is ready to run. However, Microsoft uses a few more tricks to improve performance. For example, JIT uses a different model for stacks while optimizing byte order within function calls. In addition,

JIT organizes code more efficiently than its interpreted equivalent. Future Microsoft plans include a build-time compiler capable of generating EXE files directly from a Java source file.

The Virtual Machine and Classes

One final Microsoft run-time enhancement is the way the Virtual Machine downloads class files. In Java, each class is compiled into its own **.class* file. Java programs frequently import many different classes, which the Virtual Machine loads dynamically at run-time, in a manner very similar to the way Windows loads dynamic link libraries (DLLs). Because a typical Java applet can download twenty or more separate files, this dynamic approach makes the Java build cycle very fast (because there is no link phase) and provides a means for distributed applications. This distribution is made possible because the class files can reside anywhere on the World Wide Web.

Microsoft CAB Format

The Microsoft Virtual Machine for Java supports yet another innovation, CAB, which stands for *cabinet format*. This is the same format used by Microsoft set-up programs. CAB format lets you compress the files for an entire applet into a single archive file that you can easily download.

Similarity of Java to C/C++

Whether or not you are an experienced C/C++ programmer, you will find Java's fundamental set of data types, standard operators, and logic control statements very familiar to those used in many high-level languages such as Pascal, Ada, and Modula-3. Of course, of all of Java's ancestors, C and C++ are the source of most of Java's characteristics. This similarity naturally makes it easier for a C/C++ programmer to learn Java, but it also demands a little more attention for these individuals, because Java is not identical to C/C++. The next section clarifies Java's similarities to and differences from C/C++.

UNICODE

ASCII and EBCIDIC code are quite well known, but you may never have heard of UNICODE. The first two are industry-accepted mappings between the seven or eight bits in a byte, and some human-recognizable symbol. This relationship between binary and human languages is fine as long as you want to code in English. However, the Internet is international. Fortunately, the computer industry has seen beyond cross-platform development (a hardware issue), to multi-language development (a software concern), and invented the UNICODE.

The idea behind this new encryption standard was simple: a new code was needed that can represent every written language known today, and any to be discovered! The only way to accomplish this Herculean task was to expand the number of bits used to map between the computer's binary language, and all of the rest of the world's languages. All UNICODE characters occupy 2 bytes, or 16 bits, of storage. This allows for 65,536 unique combinations of 0s and 1s, instead of just 256 (for ASCII/EBCIDIC), to which the UNICODE standards committee mapped every known language in the world today, leaving holes in the definition for yet-undiscovered or translated symbols.

You may wonder why UNICODE is important to you. All Java source files are written in UNICODE. The Java compiler takes this source code written in UNICODE format and extracts individual elements known as *tokens*. These tokens can be divided into five major categories: *identifiers*, *keywords*, *literals*, *operands*, and *separators*. In addition, the compiler removes *comments* and *white spaces* (spaces, tabs, and line feeds) that are not a part of the token set. Each of these tokens is discussed in more detail in the next section.

Comments Every professionally written program contains documentation in the form of comments. Comments detail a program's creation date, any clarifications needed to understand the algorithm, and usually the programmer's name. A good comment neither insults the intelligence of a programmer (by stating the obvious), nor assumes too much.

Every program has its own goals, such as minimum size, speed of execution, or ease of maintenance, which dictate how the source code is created and documented. A good rule of thumb is to document any line of code that you, the author of the code, would have trouble explaining after not working with the program for several weeks.

The Java compiler supports three styles of comments. The first, which uses the symbol pair /* and */, is familiar to programmers who use languages such as Pascal and C. The distinct opening and closing of this style of comment lets you easily create comments that span several lines:

```
/***************       ...       ***************/
* myfile.java                                  */
* This Java file                               */
* Created:                                     */
* Author:                                      */
* Uses:                                        */
* External Effects:                            */
****************       ...       ***************/
```

The second style, which is similar to the syntax used in C++ programs, uses the double slash //. This style differs from the first in that there is no closing comment symbol. This style of comment, then, is necessarily terminated at the end of each line. The previous comment has been rewritten in this comment style:

```
// **************       ...       ***************
// myfile.java                                  *
// This Java file                               *
// Created:                                     *
// Author:                                      *
// Uses:                                        *
// External Effects:                            *
// *************       ...       ****************
```

Be careful when using this type of comment syntax, because all code to the right of the double slashes is ignored by the compiler:

```
float fTemp; // program uses Fahrenheit temperature scale
```

Remember that, to make boxed comments, you must include the double slashes at the beginning of each comment line.

The third style of Java comment uses a unique syntax that begins with /** and ends with */. These special comments are used for the *javadoc* system, which is used to generate API documentation from the code. This book does not cover javadoc; you can find out more information from the documentation that comes with Sun's Java Developer's Kit or from Sun's Java home page (http://java.sun.com).

Identifiers The term *identifier* has a range of meanings in a program, including variable (or instance, in an object-oriented program) names, constant names, classes, and function (or method, in an object-oriented program) names. Every language has rules for how to construct legal identifiers. Java identifiers must:

- Start with a letter* (upper- or lowercase), dollar sign, or an underscore character
- Be composed of letters*, underscores, or the digits 0-9
- Include no embedded blanks
- Not be a reserved or keyword

Also, like C/C++, Java is a case-sensitive language. As a result, uppercase letters have a different meaning from their lowercase counterparts. For example, the variable *SIZE* is different from the variable *size*. This case sensitivity lets you create easily read, self-documenting source code. The following list illustrates several examples of naming conventions for legal identifiers:

```
String FirstName = "JoAnn";
String First_Name = "Charlie";
boolean Continue = true; // note: is a legal identifier
                       // since it starts with
                       // uppercase C not c, which
                       // would be the same as Java's
                       // reserved word continue and
                       // which would then make it
                       // an illegal identifier.
const int MAXIMUM_SIZE = 81;
```

Here is one quick note about choosing a style for naming identifiers. There is a style known as Hungarian notation, originated by Charles Simony from Bell Labs, Murray Hill, New Jersey. According to this naming convention, every identifier, no matter how it reads or its style, is preceded by a mnemonic relating to the identifier's data type. So for example, all Boolean variables start with the letter "b;" shorts,

* Letters are considered to include all the upper- and lowercase alphabet from A to Z, and all UNICODE characters with numbers above hex 00C0. This enables non-Latin characters such as Ç and ø to be used in names; however, characters such as ¶ are not included.

with an "s;" integers, with "i;" longs, with "l;" floats, with "f;" and so on.

The advantage of this naming convention, after you get used to it, is that you can look at any statement, *anywhere* in a program, and identify any variable's data type. This capability has two immediate advantages. First, you do not have to track down a variable's declaring statement. Second, you can verify correctly written, or detect incorrectly written, statements in source code.

Look at the following data declarations. Each variable name begins with a reminder of its data type:

```
int iValueOne = 1, iValue2 = 2, iResult;
float fResult;
```

Now, look at the following two statements for clarity of meaning:

```
iResult = iValueOne * iValueTwo;
fResult = iValueOne * iValueTwo;
```

While both statements are *legal*, certainly for any one particular application, only one is *logically* correct. But more importantly, notice how the Hungarian naming convention helps you immediately detect the matching (first statement), or mixed-mode operations (second statement) being performed. The alternative naming convention, which follows, speaks for itself—or better said, says nothing:

```
int ValueOne = 1, Value2 = 2, ResultA;
float ResultB;
```

Now, look at these two statements for clarity of meaning:

```
ResultA = ValueOne * ValueTwo;
ResultB = ValueOne * ValueTwo;
```

Without Hungarian notation, these two statements hide the data types of the source operands *ValueOne* and *ValueTwo*, along with the data types of the receiving variables, *ResultA* and *ResultB*. Desk checks of these two statements mandate a time-consuming search for each identifier's declaring statement.

Java Keywords Table 2.1 lists the Java *keywords*, or reserved words, which are demonstrated in the following chapters. Due to the popularity of the Java language, Sun Microsystems is continually adding new features to Java. However, the following list represents the stable set of commands available at the time of this writing.

Table 2.1: Java Keywords

abstract	do	implemens	package	throw
boolean	double	import	private	throws
break	else	inner	protected	transient
byte	extends	instanceof	public	try
case	final	int	rest	var
cast	finally	interface	return	void
catch	float	long	short	volatile
char	for	native	static	while
class	future	new	sure	
const	generic	null	switch	
continue	goto	operator	synchronized	
default	if	outer	this	

Standard Data Types

Because a computer understands only 0s and 1s, all computer languages define standard data types that instruct the compiler regarding how to map those 0s and 1s to values that mean something to us. These standard data types indicate whether the value is a character, string, or numeric and, for the last of these categories, something about its precision. Some languages, including Java, include additional data types that allow a programmer to represent logical Boolean states.

The Java language has five standard data types: Boolean, character, integer, float, and string. What is most important about these data types is that they are identical across all platforms, whether character (UNICODE) or numeric (IEEE floating-point format).

Literals Although not formally a standard data type, *literals* are frequently used with the standard data types for initialization or assignment purposes. There are three basic types of literals: numeric, character or string, and Boolean. Numeric literals can be subdivided into integral and floating point. The character literal refers to a single value of the UNICODE character set, whereas strings refer to collections of characters. To maintain compatibility with C/C++, the Boolean literal is included under numbers. In C/C++, there is no

Boolean data type; instead, the integers 1 and 0 are used for logical **true** and **false**.

There are several integer literals, such as 5, which would fit in an **int** variable, or one of type **byte** or **short**. A decimal integer literal larger than an **int** is automatically of type **long**. You can also force a smaller integer literal to a **long** data type by adding the letter "l" or "L" after it, as in 5l or 5L. Negative integer literals are preceded by a minus sign, as in -5. Any integer literal preceded by the number 0 is interpreted by the Java compiler as being an octal value in the numeric range of 00 to 07. Preceding an integer literal with a 0x or 0X instructs the Java compiler to view the literal in hexadecimal notation, as in 0xFFFF.

All floating-point literals contain an integer part and a decimal part. Java assigns all floating-point literals—for example, 3.22198—a precision of **double** unless forced to **float** with an appended "f" or "F," as in 12.598f. Java also allows exponential notation with the letter "e" or "E", as in 2e8 or 10E -12.

A Boolean literal is either of the keywords **true** or **false**. These keywords can be used anywhere you need a test or as the only possible values for **boolean** variables.

Java also provides string literals that represent a series of zero or more characters contained within double quotes. Java represents this type of literal in a very different way from C/C++. In C/C++, a string is an array of characters. In Java, a string literal is implemented as an object of type **String**. Here are examples of valid Java string literals:

```
"This is a complete string."
"This is a string that starts on one line and \
continues on the next line."
"This is a string with a \"Quote\" in it!"
""     /* this is an empty string */
```

Boolean Data Type Java's **boolean** data type lets you declare a variable used for logical tests, such as:

```
boolean UserWantsToContinue = true;
// initialized boolean declaration
.
.
.
while( UserWantsToContinue == true ) {
.
.
```

```
.
  if( inputValue == 10 )
    UserWantsToContinue = false;
.
.
.
}
```

This data type can only be assigned the keywords **true** or **false**. The **boolean** value is a true literal, and not a representation of the integers 0 or 1, as in C/C++. These values are also *not* strings and cannot be coerced to the **String** data type.

Character Data Type Java uses the **char** keyword to define character variables. Character literals are distinguished in your source code by the single quotation marks around them, as in ‘a’. In addition, the backslash \ character is used to represent nonprinting or conflicting characters. Character literals can be any symbol defined in the UNICODE character set. Table 2.2 lists the control code interpretation applied to symbol pairs preceded by a backslash.

Table 2.2: Control Code Interpretations

Interpretation	*Representation*	*Code Pair**
Line continuation	<newline>	\
New line	NL(LF)	\n
Horizontal tab	HT	\t
Backspace	BS	\b
Carriage return	CR	\r
Form feed	FF	\f
Backslash	\	\\
Single quotation mark	′	\′
Double quotation mark	″	\″
Octal literal	0ddd	\ddd
Hexadecimal literal	0xddd	\xd or \Xddd
Unicode literal	0xdddd	\udddd

*Note: The \a (bell) and \v (vertical tab) control code sequences so familiar to C/C++ programmers are not supported by Java.

Character variable declarations in Java take the following form:

```
char Gender; // unitialized character variable    // decla-
ration
char DepartmentCode = 'P'; // initialized character
                            // variable declaration
```

Integer Data Type Java provides four standard integer data types: **byte**, **short**, **int**, and **long**. By default, all four types use signed notation, which means they can hold either positive or negative numbers. Which type you choose for your variables depends on the range of values you expect that variable to hold; if a value becomes too big for the variable's type, Java truncates it. Table 2.3 lists the four standard integer types and their signed numeric ranges.

The following code illustrates several integer variable declarations and initializations:

```
byte ah_register = 0xFF;
short small_loop_control_variable = 0;
int small_jackpot;
long big_lottery_win = 50000000;
```

*Note: There is no **unsigned** type specifier for integer data types in Java.*

Float Data Type Java provides two floating-point precisions—**float** and **double**—which are used to represent decimal numbers with fractional parts, such as 2.358 or 49.671. Floating-point literals can be expressed in either standard or scientific notation:

```
float fValue;
```

Table 2.3: Standard Integer Types and Signed Ranges

Standard Integer Type	*Precision*	*Value Range*
byte	8 bits	–128 to +127
short	16 bits	–32,768 to +32,767
int	32 bits	–2,147,483,648 to +2,147,483,647
long	64 bits	–9223372036854775808 to +9223372036854775807

```
double dValue;
fValue = 3.14159;
dValue = 3.14159e21;
dValue = 3.14159E21;
dValue = 1.2345e-20;
```

Variables declared to be of type **float** occupy 32 bits of storage, while variables of type **double** use 64-bit precision. Appending a "f" or "F" to a floating-point literal can force a **float** precision (1.298f), while appending a "d" or "D" can permute a **double** storage allocation (2.976D).

String Data Type Java does not support an official string data type; however it does implement a **String** class, or object. Don't worry about the fact that strings are classes. Because of the nature of classes, you don't need to worry about how to implement them; they take care of themselves. You declare a string variable by preceding its name with the keyword **String**, as in:

```
String Full_Name; // uninitialized string
                  // variable
String Title = "A Tale of Two Cities"; // initialized
string variable;
```

Each string literal creates a new instance of the class **String**.

There are two kinds of string objects: the **String** class is for read-only (immutable) objects. The **StringBuffer** class is for string objects you want to modify (mutable string objects). Although strings are Java language objects, the Java compiler follows the C tradition of providing a syntactic convenience that C programmers have enjoyed with C-style strings. The Java compiler understands that a string of characters enclosed in double quotation marks is to be instantiated as a **String** object. Thus, the declaration:

```
String HelloWorld = "Hello World!";
```

instantiates an object of the **String** class behind the scenes and initializes it with a character string containing the UNICODE character representation of "Hello World!". Java has extended the meaning of the + operator to indicate string concatenation. Thus, you can write statements such as:

```
System.out.println("There are " + num + " characters in
the file.");
```

This code fragment concatenates the string "There are " with the result of converting the numeric value *num* to a string, and concatenates that with the string " characters in the file." Then it prints the result of those concatenations on the standard output. Just as with array objects, **String** objects provide a **length()** accessor method to obtain the number of characters in the string.

Placement of Variable Declarations

Where you place a variable's declaration affects where it is legally accessible within your source code. This visibility is referred to as a variable's *scope*. Java identifiers are said to have *block scope*. A *block* is defined by the two curly braces {}. The scope of a variable is from the point it is declared to the end of the block in which it is placed. For example:

```
class MyApp {
  public static void main(String args[]) {
  main
    int iValue;
    ...
  }
  public void methodA() {
    char cValue;
    ...
  }
```

In this particular example, *int iValue* has been declared in the method **main()**. Because this block does not include the *methodA()* block, any reference to *iValue* in *methodA()* would be an error. The same is true for *char cValue*. Because *cValue* is defined within *methodA()*'s block, accessing it in **main()** would be illegal.

Note: Java treats local redeclarations of same-named identifiers in the way most older high-level languages do. Reusing the same identifier name inside a block that is nested inside another block is legal. However, any reference to the identifier within the nested block refers only to the local redefinition. For example, the following code section redefines iValue within the while loop's block. For this reason, the first statement (iValue++;) *will take iValue's contents to 11, not 1, because only the local iValue is visible. However, outside the while loop, the local redeclaration of* iValue *goes out of scope. The second statement* (iValue++;) *now takes the first* iValue's *contents to 1.*

```
class MyApp {
  public static void main(String args[]) {
    int iValue = 0;
    boolean test = true;
    while( test ) {
      int iValue = 10;
      iValue++; // local redeclaration goes to 11 here
      ...
    }
  iValue++; // outer iValue goes to 1 here
  }
}
```

Casting and Object Coercions

Sometimes referred to as coercion, casting is a term inherited from the C/C++ languages. *Casting* is an operation that lets you temporarily change a variable's type or precision. One of Java's security features is the restrictions it places on run-time casting and coercion of objects and variables. These Java casting restrictions prevent the possibility of malicious system corruption. The following list details those types of casts and coercions that are legal in Java:

- Java programs cannot cast objects to the base types, such as **Object**.
- Floating-point values can be cast to integral values.
- Integral values can be cast to floating-point precision.
- Integers cannot be cast to arrays or objects.
- Java allows instances of a class to be cast to a superclass.
- Java also allows an instance of a class to be cast to a subclass with a run-time check to ensure that it is a valid instance of the subclass or one of its subclasses. A **ClassCastException** is raised if the instance isn't a valid subclass or sub-subclass.
- All other castings or coercions are illegal and cause a compile-time error.

The following example shows the syntax and use for casting:

```
int iValue;
char cValue;
iValue = (int) cValue;
```

Here, the parenthetical reference to **int** tells the compiler that you want to change the character into an integer and place it in *iValue*. On the other hand, if you need to go the other way, you write:

```
cValue = (char) iValue;
```

You must remember to take a variable's storage allocation into consideration when casting. Because both **int**s and **char**s are 32 bits, you can move from one to another without a loss of information. However, if you were to coerce a 64-bit **long** into a 32-bit **int**, you could easily truncate the value. Be careful, though, even if the two variables are the same size, such as with a 32-bit **int** and a 32-bit **float**. You would still lose information about the fractional numbers.

Java does not support automatic casting (as do C and C++). If it did, the previous statement could be written like this:

```
cValue = iValue;
```

Table 2.4 details those casts that will not result in information loss.

Logic Control

Java provides the usual set of logic control statements necessary to create meaningful algorithms. Because these control statements perform the same logical function in Java as in many programming languages,

Table 2.4: Casts That Do Not Result in Information Loss

Original Data Type	*Coerced To*
byte to	**short, char, int, long, float, double**
short to	**int, long, float, double**
char to	**int, long, float, double**
int to	**long, float, double**
long to	**float, double**
float to	**double**

the only concern here is their syntax in Java. Various control statements are covered in this section

if Statement The **if** statement looks like:

```
if( test_expression )
  single_statement;
```

or

```
if( text_expression ) {
  statement_a;
  statement_b;
statement_n;
}
```

Note: In Java, text_expression *is evaluated as a* **boolean** *data type, not a number (as in C/C++). As a result, you cannot use an integer as a shortcut, with 0 being* ***false*** *and any other value being* ***true****. In Java, you must make some relational statement in order for* test_expression *to evaluate properly. The following code would not evaluate properly in Java:*

```
int iWantsToDo = 0;
if( iWantsToDo )
  something;
```

It would have to be rewritten to something like:

```
int iWantsToDo = 0;
if( iWantsToDo == 1 )
  something;
```

if-else Statement Next in complexity is the bi-conditional **if-else** statement. Once again, the main issue here is syntax. The permutations include:

```
if( test_expression )
  single_true_statement:
else
  single_false_statement;
```

or

```
if( test_expression )
  single_true_statement:
```

```
else {
  false_statement_a:
  false_statement_b;
  false_statement_n;
}
```

or

```
if( test_expression ) {
  true_statement_a:
  true_statement_b;
  true_statement_c;
}
else
  single_false_statement;
```

or

```
if( test_expression ) {
  true_statement_a:
  true_statement_b;
  true_statement_c;
}
else {
  false_statement_a:
  false_statement_b;
  false_statement_n;
}
```

if-else if Statement For simple subrange checks, you can use the nested **if-else if** syntax:

```
if( test_expression_a )
  do_this;
  else if ( test_expression_b )
    then_do_this;
    else if( test_expression_n )
       else_do_this;
```

switch-case Statement Another alternative to nested **if-else if** statements is the Java **switch-case** statement. A **switch-case** statement lets you code multiple logic paths based on a single variable's contents.

Usually these contents fall into a specific, testable, subset of values. Be very careful, though; unlike many other high-level language selection statements, such as Pascal's **case** statement, the Java **switch-case** statement has a few peculiarities. The general form of a Java **switch-case** statement follows:

```
switch( test_expression ) {
 case constant_a:
   statements_a;
   break;
 case constant_b:
   statements_b;
   break;
   .
   .
   .
 case constant_n:
   statements_n;
   break;
 default: statements; // default - optional
}
```

There is one keyword that a novice Java programmer needs to watch carefully: **break**. If this example had been coded in Pascal and *constant_a* equaled *test_expression*, *statements_a* would have been executed, with program execution picking up with the next statement at the end of the **case** statement (below the closing brace). In Java, the situation is quite different.

In the preceding syntax, if the **break** statement had been removed from *constant_a*'s section of code, a match similar to the one used in the preceding paragraph would have left *statements_b* as the next statement to be executed. It is the **break** statement that causes the remaining portion of the **switch-case** statement to be skipped. Let's look at a few examples. Examine the following **if-else if** code segment:

```
if( iOffset == SMALL_CHANGE_UP )
  iYcoordinate =   1;

else if( iOffset == SMALL_CHANGE_DOWN )
  iYcoordinate =  -1;

else if( iOffset == LARGE_CHANGE_UP )
```

```
  iYcoordinate =   10;
else
  iYcoordinate =  -10;
```

You can rewrite this code using a **switch-case** statement:

```
switch( iOffset ) {
  case  SMALL_CHANGE_UP:
    iYcoordinate =   1;
    break;
  case  SMALL_CHANGE_DOWN:
    iYcoordinate =  -1;
    break;
  case  LARGE_CHANGE_UP:
    iYcoordinate =   10;
    break;
  default:
    iYcoordinate =  -10;
}
```

In this example, the value of *iOffset* is consecutively compared to each case value in search of a match. When one is found, *iYcoordinate* is assigned the appropriate value. Then the **break** statement is executed, skipping over the remaining cases of the **switch** statements. However, if no match is found, the default assignment is performed (iYcoordinate = –10). Because this is the last option in the **switch-case** statement, there is no need to include a **break**. A **switch-case default** is optional. Proper placement of the **break** statement within a **switch-case** statement lets you create a set of cases, all performing the same operation. See the next program:

```
class TestSwitch {
  public static void main(String args[]) {

  char a_character         = 'U';
  int NumberOfVowels       =  0 ,
      NumberOfConsonants =  0 ;

    switch( a_character ) {
      case 'a' :
      case 'A' :
      case 'e' :
      case 'E' :
```

```
        case 'i' :
        case 'I' :
        case 'o' :
        case 'O' :
        case 'u' :
        case 'U' :  NumberOfVowels++;
                        break;
        default  :  NumberOfConsonants++;
      }
    System.out.println("\nNumber of vowels = " + NumberOfVowels);
    }
}
```

Notice how the **switch-case** statement enumerates several test values that all execute the same code section and the drop-through characteristic of a purposefully missing **break** statement. Several other high-level languages have their own form of selection (the **case** statement in Pascal and the **select** statement in PL/I), which allows for several test values, all producing the same result, to be included on the same selection line using subranges. Java, however, requires a separate case for each. But notice, in this example, how the same effect has been created by not inserting a **break** statement until all possible vowels have been checked. Should *a_character* contain a consonant, all of the vowel case tests will be checked and skipped until the **default** statement is reached.

Loops

Java has a few surprises when it comes to simple types of loop control statements. Actually, the loop types themselves are fairly standard in operation. What is interesting, however, are the ways in which you can alter the logic flow within a loop, or exit a loop. Java includes the standard set of repetition control statements: **for** loops, **while** loops, and **do-while** loops (called **repeat-until** loops in several other high-level languages).

The basic difference between a **for** loop and a **while** or **do-while** loop has to do with the "known" number of repetitions. Typically, **for** loops are used whenever there is a definite predefined number of repetitions, and **while** and **do-while** loops are reserved for an "unknown" number of repetitions.

Java provides four methods for altering the repetitions in a loop. All loops can naturally terminate based on the expressed test condition. In Java, however, a loop can also terminate because of an anticipated error condition by using either a **break** (the other use for **break** statements, besides the **switch-case** use) or **exit()** statement. Loops can also have their logic control flow altered by a **break** statement or a **continue** statement.

Pre-Test for **Loops** The syntax for a **for** loop looks very similar to that used in most high-level languages:

```
for( init_loop_control; test_expression; increment_loop_control )
```

for loop execution begins with the one-time-only initialization of the loop control variable—in this example, *init_loop_control*. This is done at the start of the loop, and it is never executed again. Following this, *test_expression*, which is called the loop-terminating condition, is tested. Whenever *test_expression* evaluates to **true**, the statement or statements within the loop are executed.

If the loop was entered, then after all of the statements within the loop are executed, *increment_loop_control* is executed. However, if *test_expression* evaluates to **false**, the statement or statements within the loop are ignored, along with *increment_loop_control*, and execution continues with the statement following the end of the loop.

To check yourself on the proper use of loop control variables, answer the following question: What is the value of the loop control variable *outside* the loop? The answer is that it is undefined. Your program should never use the loop control variable anywhere else but *inside* the loop structure. Outside the loop, the variable's contents are volatile.

The indentation scheme applied to **for** loops with a compound block looks like this:

```
for( init_loop_control; test_expression;

increment_loop_control ) {
 statement_a;
 statement_b;
 statement_c;
 statement_n;
}
```

When several statements need to be executed, a pair of braces is required to tie their execution to the loop control structure. Let's examine a few examples of **for** loops. The following example sums up the first five integers. It assumes that *Total* and *ControlValue* have been predefined as integers:

```
Total = 0;
for( ControlValue = 1; ControlValue <= 5; ControlValue++ )
  Total += ControlValue;
```

After *Total* has been initialized to 0, the **for** loop is encountered. First, *ControlValue* is initialized to 1 (this is done only once); second, *ControlValue*'s value is checked against the loop-terminating condition, <= 5. Because this is **true**, a 1 is added to *Total*. Once the statement is executed, the loop control variable (*ControlValue*) is incremented by 1. This process continues four more times until *ControlValue* is incremented to 6 and the loop terminates. In Java, as in C++, the same code segment could be written as follows. See if you can detect the subtle difference:

```
for( int ControlValue = 1; ControlValue <= 5; ControlValue++ )
  Total += ControlValue;
```

Java allows the loop control variable to be declared and initialized within the **for** loop. This brings up a very sensitive issue among structured programmers, which is the proper placement of variable declarations. In Java, you can declare variables right before the statement that actually uses them. In the preceding example, because *ControlValue* is used only to generate a *Total*, with *Total* having a larger scope than *ControlValue*, the local declaration for *ControlValue* is harmless. However, look at the following code segment:

```
int Total = 0;
for( int ControlValue = 1; ControlValue <= 5; ControlValue++ )
  Total += ControlValue;
```

This would obscure the visual "desk check" of the variable *Total* because it was not declared below the function head. For the sake of structured design and debugging, localizing all variable declarations is best. Only rarely can you justify moving a variable declaration to a nonstandard place, while sacrificing easily read, easily checked, and easily modified code.

The value used to increment **for** loop control variables does not always have to be 1 or ++. The following example sums all the odd numbers up to 9:

```
OddTotal = 0;
for( OddNumber = 1; OddNumber <= 9; OddNumber += 2 );
  OddTotal += OddNumber;
```

In this example, the loop control variable *OddNumber* is initialized to 1 and is incremented by 2. Of course, **for** loops don't always have to go from a smaller value to a larger one.

Pre-Test while **Loops** **while** loops are also pre-test loops, which means that the program evaluates *test_expression* before entering the statement or statements within the body of the loop. Because of this, pre-test loops may be executed from zero to many times. The syntax for a Java **while** loop is:

```
while( test_expression )
  statement;
```

For compound blocks, the syntax is:

```
while( test_expression ) {
  statement_a;
  statement_b;
  statement_c;
  statement_n;
}
```

Usually, **while** loop control structures are used whenever an indefinite number of repetitions is expected.

Post-Test do-while **Loops** The post-test **do-while** loop is the only loop always entered at least once, with the loop condition being tested at the end of the first iteration. In contrast, **for** loops and **while** loops may execute from zero to many times, depending on the loop control variable. The syntax for a d**o-while** loop is:

```
do
 statement ;
while( test_expression );
```

For compound blocks, the syntax is:

```
do {
 action_a;
```

```
    action_b;
    action_c;
    action_n;
} while( test_expression );
```

Because **do-while** loops always execute at least one time, they are best used whenever you know you want the particular loop to be entered. For example, your program may need to present a menu to the user. Even if all the user wants to do is quit the program, a menu needs to be shown so that the user knows which key terminates the application.

Standard Operators

All the familiar C and C++ operators apply (see Table 2.5). Because Java lacks unsigned data types, the >>> operator has been added to

Table 2.5: Java Operators

<table>
<tr><th>Operators</th><th>Associativity</th></tr>
<tr><td>() [] -> :: .</td><td>left to right</td></tr>
<tr><td>! ~ + - ++ — & sizeof new delete</td><td>right to left</td></tr>
<tr><td>.* ->*</td><td>left to right</td></tr>
<tr><td>* / %</td><td>left to right</td></tr>
<tr><td>+ -</td><td>left to right</td></tr>
<tr><td><< >> >>></td><td>left to right</td></tr>
<tr><td>< <= > >=</td><td>left to right</td></tr>
<tr><td>== !=</td><td>left to right</td></tr>
<tr><td>&</td><td>left to right</td></tr>
<tr><td>^</td><td>left to right</td></tr>
<tr><td>|</td><td>left to right</td></tr>
<tr><td>&&</td><td>left to right</td></tr>
<tr><td>||</td><td>right to left</td></tr>
<tr><td>?:</td><td>left to right</td></tr>
<tr><td>= *= /= %= += -= &= ^= |= <<= >>= >>>=</td><td>right to left</td></tr>
<tr><td>,</td><td>left to right</td></tr>
</table>

the language to indicate an unsigned (logical) right shift. Java also uses the + operator for string concatenation.

Throughout the book, you will be introduced to the various operators and how their precedence level affects their performance.

Mathematical Operators Java provides a full set of operators for mathematical calculations. Unlike some other languages, Java can use the same operators on both integer and floating-point values. Java provides a set of eleven binary operators, the first five of which you probably are already familiar with and which are usable on both integer and floating-point numerical types. The basic binary mathematical operators are listed in Table 2.6.

Table 2.7 shows the set of unary operators that can be used on numerical values.

Table 2.6: Mathematical Binary Operators

Binary Operator	*Meaning*
+	Addition
-	Subtraction
*	Multiplication
/	Division
%	Modulus

Table 2.7: Mathematical Unary Operators

Unary Operator	*Meaning*
-	Negation
++	Increment
—	Decrement

Bitwise Operators In addition to the mathematical operators, Java provides several bitwise operators that can be used only with integer values (see Table 2.8).

Equality and Inequality Operators Java provides the same set of operators used in C/C++ to test for equality, inequality, and relationships of greater than, less than, and so on, as shown in Tables 2.9 and 2.10.

Table 2.8: Bitwise Operators

Bitwise Operator	*Meaning*
~	bitwise complement
&	bitwise AND gate function
|	bitwise OR gate function
^	bitwise XOR gate function
<<	left -shift operation
>>	right-shift operation
>>>	right-shift with zero fill operation

Table 2.9: Equality and Inequality Operators

Equality/Inequality Operator	*Meaning*
==	Equal
!=	Not equal

Table 2.10: Relational Operators

Relational Operator	*Meaning*
<	less-than
>	greater-than
<=	less-than-or-equal
>=	greater-than-or-equal

Relational Operators Java provides the usual complement of relational and equality operators, with a similar syntax to many popular programming languages. Each relational operator takes numeric operands (integral or floating point) and produces a Boolean result. The relational operators are designed to determine ordering, whether some quantity is greater than another, whether some letter is less than another, and so on. The equality operators do not help in determining ordering, instead they just tell you whether two values are the same or not.

Logical Operators Logical operators let you group together one or more Boolean expressions. Table 2.11 shows the six operators for performing logical operations in Java. The *short circuit* versions of & and |, namely && and ||, do not require an entire combinational expression to evaluate before returning a result. For example, for an AND gate to return **true**, all expressions must evaluate to **true**. Look at this brief example:

```
( (xCoord < maxScreenWidth) && ( yCoord < MaxScreenHeight) )
```

With short circuit AND && if *xCoord* isn't within range, *yCoord*'s expression isn't even evaluated. Using the regular Boolean AND &, however, forces the evaluation of *both* expressions. Extreme caution must be used when writing these types of statements. Take, for example, the following modification:

```
( (xCoord++ < maxScreenWidth) && ( yCoord++ < MaxScreenHeight) )
```

Table 2.11: Logical Operators

Logical Operator	*Meaning*
!	Logical inverse (NOT gate function)
&	Boolean AND gate function
|	Boolean OR gate function
^	Boolean XOR gate function
&&	short-circuit AND gate function
||	short-circuit OR gate function

This code segment could possibly generate a very nefarious bug, when *xCoord* no longer satisfies the && condition, leaving a legal *yCoord* value untested and unincremented!

Arrays

In contrast to C and C++, Java language arrays are first-class language objects. An array in Java is a real object with a run-time representation. You can declare and allocate arrays of any type, and you can allocate arrays of arrays to obtain multidimensional arrays. You declare an array of, say, *ScreenCoords* (a class you've declared elsewhere) with a declaration like this:

```
ScreenCoord  CurrentScreenCoords[];
```

This code states that *CurrentScreenCoords* is an uninitialized array of *ScreenCoords*. At this time, the only storage allocated for *CurrentScreenCoords* is a reference handle. At some future time, you must allocate the amount of storage you need, as in:

```
CurrentScreenCoords = new ScreenCoord[10];
```

This line of code allocates an array of ten references to *ScreenCoords* that are initialized to the NULL reference. Notice that this allocation of an array doesn't allocate any objects of the *ScreenCoord* class for you; you will have to also allocate the *ScreenCoord* objects, as shown here:

```
int  i;
for (i = 0;  i < 10;  i++) {
   CurrentScreenCoords[i] = new ScreenCoord();
}
```

Access to elements of *CurrentScreenCoords* can be performed via the normal C-style indexing, but all array accesses are checked to ensure that their indices are within the range of the array. An exception is generated if the index is outside the bounds of the array. To get the length of an array, use the **length()** accessor method on the array object whose length you wish to know: *CurrentScreenCoords.length()* returns the number of elements in *CurrentScreenCoords*. For instance, the code fragment:

```
howMany = CurrentScreenCoords.length();
```

assigns the value 10 to the *howMany* variable.

The C notion of a pointer to an array of memory elements is gone, and with it, the arbitrary pointer arithmetic that leads to unreliable code in C. No longer can you walk off the end of an array, possibly trashing memory and leading to the famous "delayed-crash" syndrome, where a memory-access violation today manifests itself hours or days later. Programmers can be confident that array checking in Java will lead to more robust and reliable code.

Exceptions

If a program behaves abnormally, encounters an unexpected input, or detects an anomaly in its operation, it must react. This is called *exception handling*. One very nice standardized feature of Java is its exception-handling mechanism. There are two parts to the syntax for the exception mechanism: part one involves signaling an exception, while part two sets up the exception handler. To signal an exception, your program simply uses the **throw** keyword, as in:

```
throw new MyExceptionMethod();
```

To set up an exception handler, your program uses the **try-catch** keywords. This statement syntax involves a **try** block, which is the code that is executed assuming no exception occurs, and then a series of **catch** blocks, which are executed if an exception has been **throw**n:

```
try {
      // try code block
  }
    catch (MyExceptionType ErrorOne)  {
             // catch statement(s) ErrorOne);
  }
    catch (MyExceptionType ErrorTwo)  {
             // catch statement(s) ErrorTwo);
  {
}
```

Exception handling is discussed in greater detail throughout the remaining chapters of this book.

Objects

Because many readers are undoubtedly familiar with the procedurally oriented aspects of programming languages such as Pascal, Modula-3, and C, the initial chapters of this text use this familiarity to introduce you to Java. However, Java is an object-oriented language. In C++ and

Java then, an *object* is defined as a programming abstraction that groups data with the code that operates on that data. A *class* is a template for a set of object instances. Learning how to understand, use, and develop your own objects requires additional program fundamentals, concepts, and syntax. The discussion of these topics is delayed until Chapter 4, "Java Programming Fundamentals."

FEATURES OF C/C++ NOT IN JAVA

The earlier part of this chapter concentrated on the principal features of Java. This section discusses features removed from C and C++ in the evolution of Java. The first step was to eliminate redundancy from C and C++. In many ways, the C language evolved into a collection of overlapping features, providing too many ways to say the same thing, while in many cases not providing needed features. C++, in an attempt to add "classes to C," merely added more redundancy while retaining many of the inherent problems of C.

Typedefs, Defines, or Preprocessor

Source code written in Java is simple. There is no preprocessor, no **#define** and related capabilities, no **typedef**, and, without those features, no header files. Instead of header files, Java language source files provide the definitions of other classes and their methods. A major problem with C and C++ is the amount of context you need to understand another programmer's code: you have to read all related header files, all related **#defines**, and all related **typedefs** before you can even begin to analyze a program.

In essence, programming with **#define**'s and **typedef**'s results in every programmer inventing a new programming language that's incomprehensible to anybody else, thus defeating the goals of good programming practices. In Java, you obtain the effects of **#define** by using constants. You obtain the effects of **typedef** by declaring classes—after all, a class effectively declares a new type. You don't need header files because the Java compiler compiles class definitions into a binary form that retains all the type information through to link time. By removing all this baggage, Java becomes remarkably context-free. Programmers can read and understand code and, more importantly, modify and reuse code much faster and easier.

Structures or Unions

Java has no structures or unions as complex data types. You don't need structures and unions when you have classes; you can achieve the same effect simply by declaring a class with the appropriate instance variables. The code fragment below declares a class called *ScreenCoord*:

```
class ScreenCoord extends Object {
    double  X_Coord;
    double  Y_Coord;
    methods to access the instance variables
}
```

The following code fragment declares a class called *Rectangle* that uses objects of the *ScreenCoord* class as instance variables.

```
class Rectangle extends Object {
    ScreenCoord  LowerLeft_Coord;
    ScreenCoord  UpperRight_Coord;
    methods to access the instance variables
}
```

In C, you'd define these classes as structures. In Java, you simply declare classes. You can make the instance variables as private or as public as you wish, depending on how much you wish to hide the details of the implementation from other objects.

Functions

Java has no functions. Object-oriented programming supersedes functional and procedural styles. Mixing the two styles just leads to confusion and dilutes the purity of an object-oriented language. Anything you can do with a function you can do just as well by defining a class and creating methods for that class. Consider the *ScreenCoord* class from above. Public methods have been added to set and access the instance variables:

```
class ScreenCoord extends Object {
    double  X_Coord;
    double  Y_Coord;
    public void setX( double X_Coord ) {
         this.X_Coord = X_Coord;
    }
```

```
    public void setY( double Y_Coord ) {
        this.Y_Coord = Y_Coord;
    }
    public double X_Coord( void ) {
        return X_Coord;
    }
    public double Y_Coord( void ) {
        return X_Coord;
    }
}
```

If the *X_Coord* and *Y_Coord* instance variables are private to this class, the only means to access them is via the public methods of the class. Here's how you'd use objects of the *ScreenCoord* class from within, say, an object of the *Rectangle* class:

```
class Rectangle extends Object {
    ScreenCoord  LowerLeft_Coord;
    ScreenCoord  UpperRight_Coord;
    public void setEmptyRect( void ) {
        LowerLeft_Coord.setX( 0.0 );
        LowerLeft_Coord.setY( 0.0 );
        UpperRight_Coord.setX( 0.0 );
        UpperRight_Coord.setY( 0.0 );
    }
}
```

Functions and procedures are not inherently wrong. Using classes and methods, however, you can focus on only one way to express a given task. By eliminating functions, your job as a programmer is immensely simplified: you work only with classes and their methods.

Multiple Inheritance

Multiple inheritance—and all the problems it generates—has been discarded from Java. The desirable features of multiple inheritance are provided by interfaces, which are conceptually similar to Objective C protocols. An interface is not a definition of an object. Rather, it's a definition of a set of methods that one or more objects will implement. An important issue of interfaces is that they declare only methods and constants. No variables can be defined in interfaces.

Goto Statements

Java has no goto statement. Studies illustrated that goto is (mis)used more often than not, simply "because it's there." Eliminating goto led to a simplification of the language—there are no rules about the effects of putting a goto in the middle of a **for** statement, for example. Studies on approximately 100,000 lines of C code determined that roughly 90 percent of the goto statements were used purely to obtain the effect of breaking out of nested loops. As mentioned above, multilevel **break** and **continue** remove most of the need for goto statements.

Operator Overloading

You cannot overload the standard arithmetic operators. Once again, the effects of operator overloading can be just as easily achieved by declaring a class, appropriate instance variables, and appropriate methods to manipulate those variables.

Automatic Coercions

Java prohibits C- and C++-style automatic coercions. If you want to coerce a data element of one type to a data type that would result in loss of precision, you must do so explicitly by using a cast. Consider this code fragment:

```
int  myInt;
double  myFloat = 3.14159;
myInt = myFloat;
```

The assignment of *myFloat* to *myInt* would result in a compiler error due to a possible loss of precision. Instead, you must use an explicit cast. You should re-write the code fragment as:

```
int  myInt;
double  myFloat = 3.14159;
myInt = (int)myFloat;
```

Pointers

Most studies agree that pointers are one of the primary features that enable programmers to inject bugs into their code. Given that structures are gone, and arrays and strings are objects, the need for pointers to these constructs goes away. Thus, Java has no pointers. Any task that would require arrays, structures, and pointers in C can be more easily and reliably performed by declaring objects and arrays of objects.

Instead of complex pointer manipulation on array pointers, you access arrays by their arithmetic indices. The Java run-time system checks all array indexing to ensure indices are within the bounds of the array. You no longer have dangling pointers and trashing of memory due to incorrect pointers, because there are no pointers in Java.

THE MICROSOFT C++ COMPILER AND JAVA COMPILER

Because using the Java language involves more than simply running programs, Microsoft has chosen to provide Java as an optional Microsoft C++, user-installed add-on. This makes sense for two reasons. First, you need to enter, edit, and debug Java source code, not just run Java programs. The Microsoft C++ IDE (Integrated

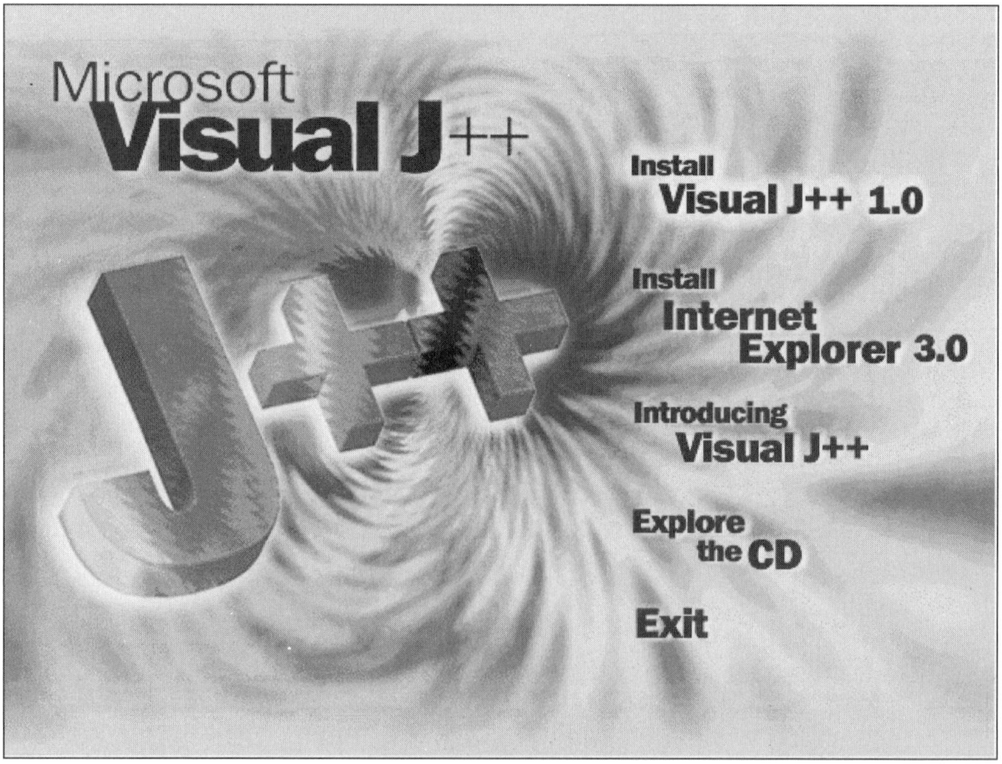

Figure 2.1: Initial set-up window.

Development Environment) works perfectly for these tasks and is already familiar to hundreds of thousands of programmers. Second, because Java is most similar to the C and C++ languages, nesting the Java development tools within Microsoft C++ makes sense.

INSTALLING THE JAVA COMPILER

To maximize the use of your system's resources, the Microsoft C++ installation program does not automatically install the Java component to the IDE. For this reason, if you want to use Java, you must run the *setup.exe* program a second time (assuming you have already installed Microsoft C++). Figure 2.1 on the previous page shows the set-up program's initial window.

1. To install Visual J++, click on **Install Visual J++ 1.0,** as seen in Figure 2.1. You will now see a window similar to Figure 2.2. Notice that the text in this window highlights

Figure 2.2: Visual J++ installation.

the fact that you may, at a later date, rerun the set-up program to change Visual J++ features.

2. Click on the Next> button to begin the installation. The window that opens shows the standard E.U.L.A. agreement (Microscoft End-User License Agreement). See Figure 2.3.
3. Click on the Yes button to continue. A window opens, as shown in Figure 2.4, in which you enter your user name and organization.
4. Click on the Next> button to open the window shown in Figure 2.5. In most cases, you should choose the Typical install option.

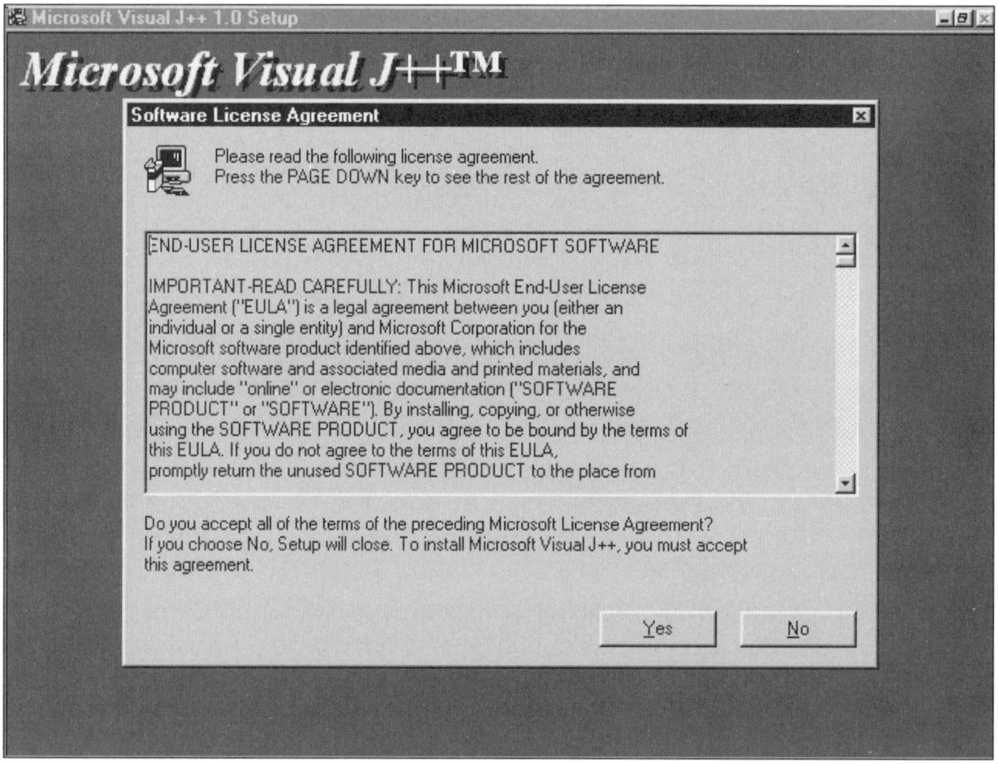

Figure 2.3: EULA message window.

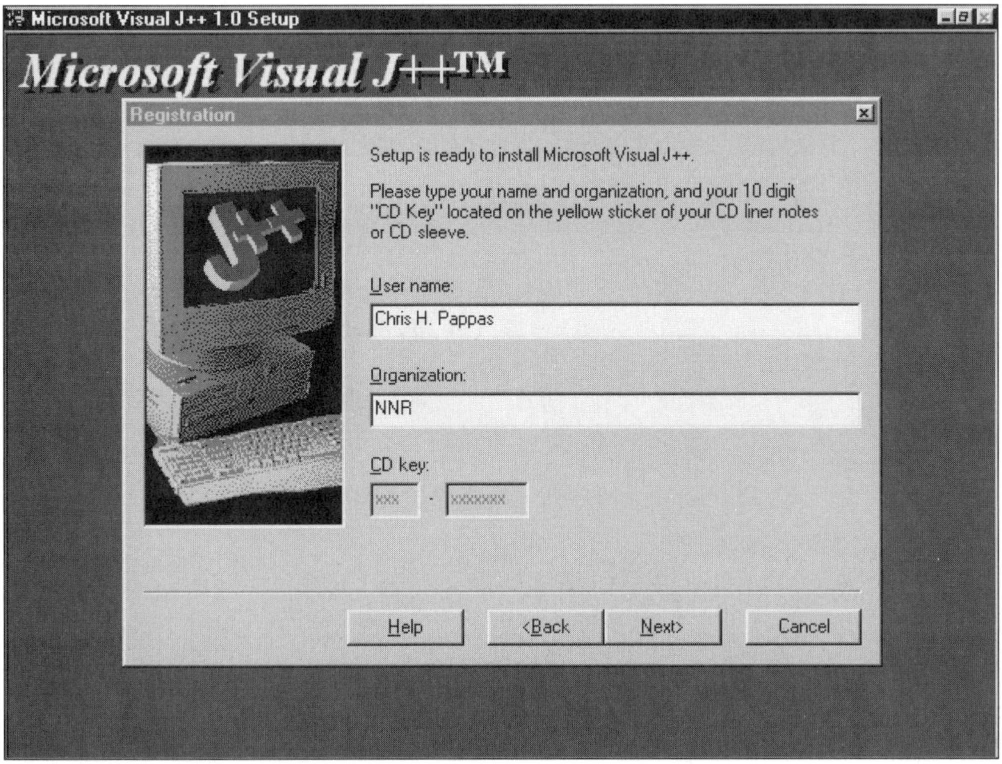

Figure 2.4: Assigning a user name and organization.

5. Click on the Next> button to open the window shown in Figure 2.6.
6. Click on the Next button to open the message window shown in Figure 2.7. Visual J++ needs to take an extra step to install the ActiveX run-time environment to give your Java program access to these powerful custom control objects.
7. Register your product. By responding to a few prompts, you can register your Microsoft Visual J++ online (see Figure 2.8).
8. Click OK to launch the Visual J++ Registration Wizard, which automates the registration procedure. (See Figure 2.9.)

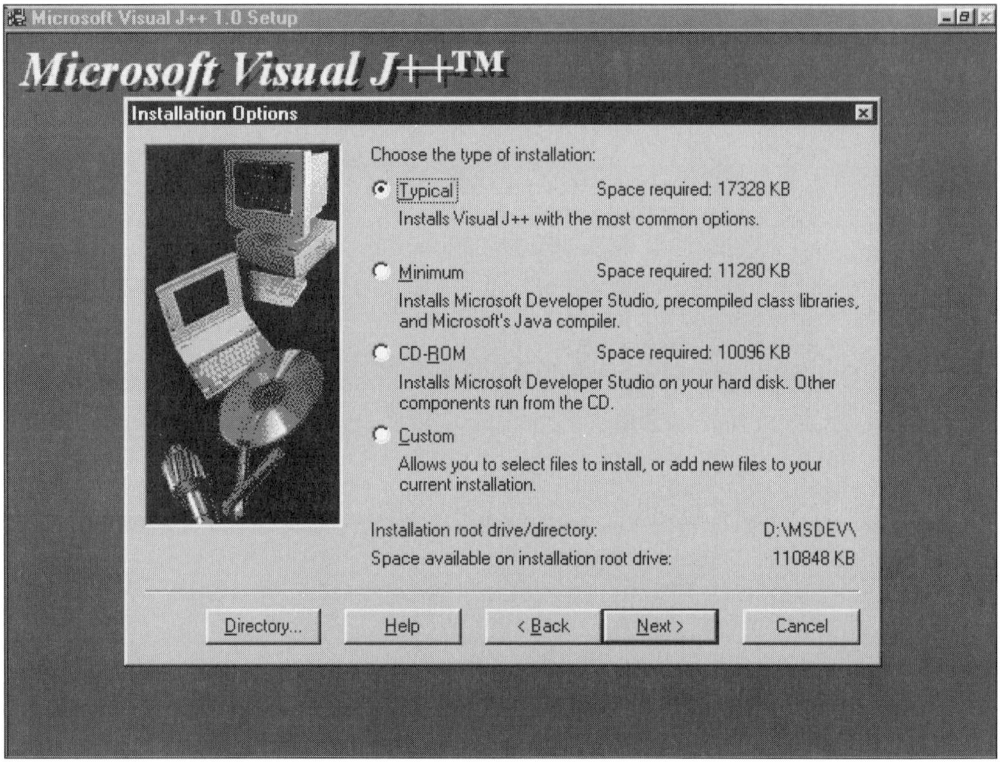

Figure 2.5: Choosing the Typical install option.

Note: The Java debugger requires a TCP/IP connection to run; if this is not present, you will get an "UnknownHostException" when launching the Java debugger. This often occurs when an IP address is obtained automatically from a service provider and you are running offline. It is possible to debug offline, but you must change the Windows95 Control Panel | Network | TCP/IP properties page and specify an IP address.

COMING TO TERMS

The following new terms have been discussed in this chapter and are presented here for your review.

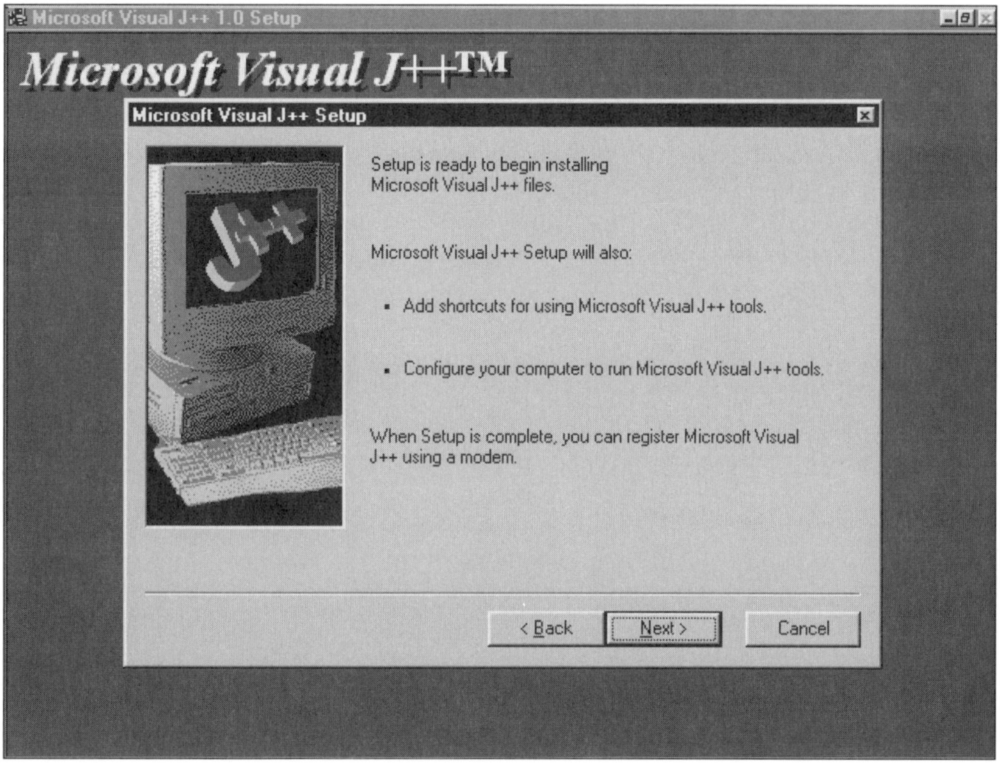

Figure 2.6: Adding Visual J++ shortcuts and tools.

block—Physically represented by brace pairs { }, which logically represent a related group of executable code statements.

coercion—Another term for the C/C++/Java cast operator, which refers to these languages' ability to allow a variable's type and precision to be temporarily changed.

exception handling—A programming language's ability to detect, and then eloquently (usually through programmer-written subroutines) recover from, what would normally be fatal error conditions.

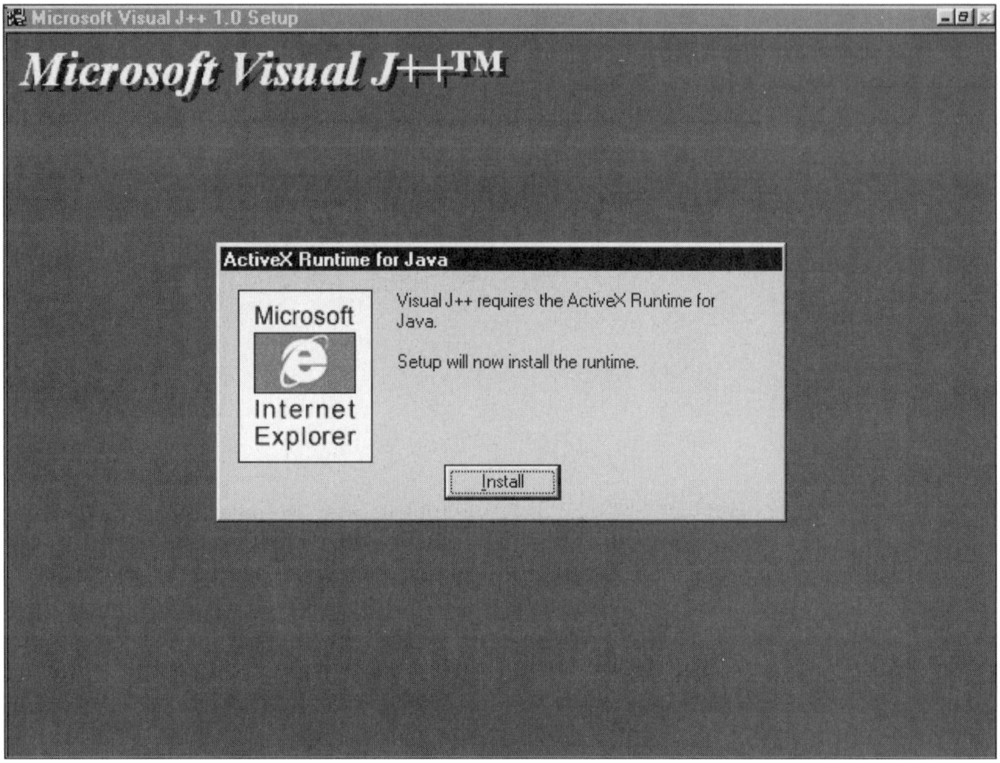

Figure 2.7: Loading the Active X run-time environment.

Hungarian notation—A style of creating identifiers whereby each variable or constant name begins with an abbreviation of its data type.

IDE—Microsoft's comprehensive program development environment with which you can enter, edit, compile, run, and debug Java programs. IDE stands for Integrated Development Environment.

identifier—The umbrella category that collectively describes variable names, constant names, and method (or function) names.

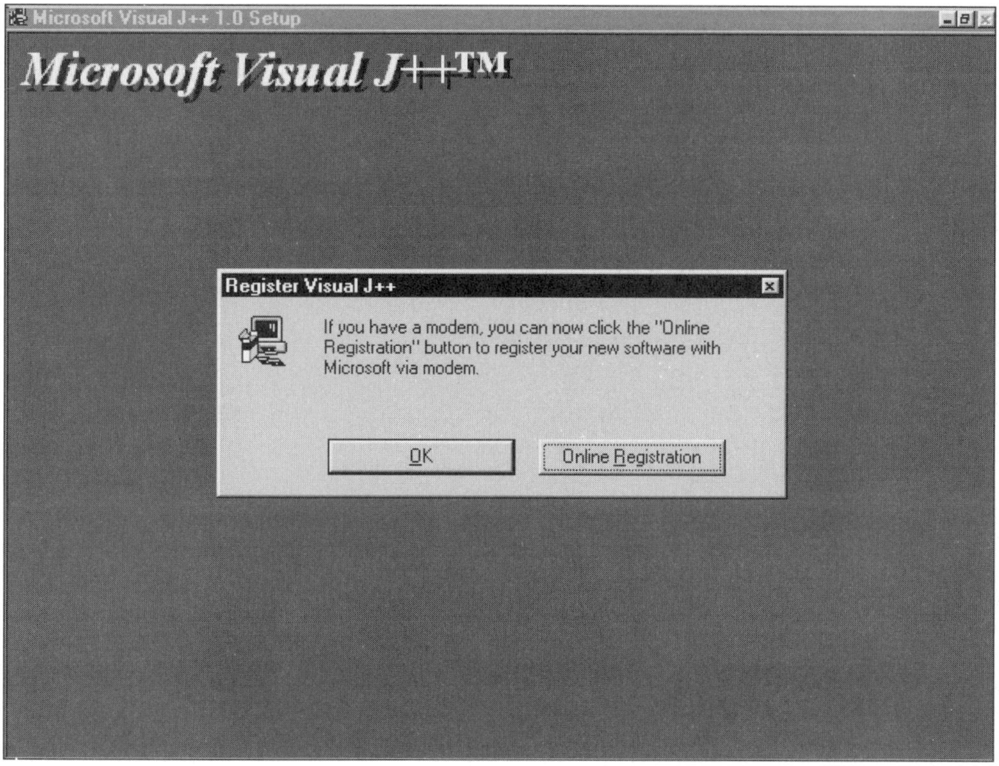

Figure 2.8: Microsoft Visual J++ online registration prompt.

literals—The term applied to the legal constant values assigned to the standard Java data types.

UNICODE—The new encryption standard that maps every known language in the world and yet-undefined languages to a 16-bit value. All Java source files are created using this new universal standard.

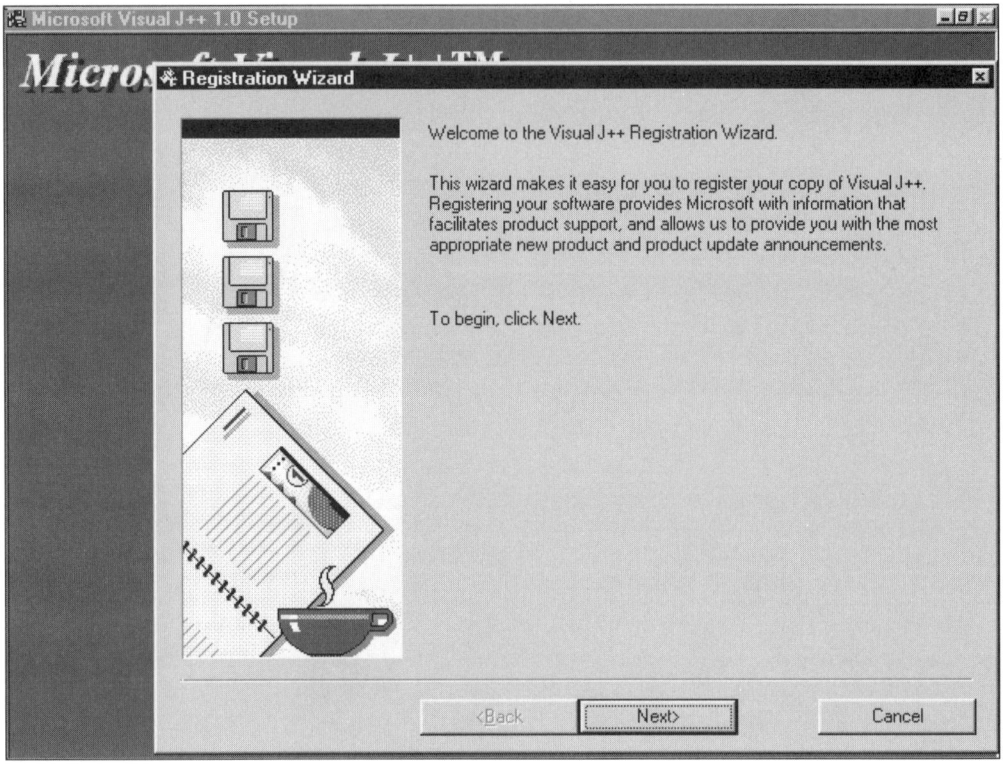

Figure 2.9: Registration Wizard.

Chapter 3

BASIC LANGUAGE FEATURES

If you have never used a Microsoft development environment, you are in for an exciting surprise. Microsoft has spent decades designing and refining program development tools that just about write an entire program for you. This is true about the Visual Basic and C/C++ compilers, and it is also true about the Visual J++ compiler/interpreter.

This chapter covers everything you need to know about writing, compiling, interpreting, running, and debugging Java applications and applets, using Microsoft's Visual J++ Java tools. Soon you will know how to generate a simple Java application or applet using Microsoft's JavaAppletWizard, with almost nothing more than mouse clicks!

WRITING YOUR FIRST JAVA APPLICATION

To begin, your Microsoft Visual J++ compiler/interpreter is shipped to you in two versions: the command line version and the integrated IDE version. Remember that Java is a full-featured programming language capable of developing standalone programs—these are called Java applications. The first program you write will be a Java application and you will use the command line Java compiler/interpreter to compile, debug, and run the application.

myfirst.java **Application**

To show you just how easy a process this is, using whatever text editor you choose, enter and save the following code:

```
/* myfirst.java                                       */
/* 4/4/96                                             */
/* Simple example application using WordPad to      */
/* enter the source code. The program will be        */
/* compiled with javac.exe, and then the program */
/* will be run using java.exe                         */

import java.util.Date;

class myfirst {
    public static void main(String args[]) {
      Date Today = new Date();
      System.out.println(Today);
    }
}
```

Use the filename *myfirst.java,* and save the file in your *Msdev//bin* subdirectory. All Java source files must have a *.java* file extension. Figure 3.1 uses the Windows 95 WordPad text editor to create and save the example source file.

Comments

This simple Java application begins with a comment block using the /* */ comment delimiter symbol pairs. Be careful not to forget to terminate your comments.

The import Statement

Here is the next statement in the program:

```
import java.util.Date;
```

This statement is closest in function to Pascal's or C/C++'s **#include** statement. What it does is pull in Java compiler–supplied class definitions.

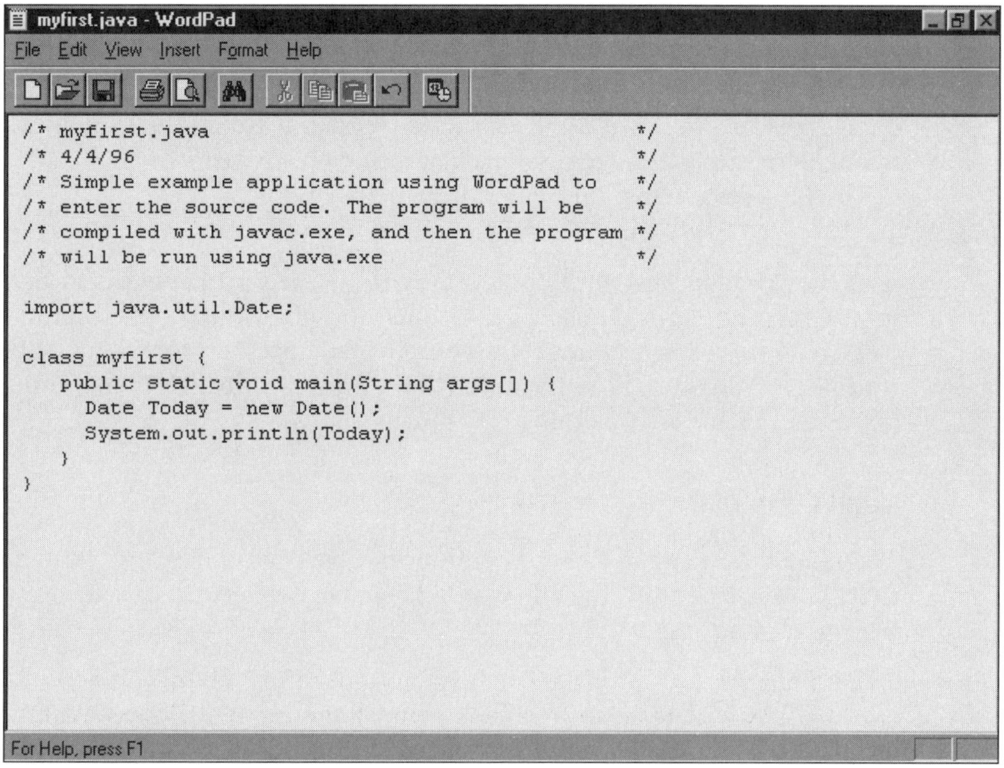

Figure 3.1: Using Microsoft Windows 95 WordPad to create Java source code.

Note: To C/C++ programmers, Java is not a two-pass compiler as C/C++ are and therefore the ***import*** *statement is not a preprocessor statement.*

After the **import** keyword comes a series of identifiers separated by periods. Many programming languages use this period . operator. In Pascal and Modula-3, this operator is used to select fields within a record. In C/C++, the operator performs the same logical function, only you would say that the operator selects members of a structure.

But in C/C++, the same operator is used in a more advanced syntax, namely selecting functions; only these functions are called *member functions* or *methods*. Member functions or methods are functions that are syntactically tied to a specific structure or class. They have been given this unique name so that programmers can distinguish between standalone functions (those written in a procedural design approach) and member functions or methods (used in object-oriented programming class or object definitions). Simply stated, an *object* in object-oriented programming is a syntactic way of bundling data declarations, called *member data*, with the functions that work with the member data, called *member functions* or *methods*.

The Java statement:

```
import java.util.Date;
```

uses the *period member operator* along with the **import** keyword to pull in Java compiler–supplied definitions for the **util.Date()** method (which, from a programmer's viewpoint, is closest in form to a subroutine or function). Finally, notice that all Java code statements must terminate with a semicolon.

Your First class

The next statement in the application involves two lines of code. The first line starting with the keyword **class** and the second line containing the closing brace }:

```
class myfirst {
      .
      .
      .
}
```

To begin your understanding of a Java **class**, think of a Pascal **record** or C/C++ **struct** definition. These keywords allow a programmer to logically relate different data types into one user-defined unit. C++ and Java **class** syntax has the identical capability, only the **class** goes one step further by allowing the syntactic bundling of **class**-specific member functions. All Java programming must be done within a **class**. The Java language does not support standalone functions. Following the coded example's use of the keyword **class** is the user-defined **class** name, in this case *myfirst*. All **class** code must be surrounded with brace pairs { . . . }.

The Required main() Method

The first statement within the class definition also involves two lines of code, the formal **main()** method definition and its matching closing brace }:

```
public static void main(String args[]) {
        .
        .
        .
}
```

The *compound block* (meaning more than one line of code surrounded by a brace pair { }) statement begins with the **public** keyword, which indicates that the method **main()** is globally accessible. Without going into too much detail too soon, the **static** keyword defines when the method **main()** is put into the symbol table and the persistence of the method **main()**. **void** is a keyword also used in C/C++ programming, and in this syntax it indicates that the method **main()** does not return any value.

Not only must all Java code be nested within a **class** definition, but all Java applications must have a method called **main()**, where program execution begins and usually terminates. The only formal argument to **main()** is *(String args[])*. The keyword **String** used in the formal argument list defines *args[]* as an array of the **String** class.

This definition allows a Java program to easily check for, and incorporate, command line arguments passed to the application. For example, the MS-DOS program *copy.exe*, when executed, expects the user to type two filenames: *file_to_copy.ext* and *file_name_of_copy.ext*. These filenames fall under the category of *command line arguments*. By putting *(String args[])* in the Java **main()** formal argument list, you give the application the ability to import and use command line arguments.

The formal argument name, *args[]*, is closest to the C/C++ **main()** formal argument *argv[]*. However, there is a difference between the two languages that C/C++ programmers need to know. In C/C++ the first string available in *argv[0]* is the name of the application, with the second string being the first command line argument. In our MS-DOS example, this means the first string is *copy.exe*, and the second string is *file_to_copy.ext*. In a Java application, you have no access to the program's name. This means that the first string, found at *args[0]*, is the name of the first command line argument—in this case, *file_to_copy.ext*.

Instantiating Your First Object

The first statement inside the sample program's **main()** method is:

```
Date Today = new Date();
```

This statement defines the member *Today* to be of type **Date** and uses the **new** keyword to dynamically allocate an instance of the method **Date()**. An *instance* of member data, or member functions, is closest to the procedural concept of creating a variable, except that instance is an object-oriented programming concept.

Simple Output with the println() Method

The Java application now has all of the member data declarations and methods necessary to query the system's clock and fill in the data members with valid information. For this reason, the next statement:

```
System.out.println(Today);
```

can simply call the **System.out.println()** method to output *Today*'s valid member data. Now that you have some understanding of how the program works, it is time to try your first compile.

Running *jvc.exe*

You'll find the Java command line compiler, named *jvc.exe*. under the *Msdev//bin* subdirectory. To run the command line compiler, switch to a DOS compatibility window and type *Jvc myfirst*, as seen below:

```
Microsoft (R) Visual J++ Compiler Version 1.00.6173
Copyright (C) Microsoft Corp 1996. All rights reserved.
```

If you entered the source file without any errors, this is all you will see. However, *jvc.exe* is capable of command line diagnostics. If you want the Java compiler to list error messages to the screen, you need to run it in verbose mode. To do this, simply type *jvc /verbose myfirst*, as seen in this next listing:

```
Microsoft (R) Visual J++ Compiler Version 1.00.6173
Copyright (C) Microsoft Corp 1996. All rights reserved.

Parsing myfirst.java:
    Loading class: [c:\windows\java\classes\classes.zip]\java\
        util\Date.class (referenced in myfirst.java)
    Loading class: [c:\windows\java\classes\classes.zip]\java\
        lang\Object.class (referenced in myfirst.java)
Compiling myfirst.java:
    Loading class: [c:\windows\java\classes\classes.zip]\java\
        lang\String.class (referenced in myfirst.java)
```

```
Loading class: [c:\windows\java\classes\classes.zip]\java\
    lang\System.class (referenced in myfirst.java)
Loading class: [c:\windows\java\classes\classes.zip]\
    java\io\PrintStream.class (referenced in myfirst.java)
Loading class: [c:\windows\java\classes\classes.zip]\
    java\io\FilterOutputStream.class (referenced in
    myfirst.java)
Loading class: [c:\windows\java\classes\classes.zip]\
    java\io\OutputStream.class (referenced in myfirst.java)
Generating file 'myfirst.class'
```

In */verbose* mode, *jvc.exe* provides a detailed step-by-step progress report on each class and statement being translated. Notice how fast this new Microsoft Java compiler processes the source file!

jvc.exe Command Line Switches

Table 3.1 lists all of the *jvc.exe* command line switches. The syntax for using *jvc.exe* looks like:

```
Usage: JVC [options] <filename>
```

Table 3.1: *jvc.exe* Command Line Switches

Jvc Switch	*Meaning*
/cp <classpath>	Set class path for compilation
/cp:p <path>	Prepend path to class path
/cp:o[-]	Print classpath
/d <directory>	Root directory for class file output
/g[-]	Full debug information (g:l, g:d)
/g:l[-]	Generate line numbers <default=none>
/g:t[-]	Generate debug tables <default=none>
/nowarn	Turns off warnings <default=warn>
/nowrite	Compile only; do not generate class files
/O[-]	Full optimization (O:I,O:J)
/O:I[-]	Optimize by inlining <default=no opt>
/O:J[-]	Optimize bytecode jumps <default=no opt>
/verbose	Print messages about compilation progress
/w{0-4}	Set warning level <default=2>
/x[-]	Disable extensions <default=enabled> '-' Turns flag off

Remember, *jvc.exe* only works on source files with a **.java* file extension.

Running myfirst.class **Using** jview.exe

Regardless of whether you ran the Java compiler in standard or verbose mode, *jvc.exe* took your Java source file, *myfirst.java*, and generated an executable file called *myfirst.class*. Most compilers generate executable files with an *.exe* file extension. However, a Java executable has a *.class* file extension.

To run your Java application, you use *jview.exe*, which is the runtime Java interpreter. At this point you are ready to execute your first Java application by typing *jview myfirst* as seen below.

```
Microsoft (R) Visual J++ Command-line Interpreter Version
1.00.6173
Copyright (C) Microsoft Corp 1996. All rights reserved.
Sun Jul 14 09:35:31 SA Pacific Standard Time 1996
```

***jview.exe* Command Line Switches** Table 3.2 lists all of the *jview.exe* command line switches. The syntax for running *jview.exe* looks like:

```
Usage: JView [options] <classname> [arguments]
```

Remember, Java compilers do not output the usual **.exe* executable files. Instead, they generate machine-independent bytecode files with a **.class* file extension. *jview.exe* will only interpret files with **.class* file extensions.

Writing Your First Java Applet

The source code for your first Java applet is not that much different from its Java application counterpart. Let's take a look at the Java applet source code line by line:

```
/* mysecond.java                                    */
/* 4/4/96                                           */
/* This second example demonstrates how to write   */
/* a simple Java applet. This requires two files   */
/* first the Java source file, and second the */
/* HTML document which will use the <APPLET> */
/* tag to refer to the Java applet being written. */
```

Table 3.2: jview.exe Command Line Switches

Jview Option	*Meaning*
/?	Display usage text
/a	Run <classname> as an applet Note: The default is to run as a standalone application if the class contains a **main();** otherwise it runs as an applet.
/cp <classpath>	Set class path
/cp:p <path>	Prepend path to class path
/cp:a <path>	Append path to class path
Classname	Class file to be executed
Arguments	Command-line arguments to be passed on to the class file if class is being run as an applet; the arguments must be in the form of: param1=value1 param2=value2 ... paramN=valueN Note: Place double quotation marks around the value if it contains spaces.

```
/* The following statement is identical to the     */
/* one used in the Java application previously     */
/* discussed.                                      */
import java.util.Date;

import java.awt.Graphics;        /* new imports    */
import java.applet.Applet;

public class mysecond extends java.applet.Applet {
  Date Today;
  String TodayAsString;

  public void paint(Graphics graphic) {
    Today = new Date();
    TodayAsString = Today.toString();
    graphic.drawString( TodayAsString, 10, 10 );
  }
}
```

Once again, the program begins with a comment block. To make this applet as similar as possible to its application counterpart, it too is going to simply output today's day, date, time, and year. For this reason, the program continues with the same **import** statement used in the Java application:

```
import java.util.Date;
```

However, the applet needs additional horsepower, which is included by the next two **import** statements:

```
import java.applet.*;
import java.awt.*;
```

You already know what the **import** statement accomplishes, but let's take a closer syntactic look at what follows the keyword—namely, *java.util.Date, java.awt.Graphics,* and *java.applet.Applet*. From previous discussions, you know that the period member operator . can select either an object's data members or, in these two statements, methods. In this analogy, then, we would be referencing *.Date, .Graphics.,* and *.Applet*. At this point, however, you may be wondering what the *java, awt,* or *applet* identifiers do.

The Java language lets you logically relate groups of **class** definitions into a side effect–proof syntax called a *package*. The three **import** statements access specific methods—*.Date, .Graphics,* and *.Applet*—within their respective packages, *java, java.awt,* and *java.applet*. Notice Sun's style of naming these identifiers. All package names begin with lowercase, while all methods (member functions tied to a specific object **class**) begin with an uppercase letter. This is not a compiler requirement, just the developer's preference. However, because Java is a case-sensitive language, having a general idea of how compiler-supplied code is written makes it that much easier to use.

The source file continues by defining the object *mysecond*, using the **class** keyword:

```
public class mysecond extends java.applet.Applet {
      .
      .
      .
}
```

The **public** keyword acknowledges the *mysecond* **class** definition as being globally accessible and could have also been placed before the **class** keyword in the previous Java application's coded example. However, unlike the application counterpart, this **class** definition contains the keyword **extends**. This keyword tells the compiler that you are going to use the imported object's members (data and function types), but that the program is going to add application-specific functionality. In this case, the applet is going to define two data members:

```
Date Today;
String TodayAsString;
```

As in C/C++, when you are declaring data members, the member's data type comes first. Here *Today*'s data type is the class **Date**, and *TodayAsString* is of class type **String**. As in the Java application example, *Today* will be used to hold the current day, date, and year. *TodayAsString* will be used to hold the same information converted to string format for output.

The applet continues by enhancing the inherited **paint()** method defined in **java.awt.Graphics**. *Inheritance* of member functions or methods is very similar to the way a record variable, in Pascal (or, in C/C++, a structure variable) inherits its formal record's declaration fields:

```
public void paint( Graphics graphic ) {
      .
      .
      .
}
```

Notice that the method's body is encapsulated within a pair of braces { }. Once again, the **public** keyword flags the compiler to this method's visibility outside the formal **class** definition. **void** means the method returns nothing—officially. *paint()* is the name of the method and the dummy argument *graphic* is of class type **Graphics**.

Because the **paint()** method is a standard member function of the **Graphics** class, the application-specific code added to it is considered an extension of the formal **paint()** method:

```
Today = new Date();
TodayAsString = Today.toString();
graphic.drawString( TodayAsString, 10, 10 );
```

Here the member function uses the **new** keyword to dynamically allocate enough memory for an instance of the method *Date()* and then assigns its memory address to *Today*. The second statement uses an inherited method, namely *toString()*, to convert *Today*'s numeric format into a string for output. Notice how easy it is to invoke an inherited object's methods (member functions) using the period member operator *Today.toString()*. The third and final statement uses the *graphic* instance's inherited *drawString()* (formally **Graphic.drawString()** member function or method—these terms are intentionally substituted for one another so that you become comfortable with either term), to output *TodayAsString*!

Writing Your First HTML File

Unfortunately, just rewriting the Java application's source code using applet syntax is not enough to create a Java applet. An applet, by definition, is meant to be embedded within an Internet Web page; and as such, it needs an HTML (Hyper Text Markup Language) invocation file. After you create a class or classes that contain your applet and compile them into class files, as you would for any other Java program, you create a Web page to hold that applet. There is a special HTML *tag* or *element* for including applets in Web pages. Java-capable browsers, such as HotJava, use the information contained in that element to locate the compiled class files and execute the applet itself. This section explains how to put Java applets in a Web page and how to serve those files to the Web at large.

You include an applet on a Web page by using the HTML element **<applet>**. The following listing shows the simplest HTML file you can create to include *mysecond.class*:

```
<title>The mysecond Applet</title>
<hr>
<applet code=mysecond.class width=200 height=200>
</applet>
```

The HTML file (which is just an ASCII text file) wraps the program's title, *The mysecond Applet,* between the opening and closing title elements, **<title>** and **</title>**. The text between the **<title>** and **</title>** elements is displayed by browsers that do not understand the **<applet>** tag (which includes most browsers that are not Java-capable). Because your Web page may be viewed in many different kinds of browsers, you should include alternate text here so that readers of your page who don't have Java will see something other than a blank line.

You'll notice that many HTML elements have an opening and closing syntax. The closing element repeats the opening HTML element but prepends a slash symbol /. The **<hr>** represents a *horizontal rule.* This element causes the Web page to display a thin highlighted separator bar and moves the program's output pointer to the beginning of a new line.

Of particular importance to the *mysecond.java* applet is the third statement. Here the **<applet code=...>** element pulls the compiled *mysecond.class* into the Web page. *width* and *height* are required and used to indicate the bounding box of the applet—that is, how big a box to draw for the applet on the Web page. (Actually, there is more syntax required for a properly written HTML file, which is discussed later in this chapter.)

Creating *mysecond.java* and the associated HTML file doesn't really look all that difficult. However, you still need to pull it all together to test it. Also, creating more Java applets would require not only a rewrite of the Java source file, but new HTML support files—which would be a time-consuming endeavor. Fortunately, Microsoft has included a Java-specific JavaAppletWizard in the IDE. A later discussion explains how to use this versatile Java development tool. First, however, let's look at two "quick'n dirty" approaches to Java program development provided by Microsoft's Development Studio.

NINE SIMPLE STEPS FOR DEVELOPING A JAVA APPLICATION

As you will see, Microsoft has provided many different approaches to creating, compiling, and interpreting Java source code, from standalone command line development cycles, simple "automatic" application and applet development, to full-blown, robust program development. You have already learned the standalone approach using a separate word processor, *jvc.exe* and *jview.exe.*

This section details the nine quick steps to Java application development using Visual J++'s IDE Editor. The nine steps are:

1. From the **File** menu, select **New** to open the **New** dialog box.
2. Select Text File and click OK. A blank text editor window opens.

3. Type the following code in the text editor:

```
public class HiThere
{
        public static void main( String args[] )
        {
                System.out.println( "Hello, Java Programmer!" );
        }
}
```

4. From the **File** menu, select **Save** to open the **Save** dialog box.
5. Type `HiThere.java` and click OK.
6. From the **Build** menu, select **Build *HiThere***. A dialog box opens, prompting you to create a default workspace.
7. Click Yes. Visual J++ creates a default workspace and builds the application.
8. From the Build menu, select **Execute**. The **Information for Running Class** dialog box opens, prompting you to select whether you want to run the class using a browser (as an applet) or using the standalone interpreter (as an application).
9. Choose the standalone interpreter. The Java application runs.

It's just that easy! Use this approach whenever you need to quickly test a piece of Java application code.

NINE SIMPLE STEPS FOR DEVELOPING A JAVA APPLET

Creating a simple Java applet is just as easy as its application counterpart, with just a few modifications. To quickly enter, edit, save, and run a Java applet, follow these basic nine steps:

1. From the **File** menu, select **New** to open the **New** dialog box.
2. Select Text File and click OK. A blank text editor window opens.
3. Type the following code in the text editor:

```
import java.awt.Graphics;

public class HiAgain extends java.applet.Applet
{
```

```
    public void paint( Graphics g )
    {
        g.drawString( "Hello, Again!", 50, 25 );
    }
}
```

4. From the **File** menu, select **Save** to open the **Save** dialog box.
5. Type `HiAgain.java` and click OK.
6. From the **Build** menu, select **Build *HiAgain***. A dialog box opens, prompting you to create a default workspace.
7. Click Yes. Visual J++ creates a default workspace and builds the applet.
8. From the **Build** menu, select **Execute**. The **Information for Running Class** dialog box opens, prompting you to select whether you want to run the class using a browser (that is, as an applet) or using the standalone interpreter (as an application).
9. Choose the browser option. The Java applet runs. Use JavaAppletWizard to generate a basic Java applet as a starting point for your own applets.

Of course, the default workspace and associated HTML file are devoid of any sophisticated capabilities. Once again, use these nine steps whenever you want to quickly enter, edit, save, compile, and run Java applet source code.

USING MICROSOFT'S JAVAAPPLETWIZARD

The standalone *jvc.exe* Java compiler and *jview.exe* interpreter are straightforward to use; these procedures are cumbersome, however, when you are writing applets. For this reason, Microsoft has included a special Java tool—the JavaAppletWizard—in the Microsoft C++ IDE (Integrated Development Environment). You begin by launching Visual J++.

Starting Visual J++

You launch Visual J++ by first selecting Microsoft Visual J++ from the main program group, and then Microsoft Developer Studio. Figure 3.2 shows the initial Visual J++ start-up window.

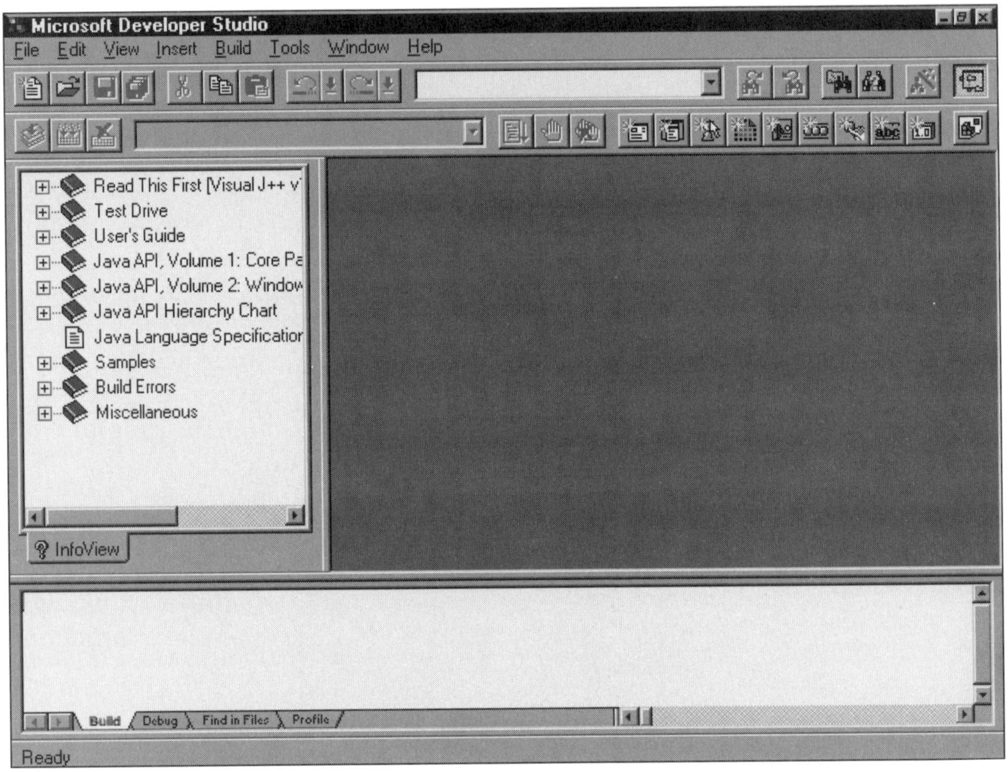

Figure 3.2: Starting Visual J++.

Notice the list of online books available to assist you in learning how to use the IDE provided by the Developer Studio.

Starting a New Java Project

To begin writing your own Java applet or application:

1. Click on the **File | New | Project Workspace** option (see Figure 3.3). The New Project workspace window appears, as shown in Figure 3.4.
2. To begin a Java project definition, give the project a location and name (here, use *mysecond)*. Accept the default for platform type, which is check marked in Figure 3.4 (Java Virtual Machine).

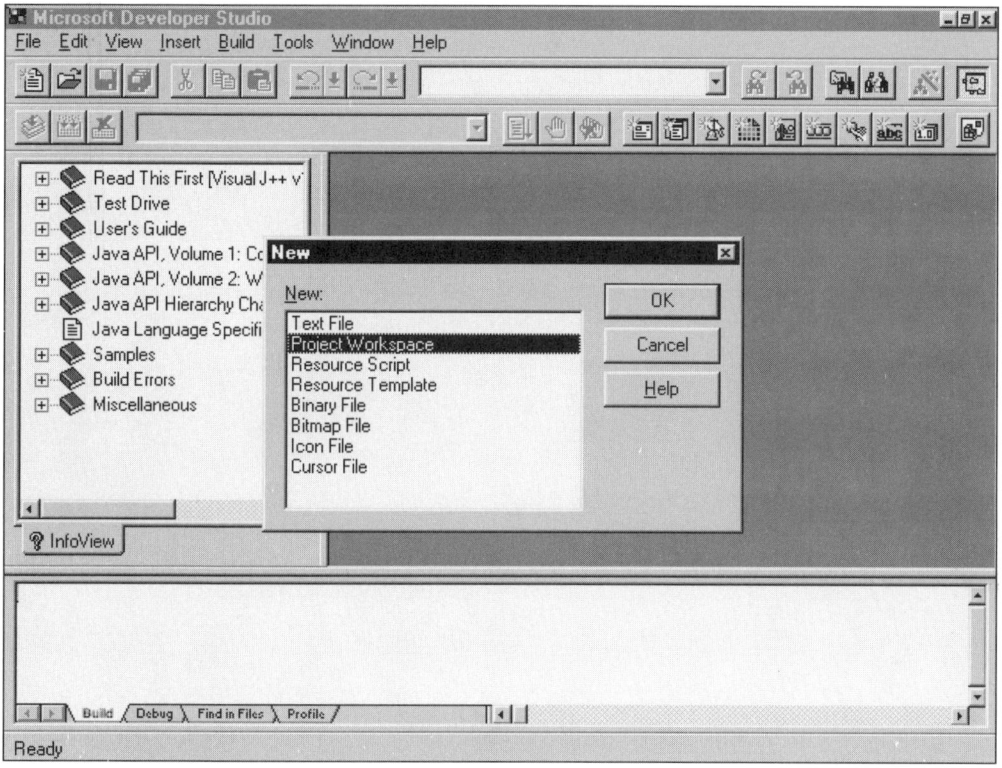

Figure 3.3: Starting a new Java project.

3. Click on the JavaAppletWizard type to launch the JavaAppletWizard for Java (see Figure 3.5). To accept these settings, click on the Create button.
4. In the first window of the JavaAppletWizard (see Figure 3.6) select the *As an applet and as an application* radiobutton. Now you can see the code automatically generated by JavaAppletWizard for creating both types of Java programs, simultaneously! Also, select the *No, thank you* option for source file comments. Now click on the Next> button.
5. On the second window of the JavaAppletWizard (Figure 3.7), select the *No, thank you* option for the sample HTML file, and change the screen resolution to match your monitor. For this example, the values 320 and 240 were changed to 640 and 480. Once again, click on the Next> button.

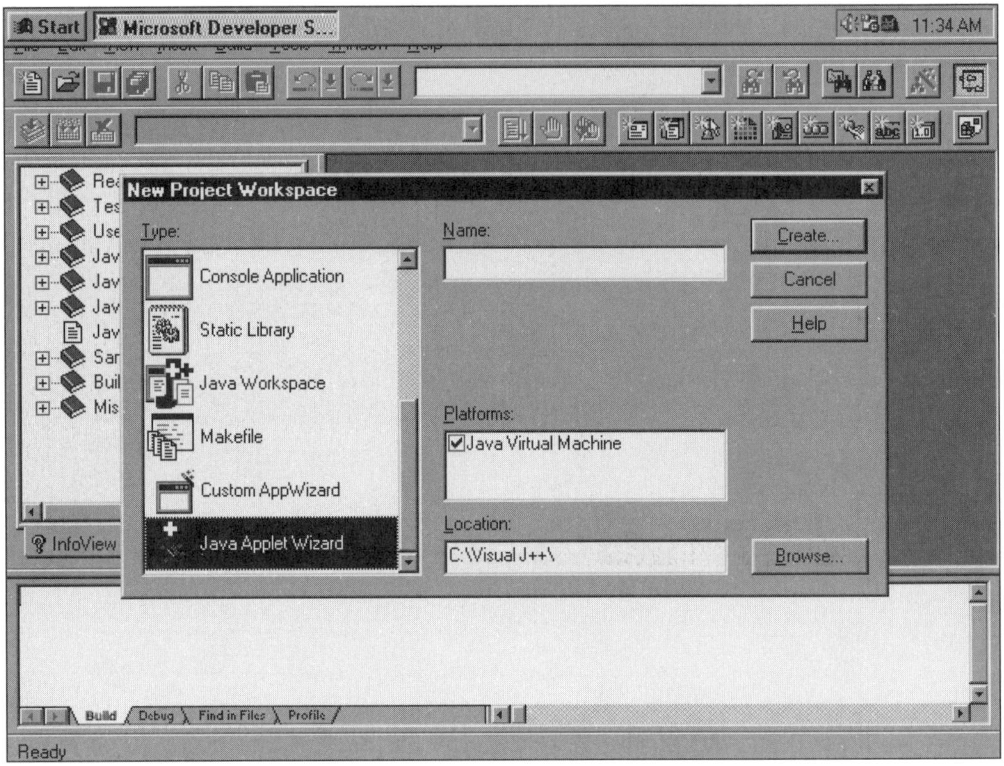

Figure 3.4: New Project Workspace window.

6. On the third window of the JavaAppletWizard (Figure 3.8) you select multithreaded program options and a mouse interface. For now, click these off by choosing the *No, thank you* radiobutton and then click on the Next> button.
7. In the JavaAppletWizard parameters window (Figure 3.9), you do not need to add any additional information for this introductory example. Click on the Next> button. Note that any information you enter in this dialog box is accessible to the Java **GetParameterInfo()** member function (method).
8. In this final window of the JavaAppletWizard (see Figure 3.10), you review the information returned by the method call **GetAppInfo()**. When you are developing a marketable prod-

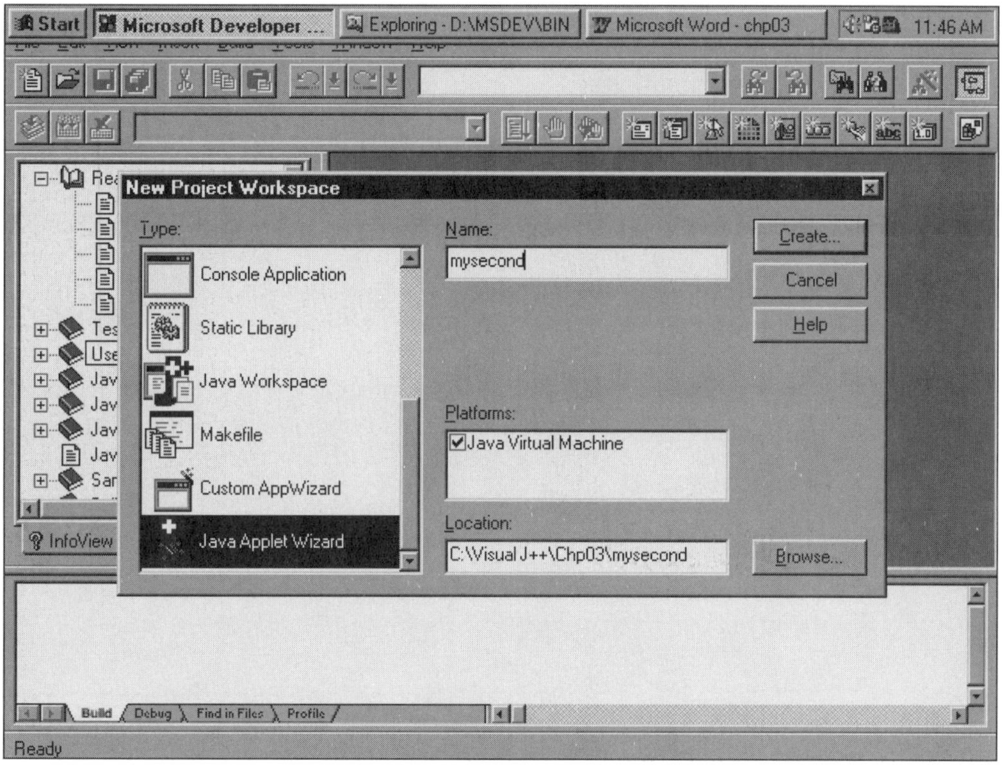

Figure 3.5: Completed information in the New Project Workspace window.

uct, this is the ideal location to present any copyright information, version numbers, service phone numbers, and so on. With this information reviewed, click on the Finish button.

9. Examine the detailed summary page highlighting all of the parameters set for this Java program (Figure 3.11). At this point, the JavaAppletWizard has all of the information necessary to create the Java program, so click on the OK button.
10. View the default development window generated by the JavaAppletWizard (Figure 3.12). This subdirectory has been created to hold everything necessary to create your program. Double-click on the *mysecond classes* folder to see an expanded directory listing (Figure 3.13).

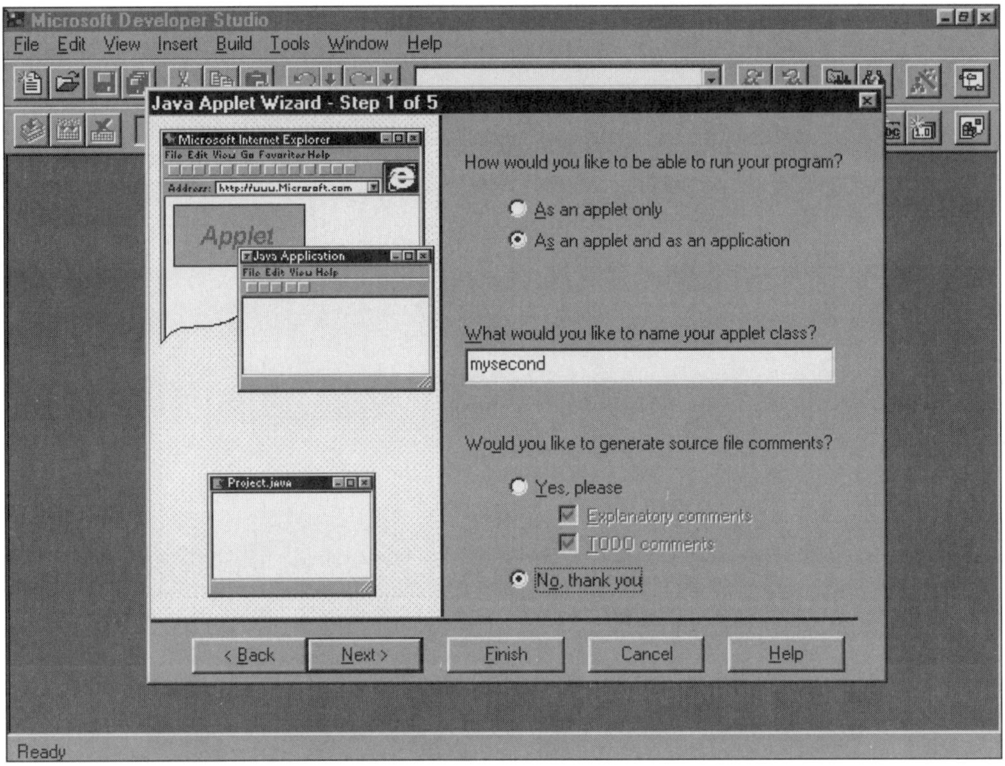

Figure 3.6: First window of the JavaAppletWizard.

11. The JavaAppletWizard generates two files: a source file, in this example *mysecond*, and a FrameClass, *mysecondFrame* (only used if the program is run as an applet). Because the default source file *mysecond* doesn't do anything except put up an empty window at run-time, you need to modify it. At this point, double-click on *mysecond* in the subdirectory window. The IDE will locate the file and automatically open it.
12. Modify the blank template so that it looks like the following listing:

```
import java.util.Date;

import java.applet.*;
```

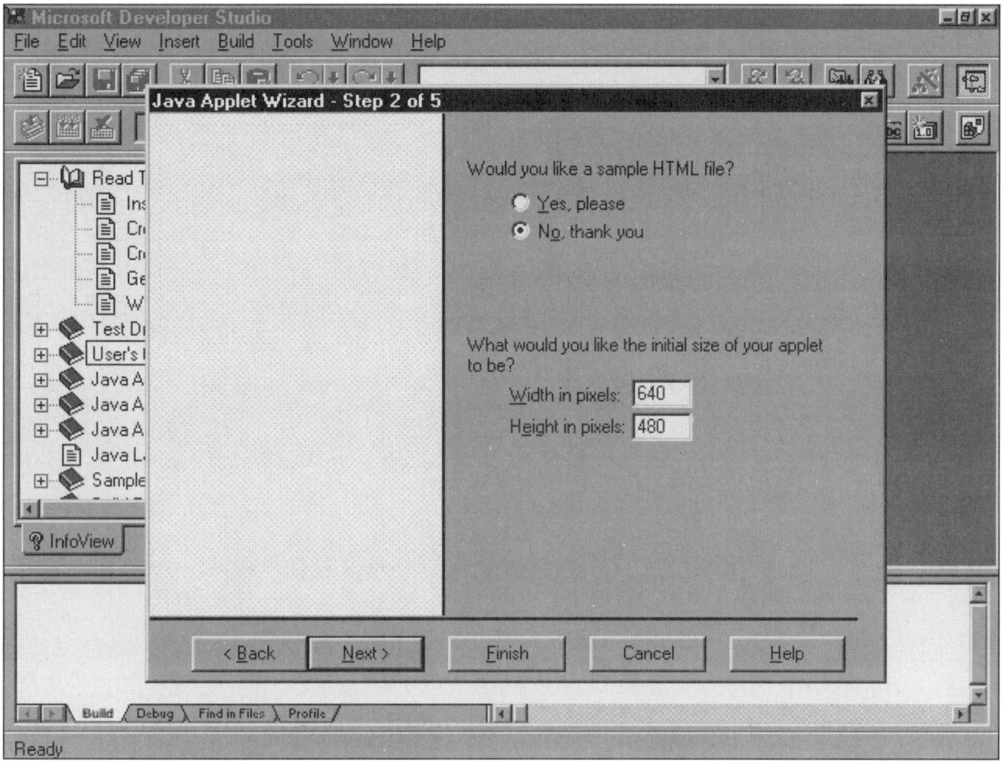

Figure 3.7: Microsoft JavaAppletWizard for Java window (*Methods* tab selected).

```
import java.awt.Graphics;
import mysecondFrame;

public class mysecond extends Applet
{
    // STANDALONE APPLICATION SUPPORT:
    //        m_fStandAlone will be set to
    //        true if applet is run standalone
    //-----------------------------------------
    boolean m_fStandAlone = false;

    Date Today;
    String TodayAsString;
```

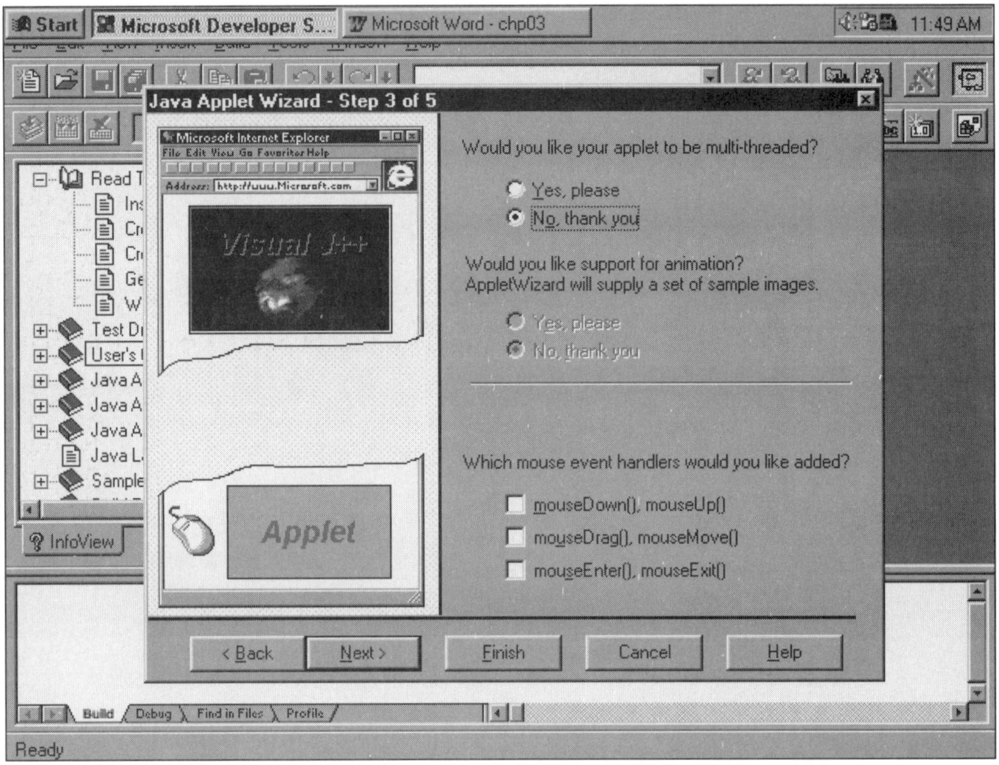

Figure 3.8: The third window of the JavaAppletWizard.

```
    public static void main(String args[])
    {
        mysecondFrame frame = new mysecondFrame("mysecond");

        // Must show Frame before we size it
        // so insets() will return valid
        // values
        //---------------------------------------------
        frame.show();
        frame.resize(frame.insets().left + frame.insets().right
+ 640,
```

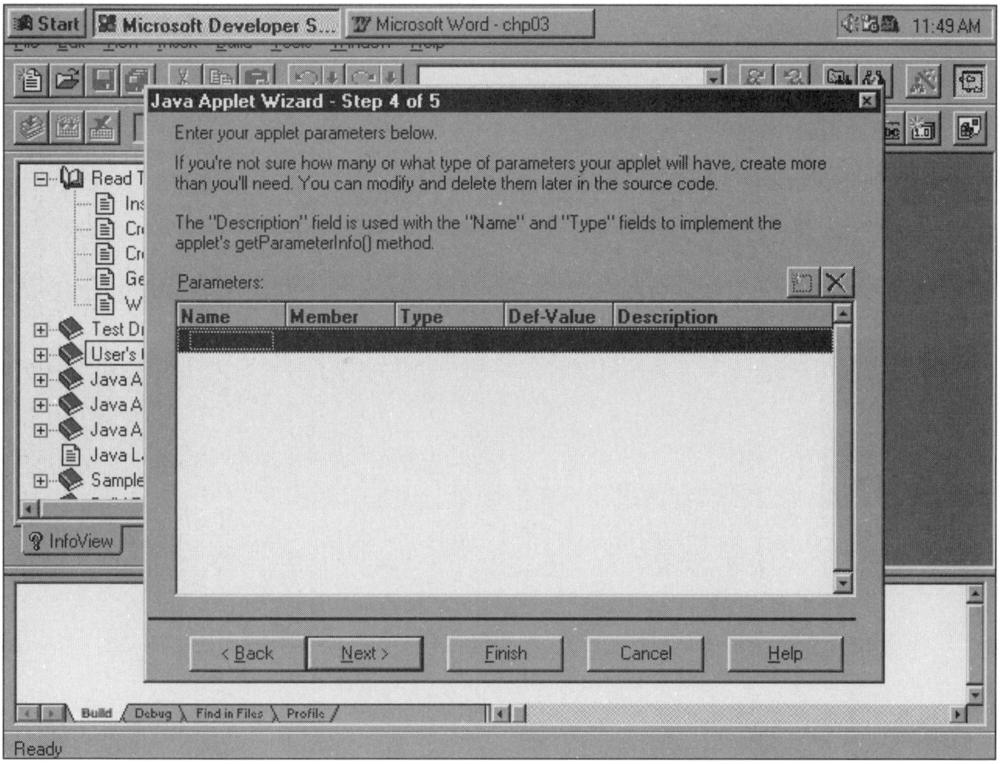

Figure 3.9: The JavaAppletWizard parameters window.

```
                              frame.insets().top  +
frame.insets().bottom +
                                         480);

           mysecond applet_mysecond = new mysecond();

           frame.add("Center", applet_mysecond);
           applet_mysecond.m_fStandAlone = true;
           applet_mysecond.init();
           applet_mysecond.start();
     }

     public mysecond()
```

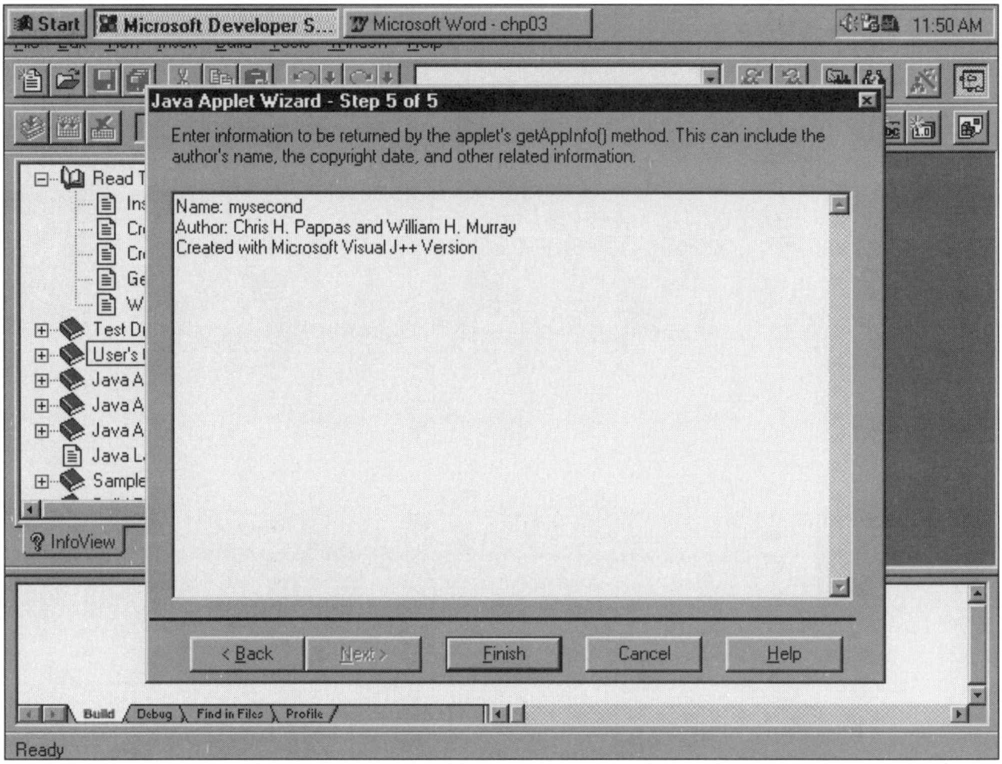

Figure 3.10: The final window of the JavaAppletWizard.

```
    {
    }

    public String getAppletInfo()
    {
        return  "Name: mysecond\r\n" +
                "Author: Chris H. Pappas and William H.
Murray\r\n" +
                "Created with Microsoft Visual  J++ Version";
    }


    public void init()
    {
```

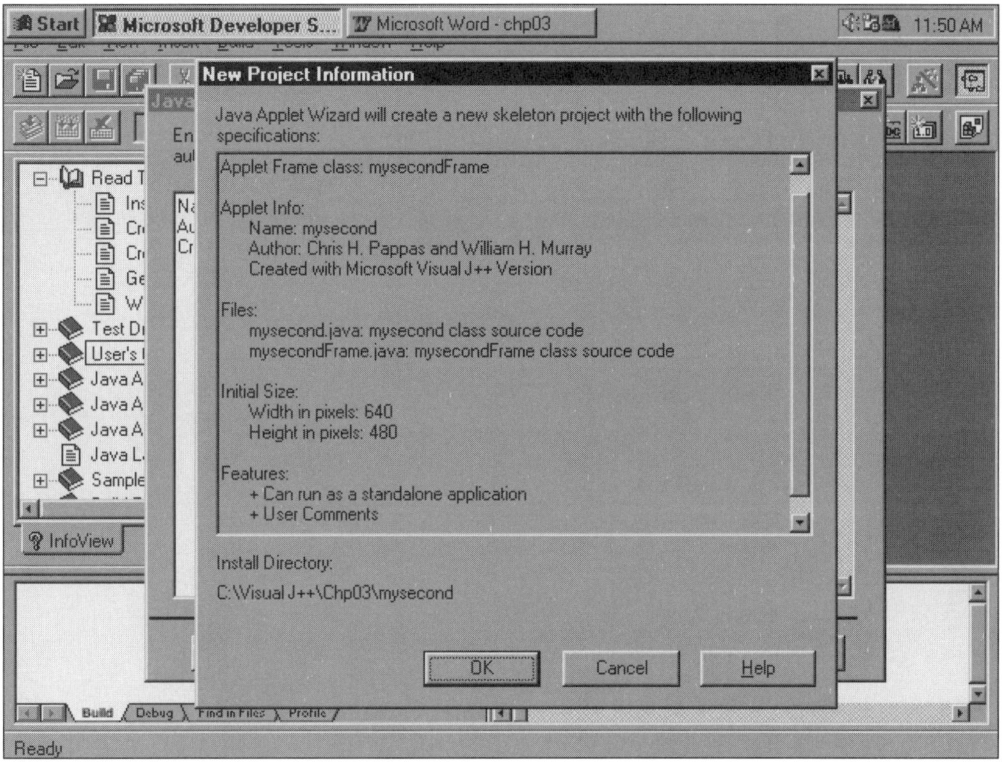

Figure 3.11: JavaAppletWizard New Project Information window.

```
// If you use a ResourceWizard-
// generated "control creator" class
// to arrange controls in your
// applet, you may want to call its
// CreateControls() method from
// within this method. Remove the
// following call to resize() before
// adding the call to
// CreateControls();
// CreateControls() does its own
// resizing.
//-------------------------------------------
resize(640, 480);
```

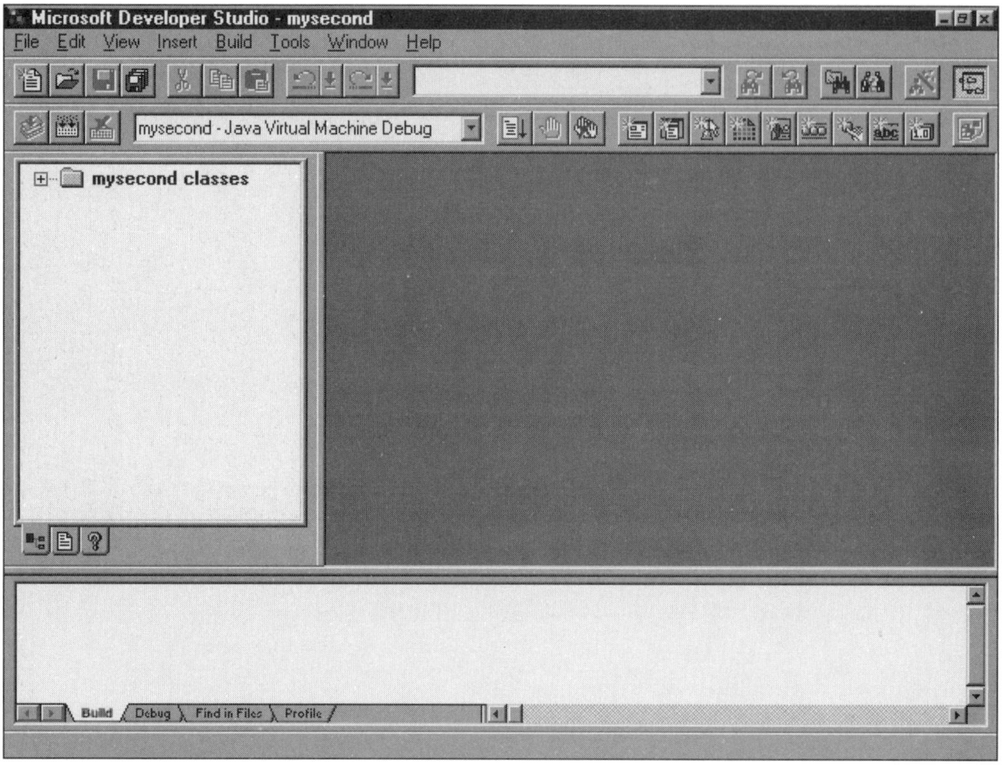

Figure 3.12: Default JavaAppletWizard program development window.

```
    }

    public void destroy()
    {
    }

    public void paint(Graphics graphic)
    {
        Today = new Date();
        TodayAsString = Today.toString();
        graphic.drawString( TodayAsString, 10, 10 );
    }

    public void start()
```

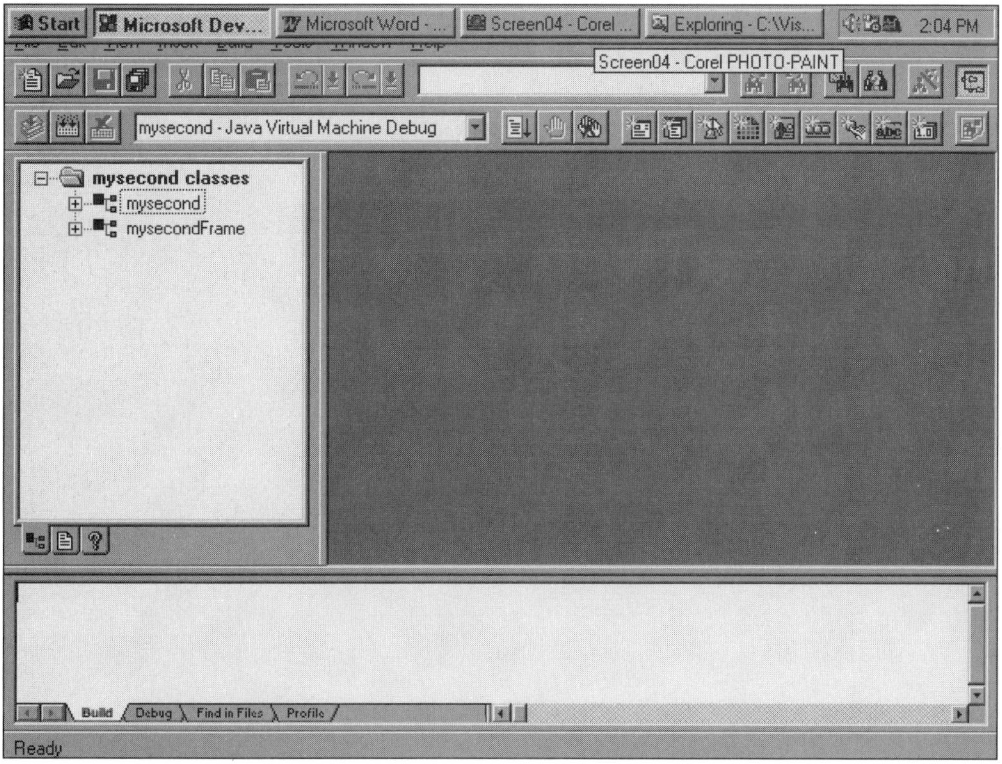

Figure 3.13: Expanded *mysecond classes* subdirectory.

```
        {
        }

        public void stop()
        {
        }

}
```

13. The top of your edit window should now look like that shown in Figure 3.14. Save your file by selecting **Save** from the **File** menu.

    The following listing contains the *mysecondFrame.java* code automatically generated by the JavaAppletWizard. Unless you have already done some object-oriented Windows pro-

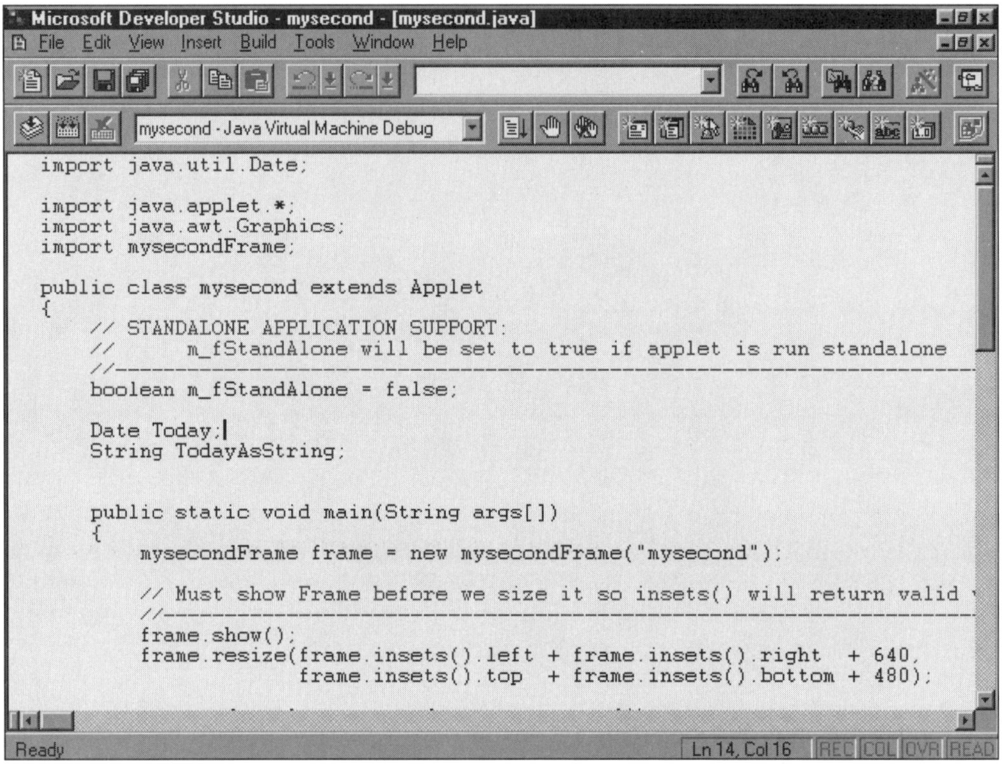

Figure 3.14: The edited JavaAppletWizard template.

gramming, the file's contents may be a bit confusing. Later chapters in the book discuss this file's purpose and syntax in greater detail:

```
import java.awt.*;

class mysecondFrame extends Frame
{
    public mysecondFrame(String str)
    {
        super (str);
    }

    public boolean handleEvent(Event evt)
    {
```

```
            switch (evt.id)
            {
                case Event.WINDOW_DESTROY:
                    dispose();
                    System.exit(0);
                    return true;

                default:
                    return super.handleEvent(evt);
            }
        }
}
```

The file contains a **Frame** class extension, *mysecondFrame,* which is specific to this program example, and two methods, *mysecondFrame()* and *handleEvent()*. These two member functions (methods) are needed to create the applet window used by the program at run-time. The good news is that, even if you do not understand the file's contents, the files work as is! Now let's take a detailed look at the automatically generated JavaAppletWizard's main file, *mysecond.java*.

Using the JavaAppletWizard's Autogenerated Java Source File

If you run the code generated by the JavaAppletWizard, all you would see is an empty applet window. This section explains the standard elements of the autogenerated code and shows how to extend the template to print today's day, time, and date. Notice how the JavaAppletWizard has inserted the authoring information into the comment block. Below the comment, you see four **import** statements:

```
import java.util.Date;

import java.applet.*;
import java.awt.Graphics;
import mysecondFrame;
```

These four **import** statements are almost identical to the Java applet written earlier without the JavaAppletWizard. Here is the difference. The Java applet has this statement:

```
import java.applet.Applet;
```

The Java JavaAppletWizard generated these statements:

```
import java.applet.*;
. . .
import mysecondFrame;
```

Many system commands, such as **dir** and **copy**, and many Windows options, such as the File Manager, let you use wildcards. *Wildcards* are symbols that the invoked utility uses for search criteria. The asterisk symbol * is one of those symbols. By changing the import extension from *.Applet* to .*, the JavaAppletWizard has generated a more general, robust **import** statement. Rather than pulling in just the **java.applet.Applet**, the statement pulls in all **java.applet.*** classes. The second **import** statement pulls in the code defining the Frame class necessary to run this program as an applet.

The next statement is generated by the JavaAppletWizard and begins the applet's **class** definition. Notice the JavaAppletWizard gives the class the same name as the Workspace file (i.e., *mysecond*).

```
public class mysecond extends Applet
{
        .
        .
        .
}
```

Note: The formal class definition could have ended at this point with **implements Runnable**. *A* **class** *that has implemented the* **Runnable** *interface can be run in a thread by passing the instance of the class to a new thread object. (Threads are discussed in the next chapter.)*

The next important statement is a member declaration for *m-_fStandAlone*. The IDE uses this member's value to determine if the program is being run as an applet (*m_fStandalone = false*) or application (*m_fStandalone = true*).

```
boolean m_fStandAlone = false;
```

The next two statements were added to the autogenerated JavaAppletWizard **class** definition to enable the template to output the day, date, and time.

```
Date systemdate;                          // added to template
String mydate;                            // added to template
```

Surprise! Do you recognize the beginning syntax in this next portion of the autogenerated JavaAppletWizard code? It is the same **main()** declaration used at the beginning of the chapter to write a standalone Java application. The JavaAppletWizard generates a source file that can be used to develop a standalone Java application, or a Java applet!

```
public static void main(String args[])
{
    mysecondFrame frame = new mysecondFrame("mysecond");
    // Must show Frame before we size it so
    // insets() will return valid
    // values
    //----------------------------------------------------
    frame.show();
    frame.resize(frame.insets().left + frame.insets().right  +
640,
                 frame.insets().top  + frame.insets().bottom +
                      480);
```

The **frame** class implements a bordered window with the applet's title, *"mysecond"*. The **show()** method displays the framed window, while the **resize()** method dimensions the window.

The next four statements instantiate the object *applet_mysecond* of **class** type *mysecond*, use the **add()** method to "center" the applet, call the instance's (*applet_mysecond*) **init()** method to initialize the object, and finally invoke the **start()** method to execute the applet. All of these methods are discussed in greater detail in later chapters.

Notice in particular that whenever this method is invoked, *m_fStandAlone* is set equal to *true*:

```
mysecond applet_mysecond = new mysecond();

frame.add("Center", applet_mysecond);
applet_mysecond.m_fStandAlone = true;
applet_mysecond.init();
applet_mysecond.start();
}
```

Below, the member function *mysecond()* is a special type of method called a constructor and is empty. A *constructor* is a special class method that is automatically invoked whenever the object is instantiated. Constructors are discussed in detail in Chapter 4. Notice that the

JavaAppletWizard has filled in the **getAppletInfo()** method (member function), with the information you provided.

```
public mysecond()
{
}

public String getAppletInfo()
{
    return "Name: mysecond\r\n" +
           "Author: Chris H. Pappas and William H. Murray\r\n" +
           "Created with Microsoft Visual J++ Version";
}
```

The next three statements were added to the autogenerated JavaAppletWizard **paint()** method to enable the template to output the day, date, and time.

```
// This routine handles the painting
public void paint(Graphics graphic)
{
  systemdate = new Date();             // added to template

  mydate = systemdate.toString();      // added to template
  graphic.drawString(mydate, 10, 10);  // added to template
}
```

At this point, you are ready to compile the project.

Compiling mysecond.java

To compile the *.java* source file created by JavaAppletWizard, you select **Rebuild All** from the **Build** menu (Figure 3.15).

The **Build *mysecond*** command is slightly different from the **Rebuild All** command. **Build** checks the dates of all source files against those of any existing **.class* files. Any updated support file is re-compiled and then added to the **.class* output file. This is fine if every file used by your workspace is stamped with the correct date information. However, should your workspace import source files across a network, it is possible that their date stamps are incorrect. In this case, the **Build** command would then *not* update your **.class* file.

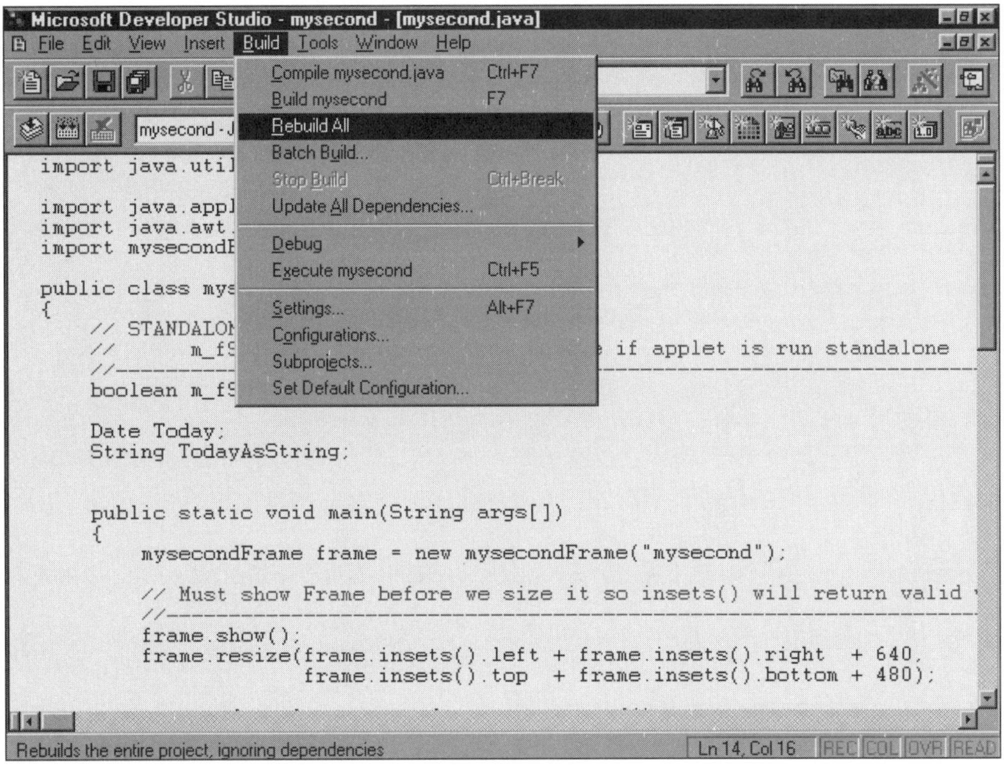

Figure 3.15: Compiling your program with the **Rebuild All option**.

For this reason, although it will take longer to reprocess interpreted files, you should *always* select the **Rebuild All** command. This command ignores date checks, recompiles all source files, and generates a totally new **.class* output file.

Assuming you have not missed any code additions to the JavaAppletWizard autogenerated code, you should see a window similar to that shown in Figure 3.16. You are now ready to run the program.

To run a program, select **Execute** from the **Build** menu (see Figure 3.17). A sample execution is shown in Figure 3.18.

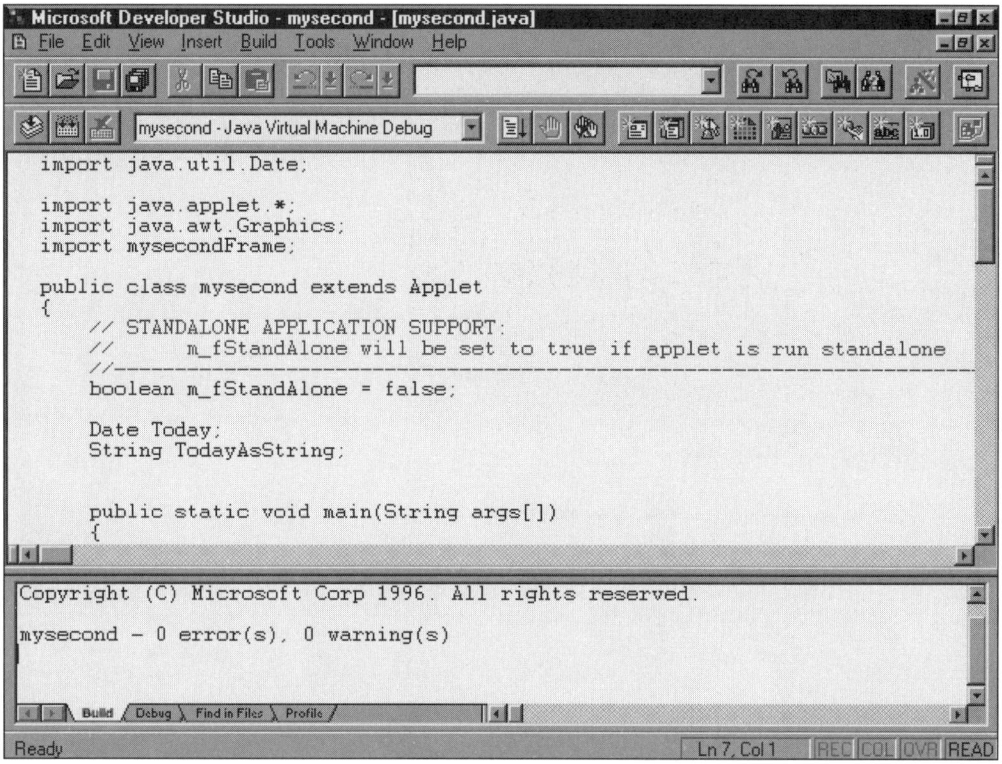

Figure 3.16: A successful recompiling of *mysecond.java* using the **Rebuild All** command.

DEBUGGING APPLETS

Unfortunately, programmers do not always write flawless code. Once again, the Microsoft IDE comes to the rescue with an integrated Java debugger. With the Java debugger you can set breakpoints (program execution STOP points), view variable contents, and class members. However, to access this information, you must have first compiled your Java source file with the compiler's debugging information check box selected.

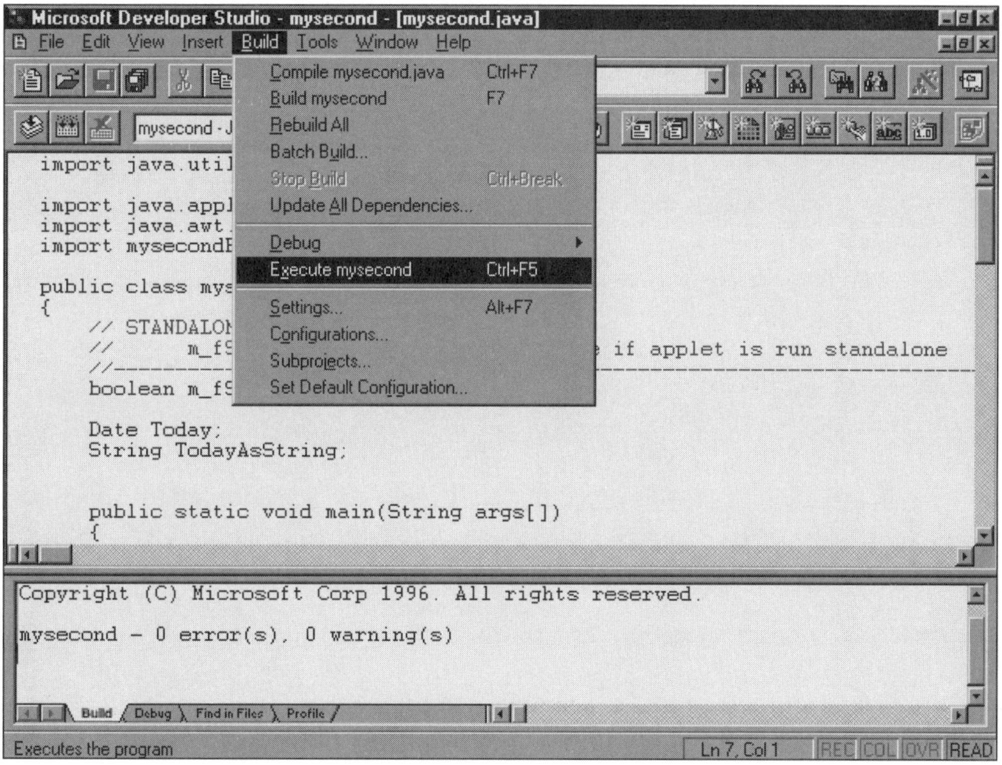

Figure 3.17: Executing *mysecond.java.*

Setting Breakpoints

Before actually starting the debugger, you need to know how to set a breakpoint. A *breakpoint* is used to tell the debugger which line of source code to stop on. This is a time-saving step because you do not always want to debug your program literally line by line.

To set a breakpoint, you put the cursor on the line in question, click the right mouse button, and select the **Insert/Remove Breakpoint** command from the pop-up menu (Figure 3.19). Note that the breakpoint is being set on the last line of code *inside* the method **paint()**.

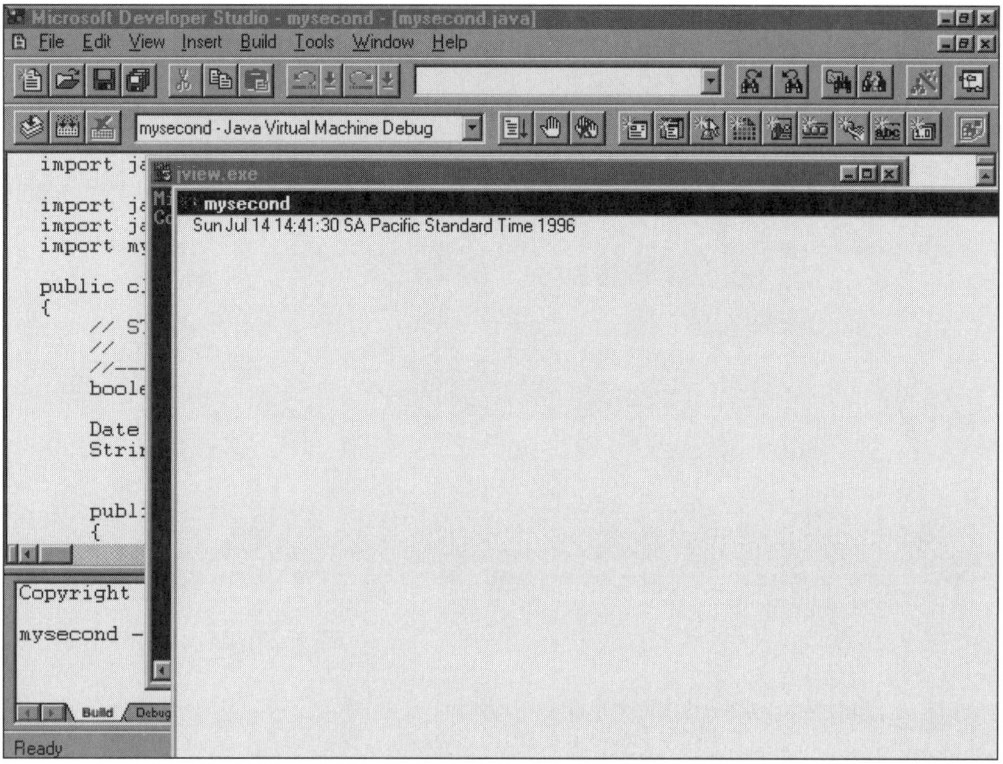

Figure 3.18: Output window for *mysecond.java*.

Running the Java Debugger to a Breakpoint

To start a Java debug session, select the command sequence **Build | Debug | Go** (see Figure 3.20). Notice the small STOP sign placed on the line containing the breakpoint.

Figure 3.21 shows the debugger tool bar, an edit window positioned to the breakpoint, and the default organization for the object inspection window.

Figure 3.22 shows a slightly modified debugger window size, highlighting the object inspection window. This window lets you view any object, its members, and their current values. To use this valuable tool,

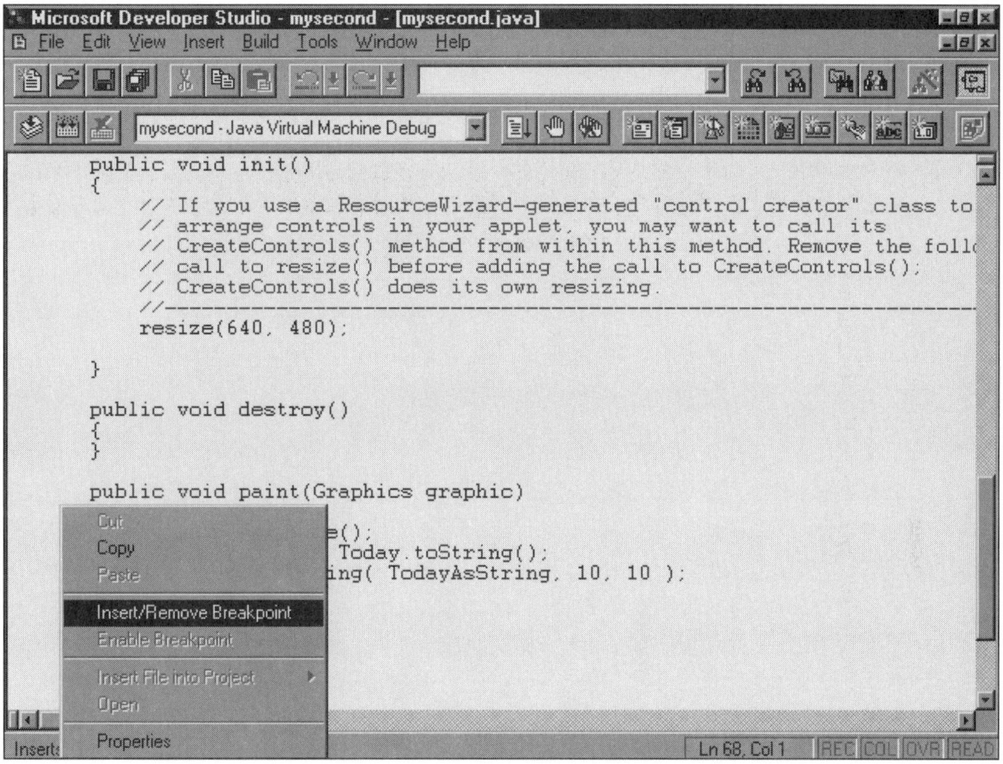

Figure 3.19: Setting a breakpoint.

simply click on the object in question and continue to expand the hierarchy tree until you see the member in question.

COMING TO TERMS

class—Java keyword used to define objects.

compound block - More than one executable statement syntactically bound to a controlling statement with a pair of matching braces { }, as in a formal class or member function definition.

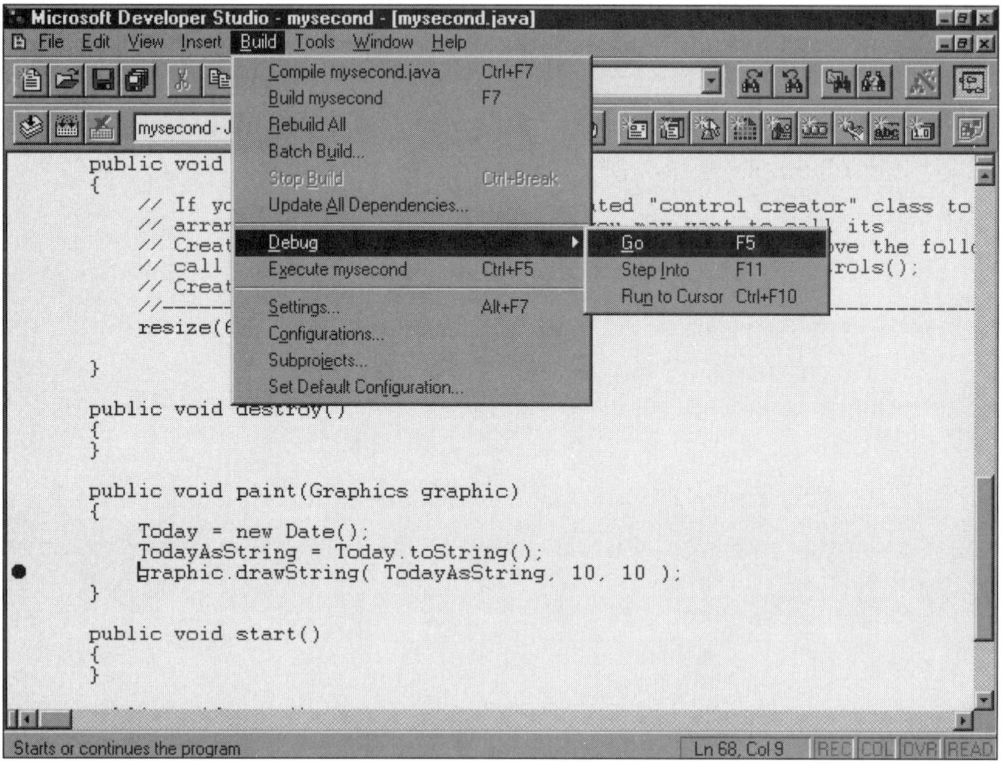

Figure 3.20: Running the debugger to a breakpoint.

extends—Tells the Java compiler that the specified class is going to have additional application-specific code added to its formal definition.

HTML—Hyper Text Markup Language. A file used to define Internet Web pages and specifically used with the Java language to host a Java applet.

import—Pulls in Java or user-supplied package and class definitions.

java.exe—The Java run-time interpreter. *java.exe* is used with compiled Java source files having a *.class* file extension.

javac.exe—The standalone Java compiler. *javac.exe* is used with Java source files having a *.java* file extension.

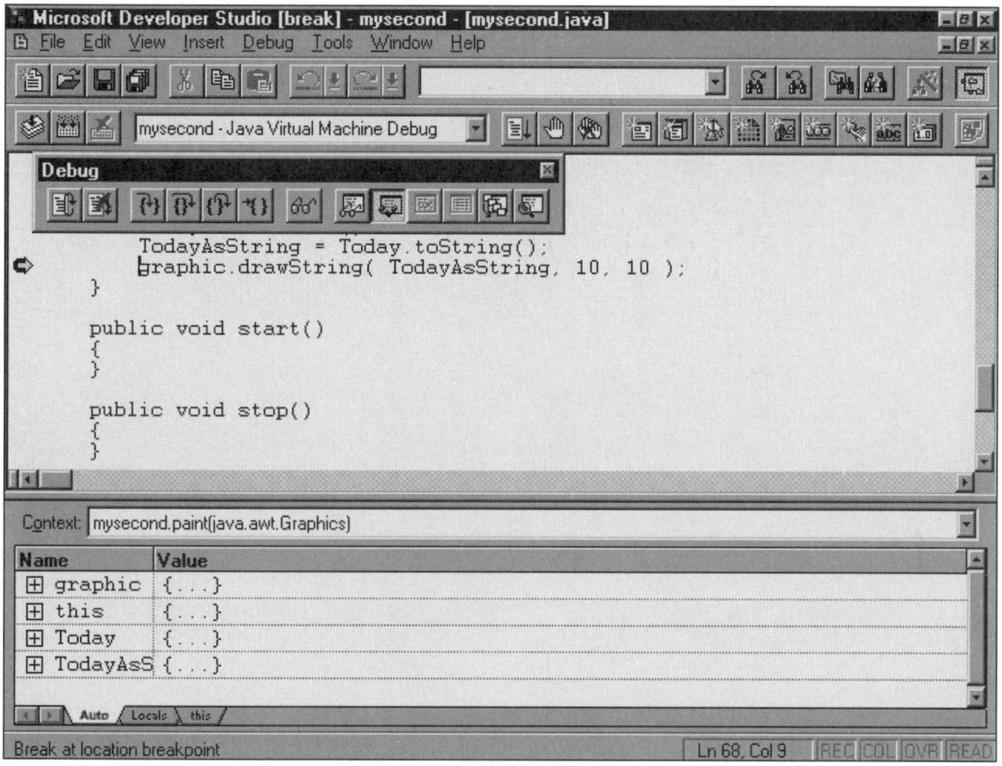

Figure 3.21: Debug information window.

member function—A function syntactically bound to a specific class. Also called a method.

method—A function syntactically bound into a specific class. Also called a member function.

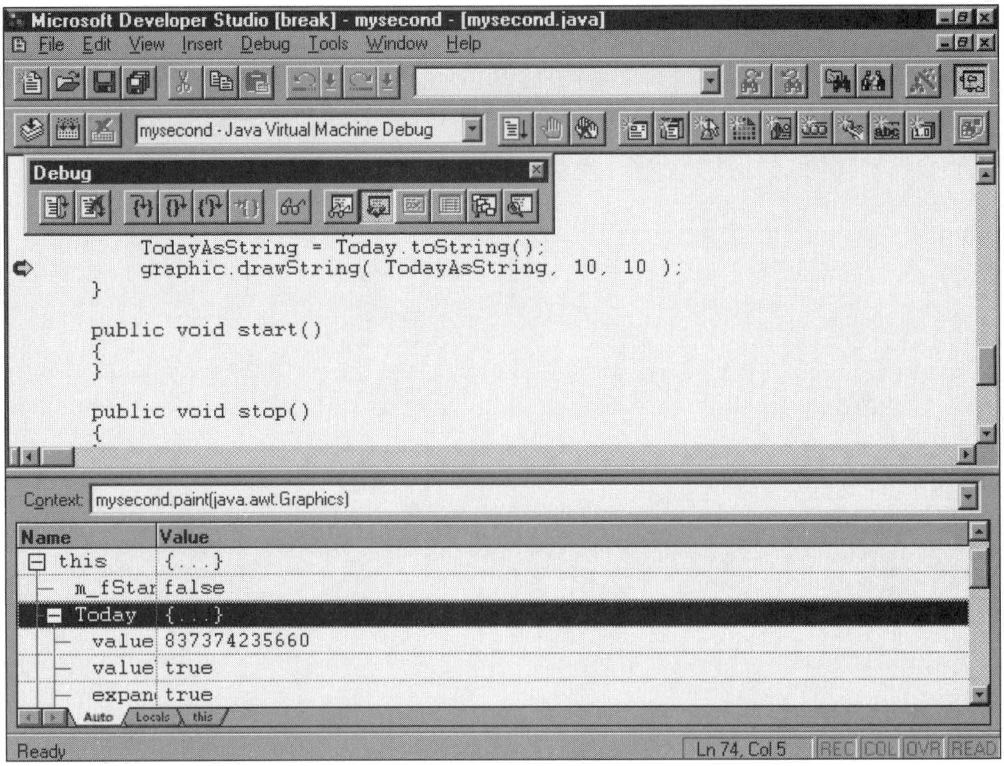

Figure 3.22: User-modified inspection window contents.

Chapter 4

JAVA PROGRAMMING FUNDAMENTALS

Chapter 2 covers the fundamental features and syntax of the Java language. Chapter 3 explains the differences between Java applications and Java applets as well as how to use Microsoft's IDE Java tools to enter, edit, compile, debug, and run Java programs. Chapter 4 is designed to finalize your conceptual and syntactic understanding of the higher-level constructs provided by the Java language.

If you are already comfortable with an object-oriented language such as Ada or C++, you will find many of the topics discussed in this chapter quite familiar. If you are new to object-oriented programming languages, Chapter 4 is particularly important. Many of the object-oriented concepts discussed in this chapter are first presented using their procedural-oriented language's underpinnings.

CLASSES AND OBJECTS

To help put the concepts involved in object-oriented programming into perspective, ask yourself the following question. Did you need to go out and purchase a new computer just to execute programs designed using object-oriented technology? Of course the answer is no. Whether the executable file you are running had procedural-design Assembly Language source code roots, or FORTRAN or

COBOL, or Pascal or C, or object-oriented-design Ada or C++ origins, once the source file was assembled or compiled, and linked into an EXE format, it ran on your computer. That's good news.

No matter how complex object-oriented design philosophy and syntax may appear, when the program is compiled, all the high-brow philosophy and syntax gets translated down to machine code. So, let's begin by demystifying objects.

First, all Java programming must be done within a class (note that in Java, there are no standalone functions). Java has the **class** keyword for this purpose. From previous chapters, you know that an object is very similar to a C/C++ structure with one addition: the structure's members can be functions (called member functions, or methods). An object really does not contain any new horsepower that a Pascal record and standalone functions would provide. It's just that object-oriented languages provide a syntax that can bundle these two constructs into one syntax that is free of side effects. The syntax for a Java class is:

```
class classTag {
     // member data declarations go here
     .
     // member function (methods) declarations go here
}
```

The Java keyword is **class** and the *classTag* field is where you supply a readable, self-documenting identifier as the name of the class. Notice that the brace pairs { } indicate that a class definition is considered a compound block.

Instantiating Java Class Member Data

If you are new to object-oriented programming, then you probably don't know the meaning of the word "instantiating." So, let's rewrite the section title, using terms that all programmers understand: Creating Fields Within a Record. *Instantiation* or *instantiating an object* is similar to the procedural programming task of creating a variable. Java member data instantiation has the same syntax as a standalone variable declaration:

```
class classTag {
  memberDataType memberDataName [, more_memberDataNames];
  // method definitions follow
}
```

The following code segment declares four data members—*Title, Age, HourlyWage,* and *WorkedThisWeek* of the class *sample*:

```
class sample {
  String  Title = "The employee's paycheck is: ";
  int     Age;
  double  HourlyWage, WorkedThisWeek;
}
```

Because by definition an object contains both data and functions that work on the data, this class definition has no functionality. All it can do is hold three types of information: **String**, **int**, and **double**.

Methods

Methods, otherwise known as member functions, are really nothing more (syntax-wise) than functions bound specifically to a specific **class** type. The general syntax for declaring methods is:

```
class classTag {
  // member data declarations
  // method declarations
     method_ReturnType methodName( [ optionalDummyArgumentList ] ) {
          // method body
          .
          .
          // return only needed when
          // method_ReturnType is not void
          [ return method_ReturnType_instance; ]
     }
}
```

Suppose you want the *sample* class to calculate an employee's weekly paycheck. The following method accomplishes this:

```
double CalculatePaycheck( ) {
    return( HourlyWage * WorkedThisWeek );
}
```

Notice that the method's body has global access to the data members *HourlyWage* and *WorkedThisWeek* and that they are not passed as actual arguments. All class data members are global to all the class' methods. However, a class' methods may define their own local variables. Typically, these variables are visible only within the defining method. The updated *sample* class now looks like:

```
class sample {
  String  Title = "The employee's paycheck is: ";
  int     Age;
  double  HourlyWage, WorkedThisWeek;

  double CalculatePaycheck( ) {
    return( HourlyWage * WorkedThisWeek );
  }
}
```

Of course, a class that stores information and calculates some result is fairly useless unless it can output those results. This next method accomplishes this task:

```
void PrintPaycheck( ) {
  System.out.print( Title );
  System.out.println( CalculatePaycheck() );
}
```

static **Methods**

A program will declare a method using the **static** Java keyword, when declaring a subroutine that can be called without having to instantiate an object. There are several reasons why you might want to do this. One of the most common reasons is to have a method that creates an object of the target class and returns it. You may also use **static** methods whenever a program needs access to "global" functions that should be associated with a specific class.

Static methods are defined the same way that normal methods are defined, except that they are preceded with the keyword **static**; the code inside the method cannot access any non-**static** member variables. In the next example, you will see how a **static** method provides utilities to the rest of a program:

```
class int Multipliers {
  static int Cube( int iValue ) {
    return iValue * iValue * iValue;
  }
```

```
    static int Square( int iValue ) {
      return iValue * iValue;
    }
  }
  .
  .
  .
  class AnyClassNeedingCubeAndSquare {
    void ThisClassMethod {
      int iValue1 = Multipliers.Cube( 5 );
      int iValue2 = Multipliers.Square( 4 );
    }
  }
```

Here you can see that two methods—*Cube* and *Square*—are defined with the **static** Java keyword. By intent, these **static** methods can be used in a number of places within a program. Because these methods do not need any data other than what they are passed as arguments, instantiating the object that contains them is unnecessary. Notice that if these methods were useful to several classes, copying them into each of the classes would be wasteful. One way to make these methods available is to make them **static** methods in your own utility class.

The syntax for calling a **static** method is straightforward:

```
classDefining_staticMethods.staticMethodName( actualArguments );
```

static **Variable Initialization**

You can also use the **static** keyword in front of member variables. Called static initialization code, these member variable declarations are executed when a class is loaded. This syntax is used most frequently to create constant data that is useful to all the instances and subclasses of the defining class. For example, the following code segment uses **static** initialization code to fill a *DescriptorTable*:

```
class Plants {
  static String Nursery[] = new String[ 4 ];
  static {
    Nursery[ 0 ] = "Rhododendron";
    Nursery[ 1 ] = "Azalea";
    Nursery[ 2 ] = "Mamosa";
```

```
    Nursery[ 3 ] = "Bradford Pear";
  }
}
```

You may also use **static** initialization code to print out debugging/error diagnostic statements. For example, for debugging purposes, the following code modification prints out a message indicating that the class was loaded successfully:

```
class Plants {
  static String Nursery[] = new String[ 4 ];
  static {
    Nursery[ 0 ] = "Rhododendron";
    Nursery[ 1 ] = "Azalea";
    Nursery[ 2 ] = "Mamosa";
    Nursery[ 3 ] = "Bradford Pear";
    System.out.println( "Class Plants successfully installed."
);
  }
}
```

This particular type of debugging is useful in that it lets you see exactly when a class gets loaded into the system.

Constructors

If you had a good introductory, language-independent design course in your formal programming education, then you understand the need to not only declare variables, but to also initialize them. In a modular design, procedural language algorithm, this is usually accomplished by a function you write.

A properly defined object also addresses this issue of member data initialization. Like its procedural counterpart, an object also uses a function to initialize the class' member data. This initialization function has a specific name: a *constructor*. However, constructors have a syntax and behavior that is different from a normal class' methods.

The syntax for an object's constructor looks like this:

```
class classTag {
  // member data declarations
  // constructor method declaration
  public classTag( [ optionalDummyArgumentList ] ) {
```

```
        // constructor statement(s)
    }
}
```

There are three major differences between a class' methods and its unique constructor method. First, the constructor's identifier (name) must match the class' *classTag*. Second, constructors do not have a return type. Third, nowhere in your Java program will you ever see the constructor method called. This is because constructors are automatically invoked any time your program instantiates the class.

The following *sample* class constructor demonstrates constructor syntax and correct logical use:

```
public sample( int AnAge, double AnHourlyWage, double
HasWorkedThisWeek ){
    Age = AnAge;
    HourlyWage = AnHourlyWage;
    WorkedThisWeek = HasWorkedThisWeek;
  }
```

Notice that the name of the constructor method, *sample,* matches the class' name, *sample.* The constructor's code takes care of receiving the arguments passed to it—*AnAge, AnHourlyWage,* and *HasWorkedThisWeek*—and assigns these values to the class' data members. This roundabout way of initializing data members has a specific purpose: to make certain that no invalid values are ever used to initialize the object. (Note that to keep this introductory example a reasonable length, the constructor does not include all of the code necessary to perform this task.)

To make the *sample* class definition a fully functional Java application, you need to add a **main()**:

```
public static void main( String args[] ) {
    sample EmployeeOne = new sample( 23, 9.85, 40.5);
    sample EmployeeTwo = new sample( 47, 12.87, 55.0);

    EmployeeOne.PrintPaycheck();
    EmployeeTwo.PrintPaycheck();
  }
```

The method's body begins by instantiating two *sample* class objects: *EmployeeOne* and *EmployeeTwo*. Remember that when you instantiate an object, you always place its data type to the left of its identifier. For standard types like integer, you use *int objectName;* for user-defined types like *class sample*, you use *sample objectName*.

To the right of the Java assignment operator, =, you see the keyword **new**. **new** dynamically allocates enough memory to instantiate a tangible object (in other words, *EmployeeOne*) of the hypothetical blueprint type *class sample*. When the object is instantiated, its constructor method is automatically invoked. So the code to the right of **new**:

```
sample( 23, 9.85, 40.5);
sample( 47, 12.87, 55.0);
```

serves two purposes. First, it tells **new** what type of object to instantiate; and second, it passes the automatically invoked constructor any necessary initialization values. The following listing shows a complete, compilable and interpretable *sample* class:

```
import java.awt.*;

class sample {
  String  Title = "The employee's paycheck is: ";
  int     Age;
  double  HourlyWage, WorkedThisWeek;import java.applet.*;
import java.awt.*;
import sampleFrame;

public class sample extends Applet
{
    // STANDALONE APPLICATION SUPPORT:
    //          m_fStandAlone will be set to
    //          true if applet is run
    //          standalone
    //-------------------------------------------
    boolean m_fStandAlone = false;

    public static void main(String args[])
    {
        sampleFrame frame = new sampleFrame("sample");

        // Must show Frame before we size
        // it so insets() will return
        // valid values
        //-------------------------------------
```

```
        frame.show();
        frame.resize(frame.insets().left +
frame.insets().right + 320,
                                 frame.insets().top  +
frame.insets().bottom +
                                  240);

        sample applet_sample = new sample();

        frame.add("Center", applet_sample);
        applet_sample.m_fStandAlone = true;
        applet_sample.init();
        applet_sample.start();
    }

    public sample()
    {
    }

    public void finalize()
    {
    }

    public String getAppletInfo()
    {
        return "Name: sample\r\n" +
               "Author: Chris H. Pappas and William H.
Murray\r\n" +
               "Created with Microsoft Visual J++";
    }

    public void init()
    {
        resize(320, 240);
    }

    public void destroy()
    {
    }
```

```
    public void paint(Graphics g)
    {
    }

    public void start()
    {
    }

    public void stop()
    {
    }

}
```

Destructors: finalize()

While the subject of constructors is still fresh in your mind, let's discuss the syntax and logical use for another unique type of class method. If a constructor method serves to initialize an object, or in more detail, provide all of the code necessary to get the object up-and-running, then a destructor performs the logical inverse. *Destructor* methods perform object cleanup.

The syntax for many object-oriented languages' destructors also involves the class' *classTag* name preceded by a tilde ~. For the *sample* class, the constructor's name was *sample*, and in C++ the destructor method's name would be *~sample*. In Java, all class destructor methods have the same name: **finalize**. Finalizer methods are called just before the object is garbage-collected and its memory reclaimed. To create a finalizer method, include a method with the following signature in your class definition:

```
void finalize() {
  // finalize method code goes here
}
```

final **Java Keyword**

You may sometimes want to refer to a value in your source code, by name, but not want to ever change the value. You could just avoid writing any code that changes the variable's contents; however, Java gives you a way to make sure that if you make a mistake and inadvertently try to change the value, the compiler will warn you of it. This is accomplished with the **final** keyword. Note that the **final** keyword is used in a number of other areas of the language.

To specify that a variable is **final**, you precede the variable's type with the **final** keyword., as in the following example:

```
class Employee {
  int DaysWorked = 5;
  double HoursWorked = 40;
  final double MinimumWage = 7.59;
}
```

A benefit of using **final** variables is that the compiler is able to optimize the byte code it creates so that it will run faster than if you were using standard non-**final** variables.

OVERLOADING

When you are learning any new programming language, the easy part is usually learning the new language's syntax. The harder part is learning the industry-accepted nuances of that language. For example, you would not solve a problem and code a solution in Assembly language exactly as you would in COBOL exactly as you would in an object-oriented language. This analogy holds true for overloading.

Simply stated, Java *overloading* allows you to define more than one class method, using the same method name. Here the syntax is not the problem, but rather, why would a programmer want to do that? The proper use of overloading is reserved for a piece of code that logically performs the same function, but that can be started off with a different number of arguments and/or different argument types. This last statement explains why Java requires all overloaded methods to have unique formal argument lists.

Take, for example, a method written to sum arrays of three numeric values. The algorithm, or series of steps needed to perform this calculation, is identical regardless of the numeric data type (**int**, **float**, or **double**), of the array. This algorithm is a perfect candidate for overloading. Notice that the following two methods have the identical sequence of events and the same number and type of statements. The only difference involves the variable's data types:

```
// Overloaded method to sum an array of three
// integers
public int SumArray( int intArray[] ) {
  int offset;
  int tempTotal = 0;

  for( offset = 0; offset < 3; offset++ )
    tempTotal += intArray[ offset ] ;

  return( tempTotal );
}

// Overloaded method to sum an array of three
// doubles
public double SumArray( double doubleArray[] ) {
  int offset;
  double tempTotal = 0;

  for( offset = 0; offset < 3; offset++ )
    tempTotal += doubleArray[ offset ] ;

  return( tempTotal );
}
```

OVERLOADING CONSTRUCTORS

A special case of overloading involves a class' constructor. Just like regular methods, a class' constructor can also take a varying number and type of arguments. Because the logical use for a constructor often involves the initialization of class data members, an overloaded class constructor usually involves varying degrees of initialization.

Take, for example, a class that calculates an employee's weekly paycheck. There could be paycheck calculations based on three criteria: employees working forty hours at the standard rate, employees working more or less than forty hours at the standard rate, and employees working more or less than forty hours at a nonstandard rate. The following code segment demonstrates how you could overload the *paycheck* class constructor to represent each type of employee:

```
public class paycheck {
  int HoursWorked;
  double Rate;

// Employees working 40 hours at standard rate
  public void paycheck() {
    HoursWorked = 40;
    Rate = 8.79;
  }

// Employees working more/less than 40 hours at standard rate
  public void paycheck( int WorkedThisWeek ) {
    HoursWorked = WorkedThisWeek;
    Rate = 8.79;
  }

// Employees working more/less than 40 hours at non-standard
rate
  public void paycheck( double CurrentRate ) {
    HoursWorked = 40;
    Rate = CurrentRate;
  }

  public void paycheck( int WorkedThisWeek, double CurrentRate
) {
    HoursWorked = WorkedThisWeek;
    Rate = CurrentRate;
  }
}
```

With these overloaded *paycheck* class constructors, you can now instantiate *paycheck* objects in three ways:

```
paycheck standardHoursStandardRate = new paycheck();
paycheck standardHoursNonStandardRate = new paycheck(10.05);
paycheck nonStandardHoursNonStandardRate = new paycheck(55,
12.00);
```

Because each of the instantiated object's argument lists is unique in the number of arguments and data type(s), the Java compiler knows which matching overloaded constructor method to invoke.

OPERATOR OVERLOADING

Many object-oriented languages not only provide method overloading, but operator overloading as well. The principle here is the same, except that it applies to the language's operators. In C++, for example, you can overload the addition operator + to concatenate null-terminated strings—something it was originally incapable of doing. *Operator overloading* lets you extend the functionality of an object-oriented language's standard set of operators. Java does not support operator overloading.

INHERITANCE

The term *inheritance* involves the definition for a new class, based on some previously defined class. The new class is technically referred to as a *subclass*, while the class that the subclass is based upon is known as a *superclass*. The subclass is then said to inherit the characteristics of its superclass.

There are many ways to refer to this inheritance relationship, with most terms having a direct logical link to family trees. For example, a subclass can be referred to as a *child class* and a superclass can be called a *parent class*. A superclass can be subclassed, and then the subclass, subclassed. In this family tree structure, the original superclass, on which both subclasses were built, can be called a *root* or *base class*. In Java, a base class definition often uses the keyword **abstract**, meaning that the base class *must* be subclassed before it can be instantiated.

Sometimes the process of deriving subclasses is called a *derivation*. In other words, you derive a subclass. However, because Java does not support multiple inheritance (through which a subclass can inherit the characteristics of two parent classes), the terms *parent class* and *child class* are infrequently used. Instead, Java uses the terms *superclass* and *subclass*. *Siblings*, a term applied to derived child classes sharing the same parent class, also has a different meaning. In Java, a child class or subclass does not have two parents. Two subclasses, sharing the same superclass, are called siblings.

Finally, a superclass can also be referred to as a subclass' *ancestor*, while a child or subclass can be referred to as a superclass' *descendant*.

Inherited Constructors: this

Some constructors you write may be coded additions to an inherited constructor. Rather than duplicating identical behavior in multiple constructor methods in your class, it makes sense to be able to just call the inherited constructor from inside the body of the derived constructor. Java provides a special keyword, **this,** for this purpose. To call a parent class' constructor, you would use a statement of the form:

```
public class subClass extends superClass {
  public subClass ( typeO argumentOne, typeT argumentTwo, typeN
argumentN ){
    this( argumentOne, argumentTwo, argumentN... );
  }
```

from within the derived constructor's method body.

THE JAVA KEYWORD this

There will be times when you are defining a method that you will want to refer to the current object's instance variables, or to pass the current object as an argument to another method. To refer to the current object in these cases, you use the Java **this** keyword. **this** refers to the current object, and you can use it anywhere that object might appear by using the period member operator (.). For example:

```
instanceData = this.myVar;
this.myMethod( this );
```

Here the *instanceData* is the instance variable for **this** object. The class then calls the method *myMethod,* and passes it the current object. The **this** object is also a legal method return type. So any method properly defined can contain within its body the final statement:

```
return this;
```

Often you can omit the **this** keyword because it is implied. For this reason, you can refer to a class' member data and methods simply by name. So, the first two statements displayed above could be rewritten as:

```
instanceData = myVar;
myMethod( this );
```

Here are two important notes. First, you can only omit the **this** keyword if there are no conflicting local variable name collisions. Second, methods defined as **static** cannot use **this** (see the description of **static** in the following section).

public, private, protected, static, abstract

The Java keywords **public**, **private**, and **protected** deal with the scope, or visibility, of class members (data or method). By default, class members are only visible to the class itself. This has the advantage of protecting against any external side effects, such as two classes using the same member names.

Any class member preceded by the **public** keyword is visible outside the class. Any class member marked **protected** (the default if left unspecified) is only accessible to the class itself, or any subclass derived from it. Any class member marked **private** is only visible in the defining class and is not accessible to any subclass derived from it.

The **static** keyword is slightly more difficult to understand. Remember that class members can be either data or methods. The **static** modifier can be legally used for both member types. Basically, the keyword tells the Java compiler that there will only be one of whatever is being defined, whether a data member or method. While this does not prevent any subclass from inheriting the class member, it does prevent the subclass from dynamically generating its own version.

No matter how many times a class is instantiated, if its formal description contains **static** members, all object instances share the *same* member. This can be very useful whenever all instances need to share the same piece of information or to use the same data member as an accumulator.

Notice that the previously described *sample* class has a **main()** method marked **static**. This makes sense because you would not want to create multiple instances of the method **main()** each time *sample* was instantiated. Java applications can only have one method called **main()**.

Of the five modifiers, **abstract** is the one you are least likely to use as a beginning Java programmer. The **abstract** keyword is only legal for class methods and tells the Java compiler that the associated method is so incomplete that a derived child class *must* add code to it. Indirectly then, any formal class definition that contains an **abstract** method cannot be instantiated. Instead, the formal class definition, by design, was meant to be derived into a subclass.

THREADS

The term *thread* applies to each execution path your program can take. Older high-level languages were written to execute only one thread at a time. Today, programmers and users alike demand that an application be more efficient. This efficiency is made possible by today's newer programming languages, which support the feature called multithreading.

With multithreaded tasks that can be performed in the background, a program can simultaneously download files while waiting for network messages or updating information. For example, the HotJava Web browser lets you browse a page and download an image via the use of threads. You can also use threads to animate an image and play sounds.

MULTITHREADING

A multithreaded Java program is capable of simultaneously running more than one execution path. The simplest example is a Java program that concurrently prints the information in a file, and sorts a table. Of course, unless your computer has more than one microprocessor in it, true concurrent processing is physically impossible. The illusion of concurrency is accomplished by swapping each thread in and out of the main processor.

Running a single-threaded program is fine when you only have to deal with small programs that have to do a single task; but what if you had a Web page with several applets that were all supposed to be running at the same time, or you wanted to run a calculation in the background while getting more user input? In this case, each of these tasks would have to be multithreaded. Java provides two methods of implementing multithreading. The first method involves creating a class that extends the **Thread** class:

```
public class myThread extends Thread {
  public void run() {
    // thread code goes here
  }
}
```

Now, to create and run an instance of your new Thread class, you write two statements. The first statement creates an instance *threadOne* of the *myThread* class:

```
myThread threadOne = new myThread();
```

The second calls the object's **start()** method:

```
threadOne.start();
```

Whenever your program wants to stop a thread, it makes a call to the threaded object's **stop()** method, as in:

```
threadOne.stop();
```

Java's thread-handling capabilities are very sophisticated and even include ways to temporarily suspend and then resume a thread. The syntax is straightforward:

```
threadOne.suspend();
threadOne.resume();
```

The second approach creates a class that **implements** the **Runnable** interface. Any class can represent a thread if it implements the **Runnable** interface and defines a **run()** method, as in:

```
public class myRunnable implements Runnable {
  public void run() {
    // thread code goes here
  }
}
```

The first line of code creates a new class called *myRunnable* that implements the **Runnable** interface. The second statement defines the required **run()** method, and would normally contain the current task's code. A class that has implemented the **Runnable** interface can be run in a thread by passing the instance of the class to a new **Thread** object, as in:

```
className classInstance = new className();
new Thread( classInstance ).start();
```

When **start()** is called, *classInstance* indirectly calls your **run()** method. Remember, you can stop the *classInstance* thread with **stop()**.

Whether To Extend or Implement

Whether you should extend the **Thread** class or implement the **Runnable** class depends, to some degree, on whether you are writing a Java application or applet. A Java applet that uses the **Runnable** interface makes use of the **run()** method to house the body of a thread. In order to run with a Web browser that is Java-compatible, an applet must be derived from the **java.applet.Applet** class. Because a class may also need to use a thread, this class cannot inherit from both the **Applet** and **Thread** classes because Java does not support multiple inheritance. For this reason, many classes choose the **Runnable** interface to implement threads.

Finding the currentThread()

The following program demonstrates how you can find out which thread is currently executing by making a call to the standard method **Thread.currentThread()**:

```
class thread {
  public static void main( String args[] ) {
    Thread currentThread = Thread.currentThread();
    currentThread.setName( "My main thread" );
    System.out.println( currentThread );
  }
}
```

The output from the program looks like:

```
Thread[My main thread,5,main]
```

Here, *My main thread* represents a user-defined, self-documenting label. The *5* (the default priority) indicates the *currentThread*'s priority, which can be anywhere from 1 to 10. The *main* is the name of the group of threads to which this thread belongs.

Thread Priorities

All Java threads are assigned a priority (from 1 - MIN_PRIORITY to 10 - MAX_PRIORITY; 5 - NORM_PRIORITY is the default), which affects when the Java thread scheduler chooses to run a thread. When threads share the same priority, they share the processor on a first-come, first-served basis. When a thread of a higher priority than any of the others comes into existence, it will get control of the processor, even if it needs to pre-empt a currently running thread to do so. For a thread of a lower priority then to gain control, the higher-priority thread needs to go to sleep (using the **sleep()** method) or wait until notified (by calling the **wait()** method).

The problem today is that thread scheduling has not been properly specified. The current implementations have radically different behavior in terms of scheduling. However, the good news is that the Windows 95 port seems to be the closest to what one would expect. Most of the inconsistencies arise when you have threads that are relying on a pre-emptive behavior, without cooperatively giving up the microprocessor.

Extending the Thread Class

You begin writing your own thread by extending the **Thread** class and overriding the **Thread.run()** method. The following *sqrRoot* class does just this:

```
import java.applet.*;
import java.awt.*;
import ThreadFrame;

public class Thread extends Applet
{
    // STANDALONE APPLICATION SUPPORT:
    //        m_fStandAlone will be set to true if applet is run
    //          standalone
    //--------------------------------------------------------------
    boolean m_fStandAlone = false;

    public static void main(String args[])
    {
        ThreadFrame frame = new ThreadFrame("Thread");

        // Must show Frame before we size it so insets() will
        // return valid values
        //----------------------------------------------------------
        frame.show();
        frame.resize(frame.insets().left + frame.insets().right
+ 320,
```

```
                    frame.insets().top  + frame
                    insets().bottom +
                          240);

        Thread applet_Thread = new Thread();

        frame.add("Center", applet_Thread);
        applet_Thread.m_fStandAlone = true;
        applet_Thread.init();
        applet_Thread.start();
    }

    public Thread()
    {
    }

    public void finalize()
    {
    }

    public String getAppletInfo()
    {
        return "Name: Thread\r\n" +
              "Author: Chris H. Pappas and William H.
                   Murray\r\n" +
              "Created with Microsoft Visual J++ Version";
    }


    public void init()
    {
        resize(320, 240);
    }

    public void destroy()
    {
    }

     public void paint(Graphics g)
     {
```

```
        }

        public void start()
        {
        }

        public void stop()
        {
        }

}
```

In this example, the class *sqrRoot* sets itself up as an infinite loop using the **Math.sqrt()** method to calculate the square root of a number and then using the **System.out.println()** method to display the result. If you were using this class and wanted to call the thread, you would create an instance of the class *sqrRoot*, just as you would any other class:

```
sqrRoot ThreadONE  = new sqrRoot();
```

To get the thread started, you make a call to its **start()** method:

```
ThreadONE.start();
```

Once activated, the *ThreadONE.start()* method automatically calls the object's *ThreadONE.run()* method and immediately returns to the **main()** program thread, which continues to execute. The following code segment from the *sqrRoot* class' **main()** method combines these features:

```
public static void main( String args[] ) {
// ...
    sqrRoot ThreadONE = new sqrRoot();
    sqrRoot ThreadTWO = new sqrRoot();
    ThreadONE.start();
    ThreadTWO.start();
// ...
      while( (ch = (char)System.in.read() ) != '\n' );
      ThreadONE.stop();
      ThreadTWO.stop();
// ...
```

The concurrency in execution comes from the fact that the *sqrRoot* thread is outputting squared values, while the **main()**'s

System.in.read() method call is simultaneously polling for user input within its loop. As soon as the user presses the carriage return and inputs the required '\n' symbol, the **while** loop terminates, allowing the *ThreadONE/TWO.stop()* methods to be called.

Implementing the Runnable Class

Whenever you want to create a multithreaded Java program, you can implement the **Runnable** class instead of extending the **Thread** class. From previous discussions, you know that a class that has implemented the **Runnable** interface can be run in a thread by passing the instance of the class to a new **Thread** object, as in:

```
className classInstance = new className();
new Thread( classInstance ).start();
```

The following code segment rewrites the extended **Thread** class used in the last example, as an implemented **Runnable** class:

```
import java.io.*;
import java.lang.*;

class squareRt implements Runnable {
  double findSquareRootOf = 4;
  boolean infiniteLoop = true;

  public void run() {
    while( infiniteLoop ) {
      System.out.println( Thread.currentThread().getName() );
      System.out.println( Math.sqrt( findSquareRootOf++ ) );
      try {
        Thread.sleep( 1000 );
      } catch ( InterruptedException ignored ) {
          return;
      }
    }
  }

  public void stop() {
    infiniteLoop = false;
  }
```

```
  public static void main( String args[] ) {
    char ch;
    squareRt ThreadONE = new squareRt();
    squareRt ThreadTWO = new squareRt();
    new Thread(ThreadONE, "Thread ONE").start();
    new Thread(ThreadTWO, "Thread TWO").start();
    try {
      while( ( ch = (char)System.in.read() ) != '\n' );
      ThreadONE.stop();
      ThreadTWO.stop();
      } catch ( IOException e ) {
          System.err.println( e );
        }
  }
}
```

Synchronized Threads

When two or more threads need concurrent access to a shared data resource, they need to access the data one at a time. Java provides unique language-level support for such synchronization. Other multithreaded systems expose a concept called a *monitor*. A monitor is an object that is used as a mutually exclusive lock, or *mutex*. Only one thread can own a monitor at a given time.

All Java objects have their own implicit monitor associated with them. The way you enter an object's monitor is by calling a method marked with the **synchronized** keyword. The entire time a thread is inside a **synchronized** method, all other threads have to wait.

The following program contains three class definitions. The first class, called *stub*, has a single method named *call*. *call* takes a single **String** argument, *stringParam*. The *call* method tries to print out the *stringParam* string after the message *Line Number 0 starting:*, and before the string *Line Number 0 done.*. The tricky part has to do with the call to *Thread.sleep(1000);*, which pauses the currently executing thread for approximately one second.

```
class stub {
  static int count = 1;
  void call( String stringParam ) {
    System.out.print("Line Number " + count + " starting: " );
```

```
        try {
         Thread.sleep( 1000 );
         System.out.print( stringParam );
         System.out.println(" : Line Number " + count++ + " done."
);
      } catch ( Exception e ) {
          return;
        }
    }
  }

  class Driver implements Runnable {
    String currentString;
    stub astub;

    public Driver( stub thisstub, String s ) {
      astub = thisstub;
      currentString = s;
      new Thread( this ).start();
    }

    public void run() {
      astub.call( currentString );
    }
  }

  class unsynch {
    public static void main( String args[] ) {
      stub astub = new stub();
      new Driver( astub, " Which came first? " );
      new Driver( astub, " The chicken,      " );
      new Driver( astub, " or the egg?       " );
    }
  }
```

The second class, *Driver*, implements a constructor that takes a reference to an instance of the *stub* class and a **String**, which are stored in *astub* and *currentString*, respectively. The constructor also creates a new thread that will call this object's **run()** method. The thread is started immediately. The **run()** method of *Driver* is also simple; it just calls the *stub* method on the *astub* instance of *stub*, passing in the *stringParam* string.

The *unsynch* class implements the **main()** method, which instantiates a single *stub* object, and three instances of *Driver*, each with a unique sentence. The same instance of *stub*, *astub*, is passed to each *Driver*. Look at a sample run from this program:

```
Line Number 1 starting: Line Number 1 starting: Line Number 1
starting:  Which came first?   : Line Number 1 done.
 or the egg?          : Line Number 2 done.
 The chicken,         : Line Number 3 done.
```

Obviously, the *Thread.sleep()* method in the *call* method allowed the threads to context-switch and mix up the output. The solution to this problem is quite simple. Use the Java keyword **synchronized** in front of the *call* method declaration:

```
synchronized void call( String stringParam ) {
```

Now, only one instance can exist at any single moment in time, thus allowing the sequence—print first part of statement, delay, print second part of statement—to run uninterrupted. When the *call* method's formal declaration is changed to include the keyword **synchronized,** the corrected program output looks like this:

```
Line Number 1 starting:  Which came first?   : Line Number 1 done.
Line Number 2 starting:  The chicken,        : Line Number 2 done.
Line Number 3 starting:  or the egg?         : Line Number 3 done.
```

JAVA.IO INPUTSTREAM AND PRINTSTREAM

Initially, most of your Java applet input will come from your computer's keyboard with output going directly to the monitor. Input and output in Java follow the C/C++ model in which input/output (I/O) support is provided by a library, not by the language itself. In Java, of course, the I/O library is a class library—the **java.io** package.

java.io contains two abstract (meaning they cannot be instantiated directly) classes targeted towards these needs: **InputStream** and **PrintStream**. Actually, the basic job of the **InputStream** class is to read bytes from whatever stream it is attached to, be it the keyboard, a disk, or the Internet. The **PrintStream** output is intended for the monitor.

java.io classes are layered by design. At the bottom level, there are basic **InputStream** and **Outputstream** classes. Added facilities such as buffering, connecting to files, printing data types other than bytes, and so on are provided by so-called *wrapper* classes. When a Java program runs, there are three streams available by default: **System.in**, **System.out**, and **System.err**, which are similar to C/C++'s **stdin**, **stdout**, and **stderr**. **System.in** defaults to the keyboard, while **System.out** and **System.err** default to the display monitor (these latter two streams are **PrintStream** objects).

Defining Your Own Stream Objects

If you do not want to use the standard **InputStream** member **System.in** and the standard **PrintStream** member **System.out,** you can set your own stream objects equal to these two **System** members. However, you should try to use the System instance variables, because they will make your code easier for other programmers to understand:

```
InputStream myInputStream = System.in;
PrintStream myOutputStream = System.out;
```

Other programmers will be familiar with the more standard **java.lang.System** protocols. The members **System.in** and **System.out** are of type **InputStream** and **OutputStream**, respectively. Notice that the **InputStream** and **OutputStream** are not created with the Java keyword **new**.

Keyboard Input with System.in.read()

One of the easiest ways for a Java program to obtain user input is with the **InputStream** method **System.in.read()**. The **read()** method automatically waits until input is available. Technically, this is called *blocking*, or waiting. More importantly, however, is how the input information is interpreted. All **InputStream** classes work with bytes, not characters. And because all Java programs use the new UNICODE standard, each time you input a character from the keyboard, you will not be processing the high-byte of two-byte UNICODE encryption for the character. There are actually three overloaded methods with the name **read()**:

```
public abstract int read()
public int read( byte byteArray[] )
public int read(byte byteArray[], int startOffset, int
     howManyBytes )
```

The first overloaded **read()** method is passed no actual arguments and returns a single byte from the input stream with **int** precision. For this reason *javac.exe* typically complains by issuing an error message if you try to put the returned integer directly into a character variable due to the discrepancy in their storage allocations.

The second overloaded version of **read()** allows a Java program to input more than one byte. The method's formal argument is a *byteArray[]*. This **read()** method places the incoming bytes into this array beginning at the 0th offset (or the first element).

The last **read()** method allows you to selectively target which consecutive bytes, within the *byteArray[]*, you would like filled. The first formal argument is the *byteArray[]* buffer to be filled. The second argument, *startOffset*, tells the method where to begin storing the bytes (remember the first byte in *byteArray[]* is at the 0th offset!). The third argument tells the method how many bytes to input. The following program demonstrates these three overloaded **read()** methods:

```
import java.applet.*;
import java.awt.*;
import ReadFrame;

public class Read extends Applet
{
     // STANDALONE APPLICATION SUPPORT:
     //        m_fStandAlone will be set to true if applet is run
     //         standalone
     //--------------------------------------------------------
     boolean m_fStandAlone = false;

     public static void main(String args[])
     {
          ReadFrame frame = new ReadFrame("Read");

          // Must show Frame before we size it so insets() will
          // return valid values
          //---------------------------------------------------
          frame.show();
```

```
        frame.resize(frame.insets().left + frame.insets().right
+ 320,
                     frame.insets().top  + frame.insets().bottom
+
                            240);

        Read applet_Read = new Read();

        frame.add("Center", applet_Read);
        applet_Read.m_fStandAlone = true;
        applet_Read.init();
        applet_Read.start();
    }

    public Read()
    {
    }

    public void finalize()
    {
    }

    public String getAppletInfo()
    {
        return "Name: Read\r\n" +
               "Author: Chris H. Pappas and William H.
Murray\r\n" +
               "Created with Microsoft Visual J++ Version";
    }


    public void init()
    {
        resize(320, 240);
    }

    public void destroy()
    {
    }
```

```
    public void paint(Graphics g)
    {
    }

    public void start()
    {
    }

    public void stop()
    {
    }

}
```

To understand the program, look at the following sample run:

```
abcdefg979899100101102103<ctrl-z>
aaaaaaaa
aaaaaaaa

bbbbbbbbbbcccc
aaaabbbbbbbbbb
```

The first use of **read()**,

```
// First overloaded read() method
while( (currentCharacter = System.in.read()) != -1 )
        buildStringByteByByte.append( currentCharacter );
  System.out.println( buildStringByteByByte );
```

processed the user input: *abcdefg* above, inputting one character at a time and appending it to *buildStringByteByByte,* until the user signaled end-of-file by pressing CTRL-Z. At this point the **println()** method output the sequential ASCII values, *979899100101102103,* of each symbol.

The second use of **read()**:

```
// Second overloaded read( byte byteArray[] ) method
      System.in.read( byteArray );
      String aString = new String( byteArray, 0 );
      System.out.println( aString );
```

input the eight *a*'s, *aaaaaaaa,* putting them into the *byteArray,* and then used the **println()** method to output the string *aaaaaaaa.*

The third **read()** method call:

```
// Third overloaded read( byte byteArray[],
      //                        int startOffset,
      //                        int howManyBytes )
      System.in.read( byteArray, 4, 10 );
      aString = new String( byteArray, 0 );
      System.out.println( aString );
```

input the user-data *bbbbbbbbbbcccc* into the *byteArray*, which now contains *aaaaaaaa*. However, the first *b* was overwritten to the fifth *byteArray* element position, at an offset of *4*, and *10* consecutive characters were then grabbed and consecutively appended to *byteArray*; because the last four *c*'s were after the 10 *b*'s, they were not appended. This time, the **println()** outputs the string *aaaabbbbbbbbbb*, leaving the originally inserted *a*'s alone.

Display Output with System.out.print()/println()

The easiest method for performing Java program output is to use the **print()** or **println()** methods of the **PrintStream** class. The difference between **print()** and **println()** is that the latter performs a line-feed, carriage-return, after performing the required output. The following three statements:

```
System.out.print( "This is all printed " );
System.out.println( "on one line. );
System.out.println( "However, this string is on its own line."
);
```

produce the following output:

```
This is all printed on one line.
However, this string is on its own line.
```

Java overloads the plus operator + so that it can concatenate **String** objects. Notice that in the following example:

```
System.out.print( "My name is: " + nameString + "." );
System.out.println("  I am " + yearsOld + " years old." );
```

each argument to the + operator is first converted to type **String** and then output. This holds true for the string variable *nameString* and the integer variable *yearsOld*. **System.out** and **System.err** are special cases of the **PrintStream** class in that they automatically flush the output buffer. For this reason, the user sees the prompts as soon as the statement is executed.

EXCEPTIONS

Not all programming languages have the ability to "eloquently" recover from certain types of run-time error conditions. Take, for example, the Pascal language. If a Pascal program statement attempts a divide-by-zero, the Pascal application instantly aborts, taking you back to the command line. Newer programming languages such as C++, Ada, and Java let you develop a program that can trap these types of fatal errors before they are dealt with by the operating system. Java code can detect errors and identify these errors to the run-time system. This capability is known as *exception handling*.

Exceptions provide a clean way for a method to abort whatever it was doing and signal to the calling method that something has gone wrong. There are three Java keywords involved in writing an exception handler: **throw**, **try**, and **catch**. However, there are only two phases to handling an exception. The first involves signaling the exception event; for this you use the **throw** keyword.

To signal an exception event, a member function simply uses the **throw** statement with an instance of an exception class, as in:

```
throw new MyHandledException();
```

The second phase involves handling the thrown exception. Here the **try** and **catch** keywords are used together. The syntax for a **try...catch** statement looks like:

```
try {
    // code that could throw the exception goes here
                .
                .
}   catch( exceptionType exceptionName ) {
      // code to handle the thrown exception goes here
                          .
                          .
}
```

The code within the **try** block is executed. If an exception is thrown within this block, any statements below the thrown exception, within the **try** block, are ignored. Program execution continues with an attempt to catch the thrown exception by finding a **catch** block that matches the specific exception. For this reason, there may be more than one **catch** block within the **try...catch** statement, as seen here:

```
try {
    // code that could throw the exception goes here
                .
                .
}   catch( exceptionType exceptionName ) {
    // code to handle the thrown exception goes here
                      .
                      .
}  catch( exceptionType exceptionName ) {
                      .
                      .
}  catch( exceptionType exceptionName ) {
                      .
                      .
}
```

Errors and other exceptional conditions are treated as distinct from the normal flow of control in the program—which, after all, they are. When an error occurs, an exception is thrown. Exceptions climb the chain of calls until they are caught or until the program exits. The catch-and-throw method of exception handling offers two significant advantages:

- First, the error condition is dealt with only where it makes sense, instead of dealing with it at every level between where it occurs and where it needs to be dealt with.
- Second, code can be written as if the operations in it will work.

A **try...catch** statement can contain a **finally** statement. The **finally** block is used to process statements that may be skipped within the method throwing the exception. For example, if a method is supposed to open, input, and then close a file, but throws an exception, it is possible that the statement to close the file will be skipped. The **finally** statement is used in conjunction with the **try** block. Basically, it ensures that if an exception occurs, any cleanup work that is necessary is taken care of because the code in the **finally** block is guaranteed to run, even if an exception is thrown. The syntax for a **try...catch...finally** statement looks like:

```
try {
    // code that could throw the exception goes here
                    .
                    .
}   catch( exceptionType exceptionName ) {
    // code to handle the thrown exception goes here
                         .
                         .
}  catch( exceptionType exceptionName ) {
                         .
                         .
}  catch( exceptionType exceptionName ) {
                         .
                         .
}  finally {
    // code that is ALWAYS executed no matter what!
                         .
                         .
}
```

Java provides a set of exceptions that it raises when errors occur within a program. The default action is to print an error message to the monitor and terminate the current execution thread. This capability is provided by the Java run-time interpreter.

Java Run-time Exceptions

Java provides a standard set of catchable exceptions designed to handle run-time errors. Table 4.1 lists the Java error, exception, and run-time exception subclasses (many of these are discussed in later chapters):

The throw Statement

The normal series of events for a **try...catch** statement involve first trying all of the statements in the **try** block, and if any exceptions are thrown, executing the statements in the **catch** block. However, to raise your own exception, you use the Java **throw** keyword. The argument to this operator is an instance of a subclass of the **Exception** class.

Table 4.1 Java Error, Exception, and Run-time Exception Subclasses

Error Subclasses	**ClassCircularityError**
	ClassFormatError
	Error
	IllegalAccessError
	IncompatibleClassChangeError
	InstantiationError
Exception Subclasses	**ClassNotFoundException**
	DataFormatException
	IllegalAccessException
	InstantiationException
	InterruptedException
	NoSuchMethodException
	RuntimeException
RuntimeException Subclass	**ArithmeticException**
	ArrayIndexOutOfBoundsException
	ArrayStoreException
	ClassCastException
	IllegalArgumentException
	IllegalThreadStateException
	IndexOutOfBoundsException
	NegativeArraySizeExcepton
	NullPointerException
	NumberFormatException
	SecurityException
	StringIndexOutOfBoundsException

The **thrown** exception aborts the method and raises the specified exception through the call stack. If there is a matching **catch** block in the caller that matches the exception or one of its superclasses, then the exception stops there and the **catch** block handles it. However, if the caller doesn't have a matching **catch** block, the exception keeps moving through the call stack until it finds a matching **catch** block. The program terminates if no matching **catch** block is found.

To create your own exception, you first need to subclass the **exception** class, which **implements** the **Throwable** interface and provides some useful features for dealing with exceptions. Specifically, the **Exception** class provides a slot for a message and executes a stack trace. The syntax for subclassing the **Exception** class looks like:

```
class myException extends Exception {
      .
      .
      .
}
```

The advantage of subclassing the **Exception** class is that the new exception type can be caught separately from other **Throwable** exception types. In Java, the exceptions a method can throw are considered part of its public interface. Users of a method need to know the exceptions it might throw so they can be prepared to handle them. For this reason, Java requires that a method definition include a list of the exceptions it can throw. The syntax for this is straightforward:

```
public class sample {
  public static void MyException() throws thisException,
       anotherException {
  }
}
```

However, before writing your own exception, look at the following *inputString()* method:

```
public static String inputString() {
  int a_character;
  String buildString = "";
  boolean moreToDo = true;
  while( moreToDo ) {
    try {
      a_character = System.in.read();
      if( ( (char) a_character == '\n' ) ||
      ( a_character == -1 ) )
        moreToDo = false;
      else
        buildString += (char)a_character;
    } catch ( IOException e ) {
        moreToDo = false;
```

```
      }
    }
    return buildString;
  }
```

The *inputString()* method is designed to input a series of characters, with a call to **System.in.read()**, build a string, character by character, until the user either presses the carriage return or generates an end-of-file. However, **System.in.read()** can automatically throw a run-time **IOException**. The *inputString()* can handle this situation, however, because the **System.in.read()** method was placed inside a **try...catch** statement, with the **catch** block setting the **while** loop control variable *moreToDo* to **false**. The *inputString()* method is a good example of an encoded subroutine that handles its own exceptions.

However, there are times when a method should not do anything at all with an exception, and instead, pass it to the calling method. In order to tell Java this, the method throwing the unhandled exception needs to broadcast this situation with a **throws** statement in its formal header. The following code segment rewrites the *inputString()* method using this syntax:

```
public static String inputString() throws IOException {
  int a_character;
  String buildString = "";
  boolean moreToDo = true;
  while( moreToDo ) {
    a_character = System.in.read();
    if( ( (char) a_character == '\n' ) || ( a_character == -1 ) )
      moreToDo = false;
    else
      buildString += (char)a_character;
  }
  return buildString;
}
```

If you are wondering which approach is better, the general rule is for a method to deal with its own exceptions rather than propagate them to the caller. If you are writing a method that overrides a parent class' method that throws no exceptions, the overriding method must catch its own exceptions. It cannot propagate them because the parent class' method did not have a **throws** clause.

The same rules that apply to exceptions thrown by Java apply to any you may write. To throw your own exception, you have to decide what type of situation to detect, and then what type of exception to throw. Take, for example, a method that is inputting bytes to a user-defined BUFFERSIZE of 512 bytes. However, end-of-file is encountered at only 256 bytes. Your method knows this is a fatal input error condition and decides to throw its own exception. You would write the method this way:

```
String inputString( inputFile in ) {
  // member data declarations;
  while( . . . ) {
    if( a_character = = -1 ) {
      if( length < BUFFSIZE ) throw new EOFException;
    }
  . . .
}
String inputString( inputFile in ) throws EOFException {
  // member data declarations;
  while( . . . ) {
    if( a_character = = -1 ) {
      if( length < BUFFSIZE ) throw new EOFException;
    }
  . . .
}
```

Whenever a standard Java error, exception, or run-time exception just won't do, you write your own subclass of the **Exception** class. For example, the following subclass definition is interested in an input file being in UNICODE (16-bit per character, not ANSI ASCII 8-bit) format:

```
class notUNICODEexception extends IOException {
  public notUNICODEexception() {}
  public notUNICODEexception( String notUNICODEmsg ) {
    super( notUNICODEmsg );
  }
}
```

When you are writing your own exception subclass, it is traditional to have both a default constructor and one that outputs an exception-specific message. The **toString()** method of the **Throwable** base class can print out this message. With your exception class defined, you are ready to throw your own exception:

```
String inputUNICODEfileString( UNICODEinputFile in )
throws notUNICODEexception {
  while( . . . ) {
    if( ...readUTF_failure ) {
      throw new notUNICODEexception();
    }
  }
}
```

INTERFACES

Interfaces, like abstract methods and classes, let a programmer develop templates that other derived classes are expected to implement. Sometimes interfaces are the only way around Java's lack of multiple-inheritance capabilities. Multiple inheritance defines an object-oriented language's ability to derive a subclass from two parent classes.

An interface is declared using the keyword **interface**. Similar to classes, interfaces are **private** by default. However, an interface's methods are always **public**. Interface data members are both **public** and **static**—that is, available to anyone and not permitted to be changed, renamed, or extended. The syntax for an interface looks like the code that follows (note that the keywords **protected** and **private** are illegal in interface definitions):

```
public interface myInterfaceName {
  // public static member data declarations go here
  // public abstract method declarations go here
}
```

You implement the interface in a class by using the **implements** keyword, as in:

```
public class className implements interfaceName {
  // class definition
}
```

A class can also implement more than one interface by using the comma operator, as in:

```
public class className implements interfaceOne, interfaceTwo,
     interfaceThree {
  // class definition
}
```

INTERFACES WITHOUT ABSTRACT METHODS

One proper and simple use for Java interfaces is shared constant declarations. Languages such as C and C++ use special syntax in files called header files for this purpose. Java does not have header files. However, a properly written interface can replace the popular C/C++ **#define** preprocessor statement. Remember that interface instance variables must be **public static final** implied (meaning not actually entered in the code) or explicitly documented (where the three keywords precede the instance variable's declaration). Also, interface instance variables must be initialized with constant values. The following interface definition contains minimum and maximum screen resolution extents, default drive, and subdirectory constants:

```
public interface constant {
  public static final int    MIN_X_COORD  =    0,
                              MIN_Y_COORD  =    0,
                              MAX_X_COORD  =  639,
                              MAX_Y_COORD  =  479;

  public static final String defaultDrive = "c:",
                              defaultPath  =
"\encyclopedia\images";
}
```

Now any class type needing to output information can use these VGA screen resolution coordinates to make certain the displayed image is within the bounds of the current settings:

```
public class encyclopediaVideoDisplay implements constant {
  // code to display *.avi files goes here
}
public class encyclopediaBitmapDisplay implements constant {
  // code to display *.bmp files goes here
}
```

INTERFACES WITH ABSTRACT METHODS

You may be asking yourself about the benefits of interfaces. By taking the time to create an interface, you can define the protocols for an abstract class without worrying about the specific implementation until later. In addition, you can share the same interface with several classes, without worrying about how the other class is handling the methods. If you inherit the properties of the interface, other users will automatically know what the method calls are for that class.

Say, for example, you have three different telephone classes: *payPhone*, *twoLineTouchTonePhone*, and *simpleHomePhone*. Each class has its own set of member declarations. However, at some point, regardless of the phone type, you want all of them to have a *dialThePhone*() method. You could create an interface and name it *canCallOut*:

```
public interface canCallOut {
  public abstract void dialThePhone();
}
```

Now, any time you use a phone, you will know that it has a *dialThePhone()* method, and what parameters it takes.

USING INTERFACES AS CLASS TYPES

You can also use the *canCallOut* class as a type itself. This enables you to create member variables and methods that can hold any of the objects that implement *canCallOut*:

```
canCallOut aCall; // example member variable

void addLongDistancePrefix( canCallOut LongDistanceCall ) {
  // method code goes here
}
```

Interface Casting

By using a class cast, you can give the previous method *addLongDistancePrefix()* an instance of the type *payPhone*:

```
payPhone CornerOfMainAndFifth = new payPhone();
addLongDistancePrefix( (canCallOut) CornerOfMainAndFifth );
```

PACKAGES

The main idea behind Java packages is the syntactical bundling of logically related class and interface definitions. Take, for example, the six packages provided by Java (see Table 4.2).

Table 4.2. Standard Java Packages

java.applet	Containing classes that let you create Java applets that will run in any Java-compatible browser
java.awt	Containing classes that let you write platform-independent GUI applications
java.io	Containing classes used to do standard input and output
java.lang	Containing essential Java classes
java.net	Containing classes to use network connections
java.util	Containing utility classes such as vectors and hashtables

Notice how each of the classes in a package serve to perform some logically related function.

IMPORTING PACKAGES

Java provides two types of syntax for accessing classes within a package. The first method uses the **import** keyword with the asterisk * wild card symbol:

```
import java.awt.*;
```

Using *java.awt.** means that all of the classes in the **java.awt** package are imported or used. However, the second method allows you to use a specific class within a package without the **import** statement by explicitly putting the name of the package before the class. For example, the statement:

```
java.util.Date;
```

allows a program to use the **java.util.Date()** method without using the **import** statement. Using the **import** statement is a shortcut that allows you to avoid affixing the package name in front of every class in the package.

JAVA PACKAGE SYNTAX

You begin a Java package definition by using the keyword **package**. The package name is specified as a list of identifiers separated by a period, with the initial name in the list indicating the class owner and developer. The period separator in the package name lists the level, or inheritance hierarchy, where each level usually represents a smaller, more specific grouping of classes.

The Java class library itself is organized along these lines. The top level is called **java**; the next level includes names such as **io**, **util**, and **awt**. If a package definition appears in a Java source file, it must be the first statement other than comments and whitespace in the compilation unit. For example, the following code segment declares the package *allSorts*. Here, each sort class is made into its own file, with each individual file containing the statement *package sorts* at the beginning of each file:

```
// file name: sorts.java
package allSorts;
  public class sorts {
    // define sorts class
  }
><><><><><><><><><><><><><><><
// file name: bubble.java
package allSorts;
  public class bubble {
    // define bubble sort
  }
><><><><><><><><><><><><><><><
// file name: selection.java
package allSorts;
  public class selection {
    // define selection sort
  }
><><><><><><><><><><><><><><><
// file name: binaryTree.java
package allSorts;
  public binaryTree {
    // define binary tree sort
  }
><><><><><><><><><><><><><><><
// file name: quickSort.java
package allSorts;
  public quickSort {
    // define quick sort
```

```
}
><><><><><><><><><><><><><><
// file name: usesSorts.java
import allSorts.*;
```

All of these files would be saved in a subdirectory called *allSorts*. The first line in each file, *package allSorts;*, indicates that the classes in the listing are part of the *allSorts* package. For source files that are part of this package, the **package** declaration must be present at the beginning of the file, before any other statement, although it can be preceded by comments or empty lines.

When the source files are compiled, Java will create a *classname.class* file for each class in the source file and, unless directed otherwise, will store the file in the same directory as the source file. The **.class* must be located in a directory that has the same name as the package, and this directory should be a subdirectory of the directory where classes that will import the package are located.

COMING TO TERMS

The following new terms have been discussed in this chapter and are presented here for your review:

ancestor—The term used to refer to a subclass, child, or sibling class' parent, base, root, or superclass.

base class—The term used to refer to the highest level of a class inheritance hierarchy tree.

child class—The term used to refer to a parent, base, or root class' subclass.

class—An object-oriented concept that allows a programmer to syntactically combine data declarations with the functions that work on those data declarations. The result is a side-effect–proof object.

constructor—A constructor is a class member function by the same name as the class. Constructors are never directly called. Instead, they are automatically invoked whenever an instance of the class is instantiated. Constructors perform the logical task of initializing class member data.

derivation/deriving—The process by which a parent, base, root, or superclass is reused to create a subclass, child, or sibling class.

descendant—The term applied to the child, sibling, or subclass of a parent, base, root, or superclass.

destructor—A destructor is the logical inverse of a *constructor* and usually cleans up an object before it is removed from memory. Destructors are then class methods and always have the name *finalize*.

exceptions—An error condition recognized by the Java run-time environment and/or program logic.

inheritance—In a procedural language, when one record's definition contains a nested record definition, the record is said to inherit the nested record's characteristics. In an object-oriented language, the same situation holds true for objects defined based on some previous object's definition. The new object is said to inherit the previously defined object's characteristics. However, since an object definition contains both member data and member functions, the inheritance is fully functional.

instantiation—In procedural programming languages, the term *instantiation* would be translated into *creating*. In a procedural language, you create a variable. In object-oriented terms, you instantiate an object. The process of creating objects is called instantiation.

interfaces—The workaround for Java's lack of multiple inheritance. Multiple inheritance defines a syntax whereby a child class inherits two or more parent class' characteristics. Java interfaces merely define the set of methods that all formal class definitions must encode, if they wish to use the interface. This allows a programmer to assume which methods will be available, no matter how many new objects are defined sharing the same interface.

member data—In a procedural language, member data would be called fields within a record. In object-oriented terms, these fields are called member data.

member function—In procedural languages, there is no equivalent to the term *member function* because procedural languages do not allow you to syntactically tie a function's definition to any particular record. In object-oriented languages, objects can contain function declarations. So that you can recognize which type of function a programmer is talking about—standalone or one tied to an object—each type has its own term. Standalone object-oriented functions are just called functions. However, functions syntactically bundled with an object are called member functions or methods. Note that Java does not have standalone functions, all coding must be done in member functions.

method—See *member function*.

multithreaded—Multiple, concurrent paths of program execution.

overloading—The term *overloading* applies to an object-oriented language's ability to define more than one member function, or method, using the same name. The idea behind this syntax is to allow a programmer to replicate an algorithm that merely operates on different data types. Java does not support another type of overloading known as operator overloading, by which a programmer can redefine a language's standard operators.

parent class—The term applied to the class definition from which a subclass, child, or sibling class is derived.

root class - The term used to refer to the highest level on a class inheritance hierarchy tree.

siblings—Two classes that share the same parent, base, or root class.

static—This Java keyword has many uses. This chapter explained how **static** is used to declare **static** methods and **static** variables. Another way to think of the keyword **static** is "I want only one of...", either one method or variable, by the specified name. This **static** code segment is then shared, as is, no matter how many times you use it.

subclass—A class definition that is based on a previously defined class.

superclass—The term used to refer to the base, parent, or root class of a subclass.

thread—A single path of program execution.

thread priority—All Java threads are assigned a priority (from 1 - **MIN_PRIORITY** to 10 - **MAX_PRIORITY;** 5 - **NORM_PRIORITY** is the default), which affects when the Java thread scheduler chooses to run a thread. When threads share the same priority, they share the processor on a first-come, first-served basis. When a thread of a higher priority than any of the others comes into existence, it will get control of the processor, even if it needs to pre-empt a currently running thread to do so.

Chapter 5

EXPLORING EXAMPLE APPLETS

In order to give you an instant up-and-running Java experience, Microsoft ships the Java compiler/interpreter with many exciting sample applets. Each applet demonstrates a particular Java capability. You can use the source code to study, modify, or even incorporate into one of your own applets because they are all shipped to you copyright free.

HOW TO USE THE JAVA PROGRAMS SHIPPED WITH VISUAL J++

To load, compile, and run the Java applets shipped with Visual J++:

1. Start Visual J++.
2. Select **Open Workspace** from the **File** menu. (Note: These steps assume that you have first copied all of the sample programs from the CD-ROM onto your hard disk. The programs are found in the *Samples/Sun - /Microsoft* subdirectories on the CD-ROM.)
3. Route the File Manager over to the drive/subdirectory containing the sample programs, for example, *c:\Msdev\Samples\Sun* or *c:\Msdev\Samples\Microsoft*.

4. Choose the subdirectory containing the particular example of interest.
5. Select the example's *.mdp* file and click Open.
6. Select **Execute** from the **Build** menu.
7. Click Yes when asked to rebuild the out-of-date files. A dialog box opens, prompting you to save a class file to run.
8. Specify the class that extends java.applet.Applet, which is the subdirectory's file with the **.class* file extension. (Note: Several of the sample program's **.class* filenames do *not* match the name for the workspace (here the terms "workspace" and "subdirectory" mean the same thing). For example, the *TumblingDuke* subdirectory's *.class* file name is *tumbleitem*. At this point, if you were to enter the class filename *TumblingDuke.class* and attempt to execute the remaining steps, you will generate a non-running combination of files. For a beginner, removing the unwanted files and starting over can be very confusing, usually resulting in your deleting the subdirectory altogether and block-copying the source files all over again! The chapter highlights where the two names Workspace/**.class* class filename, differ. If no mention is made of a difference, then assume the workspace name *matches* the class filename.)
9. With the previous caution, you are now ready to enter the class filename and click OK. That's it! You should now see the Java program running inside your default browser.

To debug the applet:

1. Exit the browser.
2. Select **Debug/Step Into** from the **Build** menu.

As of this writing, the *c:\Msdev\Samples* subdirectory contained the list of folders seen in Figure 5.1.

Notice that there are two *Sample* subdirectories, the highlighted *Sun* and *Microsoft*. As of this writing, all of the *Sun* examples are available. However, only one sample program exists in the *Microsoft* subdirectory and it is discussed in later chapters.

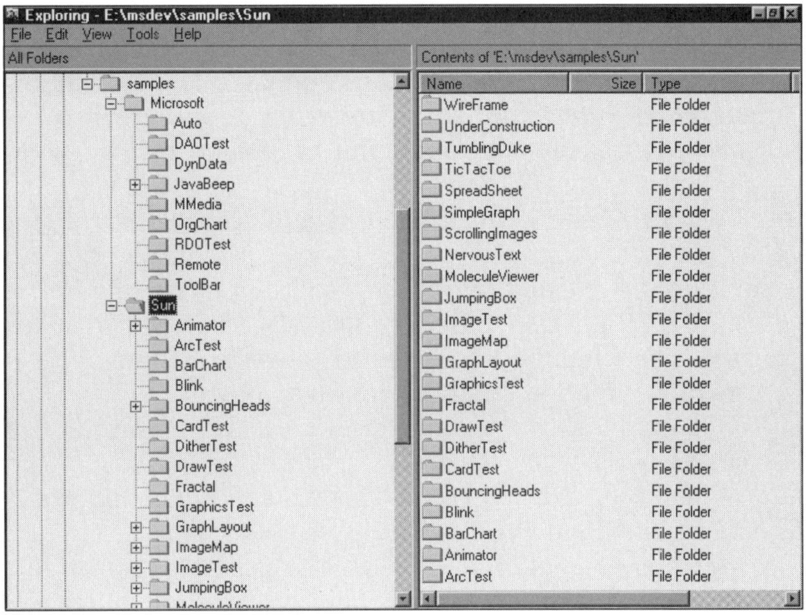

Figure 5.1: C:\Msdev\samples\Sun: Microsoft programs shipped with Visual J++.

The sample *Sun* programs cover every imaginable topic, from simple screen output, to animated screen output, to simple input, complex data input, complex data output, simple to advanced keyboard interaction, mouse interaction, graphics, video, and in case you thought the kitchen sink was left out, sound too!

Chapters 1 through 4 cover the concepts, keywords, syntax, and object-oriented design philosophies necessary to appreciate all these programs do. Because Java programming is such an enjoyable experience, an easy-to-learn language, with exciting features, take a moment at this point to sit back, relax, and experience all that Java has to offer.

This chapter does not present the programs in their alphabetical folder order, but instead organizes them logically, from simplest in concept, syntax, and design, to the more complex. This pedagogical order is used in each of the following chapters to teach you how to write your own Java programs.

PUT UP YOUR DUKES!

Here he is—Duke, the infamous animated Java mascot in all his various forms. You'll find Duke under the *Animator, TumblingDuke* (with class name *tumbleitem.class*), and *UnderConstruction* (with class name *jackhammer.class*) folders.

Figure 5.2 shows the initial screen you see when running the *animator* example program. You can choose to see Duke executing a simple animated wave and don't forget to listen (Figure 5.3).

Figure 5.4 is also under the *animator* folder and displays a flashing modern-art lighthouse. As you run each of these applets, notice the smooth animation capable with Java applets.

Figure 5.5 shows Duke executing a more complex animated jack hammer sequence (*UnderConstruction*).

Finally, Figure 5.6 shows the Duke trying out for the Summer Olympics with a gymnastic tumble (*TumblingDuke*).

Java uses simple frame flipping to generate animation in much the same way a sequence of cartoon characters are animated by flipping images drawn in each successive pose.

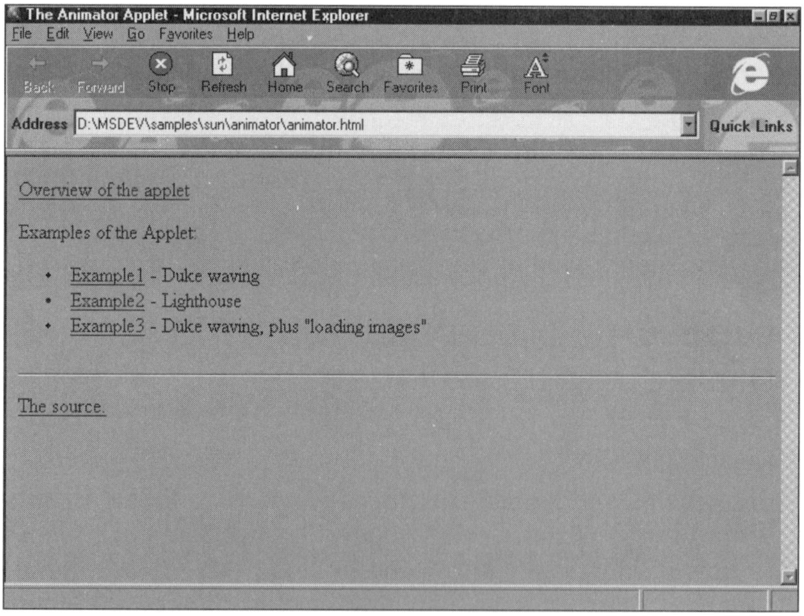

Figure 5.2: Java's Duke mascot waving a simple hello!

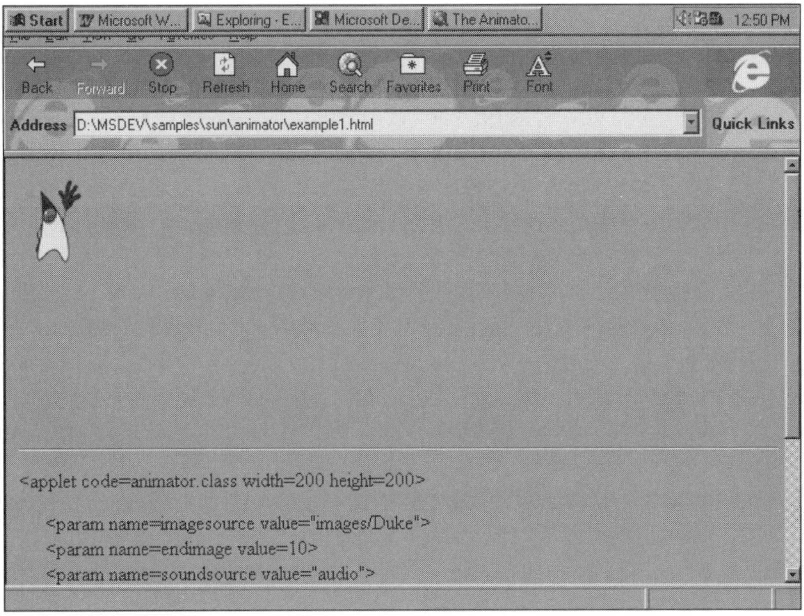

Figure 5.3: Duke waving.

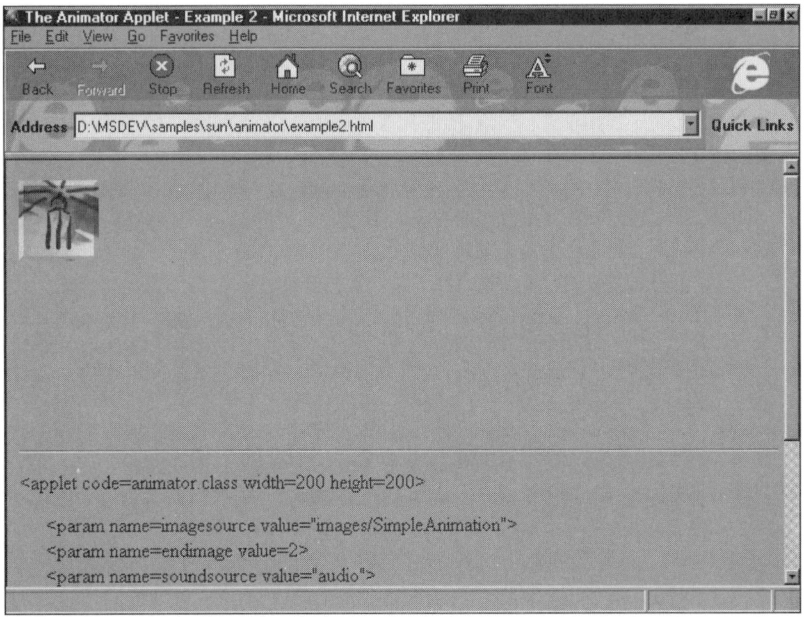

Figure 5.4: Animated modern-art flashing lighthouse.

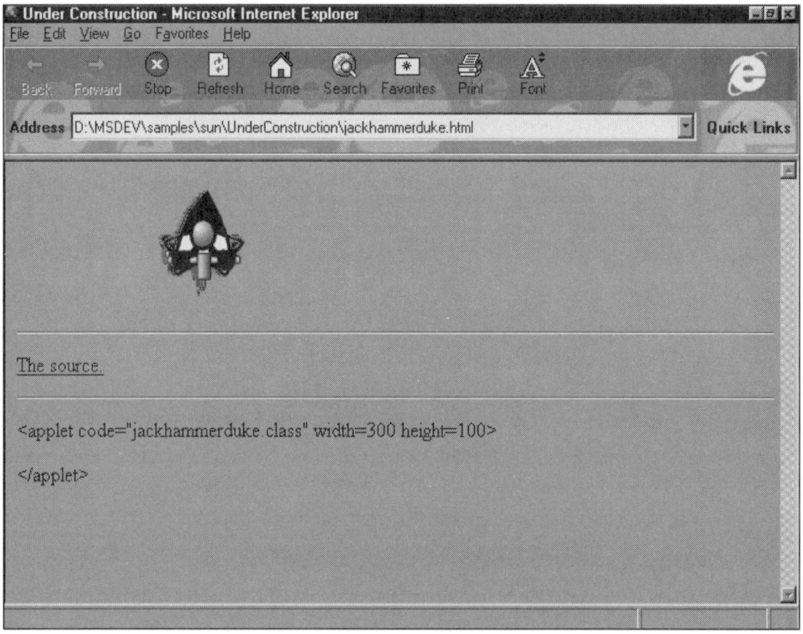

Figure 5.5: The jack hammer construction worker Duke.

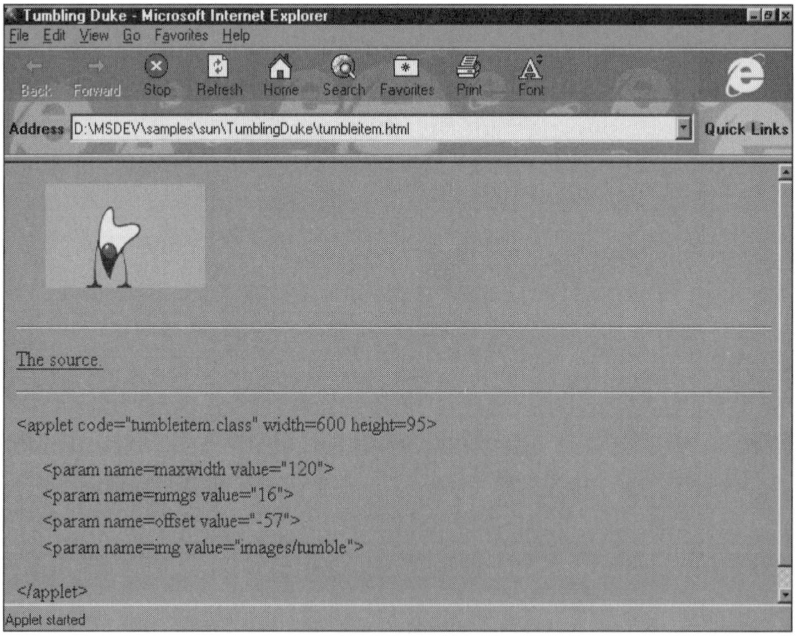

Figure 5.6: The gymnastic tumbling Duke.

ATTENTION-GRABBING JUMPING TEXT

Jazzing up a home page with some visual excitement is not just relegated to image animation. Java makes it very easy to change text color, point size, font, and yes, to animate it! Figures 5.7 (*NervousText*) and 5.8 (*Blink*) demonstrate these features. *NervousText* displays the H o t J a v a text jumping, squirming, up and down!

The *Blink.class* applet flashes words on and off, while changing their colors. Both applets present interesting text output options that will get your Web page popping.

SIMPLE STATIC GRAPHICS OUTPUT

Moving on up in complexity, this next set of applets highlights Java's capabilities for simple, static, graphics output, from plotting points, seen in Figure 5.9 (*SimpleGraph - graphapplet.class*).

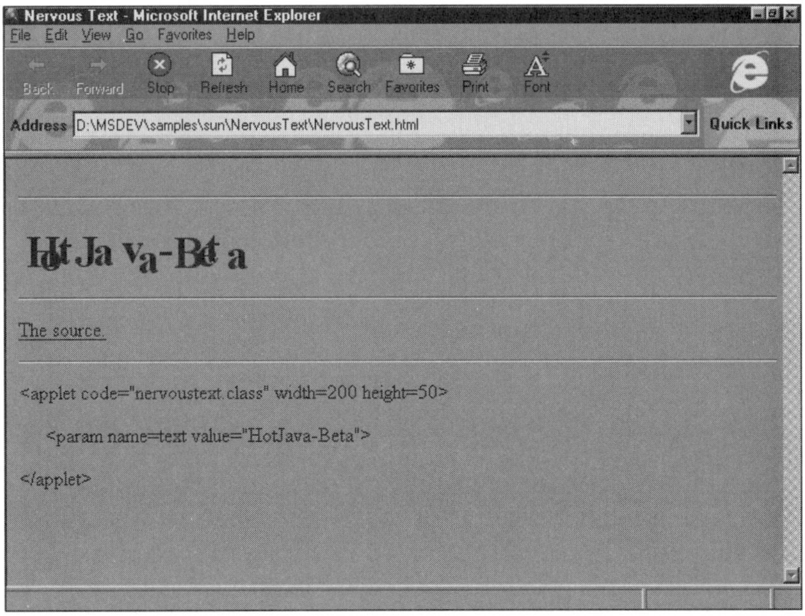

Figure 5.7: Excited, animated, eye-catching text!

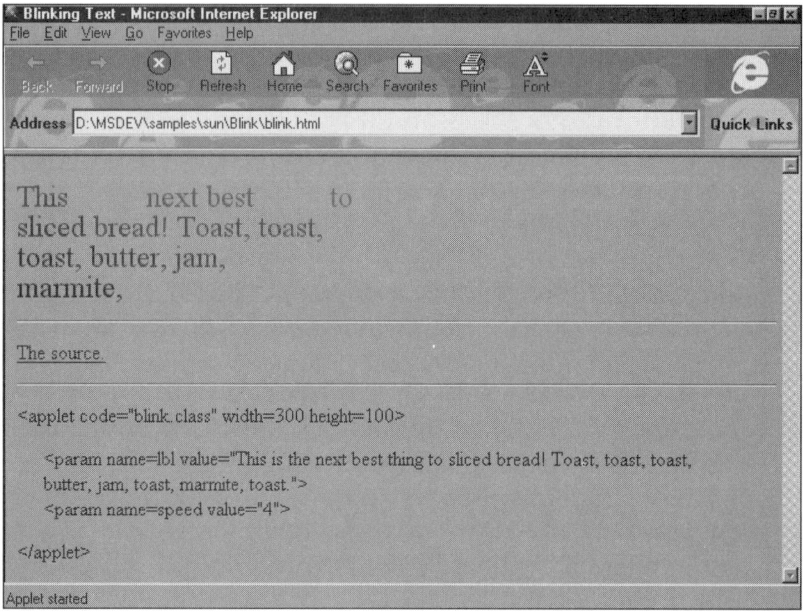

Figure 5.8: Visually enticing, colored, flashing, text output!

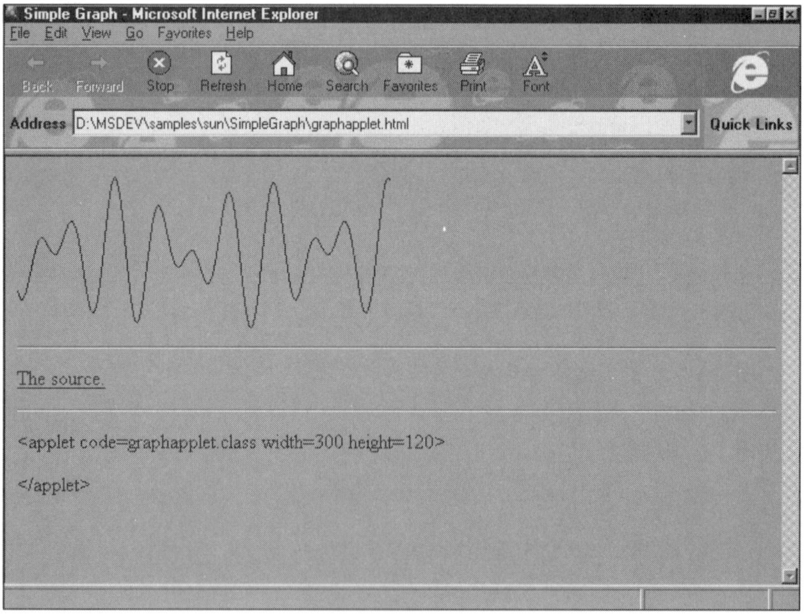

Figure 5.9: Simple, static graphics output.

The calculation and display of an interesting fractal is seen in Figure 5.10 (*\Fractal - clsfractal.class*).

And finally, a graphical bar chart (*\BarChart - chart.class*) is displayed in various colors and highlights (see Figure 5.11).

You'll discover that graphical output is easy with Java's many standard graphics classes.

INTERACTING WITH A JAVA APPLET

All of the sample applets so far have simply done their thing when run. This next set of programs interacts with the user via keyboard and mouse. The first applet demonstrates how to add PageUp, PageDown, and cursor key interaction to your Java program (see Figure 5.12 - *\ImageTest*). *ImageTest* moves the colored square (or Surfer Duke) left/right/up/down with each press of the cursor key, while increasing/decreasing the colored square's size with PageUp/PageDown.

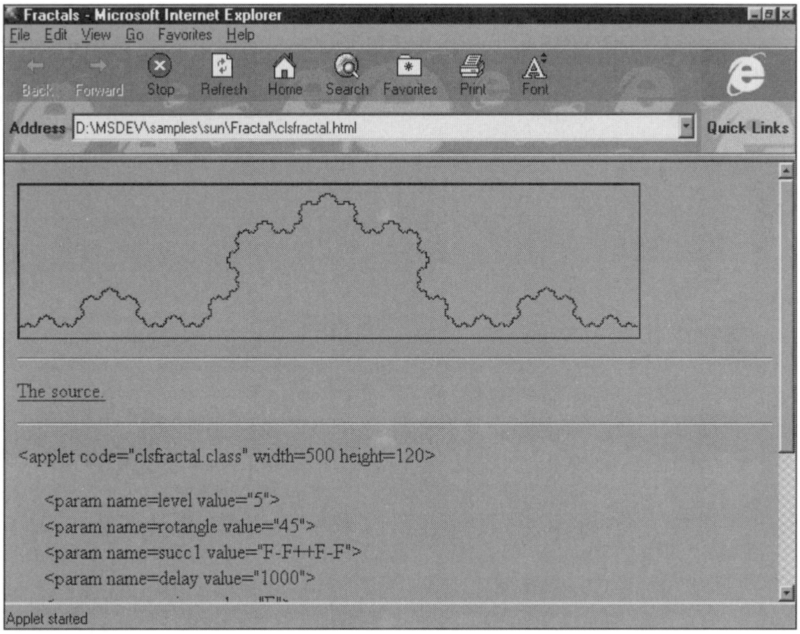

Figure 5.10: Graphing fractals.

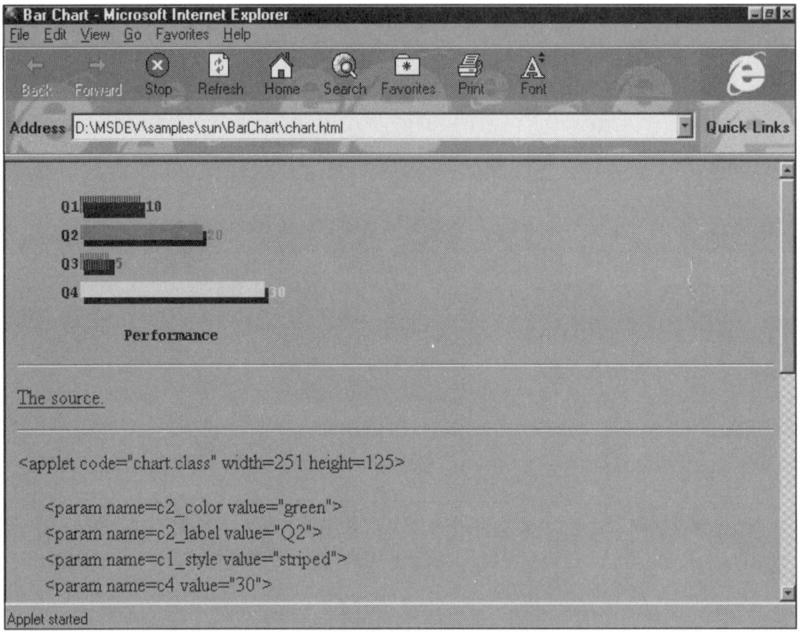

Figure 5.11: Colored, highlighted, bar chart applet.

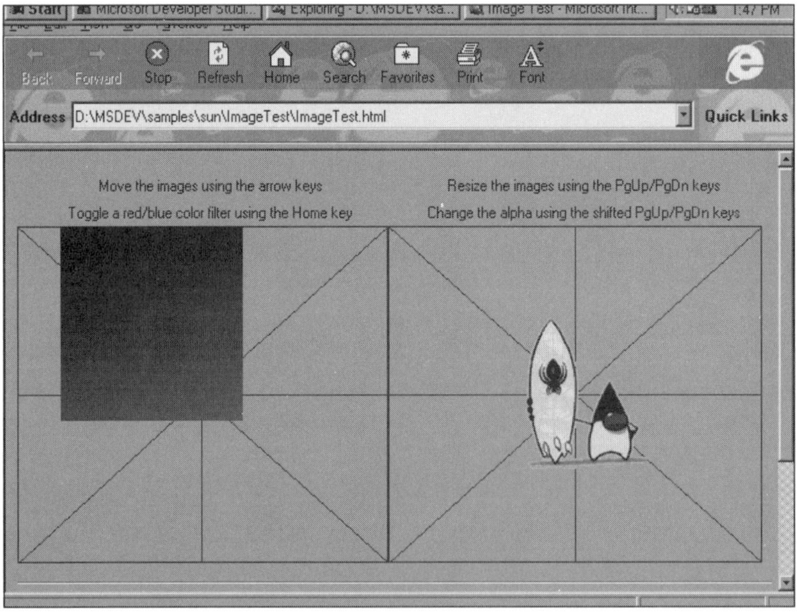

Figure 5.12: Adding a PageUp, PageDown, and cursor key interface to your applet.

The next sample program goes one better by not only recognizing the cursor keys but the mouse too. The spreadsheet applet allows both cursor key and mouse selection of spreadsheet cells, while performing an algorithmic computation (see Figure 5.13; *SpreadSheet*).

With an increasing number of kids logging on to the Internet, at younger and younger ages, don't forget them as a potential audience. This next applet creates a simple-to-use, mouse-driven, entertaining Tic Tac Toe game (see Figure 5.14; *TicTacToe*).

No one will know that YOU had fun with that one too! When someone's looking over your shoulder, run this next applet. Figure 5.15 also demonstrates a Java keyboard/mouse-user interface with a more professional adult, and serious visual interface. However, this applet goes one step further by presenting a text box entry capability for the starting and stopping angles—(*ArcTest*). The first figure shows *ArcTest* drawing the default arc.

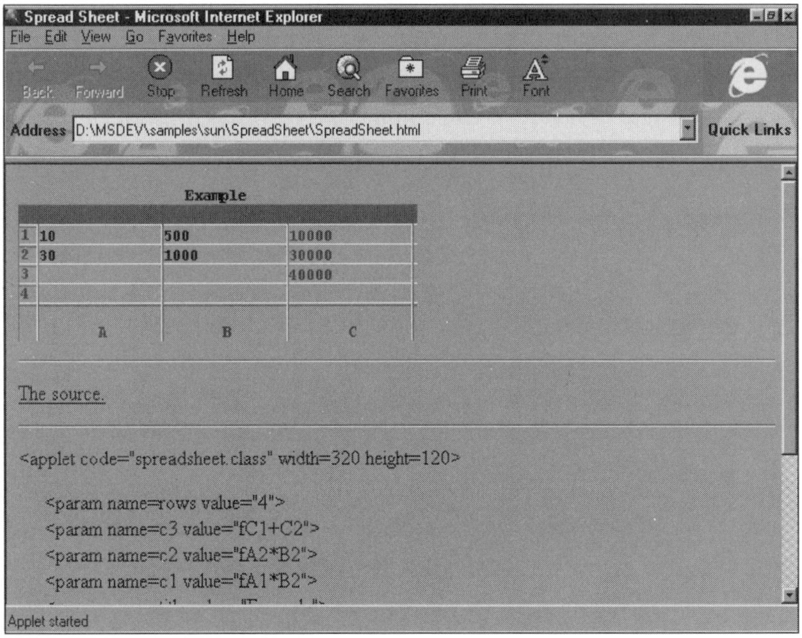

Figure 5.13: Java mouse/keyboard user interface applet.

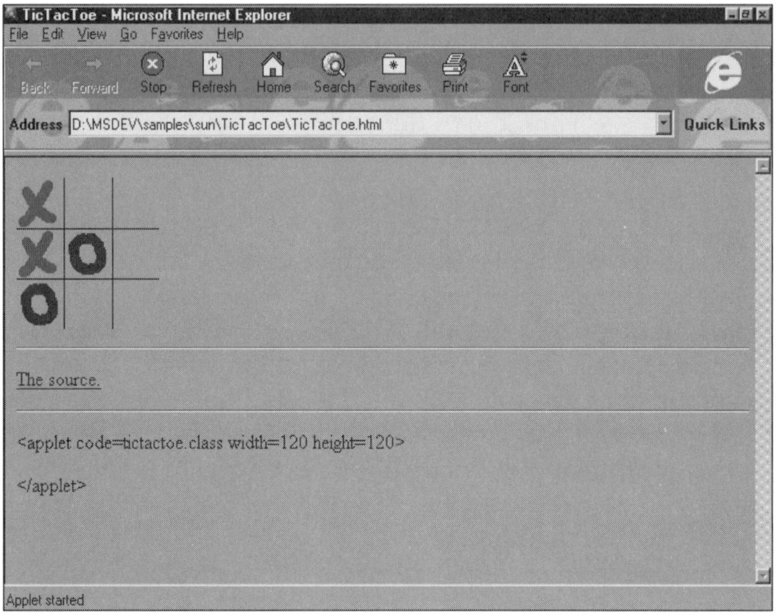

Figure 5.14: A child's favorite: mouse-driven, colored, Tic Tac Toe game.

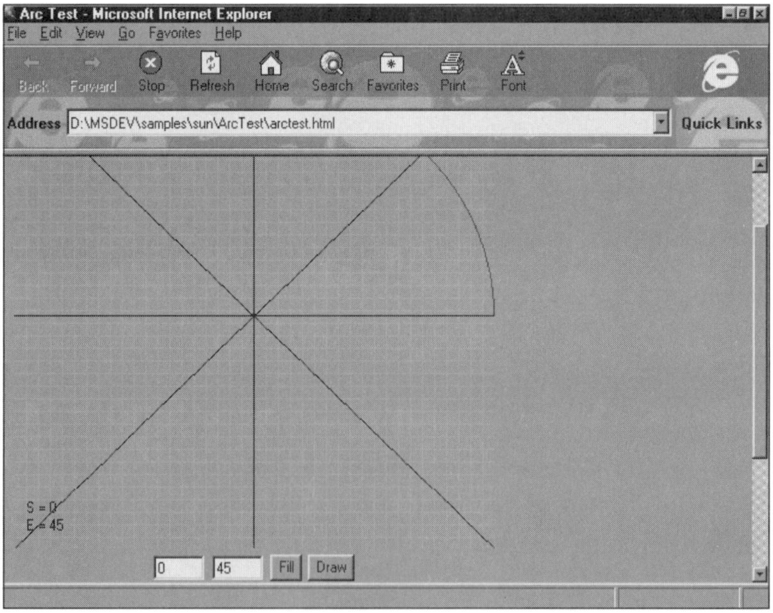

Figure 5.15: Initial *ArcTest—example1.html* with text box entry capability.

Figure 5.16 shows the applet drawing and filling the user-defined angle starting at 0 and going to 90 degrees. Then, instead of just drawing the arc (clicking the Draw button), a user can create a filled pie slice by clicking the Fill button.

ADDING A DROP-DOWN LIST BOX TO JAVA APPLETS

Whenever you want to present the user with a fixed range of options, you use a drop-down list box. Figures 5.17 through 5.21 allow the user to select from five graphical board layouts (by choosing the buttons marked one through five at the top of the applet window), move to the first, next, previous, or last board layout (using the buttons at the bottom of the applet window, or by list box selection).

Figure 5.17 shows the list box in its selected position, where the object is listing the five view options (*CardTest*).

While Figure 5.17 displayed the initial applet view, Figure 5.18 shows that the user has selected view one (seen in the collapsed drop-down list box).

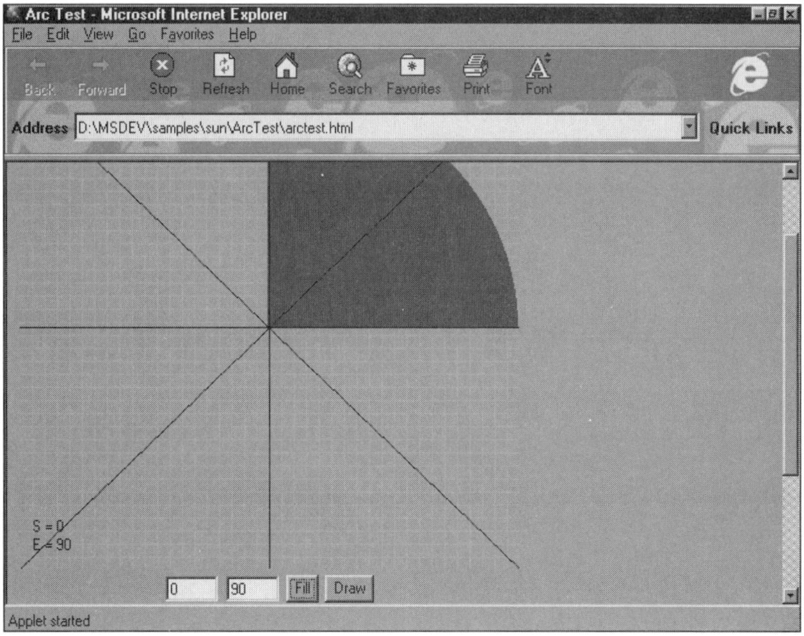

Figure 5.16: Using a text box and button applet interface.

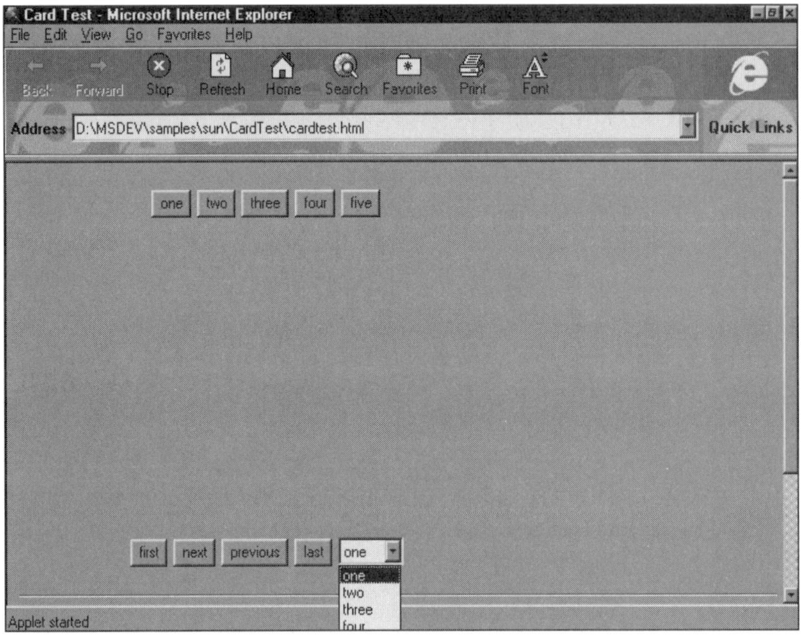

Figure 5.17: A Java applet with a drop-down list box object.

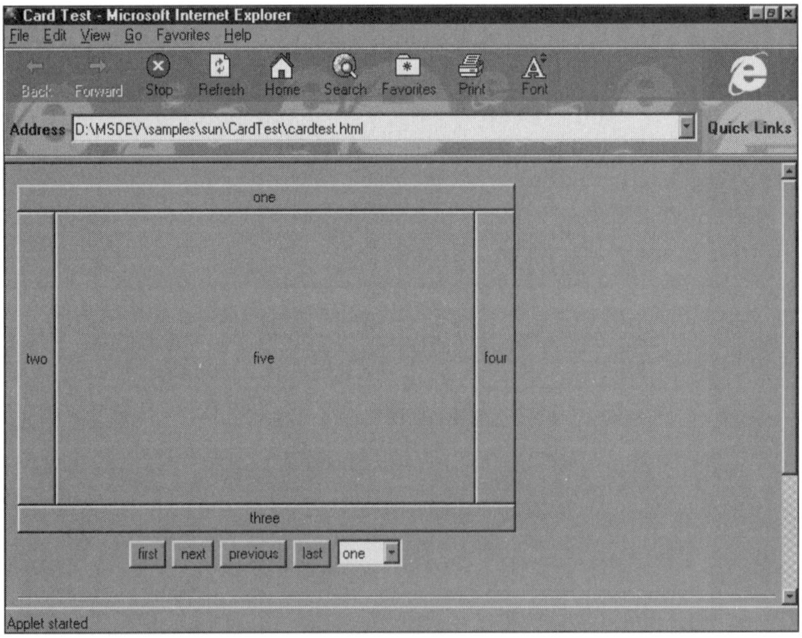

Figure 5.18: *CardTest* applet view one.

Figure 5.19 shows view two selected by pressing the next button.
Selecting the last button displays board five, as seen in Figure 5.20.
Figure 5.21 displays the fourth board layout after the user has clicked the mouse of the four button at the top of the applet window.

ALMOST ELECTRONIC PONG

If the static Tic Tac Toe game gets a little boring, try this next program. The *\JumpingBox - MouseTrack.class* applet displays a static rectangle until you move the mouse, at which point the target randomly jumps (see Figure 5.22). Your goal is to move the mouse pointer fast enough to hit the target before its next leap!

This is an excellent sample applet for precisely detecting when the mouse is moved, quickly calculating new screen coordinates, and registering back a successful strike.

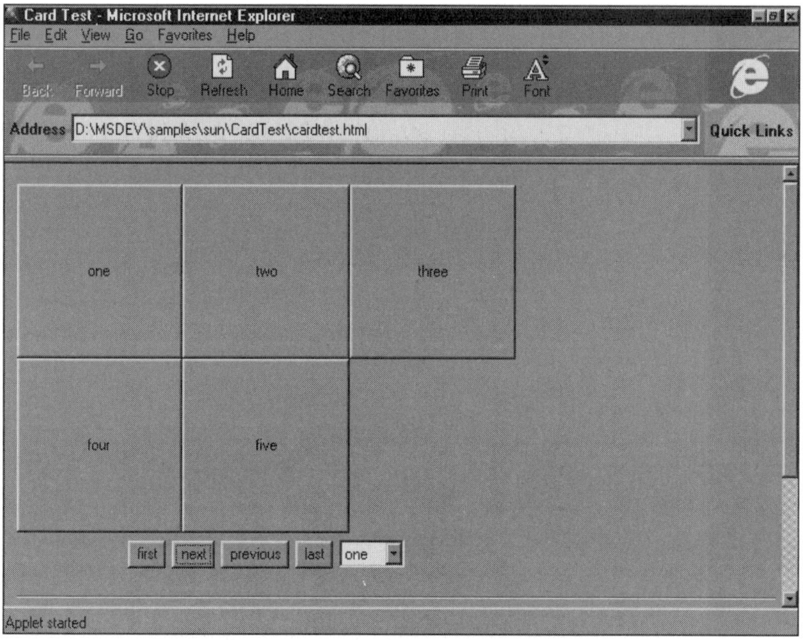

Figure 5.19: Viewing board two by pressing the next button.

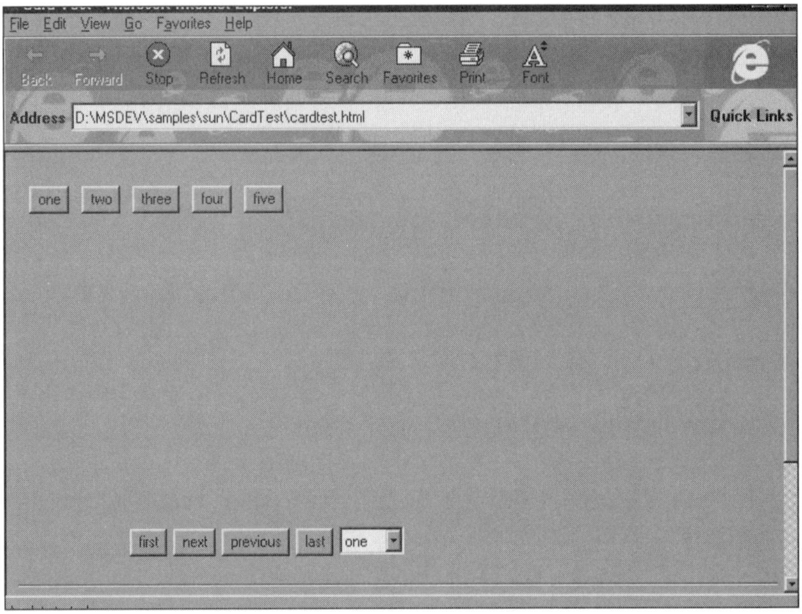

Figure 5.20: Selecting the last button to view board five.

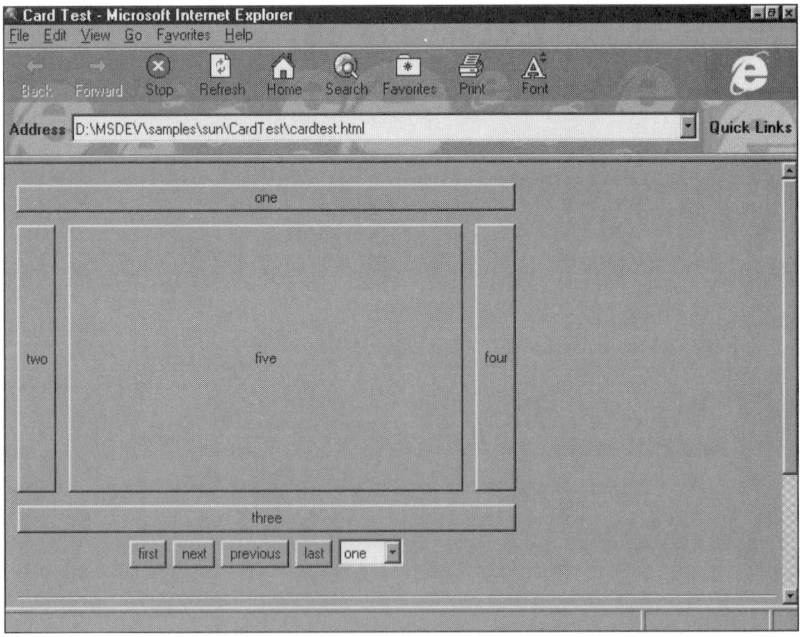

Figure 5.21: Using the four button to select the fourth board layout.

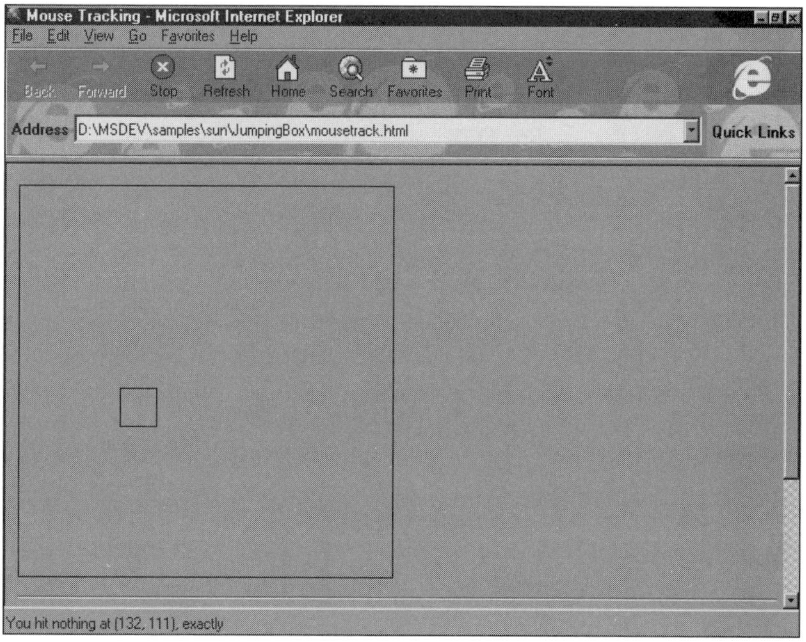

Figure 5.22: Hit the moving target applet.

HIGH-RESOLUTION SCREEN OUTPUT

Java's graphical output capabilities are not simply limited to textual enhancements, lines, colors, buttons, and bar charts. A Java applet is fully capable of using the host's display resolution. Figure 5.23 does not do this feature justice because it is reproduced in black and white. However, run on a color display, you will be very impressed with this Java applet's graphical output saturation, intensity, and resolution (*\DitherTest*).

A JAVA PAINT APPLET WITH RADIO BUTTONS

Creating an interactive paint program is easy with Java by combining color, text, buttons, list boxes, mouse interaction, and Java's point-and-line draw capabilities. Figure 5.24 shows such a program (*\DrawTest*).

This applet introduces the concept of radiobuttons. Radiobuttons let the user select one out of several, mutually exclusive options—in this case, drawing color.

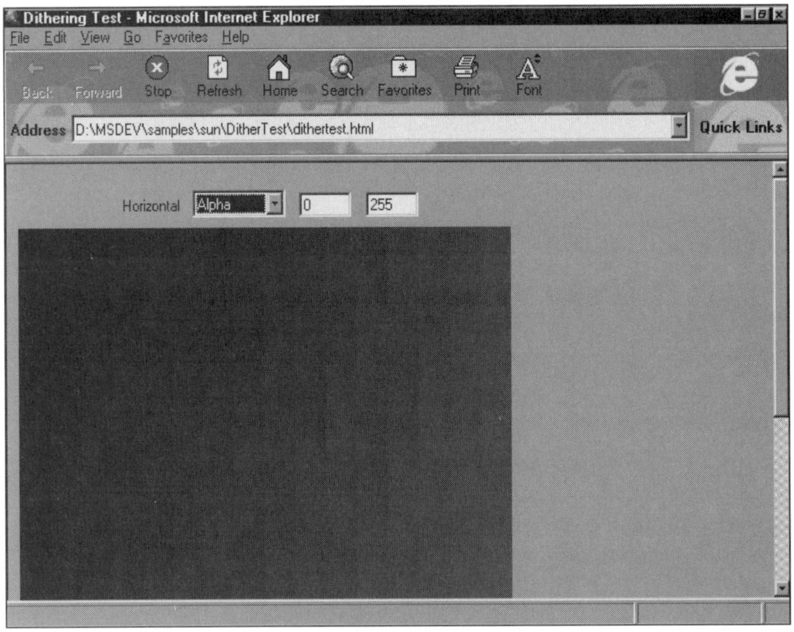

Figure 5.23: Java applet demonstrating high-resolution color output capabilities.

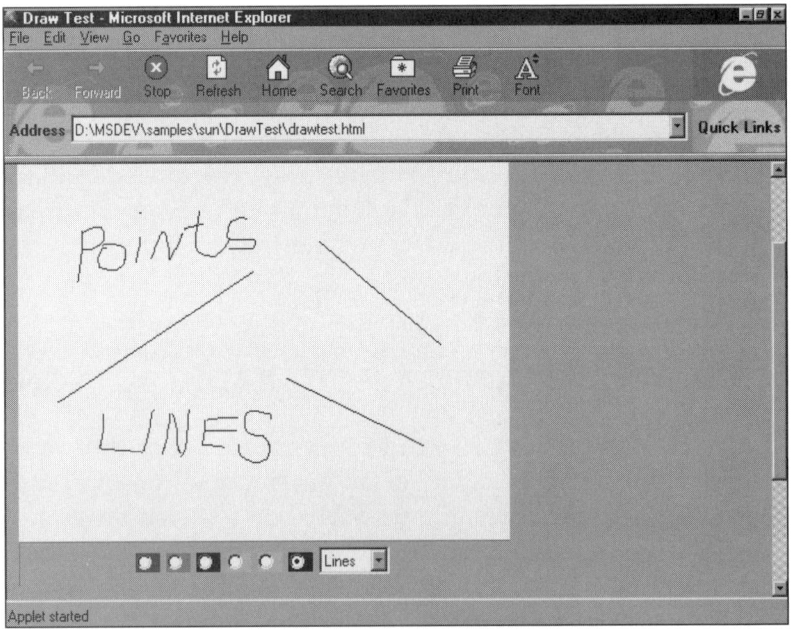

Figure 5.24: A Java Paint program using radiobuttons.

GRAPHICS TEST PATTERN APPLET

Although the *GraphicsTest* applet is capable of five unique views, only the first is displayed next. This applet (see Figure 5.25) also uses many of the previously discussed Java applet capabilities, along with circle, pie-slice, and fill graphics options (*GraphicsTest*).

ANIMATING VIDEO IMAGES

The *BounceItem* applet goes the *MouseTrack* program one better by randomly selecting an output screen coordinate, not for a rectangle, but a revolving video image! Java makes it very easy to import stored video images (see Figure 5.26) (*BouncingHeads - bounceitem .class*).

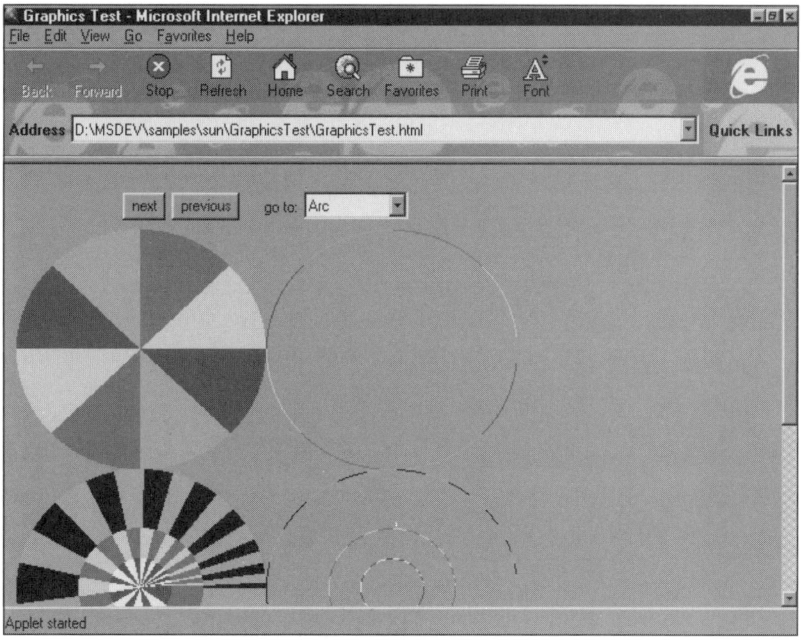

Figure 5.25: Graphics test pattern applet.

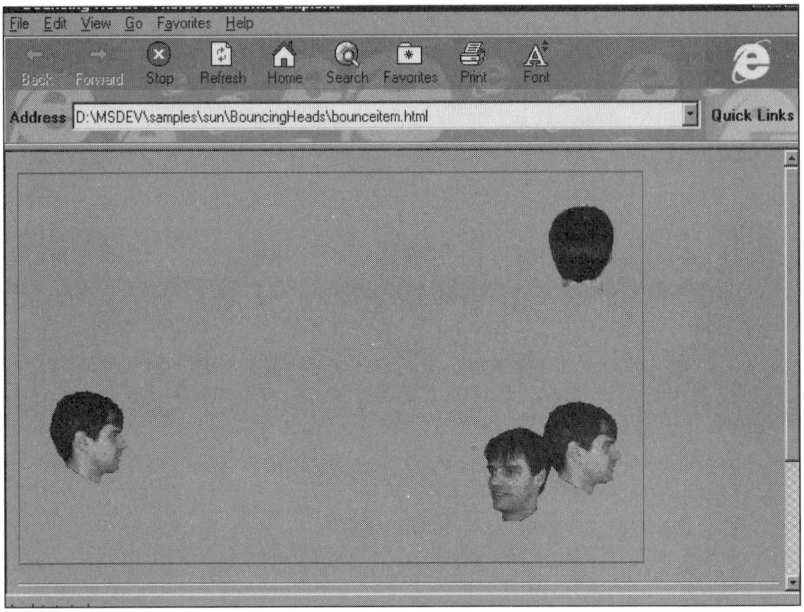

Figure 5.26: A bouncing, rotating video image applet.

GRAPHICAL VIEW OF A RELATIONAL DATABASE WITH CHECK BOXES

The *GraphLayout* applet, seen in Figure 5.27 combines all of the Java applet capabilities discussed to visually output the relationship between nodes in a sample database. The Scramble and Shake buttons mix-up and restart the image. However, this applet adds still another applet feature known as check boxes. By clicking on the Stress or Random check box objects, the user can select or deselect relational connection types (*\GraphLayout - graph.class*).

The difference between radiobuttons and check box items involves the number of items that can be concurrently selected. Radiobutton options are mutually exclusive, while any number of check box items can be simultaneously active.

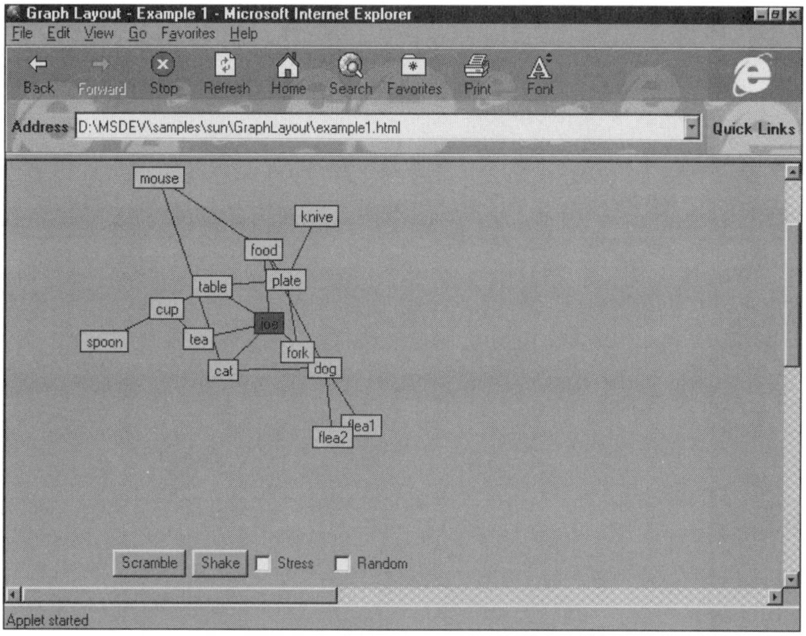

Figure 5.27: Java applet displaying text box options.

AN ANIMATED VIDEOGRAPHY LINE UP

OK, so everyone wants to get in on the act. This on-line streaming videotape applet continually displays a ticker-tape-like message of portraits, once again demonstrating the visual animation capabilities of Java applets, along with the associated personal appeal (see Figure 5.28) (*ScrollingImages - imagetape.class*).

MOLECULAR VIEWER

Figure 5.29 shows all four of the *MolecularViewer* applets running simultaneously, all using the circular solid fill graphics commands (*MolecularViewer - matrix3d.class*).

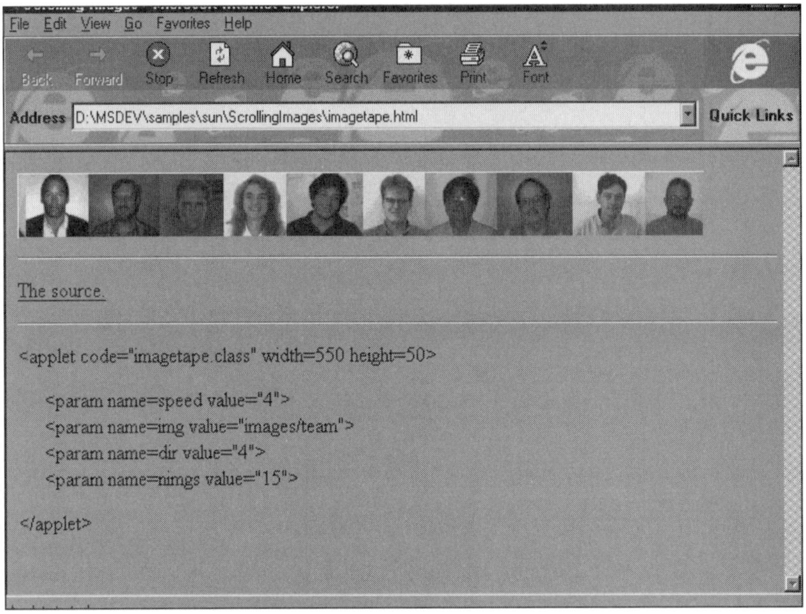

Figure 5.28: Scrolling videotape applet.

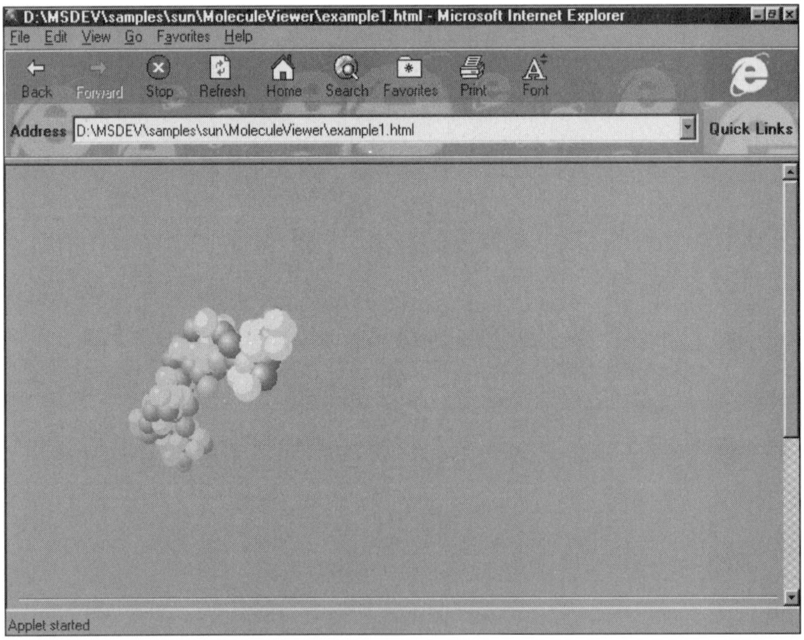

Figure 5.29: *MolecularViewer* applet.

A THREE-DIMENSIONAL MODELING WORKSTATION APPLET

This is the absolute showstopper when it comes to articulation, screen output, resolutions, algorithmic sophistication, and advanced graphical display. The *ThreeD.class* found under the \ *WireFrame* subdirectory outputs a sophisticated line drawing of a military vessel (see Figure 5.30).

By clicking the mouse above, below, to the right, and at angles to the initial image, the user can rotate the image on any axis. Of particular interest is Java's graphical capability of shading those portions of the wire frame closest to the user, and fading as the object moves off into the distance (see Figure 5.31).

Figure 5.30: Initial vessel position.

Figure 5.31: Rotated and scaled image showing Java's gradient shading capability.

LIGHTS, CAMERA, ACTION!

Now that you have seen many of the eye-catching, user-friendly features provided by a Java applet, you are ready to begin learning just how to compose one of your own. If so, skip Chapter 6, which explains additional Java tools, and go directly to Chapter 7.

Chapter 6

JAVA AND COM

Microsoft is committed to delivering top-of-the-line Java development tools, as well as the reference implementation of the Java Virtual Machine (VM) for Windows platforms. Microsoft's COM (Component Object Model) is the cornerstone of the ActiveX™ platform and tightly integrated with Java. Java is the state-of-the-art programming language that takes the run-of-the-mill and error-prone aspects of COM development and makes them easy to implement. Because Java can create and use COM objects, it is a great programming language for COM.

Note: ActiveX™ controls are OLE controls. As a result, any Java applet can be plugged into any application that supports ActiveX™ controls, including Visual Basic, Access, Delphi, and Power Builder.

All Java class COM objects are **public** and can be called remotely just like any other COM object. COM and DCOM are really the same thing. The main difference between them is the length of the wire between the two software components. Any COM object can be used remotely or locally—a feature called location independence. Thus, any COM object developed in Java can be executed on a remote server as well as on the client machine.

All COM objects, regardless of the point of origin, appear to a Java program as a standard Java class object. Java COM objects thus do not need large class libraries that wrap existing objects. Also, machine-generated "stubs" are unnecessary. Instead, existing objects can simply be called directly.

The integration of Java and COM can be achieved by making changes to the Java VM; you do not need to add new keywords or constructs to the Java language itself. The pivotal concept that makes this possible is multiple object interfaces. By integrating Java and COM, companies can preserve existing technology investments while using new technologies.

If these points sound vaguely familiar, you're right. Windows already has a vehicle—OLE—for exposing operating system components to programming languages. COM, however, is a language-independent standard for writing reusable plug-in components. For example, millions of Visual Basic programmers already use COM objects in the form of OCX (now called *ActiveX* by Microsoft). ActiveX controls work in C++, Visual Basic, Pascal, Fortran, Borland's Delphi, and the latest versions of the COBOL compilers. All of these languages use a form of COM called *automation*. These types of COM objects do little more than basic COM objects, but they do contain something very important: a type library.

COM TYPE LIBRARY

A COM object *type library* is a binary header that describes the functions and properties implemented by a COM object. This header contains everything necessary for the programming language to use the object, such as proper type checks and automatic generation of the COM calls needed to create and manipulate the object.

WINDOWS IN ANY LANGUAGE

Because Visual J++ is COM-aware, COM objects can become the vehicle through which Java programs talk to the outside world. Once Java understands COM, all that's needed to make Windows fully available to Java is to expose the Win32 API through COM objects. Note, however, that with this accomplished, Windows becomes instantly available not just to the Java language, but to *any* programming language that supports COM!

HOW COM WORKS

The basic principle behind COM objects is to make them appear just like any other Java class. At the center of this concept is the Java interface. Both COM and Java objects use interfaces in nearly an identical manner. An *interface* is an abstract class with member functions (or methods), but no member data. Also, the interface member function bodies are empty. In a way, you can think of an interface class as a "class signature," containing a named group of prototypes for class member functions that a particular class might implement as a group.

To implement the COM-Java relationship, the Java **import** statement must correctly interpret COM objects. Typically, when you import a package in Java, the Java system looks for a **.class* file of compiled Java bytecode. If it fails to find a **.class* file, Java next looks for a **.java* source file by the same name and attempts to compile it into a **.class* file. Visual J++ extends this idea to look for a COM type library, or **.tlb* file. Actually, Visual J++ will also search for **.idl* and **.odl* files and invoke *MkTypLib.exe,* or whatever compiler is necessary to generate the COM type library. As soon as a Java program imports this COM object, the methods that the object contains are identified. From Java's point of view, everything looks like normal Java code.

Take, for example, the following statement:

```
javabeep applet_javabeep = new javabeep();
```

If this were a standard Java class, Java would allocate the object from the VM's heap. But because *javabeep* is a COM object, Visual J++ instead generates a call to the *CoCreateInstance()* member function. Visual J++ knows what GUID to use (see note following), because the GUID is in the COM type library header. *CoCreateInstance()* then returns a pointer to *javabeep*'s interface, which Visual J++ uses to identify the object *applet_javabeep.*

UUID—Also called globally unique identifier (GUID), UUID is a 128-bit value that uniquely identifies objects such as OLE servers, interfaces, manager entry-point vectors, and client objects. Universally unique identifiers are used in cross-process communication, such as RPC and OLE.

However, while COM member functions map perfectly to Java member functions, COM object properties do not. Actually, COM objects have no notion of properties either. Properties are a feature of

OLE automation. Because properties syntactically resemble member data, Java accesses them by automatically generating equivalent assignment statements.

A LOOK AT JavaBeep

Although writing and using COM objects is an advanced topic beyond the scope of this text, the following example is presented to illustrate overall Java program syntax requirements for using COM. *JavaBeep* comes with your Visual J++ compiler/interpreter under the *msdev\samples\microsoft* subdirectory. *JavaBeep* is a complete Java/COM sample that you can build and run to see Java/COM support in action. The sample automatically registers a simple Beeper automation server. The Java code then uses that server to beep and create messages. You may also access *JavaBeep* through the integrated help system under the *Samples.Microsoft.JavaBeep* section.

Building JavaBeep

This section describes the steps necessary to build and execute *JavaBeep* if you have not previously copied all of the *msdev\samples\microsoft* files into your default directory:

1. To begin, click on the icon to copy the *JavaBeep* project files and then click *Copy All.* Click OK.
2. Click on the Close button and then select **Open Workspace** from the **File** menu.
3. In the **Open** dialog box, navigate to the directory into which you copied the samples (typically, *msdev\samples\microsoft\javabeep*) and then double-click the *javabeep.mdp* file to open the project.
4. Select **Execute** from the **Build** menu. When prompted for a class file name, enter *javabeep* and click OK.
5. Microsoft's Internet Explorer appears with an animation of a spinning globe. Click the mouse anywhere near the globe. Your computer should beep and the message *Hello World from Beeper* appears.
6. To view the Java code, go back to Visual J++, expand the *javabeep classes* node, and expand the *javabeep* node.

The following is a listing of *javabeep.java.* Of particular interest is the *mouseDown()* member function. If you cannot easily follow the self-documenting code, be patient. You may want to come back to this chapter after you know more about "pure" Java.

```
//**************************************************************
// javabeep.java:      Applet
//
//  This applet is a simple demonstration of calling a COM
//  object in a Java program, utilizing the ActiveX runtime for
//  Java. The COM object is the Beeper sample from the ActiveX
//  Template Library (ATL). ATL is a Template based
//  Visual C++ 4.x add on that contains a custom AppWizard
//  and various header files to generate a skeleton ActiveX
//  Control. For more information on ATL, including the source
//  code to the beeper.dll COM object, please visit
//  the Microsoft web site at:
//
//          http://www.microsoft.com/visualc/v42/atl
//
//  Most of the code of interest can be found in the
//  javabeep.mouseDown() method
//**************************************************************
import java.applet.*;
import java.awt.*;
import javabeepframe;

// Import the class files that JavaTLB generates from
// beeper.dll
import beeper.*;

//==============================================================
// Main Class for applet javabeep
//
//==============================================================
public class javabeep extends Applet implements Runnable
{
  // Beeper COM Interface variable
  IBeeper m_Beeper=null;
```

```
// THREAD SUPPORT:
//     m_javabeep  is the Thread object for the applet
//-----------------------------------------------------------------
Thread   m_javabeep = null;

// ANIMATION SUPPORT:
//     m_Graphics    used for storing the applet's Graphics
//                   context
//     m_Images[]    the array of Image objects for the
//                   animation
//     m_nCurrImage  the index of the next image to be
//                   displayed
//     m_ImgWidth    width of each image
//     m_ImgHeight   height of each image
//     m_fAllLoaded  indicates whether all images have
//                   been loaded
//     NUM_IMAGES    number of images used in the animation
//-----------------------------------------------------------------
private Graphics  m_Graphics;
private Image     m_Images[];
private int       m_nCurrImage;
private int       m_nImgWidth  = 0;
private int       m_nImgHeight = 0;
private boolean   m_fAllLoaded = false;
private final int NUM_IMAGES = 18;

// STANDALONE APPLICATION SUPPORT:
//     m_fStandAlone will be set to true if applet is
//     run standalone
//-----------------------------------------------------------------
boolean m_fStandAlone = false;

// STANDALONE APPLICATION SUPPORT
//    The main() method acts as the applet's entry point when
// it is run as a standalone application. It is ignored if
// the applet is run from within an HTML page.
//-----------------------------------------------------------------
public static void main(String args[])
{
  // Create Toplevel Window to contain applet javabeep
```

```
    //--------------------------------------------------------------
    javabeepframe frame = new javabeepframe("javabeep");

    // Must show Frame before we size it so insets() will
    // return valid values
    //---------------------------------------------------------------
    frame.show();
    frame.hide();
    frame.resize(frame.insets().left+frame.insets().right+320,
           frame.insets().top  + frame.insets().bottom + 240);

    // The following code starts the applet running within the
    // frame window.It also calls GetParameters() to retrieve
    // parameter values from the command line, and sets
    // m_fStandAlone to true to prevent init() from trying to
    // get them from the HTML page.
    //---------------------------------------------------------------
    javabeep applet_javabeep = new javabeep();

    frame.add("Center", applet_javabeep);
    applet_javabeep.m_fStandAlone = true;
    applet_javabeep.init();
    applet_javabeep.start();
    frame.show();
  }

  // javabeep Class Constructor
  //-----------------------------------------------------------------
  public javabeep()
  {
    // TODO: Add constructor code here
  }

  // APPLET INFO SUPPORT:
  //    The getAppletInfo() method returns a string describing
  // the applet's author, copyright date, or miscellaneous
  // information.
  //-----------------------------------------------------------------
```

```
public String getAppletInfo()
{
  return "Name: javabeep\r\n" +
         "Author: Microsoft Developer Support\r\n" +
         "Created with Microsoft Visual J++ Version 1.0";
}


// The init() method is called by the AWT when an applet is
// first loaded or reloaded.  Override this method to perform
// whatever initialization your applet needs, such as
// initializing data structures, loading images or fonts,
// creating frame windows, setting the layout manager, or
// adding UI components.
  //--------------------------------------------------------
public void init()
{
      // If you use a ResourceWizard-generated "control
      // creator" class to arrange controls in your applet,
      // you may want to call its CreateControls() method
      // from within this method. Remove the following call
      // to resize() before adding the call to
      // CreateControls(); CreateControls() does its
      // own resizing.
      //---------------------------------------------------
  resize(320, 240);

  // TODO: Place additional initialization code here
}

// Place additional applet clean up code here.  destroy() is
// called when your applet is terminating and being
// unloaded.
//-----------------------------------------------------------
public void destroy()
{
  // TODO: Place applet cleanup code here
}
```

```
    // ANIMATION SUPPORT
    // The imageUpdate() method is called repeatedly by the AWT
    // while images are being constructed.  The flags parameter
    // provides information about the status of images under
    // construction.  The AppletWizard's initial implementation
    // of this method checks whether the ALLBITS flag is set.
    // When the ALLBITS is set, this method knows that an image
    // is completely loaded. When all the images are completely
    // loaded, this method sets the m_fAllLoaded variable to true
    // so that animation can begin.
    //----------------------------------------------------------
    public boolean imageUpdate(Image img, int flags, int x, int
  y, int w, int h)
    {
      // Nothing to do if images are all loaded
      //--------------------------------------------------------
      if (m_fAllLoaded)
        return false;

      // Want all bits to be available before painting
      //--------------------------------------------------------
      if ((flags & ALLBITS) == 0)
        return true;

      // All bits are available, so increment loaded count of
      // fully loaded images, starting animation if all images
      // are loaded
      //--------------------------------------------------------
      if (++m_nCurrImage == NUM_IMAGES)
      {
        m_nCurrImage = 0;
        m_fAllLoaded = true;
      }

      return false;
    }

      // ANIMATION SUPPORT:
      //     Draws the next image, if all images are currently
      //     loaded
```

```
  //--------------------------------------------------------------
private void displayImage(Graphics g)
{
  if (!m_fAllLoaded)
    return;

  // Draw Image in center of applet
  //--------------------------------------------------------------
  g.drawImage(m_Images[m_nCurrImage],
         (size().width - m_nImgWidth)   / 2,
         (size().height - m_nImgHeight) / 2, null);

  // Draw a click me label
  FontMetrics fm = getFontMetrics(getFont());
  String message = new String("Click me with the mouse!");
  g.drawString(message,
         (size().width-fm.stringWidth(message))/2,
         3*(size().height)/4);
}

// javabeep Paint Handler
//--------------------------------------------------------------
public void paint(Graphics g)
{
  // ANIMATION SUPPORT:
  // The following code displays a status message until all
  // the images are loaded. Then it calls displayImage to
  // display the current image.
  //--------------------------------------------------------------
  if (m_fAllLoaded)
  {
    Rectangle r = g.getClipRect();

    g.clearRect(r.x, r.y, r.width, r.height);
    displayImage(g);
  }
  else
    g.drawString("Loading images...", 10, 20);

  // TODO: Place additional applet Paint code here
}
```

```
// the start() method is called when the page containing the
// applet first appears on the screen. The AppletWizard's
// initial implementation of this method starts execution of
// the applet's thread.
//------------------------------------------------------------
public void start()
{
  if (m_javabeep == null)
  {
    m_javabeep = new Thread(this);
    m_javabeep.start();
  }
  // TODO: Place additional applet start code here
}

// the stop() method is called when the page containing the
// applet is no longer on the screen. The AppletWizard's
// initial implementation of this method stops execution of
// the applet's thread.
//------------------------------------------------------------
public void stop()
{
  if (m_javabeep != null)
  {
    m_javabeep.stop();
    m_javabeep = null;
  }

  // TODO: Place additional applet stop code here
}

// THREAD SUPPORT
// The run() method is called when the applet's thread is
// started. If your applet performs any ongoing activities
// without waiting for user input, the code for implementing
// that behavior typically goes here. For example, for an
// applet that performs animation, the run() method
// controls the display of images.
//------------------------------------------------------------
public void run()
```

```
    {
      repaint();

      m_Graphics = getGraphics();
      m_nCurrImage   = 0;
      m_Images    = new Image[NUM_IMAGES];

      // Load in all the images
      //------------------------------------------------------------
      String strImage;

      // For each image in the animation, this method first
      // constructs a string containing the path to the image
      // file; then it begins loading the image into the m_Images
      // array.  Note that the call to getImage will return
      // before the image is completely loaded.
      //------------------------------------------------------------
      for (int i = 1; i <= NUM_IMAGES; i++)
      {
        // Build path to next image
        //---------------------------------------------------------
        strImage="images/img00"+((i < 10)?"0" : "")+i+ ".gif";
        if (m_fStandAlone)
          m_Images[i-1] =
  Toolkit.getDefaultToolkit().getImage(strImage);
        else
          m_Images[i-1] = getImage(getDocumentBase(), strImage);

        // Get width and height of one image.
        // Assuming all images are same width and height
        //---------------------------------------------------------
        if (m_nImgWidth == 0)
        {
          try
          {
            // The getWidth() and getHeight() methods of the
            // Image class return -1 if the dimensions are not
            // yet known. The following code keeps calling
            // getWidth() and getHeight() until they return
            // actual values.
```

```
        // NOTE: This is only executed once in this loop,
        //       since we are assuming all images are the
        //       same width and height.  However, since we
        //       do not want to duplicate the above image
        //       load code, the code resides in the loop.
        //-----------------------------------------------
        while ((m_nImgWidth=m_Images[i-1].getWidth(null))<0)
          Thread.sleep(1);

        while ((m_nImgHeight=m_Images[i-1].getHeight(null))<0)
          Thread.sleep(1);
      }
      catch (InterruptedException e)
      {
        // TODO: Place exception-handling code here in case
        //     an InterruptedException is thrown by
        //   Thread.sleep(), meaning that another thread has
        //   interrupted this one
      }
    }

    // Force image to fully load
    //-------------------------------------------------
    m_Graphics.drawImage(m_Images[i-1], -1000, -1000, this);
  }

  // Wait until all images are fully loaded
  //---------------------------------------------------
  while (!m_fAllLoaded)
  {
    try
    {
      Thread.sleep(10);
    }
    catch (InterruptedException e)
    {
```

```
        // TODO: Place exception-handling code here in case an
        //       InterruptedException is thrown by
        //       Thread.sleep(), meaning that another thread
        //       has interrupted this one
      }
    }

    repaint();

    while (true)
    {
      try
      {
        // Draw next image in animation
        //--------------------------------------------------------
        displayImage(m_Graphics);
        m_nCurrImage++;
        if (m_nCurrImage == NUM_IMAGES)
          m_nCurrImage = 0;

        // TODO:  Add additional thread-specific code here
        Thread.sleep(50);
      }
      catch (InterruptedException e)
      {
        // TODO: Place exception-handling code here in case an
        //       InterruptedException is thrown by
        //       Thread.sleep(), meaning that another thread
        //       has interrupted this one
        stop();
      }
    }
  }

  // MOUSE SUPPORT:
  // The mouseDown() method is called if the mouse button is
  // pressed while the mouse cursor is over the applet's
  // portion of the screen.
  //--------------------------------------------------------------
```

```
public boolean mouseDown(Event evt, int x, int y)
{
  String BeeperString = new String();

  // Check if the Beeper object exists, and create it if
  // necessary
  if(m_Beeper==null)
    m_Beeper = (IBeeper) new Beeper();

  // Call Beeper object 'Beep' method. Note that the Beep
  // object has been written such that on the sixth call to
  // Beep(), the Beep object will return an OLE error code
  // which gets thrown as a Java exception. This sample
  // catches the exception, Releases the Beeper object,
  // creates a new Beeper object, and continues
  try
  {
    m_Beeper.Beep();
  }
  catch(com.ms.com.ComException e)
  {
    // Release the Beeper object by setting m_Beeper=null
    m_Beeper=null;
    // Create a new Beeper object
    m_Beeper = (IBeeper) new Beeper();
    m_Beeper.Beep();
  }

  // Call the Beepers getCount and getItem methods
  for(int i=1;i<=m_Beeper.getCount();i++)
  {
    // Build a message string from the strings that getItem
    // returns
    BeeperString+=m_Beeper.getItem(i)+" ";
  }

  // Display the string
  m_Graphics.drawString(BeeperString,x,y);
```

```
    return true;
  }

  // MOUSE SUPPORT:
  // The mouseUp() method is called if the mouse button is
  // released while the mouse cursor is over the applet's
  // portion of the screen.
  //--------------------------------------------------------------
  public boolean mouseUp(Event evt, int x, int y)
  {
    // TODO: Place applet mouseUp code here
    return true;
  }


  // TODO: Place additional applet code here

}
```

In the program above, the following statement:

```
// Import the class files that JavaTLB generates from
// beeper.dll
import beeper.*;
```

imports the *beeper* COM object. *Beeper* implements the *IBeeper* interface (seen in the next listing from the *mouseDown()* method), which is the abstract specification for beepers:

```
// Create a new Beeper object
   m_Beeper = (IBeeper) new Beeper();
```

To use such an object in Java, you write:

```
m_Beeper.Beep();
```

Because the Microsoft Visual J++ compiler/interpreter allows the **import** statement to recognize COM objects, automatically locating the associated **.tlb*, **.idl*, and **.odl* files, it knows exactly what methods *IBeeper* contains and that *Beeper* is a COM class that implements *IBeeper*. From the outside, everything looks like normal Java code; however, internally the Visual J++ compiler and VM have to execute the translation.

USING COM OBJECTS WITH JAVA

Because your Visual J++ compiler/interpreter supports Java/COM integration, you can refer to COM objects directly from your Java source code. This makes any COM service, including those offered by programmable controls or automation objects, available from any Java program. In order to use a COM class from Java, you must first import it, which means creating a Java class that acts as a wrapper for the COM class. Visual J++ includes the Java Type Library Wizard (described below) for this purpose.

Visual J++ uses type libraries as a mechanism defined by COM to store type information; each type library contains complete type information about one or more COM entities, including classes, interfaces, and so forth.

Creating Your Own COM Objects

To create your own COM object in Java, you must first write the COM object's ODL definition. In OLE automation, this involves text files containing a description of an application's interface. Object description language (or ODL) scripts are compiled into type libraries using the *MkTypLib* tool included with the OLE Software Development Kit. Next, you implement the object just like any other Java class. When you compile the code, Visual J++ realizes that the class is really a COM object (because it finds *yourclass.odl*) and automatically generates a Windows DLL with class factory, *DllCreateClass()* member function, and other required methods.

Importing a COM Class

When you are building a Java program that uses COM objects, you can use the Java Type Library Wizard found under the **Tools** menu. To do so:

1. From the **Tools** menu, choose the **Java Type Library Wizard**.
2. Notice that the check box list displays all the type libraries registered on your machine (see \HKEY_CLASSES_ROOT\TypeLib key of the system registry).
3. Select the type library that describes the COM class(es) you want to use.

4. Click OK.
5. The Type Library Wizard, in the output window, prints the **import** statement(s) appropriate for each package it has created. You can copy and paste these **import** statements into your Java source code; as a result, you can refer to classes in those packages by their short names.

As an example, suppose *beeper.dll*, which defines the Beeper class in the example program and an *IBeeper* interface, is registered as having type library information. Running Java Type Library Wizard and selecting *beeper.dll* would create a package containing the Java class Beeper and the Java interface *IBeeper*. You can use the **import** statement in your Java source code to easily refer to classes in the beeper package. For example:

```
import beeper.*;    // import beeper package
```

This is identical to Java's syntax for importing an entire package. You could also import a single class within a type library:

```
import beeper.Beeper;
```

Again, this is identical to Java's syntax for importing a single class. The Java classes that wrap COM classes can be used just like any other Java classes. For example:

```
IBeeper myBeep = new Beeper();
int thisTone = myBeep.getSound();
myBeep.putSound(64);
myBeep.Beep();
```

The above code declares an instance of the COM class *Beeper*, gets and sets the value of a property of the object, and then calls a method on the object. Note that the **import** statement is not strictly necessary. Recall that in Java, any class can be referenced using its fully qualified name (for example, **java.util.Date**), as long as a class fitting that name can be found when searching the class path. The **import** statement merely allows you to refer to the class using its short name (for example, **Date**). The same is true for COM classes. The **import** statement is not required in order to use the class; it simply allows the class to be referenced using its short name. Any COM class can always be referenced using its fully qualified name (*beeper.Beeper*, in the above example).

JAVA TYPE LIBRARY WIZARD

You can use the Java Type Library Wizard to report everything that has a registry entry under HKEY_CLASSES_ROOT\TypeLib. This report is not restricted to just **.tlb* files; because **.olb*, **.ocx*, **.dll*, and **.exe* files can all contain type library information. For each type library, the Java Type Library Wizard creates a directory below *\windows\java\lib* (or *\winnt\java\lib*, if you're running Windows NT 4.0) having the same name as the type library.

The Java Type Library Wizard fills that directory with **.class* files, one for each COM class and interface described in the type library. All the generated classes and interfaces are part of a Java package having the name as the type library file. For example, to return to the *beeper* example, running the Java Type Library Wizard on *beeper.dll* would create the files *beeper.class* and *ibeeper.class* and place them in the directory *\windows\java\lib\beeper*. Because *\windows\java\lib* is on the class path, the compiler can find the beeper directory and its contents, and the statement *import beeper.** allows you to refer to the classes by their short names.

For each **.class* file generated by the Java Type Library Wizard, there is a special attribute identifying it as a wrapper for a COM class. When the Java Support in Internet Explorer sees this attribute on a class, it translates all Java method calls on the class into COM function calls on the COM class. For a COM interface that defines properties, the Java wrapper defines two methods for each property, named **get()** and **put()**. Once you have run the Java Type Library Wizard for a given type library, you don't need to re-run the wizard unless the type library has changed. Once the wizard has generated **.class* files from a type library, the type library is no longer needed.

When distributing an applet that uses COM, you only need to provide the **.ocx*, **.dll*, or *.exe* file for the COM objects, plus the **.class* files that wrap them, not the **.tlb* file. (You must, of course, include the **.class* files for the applet itself. You must also register the COM object appropriately.) When using COM from applets embedded on a web page, the **.ocx* or **.dll* files that implement the COM object should be code signed, as well as any applets that make calls to them.

You may also use the command line version of the Java Type Library Wizard called *JavaTLB.exe*. *JavaTLB.exe* generates Java class wrappers out of type library information. To run *JavaTLB.exe,* type:

```
JavaTLB myfile
```

where *myfile* is the name of the **.tlb* file, or **.ocx*, **.dll*, or **.exe* file containing the type library information. This will create the appropriate subdirectory and **.class* files under *\windows\java\lib*.

TYPE MAPPINGS BETWEEN JAVA AND COM

Microsoft's Java support within the Internet Explorer allows a Java program to access any construct that can be defined in a type library. Naturally, any COM constructs that cannot be defined in a type library are inaccessible to Java programs. There are five basic types that can be defined in ODL. These map in Java as defined below:

- All COM classes, defined using the **coclass** keyword, are visible as classes in Java.
- Interfaces, defined using the **interface** keyword, are visible in Java as interfaces.
- Dispatch interfaces, defined using the **dispinterface** keyword, are visible in Java as interfaces; properties in the dispatch interface are accessible through two methods named **get()** and **put()**.
- All structures, defined using the **typedef** keyword, are visible in Java as classes.
- All module statements, defined using the **module** keyword, are ignored.

Table 6.1 details how ODL types map to their Java counterparts.

Whether you choose to be a Java purist, or welcome integrating COM into Java files, you cannot deny that Microsoft's Visual J++ is a viable tool for developing everything from standalone Java programs to full-bore graphics viewers, animation players, credit card transactors, stock quote grabbers, grid controls, text editors, and audio and video players, through COM and an entire industry of ActiveX controls.

Table 6.1: ODL Types and Their Java Equivalents

ODL Type	*Java Equivalent*
boolean	boolean
char	char
double	double
int	int
float	float
long	int
short	short
unsigned char	byte
wchar_t (UNICODE)	short
BSTR	class java.lang.String
CURRENCY	long
DATE	double
SCODE/HRESULT	int (see also class com.ms.com.ComException)
VARIANT	class com.ms.com.Variant
IDispatch *	class java.lang.Object
IUnknown *	class java.lang.Object
SAFEARRAY(<typename>)	array of <typename>
<typename> *	one-element array of <typename>
void	void
LPSTR	class java.lang.String

Chapter 7

THE PROGRAMMING ENVIRONMENT

Previous chapters cover how to create simple Java applets and applications with Microsoft J++. This chapter explores further details about the various features of the Java language and programming environment. Later chapters explain how to write robust Java code that lets you add animation, color, control, dialog box, font, graphic, menu, mouse, and sound capabilities to your J++ projects.

Many people reading this book have probably written Windows applications using the Microsoft C++ compiler and the standard Windows API functions. Thus, where appropriate, important similarities and differences between the Microsoft Windows API and the Microsoft J++ API are highlighted.

THE DEFAULT

Programming environments such as MS-DOS, Windows, and Java have a default set of features. These features can include the window size, background color, printing color, drawing color, and so on. For example, if you create a simple "Hello World" in C or C++, your text will print on a black DOS screen with a white default system font. Likewise, if you are developing a similar Windows application, expect to see your text printed in black with the default

Windows font. The Windows background color will be white with the window's size initially determined by the operating system. What about Microsoft's J++ implementation? A simple way to answer that question is to develop a basic application and investigate the resulting graphical environment when the application is executed.

A Basic J++ Application

Let's build a simple application using Microsoft's J++ tools and Java Applet Wizard. We'll use this application to investigate the default Java graphical environment provided by Microsoft's J++.

Creating a Java Application From within the Microsoft J++ compiler, you follow these steps to create a Java application similar to the example provided:

1. From the main menu, select **File | New | Project Workspace**.
2. Set the Project Name, Platform, Location, and Type, as shown in Figure 7.1, and launch the Java Applet Wizard.
3. A J++ Project is started. The first step in a five-step process, similar to Figure 7.2, opens (see Figure 7.2). For this example, mark the selections as shown in Figure 7.2.
4. Click the Next> button to move to step 2 (see Figure 7.3). Do not request an HTML file at this time. Set the initial window size to 640 × 480.
5. Click the Next> button to move to step 3 (see Figure 7.4). Set the options to match those shown in the figure. In this example, the application is not multithreaded, nor does it require animation or include mouse support.
6. Click the Next> button to move to step 4. This application requires no additional applet parameters. Leave this area blank, as shown in Figure 7.5.
7. Click the Next> to move to step 5. At this step, you can modify the applications name, author, and so on. Figure 7.6 shows the screen as modified for this example.
8. Click the Finish button to complete the design process and view the skeleton project description. The project information shown in Figure 7.7 describes this project.

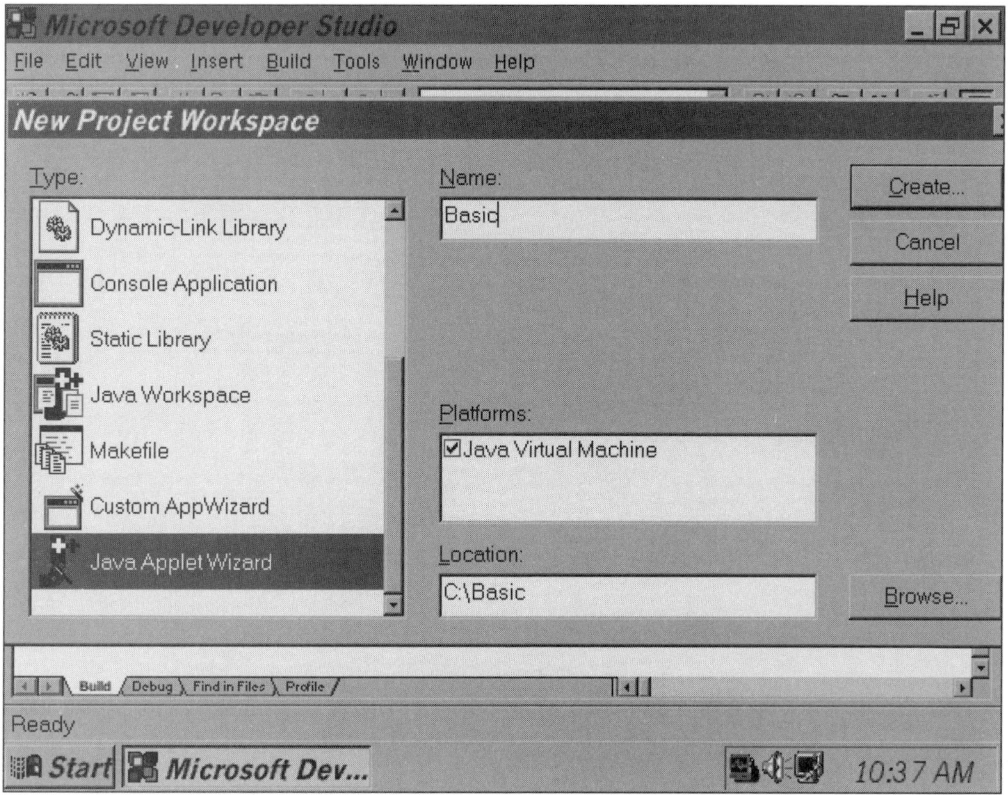

Figure 7.1: Use the New Project Workspace dialog box to set the name, platform, location, and type for the new Java application.

9. Click the Okay button to generate and save this project code. Microsoft J++ returns you to the initial window.

If you now select **Project Workspace** from the **View** menu, you will be able to select (from the File View), view, and modify the *Basic.java* and *BasicFrame.java* files created by the Java Applet Wizard. Figure 7.8 shows the *Basic.java* file in the Visual J++ editor.

The following code listing is the code generated by the Java Applet Wizard with just one modification shown in a bold font.

```
import java.applet.*;
import java.awt.*;
```

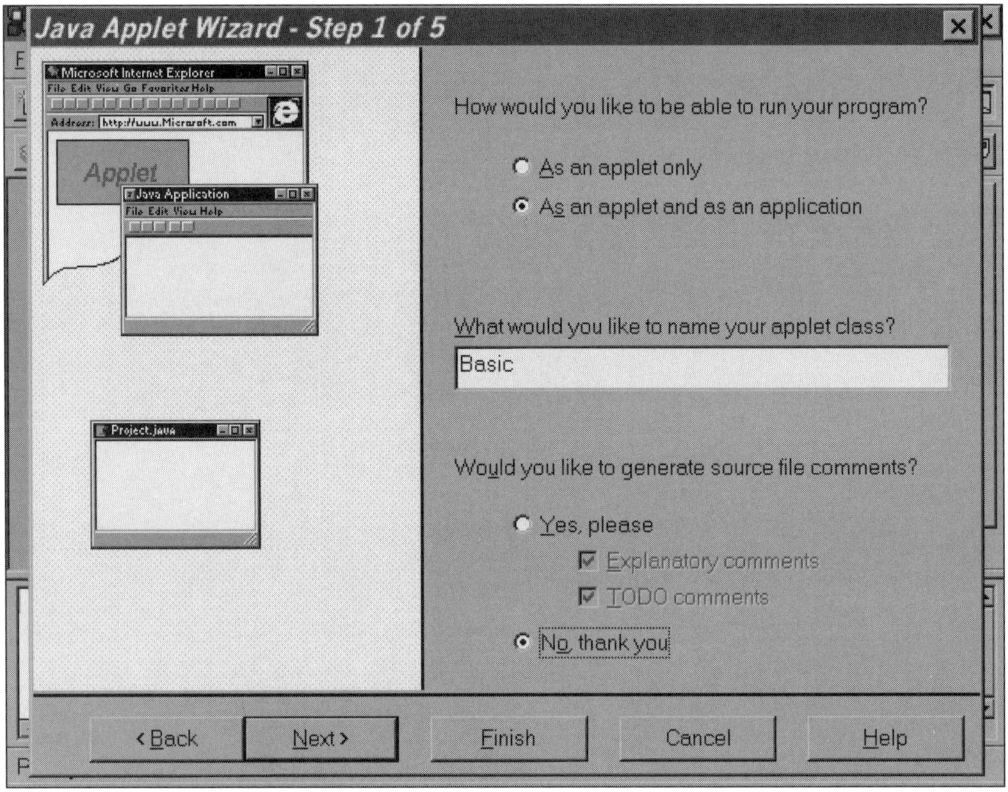

Figure 7.2: The Java Applet Wizard: Step 1 of 5 lets you create applets and applications. Do you want to include comments?

```
import BasicFrame;

public class Basic extends Applet
{
  // STANDALONE APPLICATION SUPPORT:
  //    m_fStandAlone will be set to true if applet is run
  //    standalone
  //-------------------------------------------------------------
  boolean m_fStandAlone = false;

  public static void main(String args[])
  {
```

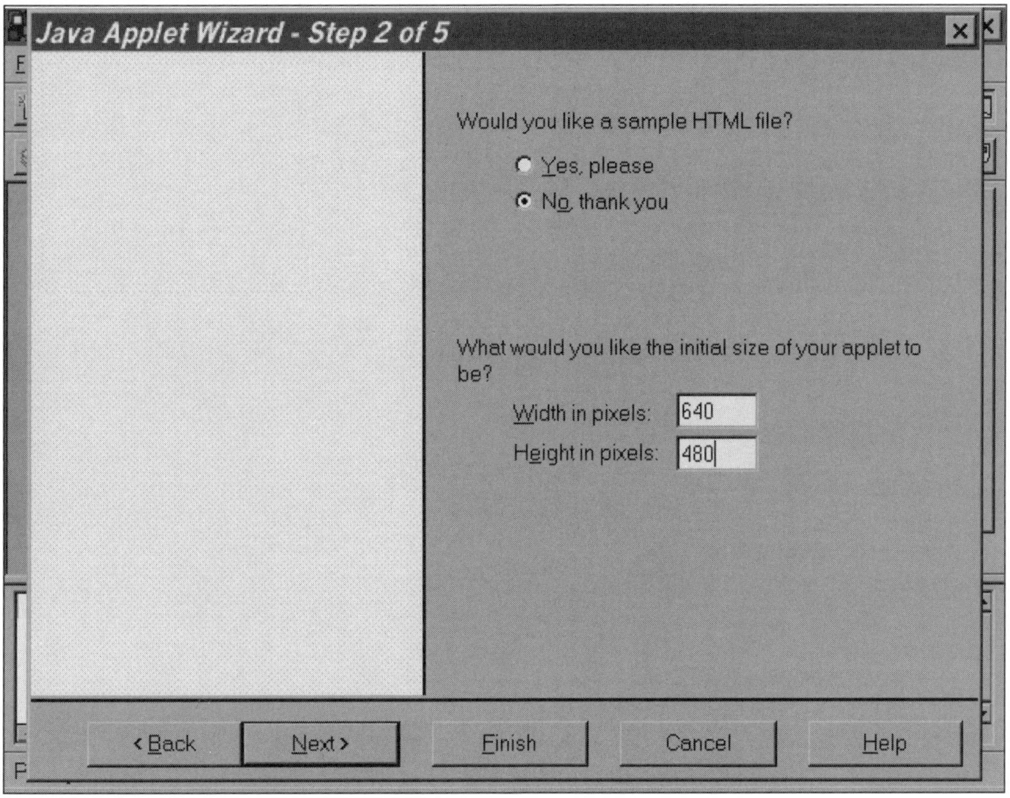

Figure 7.3: The Java Applet Wizard: Step 2 of 5 can generate an HTML file for applets and set the initial screen size for the project.

```
BasicFrame frame = new BasicFrame("Basic");

// Must show Frame before we size it so insets() will
// return valid values
//--------------------------------------------------------------
frame.show();
frame.resize(frame.insets().left+frame.insets().right+640,
        frame.insets().top  + frame.insets().bottom + 480);

Basic applet_Basic = new Basic();

frame.add("Center", applet_Basic);
```

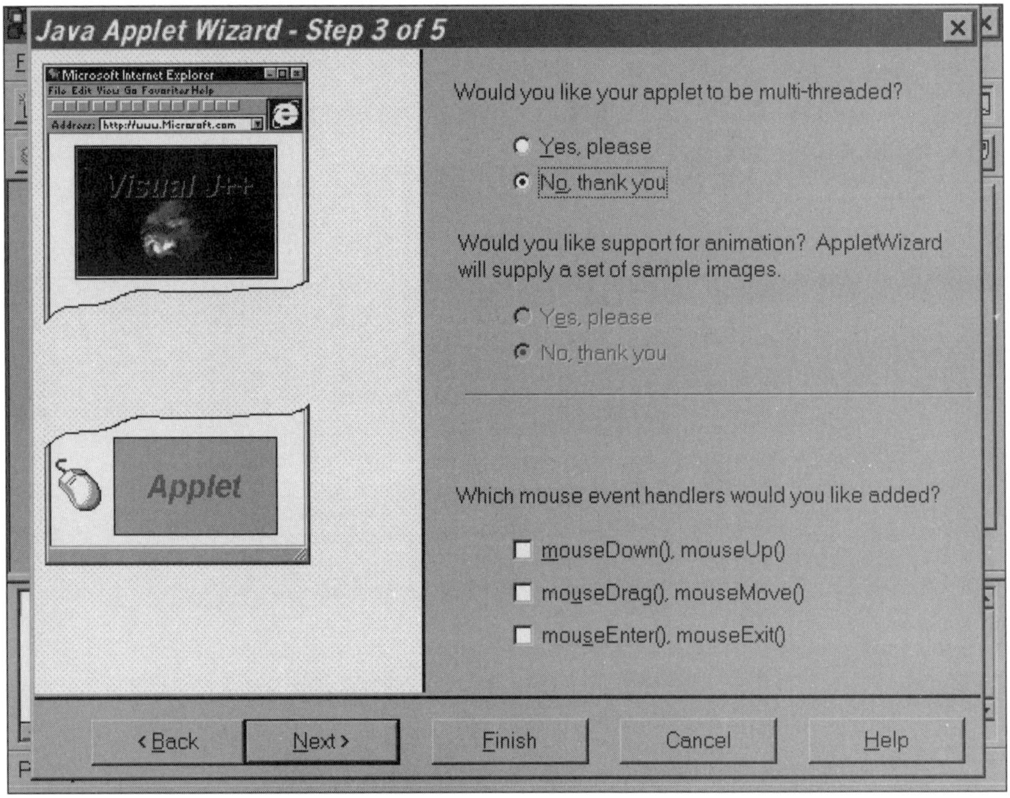

Figure 7.4: The Java Applet Wizard: Step 3 of 5 allows multithreading and mouse support to be included.

```
        applet_Basic.m_fStandAlone = true;
        applet_Basic.init();
        applet_Basic.start();
    }

    public Basic()
    {
    }

    public void finalize()
    {
    }
```

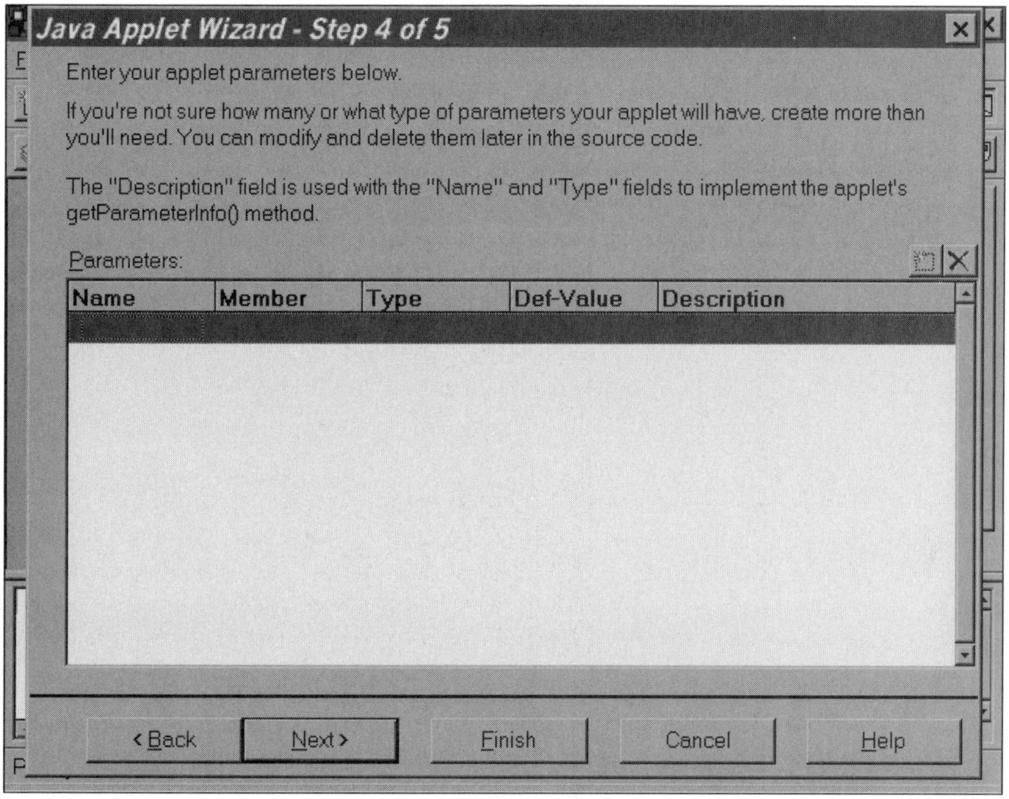

Figure 7.5: The Java Applet Wizard: Step 4 of 5 allows additional programming parameters to be included. None is needed at this time.

```
public String getAppletInfo()
{
  return "Name: Basic\r\n" +
    "Author: Chris H. Pappas and William H. Murray\r\n" +
    "Created with Microsoft Visual J++";
}

public void init()
{
  resize(640, 480);
}
```

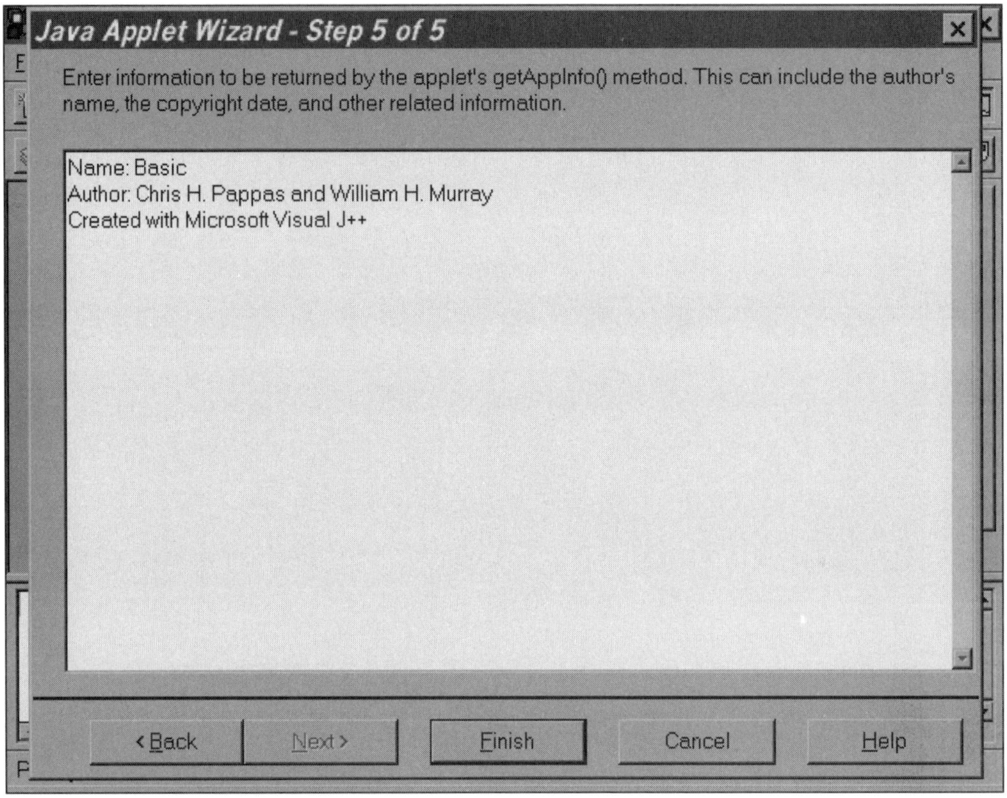

Figure 7.6: The Java Applet Wizard: Step 5 of 5 allows project information to be included and modified.

```
public void destroy()
{
}

public void paint(Graphics g)
{
  g.drawString("Here is sample text to draw.", 10, 10);
  g.drawOval(20, 20, 100, 150);
  g.fillOval(340, 20, 100, 150);
}

public void start()
```

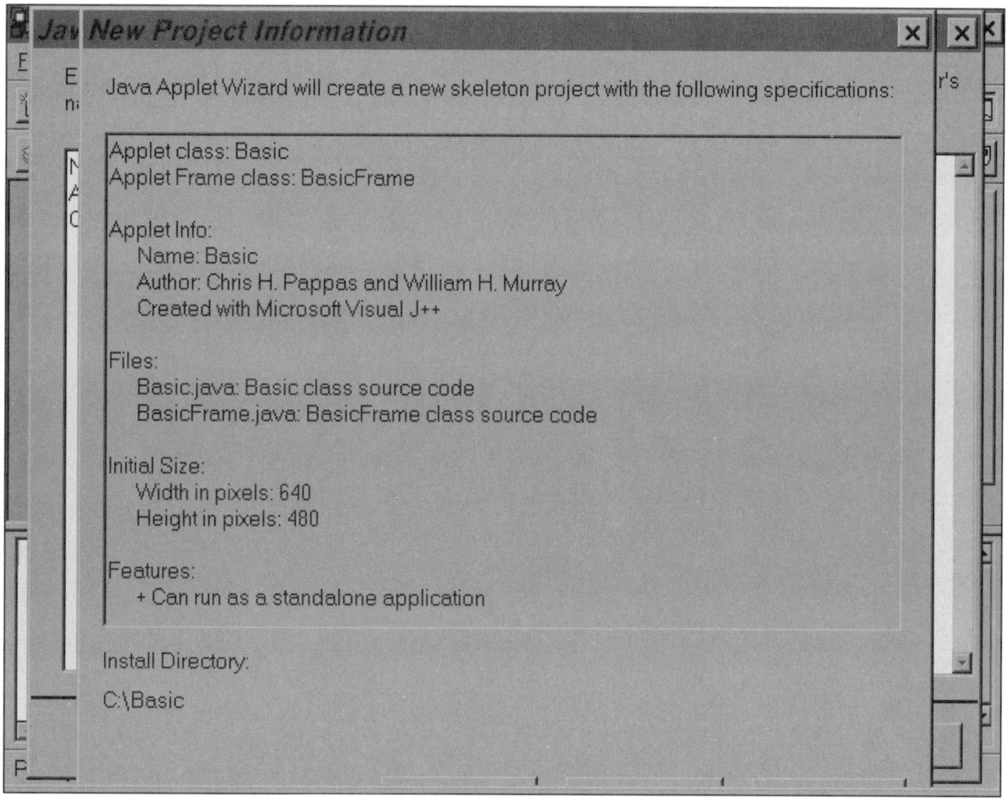

Figure 7.7: The New Project Information dialog box reviews the results of the options chosen for the project. This information will create a project file, Basic.java file, and BasicFrame.java file.

```
    {
    }

    public void stop()
    {
    }
}
```

If you are working along with this example, modify your code to match the code in the listing. You are now ready to build the complete Java application.

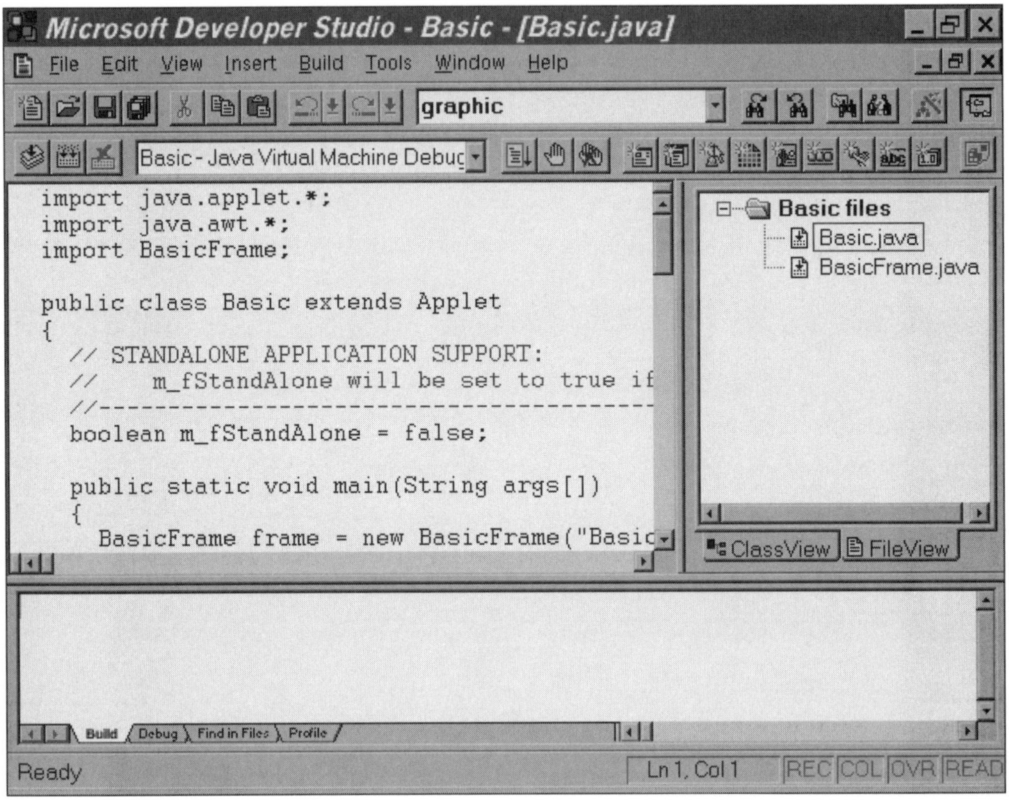

Figure 7.8: The code created by the Java Applet Wizard can be edited with the Microsoft J++ editor.

Building a Java Application Building a Java application is simple and can be done directly from the Microsoft Developer Studio editor shown in Figure 7.8. Select **Build | Rebuild All** from the **Build** menu. Your code will be compiled quickly. Figure 7.9 shows the results of the build operation.

If your build operation was successful, you are now ready to launch the basic Java application you just compiled.

Launching the Application A successfully compiled Java application can be launched directly from within the Microsoft Developer Studio editor. From the main menu bar, select **Build | Execute**, as shown in Figure 7.10.

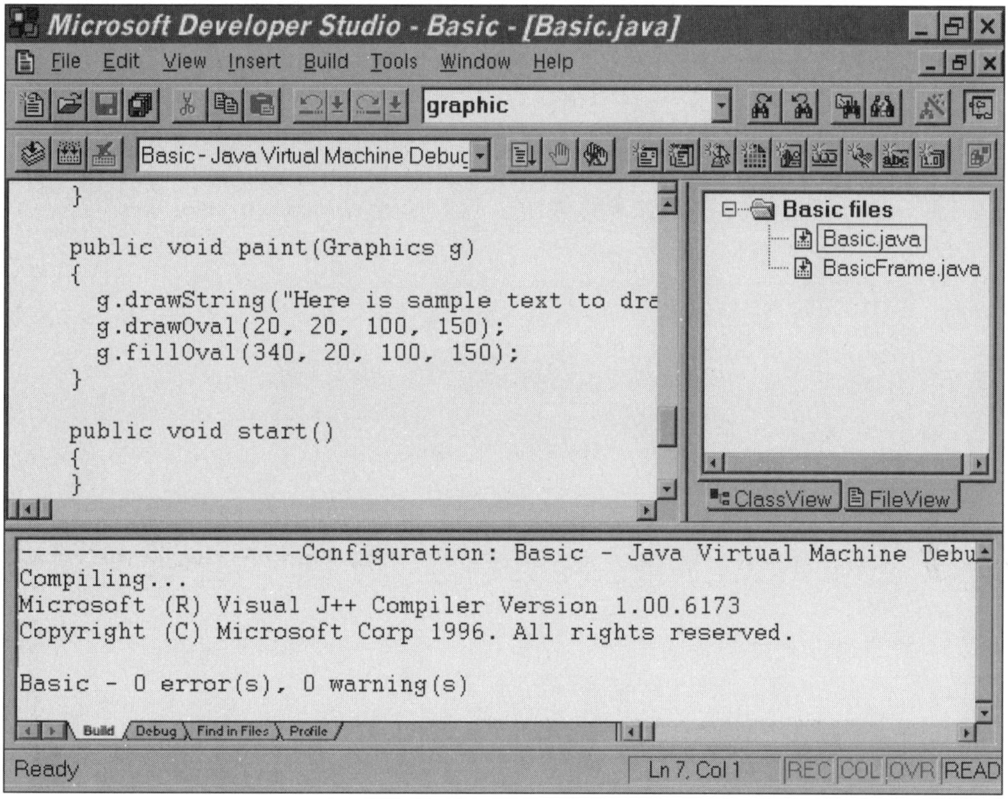

Figure 7.9: The results of the build operation are sent to the screen.

If a dialog box requests additional information, you will need to enter the name of the project. However, for most cases in this book, that step will not be necessary.

Figure 7.11 shows the window created by the Simple.class when it is executed.

Figure 7.11 does not tell us too much about our default environment, or does it? The next section investigates what you have learned from this application.

Environment Clues Revealed

Figure 7.11 shows you that you should expect nothing more than a standard Windows title bar and system menu options from your

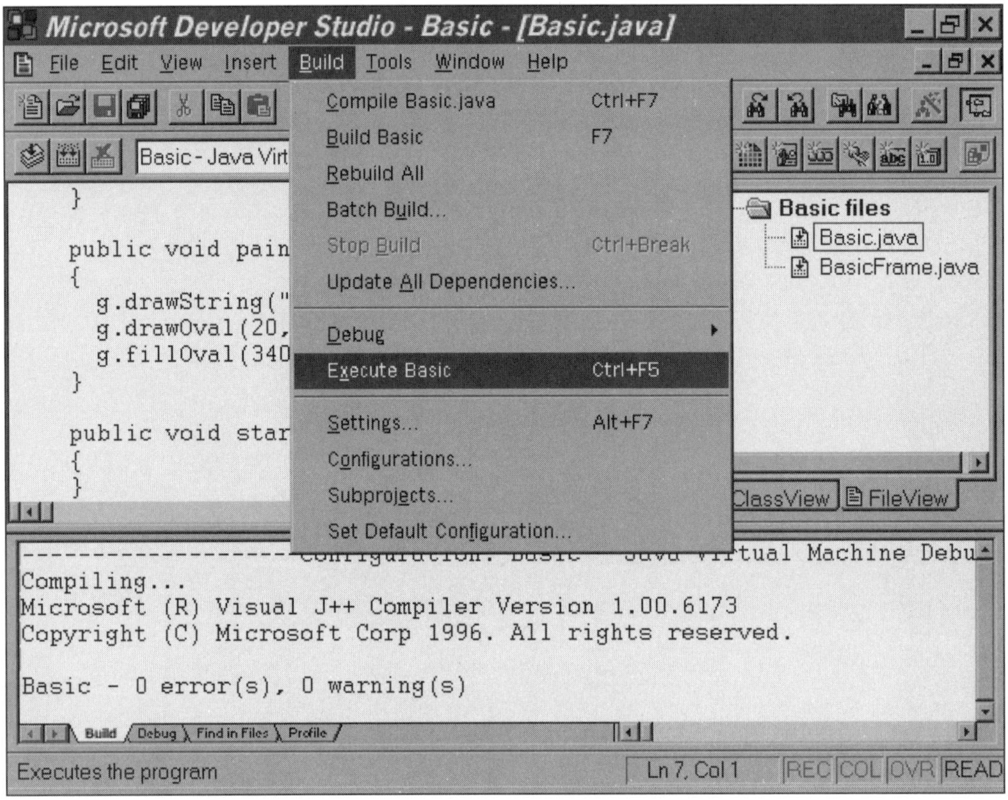

Figure 7.10: A Java application can be launched from the Project window.

environment. Actually, the initial window size can be forced to a specific size. The Java Applet Wizard let us set the initial screen size to 640 × 480—a standard VGA screen. Here is the portion of code that was generated for that purpose.

```
resize(640, 480);
```

It is also possible to change the size and position of a window with the **reshape()** member function:

```
reshape(100, 100, 200, 100);
```

If this member function is used, at the appropriate location, the launched application will start drawing a window 100 pixels from the left side of the screen and 100 pixels from the top of the screen. The window will be 200 pixels wide and 100 pixels high.

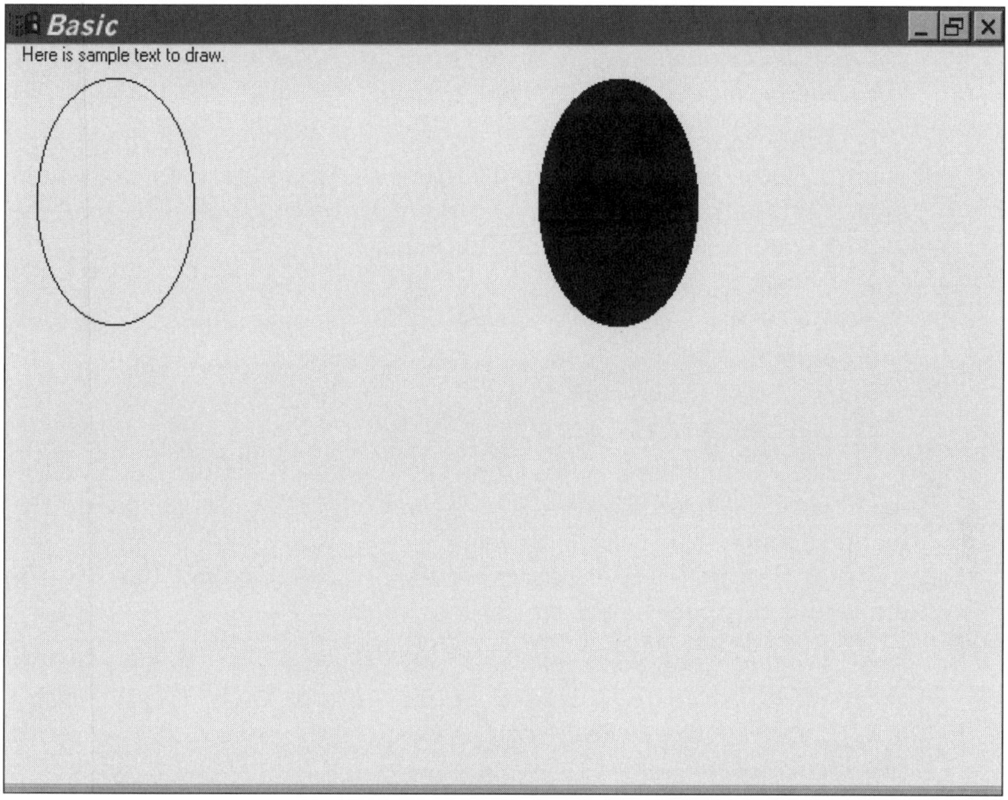

Figure 7.11: The Simple Java application's window.

Note: Windows programmers will notice that the third and fourth parameters specified in the ***reshape()*** *member function (method) call gives the actual width and height of the window. Under Windows, these parameters usually represent the window's extent. When you are programming with Windows API functions, the width is determined by finding the difference between the third and first parameters and the height by finding the difference between the fourth and second parameters.*

Examine Figure 7.11 again. First, notice the default background color provided by the Microsoft Java Applet Wizard. Microsoft chose white as the background color. The default drawing color is black. This means that text is drawn to the screen in a black font. Lines are drawn with a black pen and shapes that are filled are filled with a black brush.

Note: Windows programmers are familiar with similar environment characteristics. They would say that the text color is black, the default pen color is black, and the fill brush is a solid black brush.

Java programmers do not talk of pens and brushes. We draw various graphics primitives by first setting the drawing color and then drawing the graphics shape. The point to be made here is that the default color for text, lines, and fills is black.

The code to draw the text and graphics figures is simple and straightforward.

```
g.drawString("Here is sample text to draw.", 10, 10);
g.drawOval(20, 20, 100, 150);
g.fillOval(340, 20, 100, 150);
```

These specific member functions are discussed in more detail in the next chapter. Currently, the focus is on the parameters passed to the member functions.

Figure 7.12 shows coordinates for a VGA screen. Notice that the origin is in the upper-left corner of the window.

Note: Windows programmers know that they have six drawing modes available to them. Java is limited to one drawing mode. It is Windows MM_Text mode (the default) that is most closely associated with Java's coordinate system.

The **drawString()** member function is used to draw the text string to the window. The coordinates specify the starting X and Y positions of the string.

The **drawOval()** and **fillOval()** member functions draw two shapes in the window. The first two parameters of each member function specify the starting point of each shape on the previously mentioned coordinate system. The second two parameters specify the actual width and height of the shape.

Note: Windows programmers will again notice that the third and fourth parameters specified in the Java member functions give the literal width and height of the graphics shape. Under Windows, these parameters usually represent the extent of the graphics shape measured from the first two parameters.

Many graphics shapes, as explained in the next chapter, are drawn as if they are contained within a *bounding* rectangle. When this is the case, the parameters specified in the Java graphics member functions

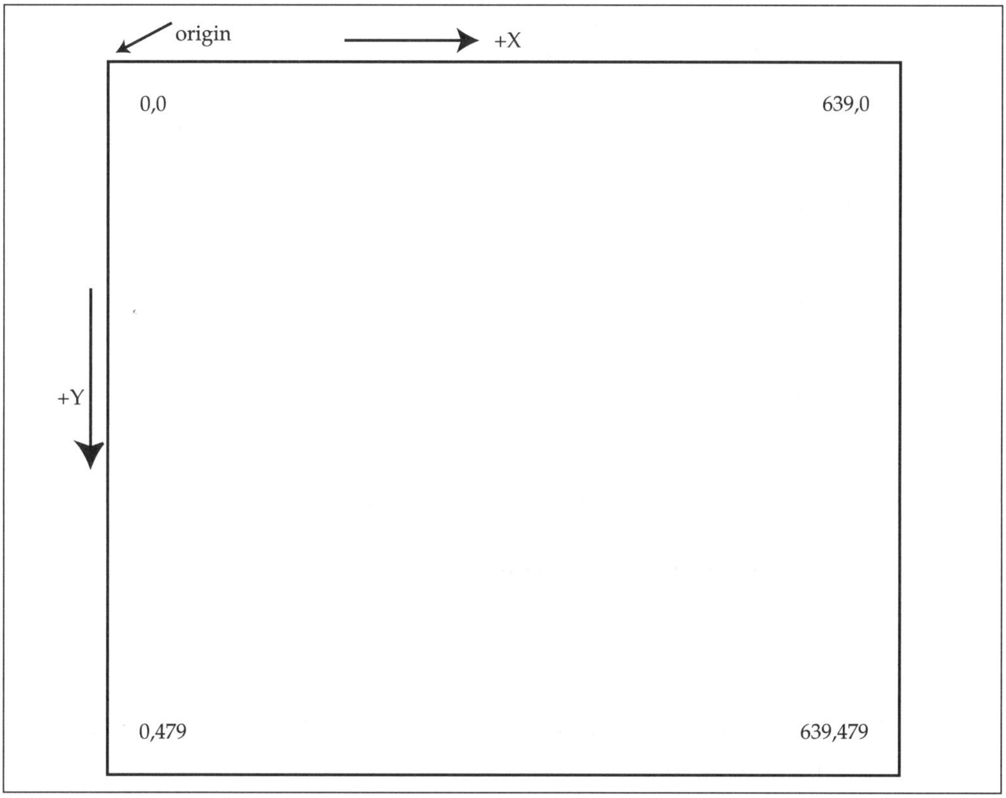

Figure 7.12: The graphics coordinate system with values specific to a VGA window.

are those for the bounding rectangle. Figure 7.13 shows how the shape created by the **drawOval()** member function is contained within a bounding rectangle.

The coordinate system and the graphics primitives used in this chapter are described in the Java Graphics class. The next section investigates the available Java classes.

JAVA CLASSES

Java's many classes provide the member functions necessary for creating applications. For example, the AWT (Abstract Window Toolkit)

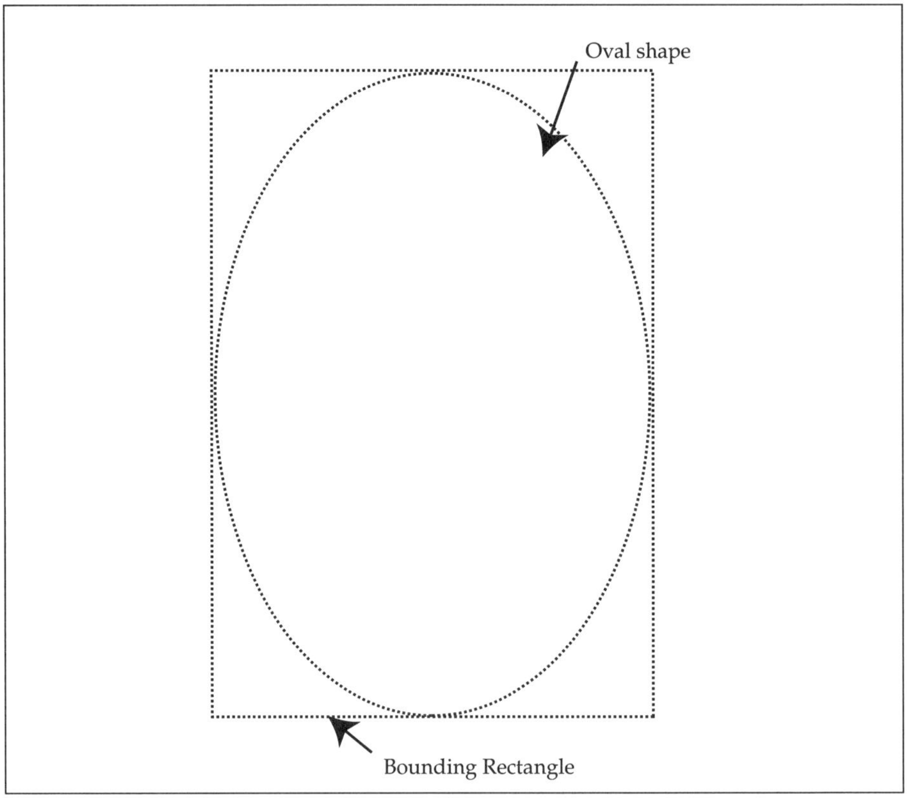

Figure 7.13: The size of graphics shapes are specified with respect to a bounding rectangle.

classes are included in your Java code, created by the Java Applet Wizard, with the following portion of code.

```
import java.awt.*;
```

If you were only using member functions in the Graphics class, that line of code could have been replaced with:

```
import java.awt.Graphics;
```

The following listing gives all of the standard AWT Java classes available to us. Many of these classes are discussed in later chapters.

```
AWTError.class
AWTException.class
BorderLayout.class
Button.class
```

```
Canvas.class
CardLayout.class
Checkbox.class
CheckboxGroup.class
CheckboxMenuItem.class
Choice.class
Color.class
Component.class
Container.class
Dialog.class
Dimension.class
Event.class
FileDialog.class
FlowLayout.class
Font.class
FontMetrics.class
Frame.class
Graphics.class
GridBagConstraints.class
GridBagLayout.class
GridBagLayoutInfo.class
GridLayout.class
Image.class
ImageMediaEntry.class
Insets.class
Label.class
LayoutManager.class
List.class
MediaEntry.class
MediaTracker.class
Menu.class
MenuBar.class
MenuComponent.class
MenuContainer.class
MenuItem.class
Panel.class
Point.class
Polygon.class
Rectangle.class
Scrollbar.class
```

```
TextArea.class
TextComponent.class
TextField.class
Toolkit.class
Window.class
```

The sample code, listed earlier in this chapter, made use of the Graphics class. In order to draw on the screen, the **paint()** member function is overridden.

```
public void paint(Graphics g)
```

This member function uses an argument, *g*, which is an instance of the Graphics class. The default argument name is supplied by the Microsoft Java Applet Wizard. The next chapter covers the member functions provided in the Graphics class for drawing graphics primitives. These simple graphics shapes form the foundation for all graphical drawing done on the screen.

There are additional classes, outside of the AWT, available to the programmer. You might examine the following subdirectories on your hard disk:

```
c:\MSDEV\classes\java\applet
c:\MSDEV\classes\java\AWT
c:\MSDEV\classes\java\IO
c:\MSDEV\classes\java\LANG
c:\MSDEV\classes\java\NET
c:\MSDEV\classes\java\UTIL
```

COMING TO TERMS

reshape()—A member function that can be used to size the graphical drawing area of an applet or application.

resize()—A member function that can be used to set the initial size of an application's window.

coordinate system—Defines the capabilities and constraints of the drawing surface for Java member functions.

default coordinate system—Describes those coordinate system capabilities and constraints initially set in the Java environment.

bounding rectangle—An imaginary rectangular shape used to describe the extents of many Java graphic shapes.

Chapter 8

USING GRAPHICS PRIMITIVES

Chapter 7 described how to create a simple Java application while investigating the default Java environment produced with Visual J++. This chapter provides more detail about the Java Graphics class and specifically the various member functions (methods) available for drawing basic graphics shapes. These basic shapes supported by this Java class are called *graphics drawing primitives*. Graphics primitives form the foundation for all drawing done in Java and include arcs, lines, ovals, polygons, rectangles, and so on.

If you have written Windows applications with the Microsoft Visual C++ compiler and used Windows graphics drawing primitives, you will feel right at home with the Java graphics drawing primitives. The similarities and differences between these two groups are highlighted throughout this chapter.

Note that each important example in this chapter is code complete. That is, it is formed with the Visual J++ Java Applet Wizard and modified to produce the desired Java application. No guesswork is necessary regarding how to implement these graphics primitives.

BUILDING APPLICATIONS

The applications in this chapter can be built with the Java Applet Wizard. For a step-by-step approach for developing applications in this manner, refer to Chapter 7 for additional details.

Complete coding examples are given for almost all of the drawing primitives discussed in this chapter. This Java code can be entered, compiled, and executed as a standalone application. If you encounter errors during the compile or run process that are not related to a typing error, you have probably forgotten one of the steps detailed in Chapter 7.

Note: Windows programmers will notice that a majority of the Java graphics primitives are passed a starting x,y coordinate point. This is the point from which the graphics shape will be drawn. Frequently, the next two values are for width and height. The width and height values are measured with respect to the starting point and represent the width and height of the object.

Windows graphics primitives, on the other hand, do not specify the width and height. The third and fourth parameters, in a similar Windows function, represent the end points of the shape. Thus, width is calculated by subtracting the first parameter from the third parameter and height by subtracting the second parameter from the fourth.

clearRect(int x, int y, int width, int height)

This member function clears the specified rectangle by filling it with the current background color. This action takes place on the current drawing surface.

The following example illustrates the **clearRect()** member function by drawing a shape to the screen and then clearing the upper-left quarter of the window.

```
import java.applet.*;
import java.awt.*;
import RectClearFrame;

public class RectClear extends Applet
{
  // STANDALONE APPLICATION SUPPORT:
  //  m_fStandAlone will be set to true if applet is run
  //  standalone
  //-------------------------------------------------------------
  boolean m_fStandAlone = false;

  public static void main(String args[])
  {
```

```
    RectClearFrame frame = new RectClearFrame("RectClear");

    // Must show Frame before we size it so insets() will
    // return valid values
    //----------------------------------------------------------
    frame.show();
    frame.resize(frame.insets().left+frame.insets().right+640,
           frame.insets().top  + frame.insets().bottom + 480);

    RectClear applet_RectClear = new RectClear();

    frame.add("Center", applet_RectClear);
    applet_RectClear.m_fStandAlone = true;
    applet_RectClear.init();
    applet_RectClear.start();
  }

  public RectClear()
  {
  }

  public void finalize()
  {
  }

  public String getAppletInfo()
  {
    return "Name: RectClear\r\n" +
           "Author: Chris H. Pappas and  William H. Murray\r\n"+
           "Created with Microsoft Visual J++";
  }


  public void init()
  {
    resize(640, 480);

  }

  public void destroy()
  {
```

```
  }

  public void paint(Graphics g)
  {
    g.fillOval(100,100,439,279);
    g.clearRect(0,0,319,239);
  }

  public void start()
  {
  }

  public void stop()
  {
  }

}
```

The following portion of code is supplied by Visual J++ to support standalone applications, such as this example.

```
import java.awt.*;

class RectClearFrame extends Frame
{
  public RectClearFrame(String str)
  {
    super (str);
  }

  public void finalize()
  {
  }

  public boolean handleEvent(Event evt)
  {
    switch (evt.id)
    {
      case Event.WINDOW_DESTROY:
        dispose();
        System.exit(0);
```

```
            return true;

          default:
            return super.handleEvent(evt);
        }
    }
}
```

Figure 8.1 shows the results of this simple application, with the upper-left quarter of the screen cleared.

clipRect(int x, int y, int width, int height)

This member function clips to a rectangle. The clipping area is formed by the intersection of the current clipping area and that of the given rectangle specified by the member function. Graphic operations only have effect within the clipping area.

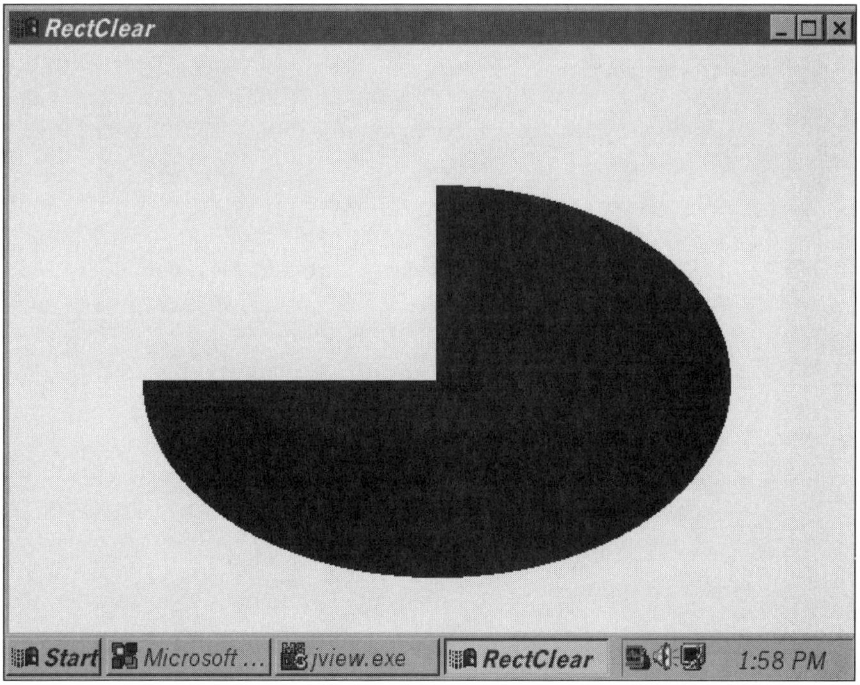

Figure 8.1: The clearRect() member function, which clears the upper-left quarter of the screen.

Here, *x* represents the x screen coordinate and *y* the y screen coordinate for the starting point. *width* represents the width and *height* the height of the clipping rectangle.

In the following listing, the **clipRect()** member function is used to clip the graphics image so that only the portion of the image in the upper-left quarter of the window is visible.

```
import java.applet.*;
import java.awt.*;
import RectClipFrame;

public class RectClip extends Applet
{
  // STANDALONE APPLICATION SUPPORT:
  //   m_fStandAlone will be set to true if applet is run
  //   standalone
  //--------------------------------------------------------------
  boolean m_fStandAlone = false;

  public static void main(String args[])
  {
    RectClipFrame frame = new RectClipFrame("RectClip");

    // Must show Frame before we size it so insets() will
    // return valid values
    //----------------------------------------------------------
    frame.show();
    frame.resize(frame.insets().left+frame.insets().right+640,
           frame.insets().top  + frame.insets().bottom + 480);

    RectClip applet_RectClip = new RectClip();

    frame.add("Center", applet_RectClip);
    applet_RectClip.m_fStandAlone = true;
    applet_RectClip.init();
    applet_RectClip.start();
  }

  public RectClip()
  {
  }

  public void finalize()
```

```
  {
  }

  public String getAppletInfo()
  {
    return "Name: RectClip\r\n" +
           "Author: Chris H. Pappas and William H. Murray\r\n"+
           "Created with Microsoft Visual J++";
  }


  public void init()
  {
    resize(640, 480);
  }

  public void destroy()
  {
  }

  public void paint(Graphics g)
  {
    g.clipRect(0,0,319,239);
    g.fillOval(100,100,439,279);
  }

  public void start()
  {
  }

  public void stop()
  {
  }

}
```

The following portion of code is supplied by Visual J++ to support standalone applications, such as this example.

```
import java.awt.*;

class RectClipFrame extends Frame
{
```

```
  public RectClipFrame(String str)
  {
    super (str);
  }

  public void finalize()
  {
  }

  public boolean handleEvent(Event evt)
  {
    switch (evt.id)
    {
      case Event.WINDOW_DESTROY:
        dispose();
        System.exit(0);
        return true;

      default:
        return super.handleEvent(evt);
    }
  }
}
```

Figure 8.2 shows the resulting figure as it is drawn to the screen.

copyArea(int x, int y, int width, int height, int dx, int dy)

This member function copies a portion of the screen. Here *x* represents the x screen coordinate and *y* the y screen coordinate for the starting point. *width* represents the width and *height* the height of the area to be copied. Here *dx* represents the horizontal distance and *dy* the vertical distance.

The following example shows how the **copyArea()** member function can be used to replicate graphics shapes. One graphics shape is drawn, and then copied and drawn again by the **copyArea()** member function.

```
import java.applet.*;
import java.awt.*;
import AreaCopyFrame;
```

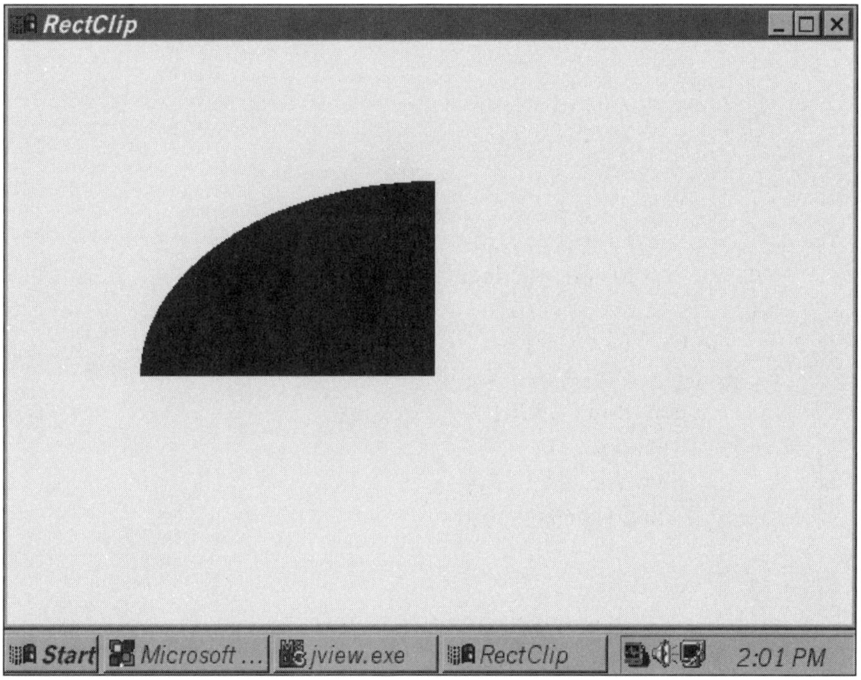

Figure 8.2: The clipRect() member function, which is used to clip a portion of the screen.

```
public class AreaCopy extends Applet
{
  // STANDALONE APPLICATION SUPPORT:
  //     m_fStandAlone will be set to true if applet is run
  //     standalone
  //-----------------------------------------------------------
  boolean m_fStandAlone = false;

  public static void main(String args[])
  {
    AreaCopyFrame frame = new AreaCopyFrame("AreaCopy");

    // Must show Frame before we size it so insets() will
    // return valid values
    //-------------------------------------------------------
```

```
    frame.show();
    frame.resize(frame.insets().left+frame.insets().right+640,
           frame.insets().top  + frame.insets().bottom + 480);

    AreaCopy applet_AreaCopy = new AreaCopy();

    frame.add("Center", applet_AreaCopy);
    applet_AreaCopy.m_fStandAlone = true;
    applet_AreaCopy.init();
    applet_AreaCopy.start();
  }

  public AreaCopy()
  {
  }

  public void finalize()
  {
  }

  public String getAppletInfo()
  {
    return "Name: AreaCopy\r\n" +
           "Author: Chris H. Pappas and William H. Murray\r\n"+
           "Created with Microsoft Visual J++";
  }

  public void init()
  {
    resize(640, 480);
  }

  public void destroy()
  {
  }

  public void paint(Graphics g)
  {
    g.fillRect(100, 100, 119, 39);
    g.copyArea(0, 0, 319, 239, 320, 240);
  }
```

```
  public void start()
  {
  }

  public void stop()
  {
  }

}
```

The following portion of code is supplied by Visual J++ to support standalone applications, such as this example.

```
import java.awt.*;

class AreaCopyFrame extends Frame
{
  public AreaCopyFrame(String str)
  {
    super (str);
  }

  public void finalize()
  {
  }

  public boolean handleEvent(Event evt)
  {
    switch (evt.id)
    {
      case Event.WINDOW_DESTROY:
        dispose();
        System.exit(0);
        return true;

      default:
        return super.handleEvent(evt);
    }
  }
}
```

Figure 8.3 shows the screen after the **copyArea()** function has duplicated the original graphics shape.

draw3DRect(int x, int y, int width, int height, boolean raised)

This member function draws a highlighted three-dimensional rectangle. Here *x* represents the x screen coordinate and *y* the y screen coordinate for the starting point. *width* represents the width and *height* the height of the three-dimensional rectangle. *raised* is a boolean that specifies if the rectangle is or is not raised. The current drawing color is used.

The following listing illustrates the use of the **draw3DRect()** member function. One shape is drawn with the boolean set to **false** and the other shape with the boolean set to **true**.

Figure 8.3: The copyArea() member function, which can be used to replicate portions of the screen.

```
import java.applet.*;
import java.awt.*;
import Rect3DFrame;

public class Rect3D extends Applet
{
  // STANDALONE APPLICATION SUPPORT:
  //    m_fStandAlone will be set to true if applet is run
  //    standalone
  //--------------------------------------------------------------
  boolean m_fStandAlone = false;

  public static void main(String args[])
  {
    Rect3DFrame frame = new Rect3DFrame("Rect3D");

    // Must show Frame before we size it so insets() will
    // return valid values
    //------------------------------------------------------------
    frame.show();
    frame.resize(frame.insets().left+frame.insets().right+640,
           frame.insets().top  + frame.insets().bottom + 480);

    Rect3D applet_Rect3D = new Rect3D();

    frame.add("Center", applet_Rect3D);
    applet_Rect3D.m_fStandAlone = true;
    applet_Rect3D.init();
    applet_Rect3D.start();
  }

  public Rect3D()
  {
  }

  public void finalize()
  {
  }

  public String getAppletInfo()
```

```
  {
    return "Name: Rect3D\r\n" +
           "Author: Chris H. Pappas and William H. Murray\r\n"+
           "Created with Microsoft Visual J++";
  }

  public void init()
  {
    resize(640, 480);
  }

  public void destroy()
  {
  }

  public void paint(Graphics g)
  {
    g.setColor(Color.cyan);
    g.draw3DRect(50,50,219,139,false);
    g.draw3DRect(369,289,219,139,true);
  }

  public void start()
  {
  }

  public void stop()
  {
  }

}
```

The following portion of code is supplied by Visual J++ to support standalone applications, such as this example.

```
import java.awt.*;

class Rect3DFrame extends Frame
{
  public Rect3DFrame(String str)
  {
    super (str);
```

```
    }

    public void finalize()
    {
    }

    public boolean handleEvent(Event evt)
    {
      switch (evt.id)
      {
        case Event.WINDOW_DESTROY:
          dispose();
          System.exit(0);
          return true;

        default:
          return super.handleEvent(evt);
      }
    }
}
```

Figure 8.4 shows the screen after the two three-dimensional shapes have been drawn. Notice that the three-dimensional effect is subtle due to the thin line segments. The effect will change as you change drawing colors.

drawArc(int x, int y, int width, int height, int startAngle, int arcAngle)

This member function is used to draw an arc that is bounded by the given rectangle. Drawing starts at *startAngle* and proceeds a total angular distance given by *arcAngle*. Angles start on the positive x-axis. Positive angles are measured counterclockwise. Here *x* represents the x screen coordinate and *y* the y screen coordinate for the starting point. *width* represents the width and *height* the height of the bounding rectangle. *startAngle* marks the start of arc and *arcAngle* the total angular distance of the arc. Angles are measured in degrees. The current drawing color is used.

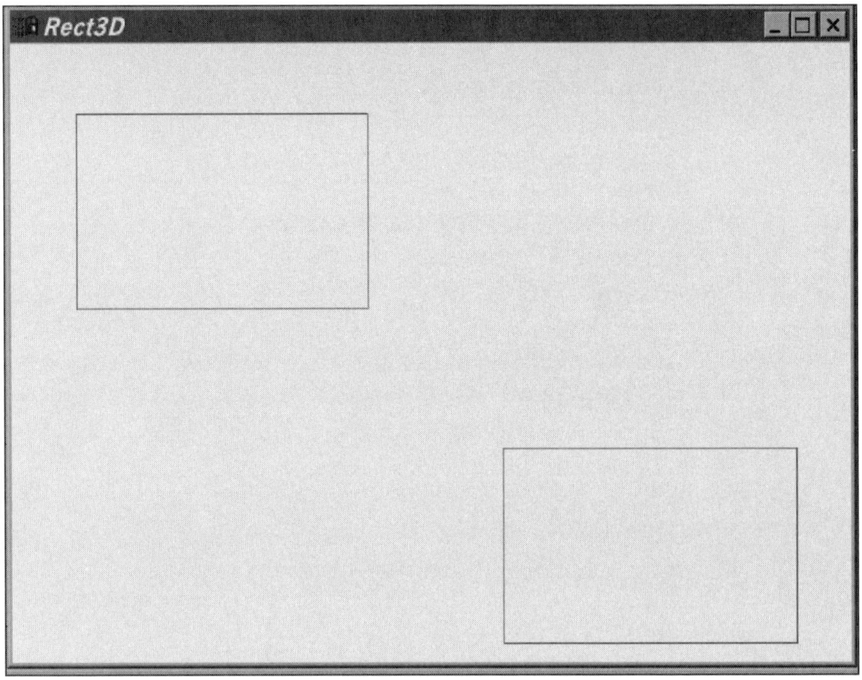

Figure 8.4: The draw3DRect() function, which can make rectangular shapes appear with a three-dimensional quality.

Note: Windows programmers will see that angular measurements are specified in degrees. This is an improvement over the convoluted method used for similar Windows API functions.

The next listing illustrates the use of the **drawArc()** member function by drawing four different arc segments on the screen.

```
import java.applet.*;
import java.awt.*;
import ArcFrame;

public class Arc extends Applet
{
  // STANDALONE APPLICATION SUPPORT:
  //     m_fStandAlone will be set to true if applet is run
  //     standalone
  //--------------------------------------------------------------
  boolean m_fStandAlone = false;
```

```
public static void main(String args[])
{
  ArcFrame frame = new ArcFrame("Arc");

  // Must show Frame before we size it so insets() will
  // return valid values
  //----------------------------------------------------------
  frame.show();
  frame.resize(frame.insets().left+frame.insets().right+640,
         frame.insets().top  + frame.insets().bottom + 480);

  Arc applet_Arc = new Arc();

  frame.add("Center", applet_Arc);
  applet_Arc.m_fStandAlone = true;
  applet_Arc.init();
  applet_Arc.start();
}

public Arc()
{
}

public void finalize()
{
}

public String getAppletInfo()
{
  return "Name: Arc\r\n" +
         "Author: Chris H. Pappas and William H. Murray\r\n"+
         "Created with Microsoft Visual J++";
}

public void init()
{
  resize(640, 480);
}

public void destroy()
{
```

```
  }

  public void paint(Graphics g)
  {
    g.drawArc(119, 120, 50, 50, 0, 90);
    g.drawArc(439, 120, 50, 50, 90, 180);
    g.drawArc(119, 339, 50, 100, 180, 270);
    g.drawArc(439, 339, 100, 50, 45, 135);
  }

  public void start()
  {
  }

  public void stop()
  {
  }

}
```

The following portion of code is supplied by Visual J++ to support standalone applications, such as this example.

```
import java.awt.*;

class ArcFrame extends Frame
{
  public ArcFrame(String str)
  {
    super (str);
  }

  public void finalize()
  {
  }

  public boolean handleEvent(Event evt)
  {
    switch (evt.id)
    {
      case Event.WINDOW_DESTROY:
        dispose();
```

```
          System.exit(0);
          return true;

        default:
          return super.handleEvent(evt);
      }
    }
  }
```

Figure 8.5 shows the results of this application and the **drawArc()** member function. Remember that the last two parameters passed to **drawArc()** specify the starting angle and the angular span of the arc.

drawLine(int x1, int y1, int x2, int y2)

This member function is used to draw a line from the coordinate positions *x1,y1* to *x2,y2*. Here *x1* represents the x screen coordinate and *y1*

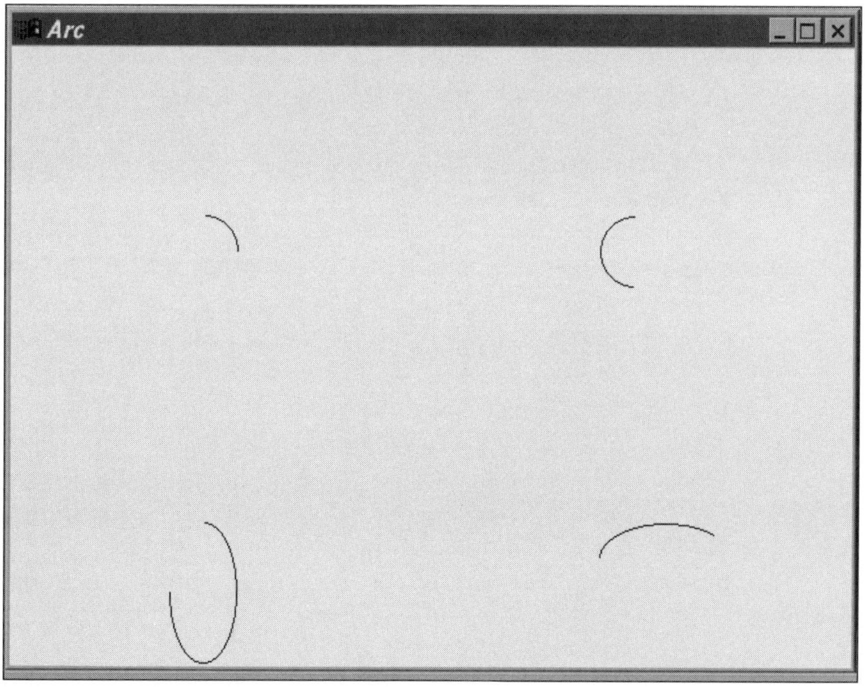

Figure 8.5: Several drawArc() member function calls illustrate the versatility of this member function.

the y screen coordinate for the starting point. Likewise, *x2* represents the x screen coordinate and *y2* the y screen coordinate for the ending point. The current drawing color is used.

The following listing illustrates the **drawLine()** member function. Four separate line segments are drawn on the screen.

```
import java.applet.*;
import java.awt.*;
import LineFrame;

public class Line extends Applet
{
  // STANDALONE APPLICATION SUPPORT:
  //     m_fStandAlone will be set to true if applet is run
  //     standalone
  //--------------------------------------------------------------

  boolean m_fStandAlone = false;

  public static void main(String args[])
  {
    LineFrame frame = new LineFrame("Line");

    // Must show Frame before we size it so insets() will
    // return valid values
    //------------------------------------------------------------
    frame.show();
    frame.resize(frame.insets().left+frame.insets().right+640,
           frame.insets().top  + frame.insets().bottom + 480);

    Line applet_Line = new Line();

    frame.add("Center", applet_Line);
    applet_Line.m_fStandAlone = true;
    applet_Line.init();
    applet_Line.start();
  }

  public Line()
  {
```

```
    }

    public void finalize()
    {
    }

    public String getAppletInfo()
    {
      return "Name: Line\r\n" +
             "Author: Chris H. Pappas and William H. Murray\r\n"+
             "Created with Microsoft Visual J++";
    }

    public void init()
    {
      resize(640, 480);
    }

    public void destroy()
    {
    }

    public void paint(Graphics g)
    {
      g.drawLine(50, 120, 220, 120);  // horizontal
      g.drawLine(480, 50, 480, 139);  // vertical
      g.drawLine(50, 289, 219, 379);  // diagonal
      g.drawLine(369, 439, 589, 279); // diagonal
    }

    public void start()
    {
    }

    public void stop()
    {
    }

}
```

The following portion of code is supplied by Visual J++ to support standalone applications, such as this example.

```
import java.awt.*;

class LineFrame extends Frame
{
  public LineFrame(String str)
  {
    super (str);
  }

  public void finalize()
  {
  }

  public boolean handleEvent(Event evt)
  {
    switch (evt.id)
    {
      case Event.WINDOW_DESTROY:
        dispose();
        System.exit(0);
        return true;

      default:
        return super.handleEvent(evt);
    }
  }
}
```

Figure 8.6 shows four separate line segments drawn in each quarter of the window.

drawOval(int x, int y, int width, int height)

This member function is used to draw an oval inside the given bounding rectangle. Here *x* represents the x screen coordinate and *y* the y screen coordinate for the starting point. *width* represents the width and *height* the height of the oval shape. The current drawing color is used.

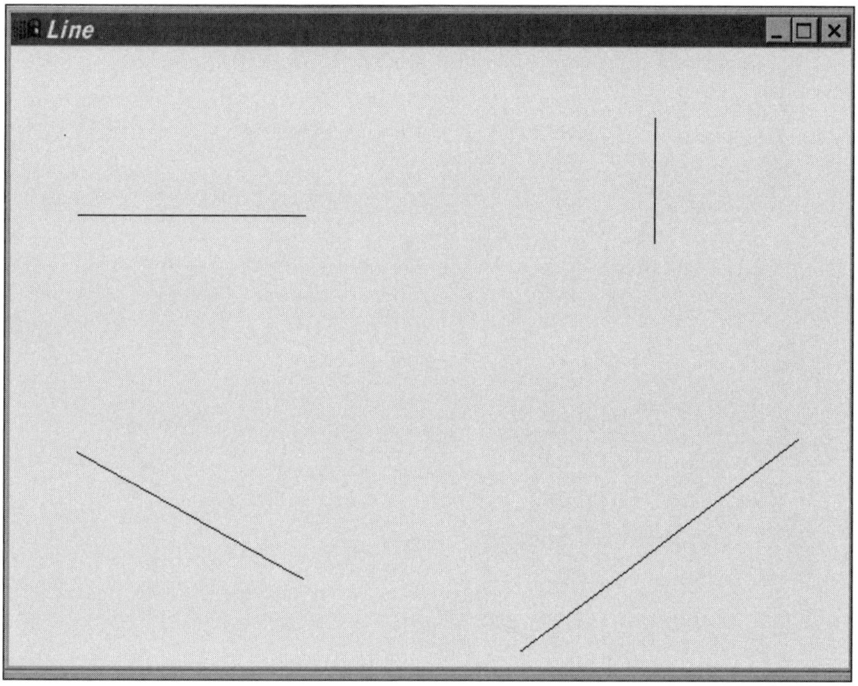

Figure 8.6: The drawLine() member function is used to draw four line segments.

*Note: The Java **drawOval()** member function is most closely associated with the Windows **Ellipse()** API function.*

This listing illustrates the use of the **drawOval()** member function. This is the member function you'll use to draw ovals, ellipses, and circles.

```
import java.applet.*;
import java.awt.*;
import OvalFrame;

public class Oval extends Applet
{
  // STANDALONE APPLICATION SUPPORT:
  //    m_fStandAlone will be set to true if applet is run
  //    standalone
  //--------------------------------------------------------------
  boolean m_fStandAlone = false;

  public static void main(String args[])
```

```
{
  OvalFrame frame = new OvalFrame("Oval");

  // Must show Frame before we size it so insets() will
  // return valid values
  //----------------------------------------------------------
  frame.show();
  frame.resize(frame.insets().left+frame.insets().right+640,
          frame.insets().top  + frame.insets().bottom + 480);

  Oval applet_Oval = new Oval();

  frame.add("Center", applet_Oval);
  applet_Oval.m_fStandAlone = true;
  applet_Oval.init();
  applet_Oval.start();
}

public Oval()
{
}

public void finalize()
{
}

public String getAppletInfo()
{
  return "Name: Oval\r\n" +
         "Author: Chris H. Pappas and William H. Murray\r\n"+
         "Created with Microsoft Visual J++";
}

public void init()
{
  resize(640, 480);
}

public void destroy()
{
}
```

```
  public void paint(Graphics g)
  {
    g.drawOval(50, 50, 539, 379);
    g.drawOval(100, 100, 439, 279);
    g.drawOval(150, 150, 339, 179);
    g.drawOval(200, 200, 239, 79);
  }

  public void start()
  {
  }

  public void stop()
  {
  }

}
```

The following portion of code is supplied by Visual J++ to support standalone applications, such as this example.

```
import java.awt.*;

class OvalFrame extends Frame
{
  public OvalFrame(String str)
  {
    super (str);
  }

  public void finalize()
  {
  }

  public boolean handleEvent(Event evt)
  {
    switch (evt.id)
    {
      case Event.WINDOW_DESTROY:
        dispose();
        System.exit(0);
        return true;
```

```
        default:
          return super.handleEvent(evt);
      }
    }
  }
```

Figure 8.7 shows an interesting pattern of decreasing oval sizes in the window.

drawPolygon(int xPoints[], int yPoints[], int nPoints)
drawPolygon(Polygon p)

This member function is used to draw a polygon. The starting and ending points for the polygon's line segments can be described in two arrays. *xPoints[]* holds the x coordinate points and *yPoints[]* the y coordinate points. *nPoints* is the total number of points.

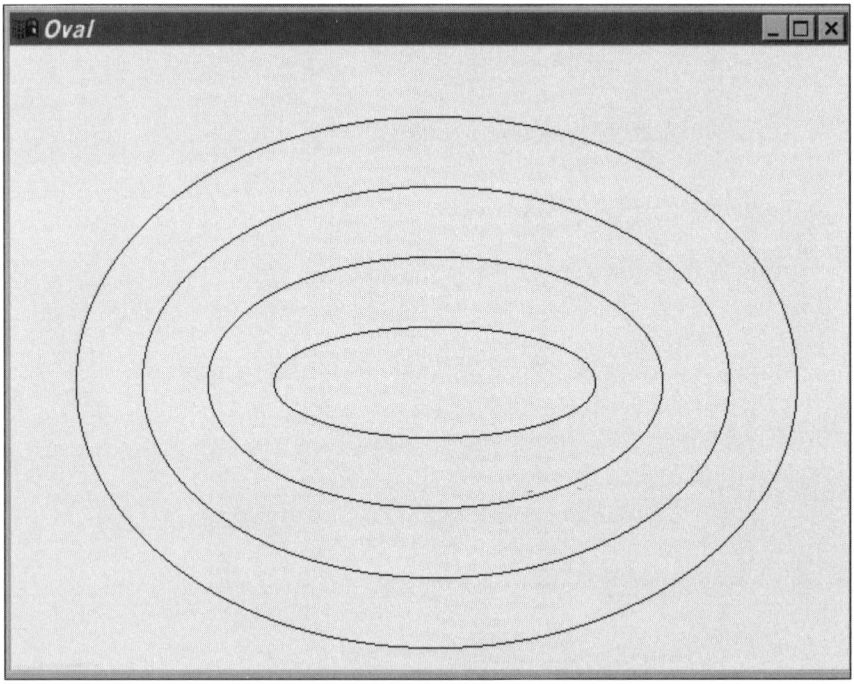

Figure 8.7: The drawOval() member function can be used to draw ellipses and circles.

An alternative method is to specify the polygon as an instance of the Polygon class. This is useful if additional points may be added after the polygon is drawn.

Polygon shapes are not automatically closed by Java. The current drawing color is used.

The following listing illustrates the use of both variations of the **drawPolygon()** member function.

```
import java.applet.*;
import java.awt.*;
import PolyFrame;

public class Poly extends Applet
{
  // STANDALONE APPLICATION SUPPORT:
  //    m_fStandAlone will be set to true if applet is run
  //    standalone
  //-------------------------------------------------------
  boolean m_fStandAlone = false;

  public static void main(String args[])
  {
    PolyFrame frame = new PolyFrame("Poly");

    // Must show Frame before we size it so insets() will
    // return valid values
    //-----------------------------------------------------
    frame.show();
    frame.resize(frame.insets().left+frame.insets().right+640,
           frame.insets().top  + frame.insets().bottom + 480);

    Poly applet_Poly = new Poly();

    frame.add("Center", applet_Poly);
    applet_Poly.m_fStandAlone = true;
    applet_Poly.init();
    applet_Poly.start();
  }

  public Poly()
```

```
{
}

public void finalize()
{
}

public String getAppletInfo()
{
  return "Name: Poly\r\n" +
         "Author: Chris H. Pappas and William H. Murray\r\n"+
         "Created with Microsoft Visual J++ ";
}

public void init()
{
  resize(640, 480);
}

public void destroy()
{
}

public void paint(Graphics g)
{
  // technique A (outer polygon)
  int Axpts[] = {319, 400, 600, 200, 25};
  int Aypts[] = {10, 30, 400, 290, 100};
  int Anumpts = Aypts.length;
  g.drawPolygon(Axpts, Aypts, Anumpts);

  // technique B (inner polygon)
  int Bxpts[] = {300, 400, 500, 300, 125};
  int Bypts[] = {100, 70, 350, 200, 150};
  int Bnumpts = Bypts.length;
  Polygon mypoly = new Polygon(Bxpts, Bypts, Bnumpts);
  mypoly.addPoint(150, 175);  // add new points
  mypoly.addPoint(175, 150);
  g.drawPolygon(mypoly);
}
```

```
  public void start()
  {
  }

  public void stop()
  {
  }

}
```

The following portion of code is supplied by Visual J++ to support standalone applications, such as this example.

```
import java.awt.*;

class PolyFrame extends Frame
{
  public PolyFrame(String str)
  {
    super (str);
  }

  public void finalize()
  {
  }

  public boolean handleEvent(Event evt)
  {
    switch (evt.id)
    {
      case Event.WINDOW_DESTROY:
        dispose();
        System.exit(0);
        return true;

      default:
        return super.handleEvent(evt);
    }
  }
}
```

Figure 8.8 illustrates the use of both versions of the **drawPolygon()** member function. Notice in the figure that two separate shapes are drawn to the screen, one inside the other. Also notice that neither figure is closed.

drawRect(int x, int y, int width, int height)

This member function is used to draw the outline of a rectangle. Here *x* represents the x screen coordinate and *y* the y screen coordinate for the starting point. *width* represents the width and *height* the height of the rectangular shape. The current drawing color is used.

The following listing illustrates the use of the **drawRect()** member function. In this example, four rectangles are drawn to the screen, from largest to smallest.

```
import java.applet.*;
import java.awt.*;
```

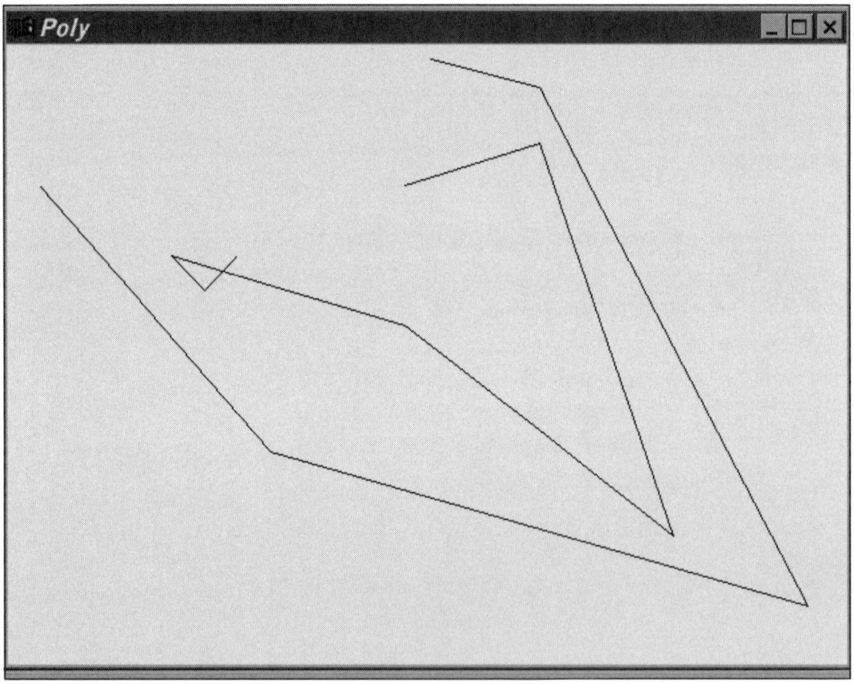

Figure 8.8: The drawPolygon() member function can be used to draw multiple-sided shapes to the window.

```
import RectFrame;

public class Rect extends Applet
{
  // STANDALONE APPLICATION SUPPORT:
  //    m_fStandAlone will be set to true if applet is run
  //    standalone
  //--------------------------------------------------------------
  boolean m_fStandAlone = false;

  public static void main(String args[])
  {
    RectFrame frame = new RectFrame("Rect");

    // Must show Frame before we size it so insets() will
    // return valid values
    //------------------------------------------------------------
    frame.show();
    frame.resize(frame.insets().left+frame.insets().right+640,
           frame.insets().top  + frame.insets().bottom + 480);

    Rect applet_Rect = new Rect();

    frame.add("Center", applet_Rect);
    applet_Rect.m_fStandAlone = true;
    applet_Rect.init();
    applet_Rect.start();
  }

  public Rect()
  {
  }

  public void finalize()
  {
  }

  public String getAppletInfo()
  {
```

```
    return "Name: Rect\r\n" +
           "Author: Chris H. Pappas and William H. Murray\r\n"+
           "Created with Microsoft Visual J++ ";
  }

  public void init()
  {
    resize(640, 480);
  }

  public void destroy()
  {
  }

  public void paint(Graphics g)
  {
    g.drawRect(50, 50, 539, 379);
    g.drawRect(100, 100, 439, 279);
    g.drawRect(150, 150, 339, 179);
    g.drawRect(200, 200, 239, 79);
  }

  public void start()
  {
  }

  public void stop()
  {
  }

}
```

The following portion of code is supplied by Visual J++ to support standalone applications, such as this example.

```
import java.awt.*;

class RectFrame extends Frame
{
  public RectFrame(String str)
  {
    super (str);
  }
```

```
  public void finalize()
  {
  }

  public boolean handleEvent(Event evt)
  {
    switch (evt.id)
    {
      case Event.WINDOW_DESTROY:
        dispose();
        System.exit(0);
        return true;

      default:
        return super.handleEvent(evt);
    }
  }
}
```

Figure 8.9 shows the four rectangular shapes drawn to the screen.

drawRoundRect(int x, int y, int width, int height, int arcWidth, int arcHeight)

This member function is used to draw the outline of a rectangle with rounded corners. Here *x* represents the x screen coordinate and *y* the y screen coordinate for the starting point. *width* represents the width and *height* the height of the rectangular shape. Rounding is specified with the *arcWidth* and *arcHeight* values. The current drawing color is used.

The following listing illustrates the use of the **drawRoundRect()** member function. In this example, four rectangles, with various degrees of rounding, are drawn to the screen.

```
import java.applet.*;
import java.awt.*;
import RectRndFrame;

public class RectRnd extends Applet
{
```

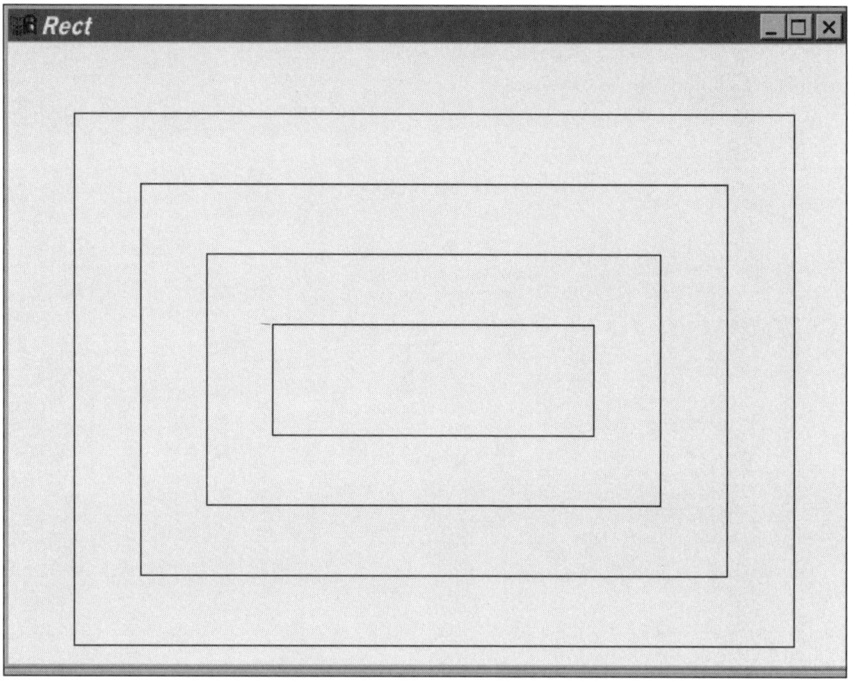

Figure 8.9: The drawRect() member function is used to draw these four rectangles to the screen.

```
// STANDALONE APPLICATION SUPPORT:
//   m_fStandAlone will be set to true if applet is run
//   standalone
//--------------------------------------------------------
boolean m_fStandAlone = false;

public static void main(String args[])
{
  RectRndFrame frame = new RectRndFrame("RectRnd");

  // Must show Frame before we size it so insets() will
  // return valid values
  //------------------------------------------------------
  frame.show();
  frame.resize(frame.insets().left+frame.insets().right+640,
         frame.insets().top  + frame.insets().bottom + 480);

  RectRnd applet_RectRnd = new RectRnd();
```

```
  frame.add("Center", applet_RectRnd);
  applet_RectRnd.m_fStandAlone = true;
  applet_RectRnd.init();
  applet_RectRnd.start();
}

public RectRnd()
{
}

public void finalize()
{
}

public String getAppletInfo()
{
  return "Name: RectRnd\r\n" +
         "Author: Chris H. Pappas and William H. Murray\r\n"+
         "Created with Microsoft Visual J++ ";
}

public void init()
{
  resize(640, 480);
}

public void destroy()
{
}

public void paint(Graphics g)
{
  g.drawRoundRect(50, 50, 539, 379, 0, 0);
  g.drawRoundRect(100, 100, 439, 279, 30, 30);
  g.drawRoundRect(150, 150, 339, 179, 30, 90);
  g.drawRoundRect(200, 200, 239, 79, 90, 30);
}

public void start()
```

```
  {
  }

  public void stop()
  {
  }

}
```

The following portion of code is supplied by Visual J++ to support standalone applications, such as this example.

```
import java.awt.*;

class RectRndFrame extends Frame
{
  public RectRndFrame(String str)
  {
    super (str);
  }

  public void finalize()
  {
  }

  public boolean handleEvent(Event evt)
  {
    switch (evt.id)
    {
      case Event.WINDOW_DESTROY:
        dispose();
        System.exit(0);
        return true;

      default:
        return super.handleEvent(evt);
    }
  }
}
```

Figure 8.10 shows four rounded rectangles. The largest rectangle has no rounding. The second largest rectangle uses values to symmetrically round the corners. The two smallest rectangles vary the amount of vertical and horizontal rounding.

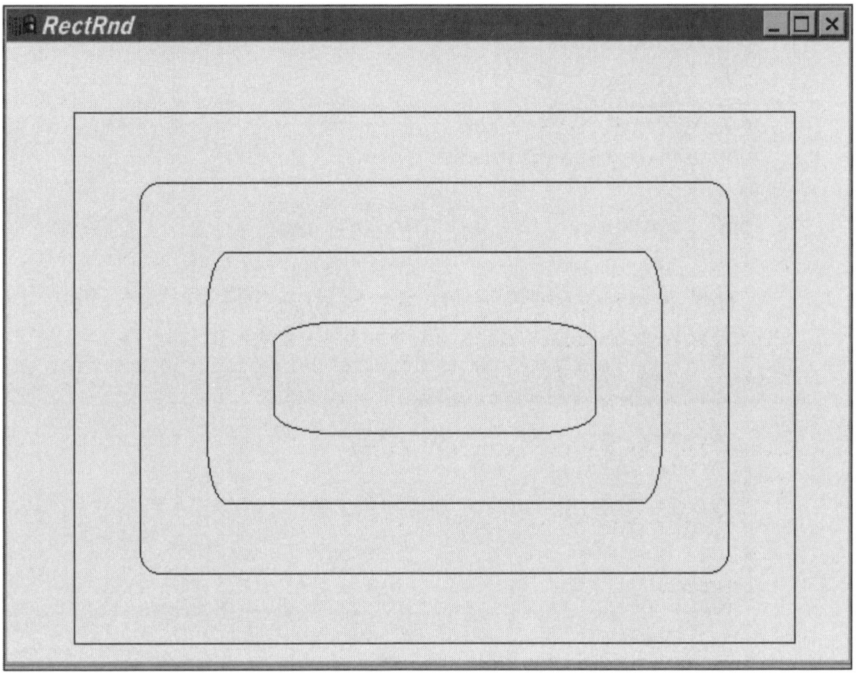

Figure 8.10: The drawRoundRect() function rounds the corners of a rectangular shape.

fill3DRect(int x, int y, int width, int height, boolean raised)

This member function is used to draw and fill a highlighted three-dimensional rectangle. Here *x* represents the x screen coordinate and *y* the y screen coordinate for the starting point. *width* represents the width and *height* the height of the rectangular shape. *raised* is a boolean that specifies if the three-dimensional rectangle is or is not raised. The current drawing color is used to draw and fill this shape.

The following listing illustrates the use of the **fill3DRect()** member function. The total three-dimensional effect is dependent on the size of the rectangle and the drawing and fill color selected.

```
import java.applet.*;
import java.awt.*;
import Rect3DFillFrame;

public class Rect3DFill extends Applet
{
```

```
// STANDALONE APPLICATION SUPPORT:
//    m_fStandAlone will be set to true if applet is run
//    standalone
//--------------------------------------------------------
boolean m_fStandAlone = false;

public static void main(String args[])
{
  Rect3DFillFrame frame = new Rect3DFillFrame("Rect3DFill");

  // Must show Frame before we size it so insets() will
  // return valid values
  //------------------------------------------------------
  frame.show();
  frame.resize(frame.insets().left+frame.insets().right+640,
         frame.insets().top  + frame.insets().bottom + 480);

  Rect3DFill applet_Rect3DFill = new Rect3DFill();

  frame.add("Center", applet_Rect3DFill);
  applet_Rect3DFill.m_fStandAlone = true;
  applet_Rect3DFill.init();
  applet_Rect3DFill.start();
}

public Rect3DFill()
{
}

public void finalize()
{
}

public String getAppletInfo()
{
  return "Name: Rect3DFill\r\n" +
         "Author: Chris H. Pappas and William H. Murray\r\n"+
         "Created with Microsoft Visual J++";
}

public void init()
```

```
  {
    resize(640, 480);
  }

  public void destroy()
  {
  }

  public void paint(Graphics g)
  {
    g.setColor(Color.cyan);
    g.fill3DRect(50,50,219,139,false);
    g.fill3DRect(369,289,219,139,true);
  }

  public void start()
  {
  }

  public void stop()
  {
  }

}
```

The following portion of code is supplied by Visual J++ to support standalone applications, such as this example.

```
import java.awt.*;

class Rect3DFillFrame extends Frame
{
  public Rect3DFillFrame(String str)
  {
    super (str);
  }

  public void finalize()
  {
  }

  public boolean handleEvent(Event evt)
  {
```

```
        switch (evt.id)
        {
          case Event.WINDOW_DESTROY:
            dispose();
            System.exit(0);
            return true;

          default:
            return super.handleEvent(evt);
        }
      }
    }
```

Figure 8.11 shows the results of two calls to the **fill3DRect()** member function. One call is made with the boolean value set to **true** and the other with this value set to **false**.

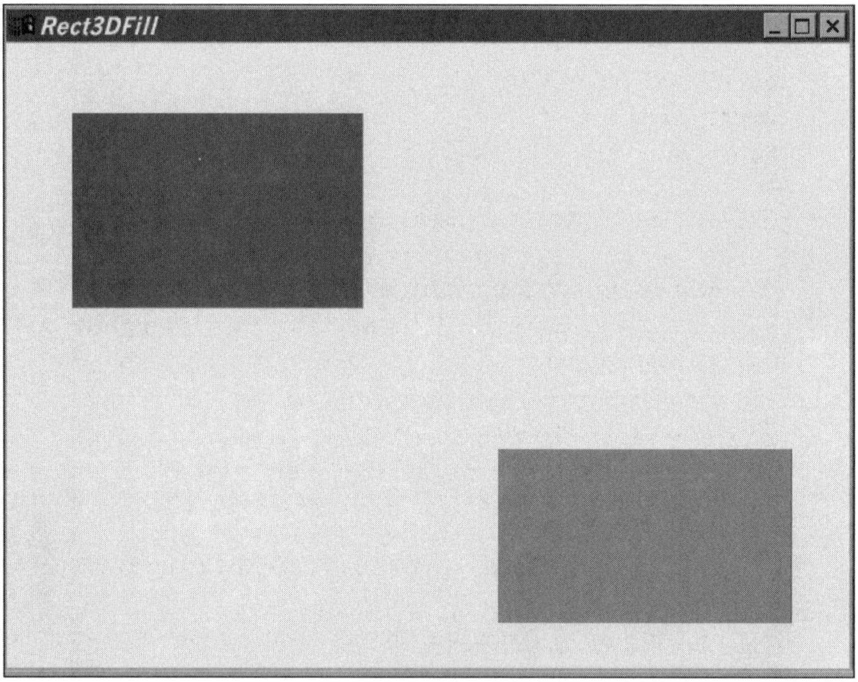

Figure 8.11: A filled three-dimensional image results from the fill3DRect() member function.

fillArc(int x, int y, int width, int height, int startAngle, int arcAngle)

This member function is used to draw and fill an arc. Drawing starts at *startAngle* and proceeds a total angular distance given by *arcAngle*. Angles start on the positive x-axis. Positive angles are measured counterclockwise. Here *x* represents the x screen coordinate and *y* the y screen coordinate for the starting point. *width* represents the width and *height* the height of the bounding rectangle. *startAngle* marks the start of arc and *arcAngle* the total angular distance of the arc. The figure is closed between the starting point and ending point. Angles are measured in degrees. The current drawing color is used to draw and fill the arc segment.

Note: Windows programmers will see that angular measurements are specified in degrees. This is an improvement over the convoluted method used for similar Windows API functions.

The following listing illustrates the **fillArc()** member function by drawing and closing four arc segments on the screen.

```
import java.applet.*;
import java.awt.*;
import ArcFillFrame;

public class ArcFill extends Applet
{
  // STANDALONE APPLICATION SUPPORT:
  //   m_fStandAlone will be set to true if applet is run
  //   standalone
  //--------------------------------------------------------------
  boolean m_fStandAlone = false;

  public static void main(String args[])
  {
    ArcFillFrame frame = new ArcFillFrame("ArcFill");

    // Must show Frame before we size it so insets() will
    // return valid values
    //----------------------------------------------------------
    frame.show();
```

```
      frame.resize(frame.insets().left+frame.insets().right+640,
               frame.insets().top  + frame.insets().bottom + 480);

      ArcFill applet_ArcFill = new ArcFill();

      frame.add("Center", applet_ArcFill);
      applet_ArcFill.m_fStandAlone = true;
      applet_ArcFill.init();
      applet_ArcFill.start();
    }

    public ArcFill()
    {
    }

    public void finalize()
    {
    }

    public String getAppletInfo()
    {
      return "Name: ArcFill\r\n" +
               "Author: Chris H. Pappas and William H. Murray\r\n"+
               "Created with Microsoft Visual J++";
    }

    public void init()
    {
      resize(640, 480);
    }

    public void destroy()
    {
    }

    public void paint(Graphics g)
    {
      g.fillArc(119, 120, 50, 50, 0, 90);
      g.fillArc(439, 120, 50, 50, 90, 180);
      g.fillArc(119, 339, 50, 100, 180, 270);
      g.fillArc(439, 339, 100, 50, 45, 135);
```

```
  }

  public void start()
  {
  }

  public void stop()
  {
  }

}
```

The following portion of code is supplied by Visual J++ to support standalone applications, such as this example.

```
import java.awt.*;

class ArcFillFrame extends Frame
{
  public ArcFillFrame(String str)
  {
    super (str);
  }

  public void finalize()
  {
  }

  public boolean handleEvent(Event evt)
  {
    switch (evt.id)
    {
      case Event.WINDOW_DESTROY:
        dispose();
        System.exit(0);
        return true;

      default:
        return super.handleEvent(evt);
    }
  }
}
```

Figure 8.12 shows four separate filled arc segments. The **fillArc()** member function closes each arc segment before filling it with the current draw and fill color.

fillOval(int x, int y, int width, int height)

This member function is used to draw and fill an oval shape bounded by the specified rectangle. Here *x* represents the x screen coordinate and *y* the y screen coordinate for the starting point. *width* represents the width and *height* the height of the oval shape. The current drawing color is used to draw and fill this shape.

*Note: The Java **fillOval()** member function is most closely associated with the Windows **Ellipse()** API function.*

The following listing illustrates the use of the **fillOval()** member function to draw four filled oval shapes to the window.

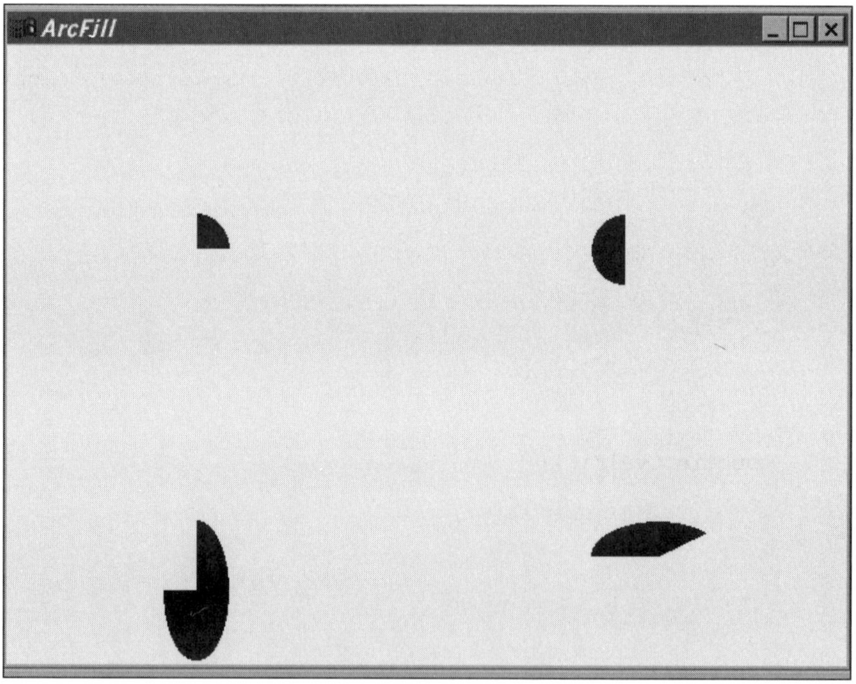

Figure 8.12: The fillArc() member function can draw and fill arc segments with the current draw and fill color.

```
import java.applet.*;
import java.awt.*;
import OvalFillFrame;

public class OvalFill extends Applet
{
  // STANDALONE APPLICATION SUPPORT:
  //   m_fStandAlone will be set to true if applet is run
  //   standalone
  //--------------------------------------------------------------
  boolean m_fStandAlone = false;

  public static void main(String args[])
  {
    OvalFillFrame frame = new OvalFillFrame("OvalFill");

    // Must show Frame before we size it so insets() will
    // return valid values
    //--------------------------------------------------------------
    frame.show();
    frame.resize(frame.insets().left+frame.insets().right+640,
           frame.insets().top  + frame.insets().bottom + 480);

    OvalFill applet_OvalFill = new OvalFill();

    frame.add("Center", applet_OvalFill);
    applet_OvalFill.m_fStandAlone = true;
    applet_OvalFill.init();
    applet_OvalFill.start();
  }

  public OvalFill()
  {
  }

  public void finalize()
  {
  }

  public String getAppletInfo()
```

```
  {
    return "Name: OvalFill\r\n" +
           "Author: Chris H. Pappas and William H. Murray\r\n"+
           "Created with Microsoft Visual J++";
  }

  public void init()
  {
    resize(640, 480);
  }

  public void destroy()
  {
  }

  public void paint(Graphics g)
  {
    g.fillOval(50, 50, 539, 379);
    g.setColor(Color.yellow);
    g.fillOval(100, 100, 439, 279);
    g.setColor(Color.red);
    g.fillOval(150, 150, 339, 179);
    g.setColor(Color.cyan);
    g.fillOval(200, 200, 239, 79);
  }

  public void start()
  {
  }

  public void stop()
  {
  }

}
```

The following portion of code is supplied by Visual J++ to support standalone applications, such as this example.

```
import java.awt.*;

class OvalFillFrame extends Frame
{
```

```
  public OvalFillFrame(String str)
  {
    super (str);
  }

  public void finalize()
  {
  }

  public boolean handleEvent(Event evt)
  {
    switch (evt.id)
    {
      case Event.WINDOW_DESTROY:
        dispose();
        System.exit(0);
        return true;

      default:
        return super.handleEvent(evt);
    }
  }
}
```

Figure 8.13 shows four separate ovals drawn to the window. The **setColor()** member function, which is covered in greater detail in the next chapter, changes the draw and fill color before the oval is drawn.

fillPolygon(int xPoints[], int yPoints[], int nPoints) fillPolygon(Polygon p)

This member function is used to draw and fill a polygon. The starting and ending points for the polygon's line segments can be described in two arrays. *xPoints[]* holds the x coordinate points and *yPoints[]* the y coordinate points. *nPoints* is the total number of points.

An alternative method is to specify the polygon as an instance of the Polygon class. This is useful if additional points may be added after the polygon is drawn.

Filled polygon shapes are automatically closed by Java and filled with the current drawing color.

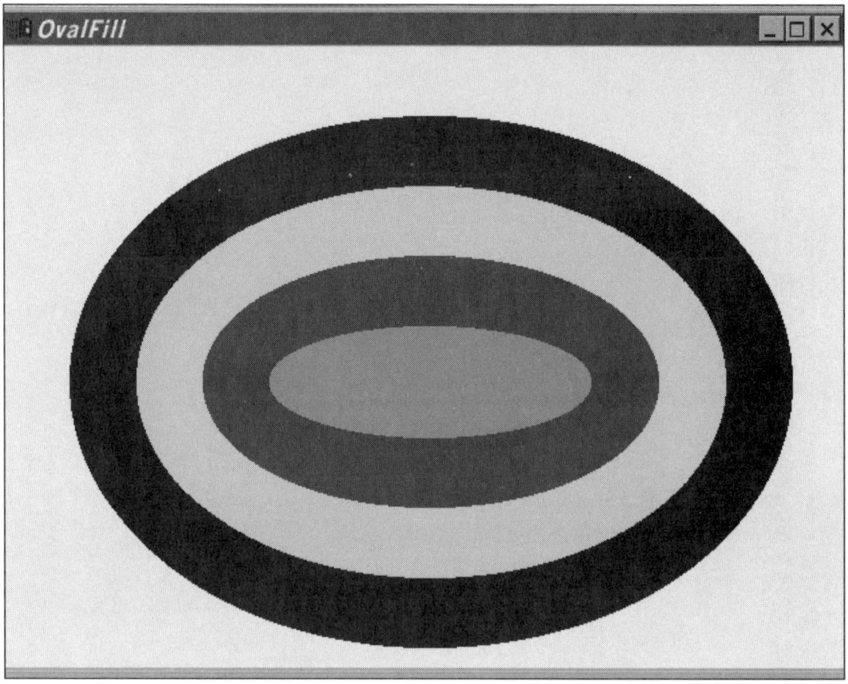

Figure 8.13. The fillOval() member function can be used to draw and fill ellipses and circles.

The following listing illustrates the use of both variations of the **fillPolygon()** member function.

```
import java.applet.*;
import java.awt.*;
import PolyFillFrame;

public class PolyFill extends Applet
{
  // STANDALONE APPLICATION SUPPORT:
  //   m_fStandAlone will be set to true if applet is run
  //   standalone
  //--------------------------------------------------------------
  boolean m_fStandAlone = false;

  public static void main(String args[])
  {
    PolyFillFrame frame = new PolyFillFrame("PolyFill");
```

```
    // Must show Frame before we size it so insets() will
    // return valid values
    //------------------------------------------------------------
    frame.show();
    frame.resize(frame.insets().left+frame.insets().right+640,
            frame.insets().top  + frame.insets().bottom + 480);

    PolyFill applet_PolyFill = new PolyFill();

    frame.add("Center", applet_PolyFill);
    applet_PolyFill.m_fStandAlone = true;
    applet_PolyFill.init();
    applet_PolyFill.start();
  }

  public PolyFill()
  {
  }

  public void finalize()
  {
  }

  public String getAppletInfo()
  {
    return "Name: PolyFill\r\n" +
           "Author: Chris H. Pappas and William H. Murray\r\n"+
           "Created with Microsoft Visual J++";
  }

  public void init()
  {
    resize(640, 480);
  }

  public void destroy()
  {
  }

  public void paint(Graphics g)
```

```
  {
    // technique A (outer polygon)
    int Axpts[] = {319, 400, 600, 200, 25};
    int Aypts[] = {10, 30, 400, 290, 100};
    int Anumpts = Aypts.length;
    g.fillPolygon(Axpts, Aypts, Anumpts);

    // technique B (inner polygon)
    g.setColor(Color.yellow);
    int Bxpts[] = {300, 400, 500, 300, 125};
    int Bypts[] = {100, 70, 350, 200, 150};
    int Bnumpts = Bypts.length;
    Polygon mypoly = new Polygon(Bxpts, Bypts, Bnumpts);
    mypoly.addPoint(150, 175);  // add new points
    mypoly.addPoint(175, 150);
    g.fillPolygon(mypoly);
  }

  public void start()
  {
  }

  public void stop()
  {
  }

}
```

The following portion of code is supplied by Visual J++ to support standalone applications, such as this example.

```
import java.awt.*;

class PolyFillFrame extends Frame
{
  public PolyFillFrame(String str)
  {
    super (str);
  }

  public void finalize()
  {
  }
```

```
  public boolean handleEvent(Event evt)
  {
    switch (evt.id)
    {
      case Event.WINDOW_DESTROY:
        dispose();
        System.exit(0);
        return true;

      default:
        return super.handleEvent(evt);
    }
  }
}
```

Figure 8.14 illustrates the use of both versions of the **fillPolygon()** member function. Notice in the figure that two separate shapes are drawn to the screen, one inside the other. Also notice that both figures have been closed by the **fillPolygon()** member function.

Figure 8.14: The fillPolygon() member function can produce dramatic graphics results.

fillRect(int x, int y, int width, int height)

This member function is used to draw and fill a rectangular shape. Here *x* represents the x screen coordinate and *y* the y screen coordinate for the starting point. *width* represents the width and *height* the height of the rectangular shape. The current drawing color is used to draw and fill this shape.

The following listing illustrates the use of the **fillRect()** member function to draw four filled rectangular shapes to the window.

```
import java.applet.*;
import java.awt.*;
import RectFillFrame;

public class RectFill extends Applet
{
  // STANDALONE APPLICATION SUPPORT:
  //    m_fStandAlone will be set to true if applet is run
  //    standalone
  //----------------------------------------------------------------
  boolean m_fStandAlone = false;

  public static void main(String args[])
  {
    RectFillFrame frame = new RectFillFrame("RectFill");

    // Must show Frame before we size it so insets() will
    // return valid values
    //--------------------------------------------------------------
    frame.show();
    frame.resize(frame.insets().left+frame.insets().right+640,
          frame.insets().top  + frame.insets().bottom + 480);

    RectFill applet_RectFill = new RectFill();

    frame.add("Center", applet_RectFill);
    applet_RectFill.m_fStandAlone = true;
    applet_RectFill.init();
    applet_RectFill.start();
  }
```

```
public RectFill()
{
}

public void finalize()
{
}

public String getAppletInfo()
{
  return "Name: RectFill\r\n" +
         "Author: Chris H. Pappas and William H. Murray\r\n"+
         "Created with Microsoft Visual J++";
}

public void init()
{
  resize(640, 480);
}

public void destroy()
{
}

public void paint(Graphics g)
{
  g.fillRect(50, 50, 539, 379);
  g.setColor(Color.yellow);
  g.fillRect(100, 100, 439, 279);
  g.setColor(Color.red);
  g.fillRect(150, 150, 339, 179);
  g.setColor(Color.cyan);
  g.fillRect(200, 200, 239, 79);
}

public void start()
{
}

public void stop()
```

```
    {
    }

}
```

The following portion of code is supplied by Visual J++ to support standalone applications, such as this example.

```
import java.awt.*;

class RectFillFrame extends Frame
{
  public RectFillFrame(String str)
  {
    super (str);
  }

  public void finalize()
  {
  }

  public boolean handleEvent(Event evt)
  {
    switch (evt.id)
    {
      case Event.WINDOW_DESTROY:
        dispose();
        System.exit(0);
        return true;

      default:
        return super.handleEvent(evt);
    }
  }
}
```

Figure 8.15 shows four separate rectangles drawn to the window. The **setColor()** member function is again used to change the draw and fill color before each rectangle is drawn.

Figure 8.15: The fillRect() member function is used to draw four rectangles in the window.

fillRoundRect(int x, int y, int width, int height, int arcWidth, int arcHeight)

This member function is used to draw and fill a rectangle with rounded corners. Here *x* represents the x screen coordinate and *y* the y screen coordinate for the starting point. *width* represents the width and *height* the height of the rectangular shape. Rounding is specified with the *arcWidth* and *arcHeight* values. The current drawing color is used to draw and fill this shape.

The following listing illustrates the use of the **fillRoundRect()** member function to draw four filled rounded rectangular shapes to the window.

```
import java.applet.*;
import java.awt.*;
import RndRectFillFrame;
```

```
public class RndRectFill extends Applet
{
  // STANDALONE APPLICATION SUPPORT:
  //   m_fStandAlone will be set to true if applet is run
  //   standalone
  //--------------------------------------------------------------
  boolean m_fStandAlone = false;

  public static void main(String args[])
  {
    RndRectFillFrame frame = new
RndRectFillFrame("RndRectFill");

    // Must show Frame before we size it so insets() will
    // return valid values
    //-------------------------------------------------------
    frame.show();
    frame.resize(frame.insets().left+frame.insets().right+640,
           frame.insets().top  + frame.insets().bottom + 480);

    RndRectFill applet_RndRectFill = new RndRectFill();

    frame.add("Center", applet_RndRectFill);
    applet_RndRectFill.m_fStandAlone = true;
    applet_RndRectFill.init();
    applet_RndRectFill.start();
  }

  public RndRectFill()
  {
  }

  public void finalize()
  {
  }

  public String getAppletInfo()
  {
    return "Name: RndRectFill\r\n" +
           "Author: Chris H. Pappas and William H. Murray\r\n"+
           "Created with Microsoft Visual J++";
  }
```

```
    public void init()
    {
      resize(640, 480);
    }

    public void destroy()
    {
    }

    public void paint(Graphics g)
    {
      g.fillRoundRect(50, 50, 539, 379, 0, 0);
      g.setColor(Color.yellow);
      g.fillRoundRect(100, 100, 439, 279, 60, 60);
      g.setColor(Color.red);
      g.fillRoundRect(150, 150, 339, 179, 60, 100);
      g.setColor(Color.cyan);
      g.fillRoundRect(200, 200, 239, 79, 100, 60);
    }

    public void start()
    {
    }

    public void stop()
    {
    }

}
```

The following portion of code is supplied by Visual J++ to support standalone applications, such as this example.

```
import java.awt.*;

class RndRectFillFrame extends Frame
{
  public RndRectFillFrame(String str)
  {
    super (str);
  }
```

```
  public void finalize()
  {
  }

  public boolean handleEvent(Event evt)
  {
    switch (evt.id)
    {
      case Event.WINDOW_DESTROY:
        dispose();
        System.exit(0);
        return true;

      default:
        return super.handleEvent(evt);
    }
  }
}
```

Figure 8.16 shows four filled rounded rectangles. The largest rectangle has no rounding. The second largest rectangle uses values to symmetrically round the corners. The two smallest rectangles vary the amount of vertical and horizontal rounding.

getClipRect()

This member function is used to obtain the bounding rectangle of the current clipping area.

setPaintMode()

This member function is used to set the paint mode to overwrite the destination with the current color.

setXORMode(Color c1)

This member function is used to set the paint mode to alternate between the current color and a new color. The new color is given as *c1*. Pixels using the current color are changed to the new color. Pixels

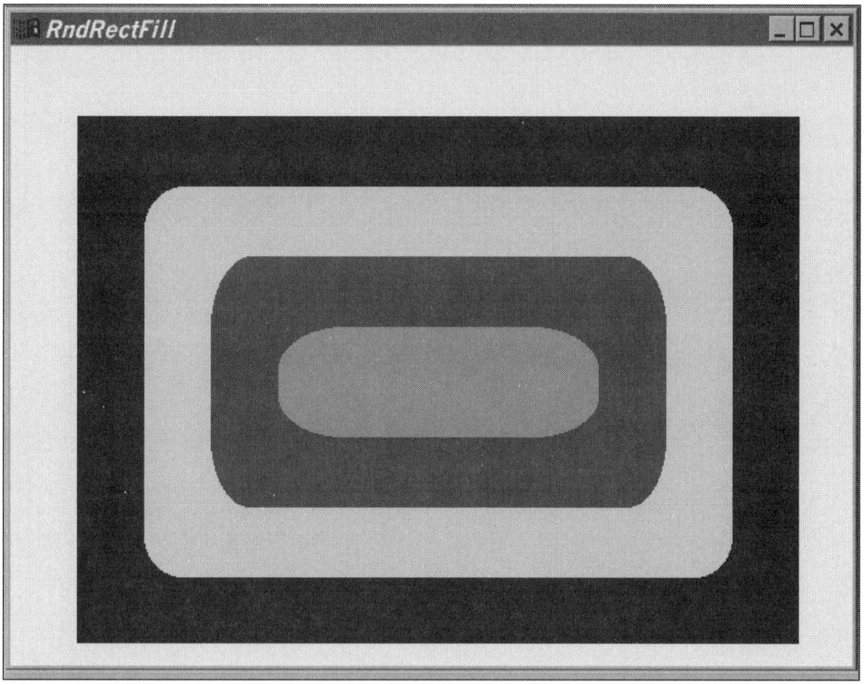

Figure 8.16: The fillRoundRect() member function is used to draw four rounded rectangular shapes to the window.

that are the current color are changed to the current color. Other colors are translated in an unpredictable manner.

translate(int x, int y)

This member function is used to set the origin of the graphics context. Here *x* represents the new x coordinate and *y* the new y coordinate. Once changed, only subsequent graphics are drawn with respect to this new origin.

The following listing illustrates how the origin can be translated to a new screen position with a call to the **translate()** member function.

```
import java.applet.*;
import java.awt.*;
import TransFrame;

public class Trans extends Applet
{
```

```
// STANDALONE APPLICATION SUPPORT:
//   m_fStandAlone will be set to true if applet is run
//   standalone
//--------------------------------------------------------------
boolean m_fStandAlone = false;

public static void main(String args[])
{
  TransFrame frame = new TransFrame("Trans");

  // Must show Frame before we size it so insets() will
  // return valid values
  //------------------------------------------------------------
  frame.show();
  frame.resize(frame.insets().left+frame.insets().right+640,
         frame.insets().top  + frame.insets().bottom + 480);

  Trans applet_Trans = new Trans();

  frame.add("Center", applet_Trans);
  applet_Trans.m_fStandAlone = true;
  applet_Trans.init();
  applet_Trans.start();
}

public Trans()
{
}

public void finalize()
{
}

public String getAppletInfo()
{
  return "Name: Trans\r\n" +
         "Author: Chris H. Pappas and William H. Murray\r\n"+
         "Created with Microsoft Visual J++";
}

public void init()
```

```
  {
    resize(640, 480);
  }

  public void destroy()
  {
  }

  public void paint(Graphics g)
  {
    g.drawOval(50,50,100,250);
    g.translate(369,0);
    g.drawOval(50,50,100,250);
  }

  public void start()
  {
  }

  public void stop()
  {
  }

}
```

The following portion of code is supplied by Visual J++ to support standalone applications, such as this example.

```
import java.awt.*;

class TransFrame extends Frame
{
  public TransFrame(String str)
  {
    super (str);
  }

  public void finalize()
  {
  }

  public boolean handleEvent(Event evt)
  {
```

```
    switch (evt.id)
    {
      case Event.WINDOW_DESTROY:
        dispose();
        System.exit(0);
        return true;

      default:
        return super.handleEvent(evt);
    }
  }
}
```

Figure 8.17 shows two oval shapes.

If you examine the listing, however, both member function calls use the same parameters. Normally, this would mean that one shape would be drawn on top of the other shape. However, between those

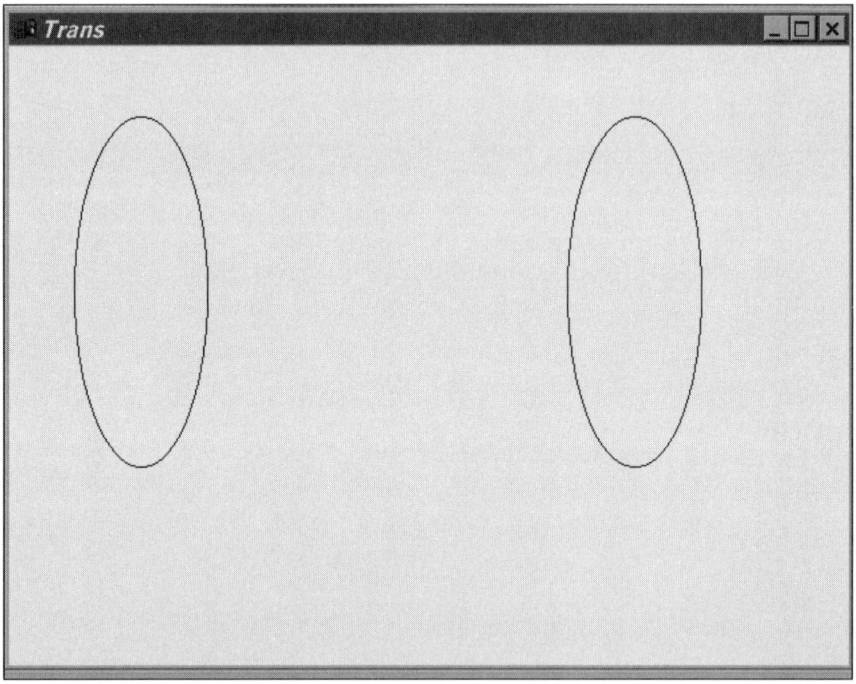

Figure 8.17: The translate() member function is used to move the origin on the current drawing surface.

two function calls was a call to the **translate()** member function, translating the origin to a new position in the window.

Note: The Java ***translate()*** *member function is most closely associated with the Windows* ***SetViewportOrgEx()*** *API function.*

COMING TO TERMS

boolean—A boolean value can either be **true** or **false.** In this chapter, several member functions use boolean values to indicate if a three-dimensional image is or is not raised.

drawing primitives—Drawing primitives are the fundamental drawing shapes, such as lines, rectangles, ovals and so on, used to create graphics images.

origin—The origin is the starting place (0,0) for the graphics coordinate system. With Java, the origin is, by default, in the upper-left corner of the window. The origin can be moved with the **translate()** member function.

Chapter 9

ADDING COLOR CAPABILITIES

Chapter 8 explained how to use the various graphics drawing primitives described in the Java Graphics base class. This chapter lets you continue to experiment with those drawing primitives as you investigate the features of the Java Color base class. This class encapsulates RGB colors in a manner that is similar to the techniques used in Visual C and C++ Windows applications. Java provides a stock palette of thirteen colors but also lets you specify a unique combination of red, green, and blue.

This chapter provides the first steps toward developing more robust applications by creating simple applications involving graphics and colors. These simple applications, along with those introduced in Chapter 10, form the basis for the presentation graphics applications discussed and developed in Chapter 15.

JAVA'S STOCK PALETTE

One popular technique for specifying colors allows red, green, and blue colors (RGB) to be specified as integer values ranging from 0 to 255. Black is specified as (0, 0, 0), while white is specified as (255, 255, 255). Java provides a stock palette of thirteen colors specified in this manner, as shown in Table 9.1.

Table 9.1: Java's Stock Palette of Colors

Color	*Name*	*RGB Mixture*
black	Color.black	(0, 0, 0)
blue	Color.blue	(0, 0, 255)
cyan	Color.cyan	(0, 55, 255)
dark gray	Color.darkGray	(64, 64, 64)
gray	Color.gray	(128, 128, 128)
green	Color.green	(0, 255, 0)
light gray	Color.lightGray	(192, 192, 192)
magenta	Color.magenta	(255, 0, 255)
orange	Color.orange	(255, 200, 0)
pink	Color.pink	(255, 175, 175)
red	Color.red	(255, 0, 0)
white	Color.white	(255, 255, 255)
yellow	Color.yellow	(255, 255, 0)

Note: Visual C and C++ Windows programmers should be familiar with the RGB method of setting colors. It is one of the popular ways Windows pen and brush colors are specified.

Java draws text and lines and does fills with the current brush. To change the current brush to a different color (remember that black is the default color), you can use the **setColor()** member function. For example, to draw a fill oval shape in green, you would use code similar to the following:

```
graphic.setColor(Color.green);
graphic.fillOval(10, 10, 200, 200);
```

To change the drawing or fill color, call the **setColor()** member function once again.

JAVA'S CUSTOM PALETTE OPTIONS

If one of the stock colors does not suit your needs, there are over 16 million color combinations available with this method of specifying color values:

$256 \times 256 \times 256 = 16{,}777{,}216$ possible combinations

The only restriction on creating a large custom palette is, of course, your color adapter and monitor. If your hardware can't match your software specifications, Windows will match the best color it is capable of producing to your specifications. This often results in a dithering effect.

To specify a custom color, a new color object needs to be created. The following portion of code illustrates how you might create a vivid light blue brush.

```
Color lightBlue = new Color(85, 170, 255);
graphic.setColor(lightBlue);
graphic.fillRect(10, 10, 200, 200);
```

Java's Color class is overloaded. In addition to passing color values as integers ranging from 0 to 255, you can pass float values ranging from 0.0 to 1.0. In this manner, the previously created light blue brush could have been specified as:

```
Color lightBlue = new Color(0.333, 0.666, 1.0);
```

The float values are converted internally by the class to integer values by multiplying the float value by 255. Thus:

$0.333 \times 255 = 85$

$0.666 \times 255 = 170$

$1.0 \times 255 = 255$

The resulting values match the original values used to create a light blue color.

MANIPULATING COLORS WITH MEMBER FUNCTIONS

A number of member functions (methods) described in the Color class and other Java classes are intended for manipulating colors. This section examines the member functions of this type that are used most frequently. Several short pieces of programming code are provided to support the discussion.

Using brighter() and darker()

These member functions can be used to quickly increase or decrease the brightness of a specified color. The brightness increases or decreases by a factor of 0.7 when the member function is called. Here is a complete Java application that illustrates the use of both member functions.

```
import java.applet.*;
import java.awt.*;
import BrDkFrame;

public class BrDk extends Applet
{
  // STANDALONE APPLICATION SUPPORT:
  //   m_fStandAlone will be set to true if applet is run
  //   standalone
  //--------------------------------------------------------------
  boolean m_fStandAlone = false;

  public static void main(String args[])
  {
    BrDkFrame frame = new BrDkFrame("BrDk");

    // Must show Frame before we size it so insets() will
    // return valid values
    //------------------------------------------------------------
    frame.show();
    frame.resize(frame.insets().left+frame.insets().right+640,
           frame.insets().top  + frame.insets().bottom + 480);

    BrDk applet_BrDk = new BrDk();

    frame.add("Center", applet_BrDk);
    applet_BrDk.m_fStandAlone = true;
    applet_BrDk.init();
    applet_BrDk.start();
  }

  public BrDk()
  {
  }

  public void finalize()
  {
```

```
}

public String getAppletInfo()
{
  return "Name: BrDk\r\n" +
         "Author: Chris H. Pappas and William H. Murray\r\n"+
         "Created with Microsoft Visual J++";
}

public void init()
{
  resize(640, 480);
}

public void destroy()
{
}

public void paint(Graphics g)
{
  Color mycolor = new Color(0, 0, 178);

  g.setColor(mycolor);
  g.fillOval(0, 0, 100, 100);

  g.setColor(mycolor.brighter());
  g.fillOval(80, 0, 100, 100);

  g.setColor(mycolor.darker());
  g.fillOval(40, 60, 100, 100);
}

public void start()
{
}

public void stop()
{
}
```

```
}
```

The following listing is produced by the J++ Applet Wizard in order to support standalone applications.

```
import java.awt.*;

class BrDkFrame extends Frame
{
  public BrDkFrame(String str)
  {
    super (str);
  }

  public void finalize()
  {
  }

  public boolean handleEvent(Event evt)
  {
    switch (evt.id)
    {
      case Event.WINDOW_DESTROY:
        dispose();
        System.exit(0);
        return true;

      default:
        return super.handleEvent(evt);
    }
  }
}
```

In this example, a blue color object is created and named *mycolor*. An oval shape is filled with this color. Next, the brightness of the color is increased by the use of the **brighter()** member function. Another oval shape is filled with the brighter color. Figure 9.1 illustrates these subtle changes in brightness.

Finally, the process is repeated once again with the use of the **darker()** member function.

Figure 9.1: The brighter() and darker() member functions can make a color brighter or darker.

Using getBackground(), getForeground(), setBackground(), and setForeground()

These member functions can be used to get or change the background and foreground colors of an application. When the **setForeground()** member function is called, all graphics are drawn or filled with the specified foreground color. Likewise, the **setBackground()** member function will change the background color to the specified value. These member functions are described in the Java Component class.

Here is an example that tests the **setForeground()** and **setBackground()** member functions.

```
import java.applet.*;
import java.awt.*;
import ForeBackFrame;
```

```
public class ForeBack extends Applet
{
  // STANDALONE APPLICATION SUPPORT:
  //    m_fStandAlone will be set to true if applet is run
  //    standalone
  //--------------------------------------------------------------
  boolean m_fStandAlone = false;

  public static void main(String args[])
  {
    ForeBackFrame frame = new ForeBackFrame("ForeBack");

    // Must show Frame before we size it so insets() will
    // return valid values
    //------------------------------------------------------------

    frame.setForeground(Color.blue);
    frame.setBackground(Color.white);
    frame.reshape(0, 0, 639, 479);

    frame.show();
    frame.resize(frame.insets().left+frame.insets().right+640,
           frame.insets().top  + frame.insets().bottom + 480);

    ForeBack applet_ForeBack = new ForeBack();

    frame.add("Center", applet_ForeBack);
    applet_ForeBack.m_fStandAlone = true;
    applet_ForeBack.init();
    applet_ForeBack.start();
  }

  public ForeBack()
  {
  }

  public void finalize()
  {
  }
```

```
    public String getAppletInfo()
    {
      return "Name: ForeBack\r\n" +
             "Author: Chris H. Pappas and William H. Murray\r\n"+
             "Created with Microsoft Visual J++";
    }

    public void init()
    {
      resize(640, 480);
    }

    public void destroy()
    {
    }

    public void paint(Graphics g)
    {
      g.drawOval(10, 10, 100, 100);
      g.fillOval(150, 150, 100, 100);
    }

    public void start()
    {
    }

    public void stop()
    {
    }

}
```

The bolded sections in the previous listing represent the code added to the Visual J++ Applet Wizard code.

The following listing is produced by the J++ Applet Wizard in order to support standalone applications.

```
import java.awt.*;

class ForeBackFrame extends Frame
{
```

```
    public ForeBackFrame(String str)
    {
      super (str);
    }

    public void finalize()
    {
    }

    public boolean handleEvent(Event evt)
    {
      switch (evt.id)
      {
        case Event.WINDOW_DESTROY:
          dispose();
          System.exit(0);
          return true;

        default:
          return super.handleEvent(evt);
      }
    }
}
```

Figure 9.2 shows a new background color and two shapes drawn with a new foreground color.

Using getColor() and setColor()

These member functions are the backbone of the Color class. The **getColor()** member function can be used to obtain the current drawing or fill color, while the **setColor()** member function is used to set the current drawing or fill color.

Here is a small portion of code that could be inserted in the **paint()** method. It illustrates the use of the **setColor()** member function.

```
Color lightBlue = new Color(85, 170, 255);
g.setColor(lightBlue);
g.fillOval(10, 10, 200, 200);

g.setColor(Color.yellow);
g.fillRect(300,300, 200, 200);
```

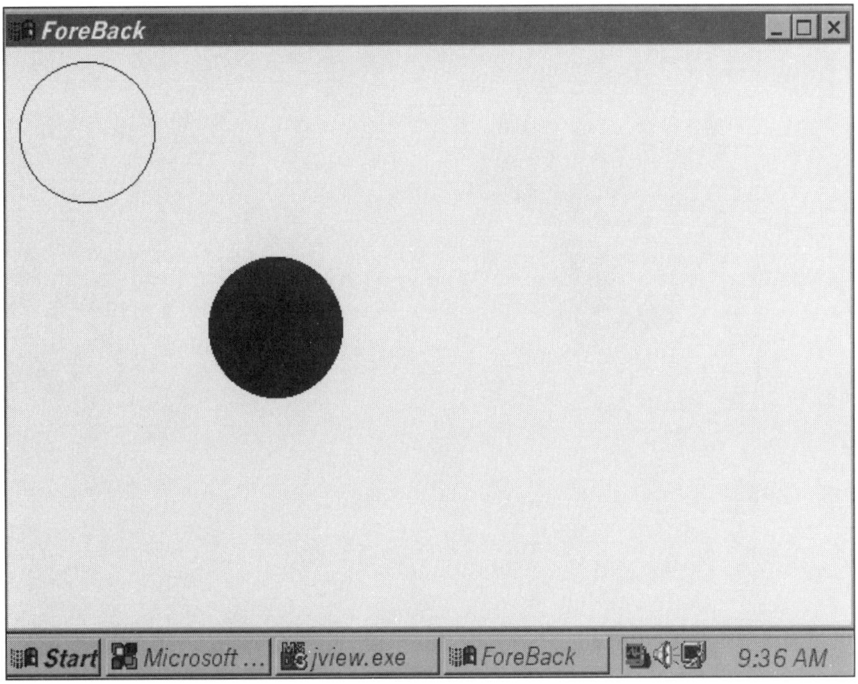

Figure 9.2: setForeground() and setBackground() member functions can be used to make global changes in the drawing/fill colors as well as in the background color of the drawing surface.

In the first portion of this example, the **setColor()** member function is used to fill an oval shape with a new light blue custom color. In the final portion of the example, **setColor()** is again used to fill a rectangular shape with a stock yellow color. Figure 9.3 illustrates the results of this portion of code.

Using getHSBColor()

This member function is used to generate a Color object based on HSB (hue, saturation, and brightness) values. The syntax for this function is:

```
Color getHSBColor(float h, float s, float b);
```

Here *h* represents the hue component, *s* the saturation component, and *b* the brightness component. The following portion of code shows how this member function might be called.

Figure 9.3: The setColor() member function allows the drawing and fill colors to be changed.

```
g.setColor(Color.getHSBColor((float) 0.35, (float) 0.7,
                              (float) 1.0));
g.fillRect(100, 100, 200, 200);
```

The color that is returned, which is used to fill the rectangular shape, is a bright green. Figure 9.4 shows the results of calling the **getHSBColor()** member function.

Using getRed(), getGreen(), getBlue()

These member functions return information, as an integer, on specific RGB values of an identified color. In the following portion of code, a lightBlue color object is defined. The green component of the new color is returned to the *mycolor* variable with a call to the **getGreen()** member function.

```
int mycolor;
Color lightBlue = new Color(66, 127, 255);
```

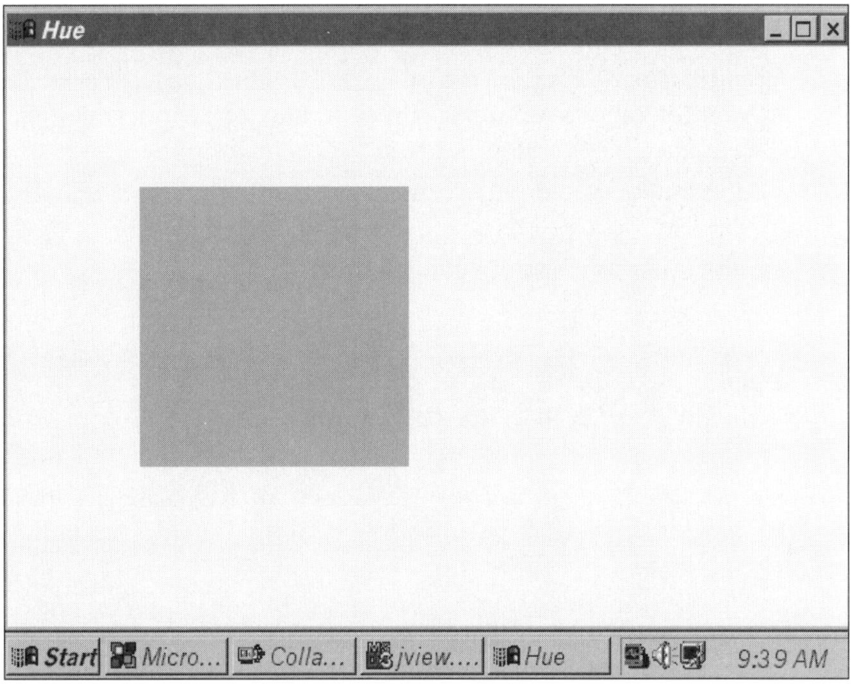

Figure 9.4: The rectangular shape is filled with a color resulting from a call to the getHSBColor() member function.

```
mycolor = lightBlue.getGreen();
g.drawString(String.valueOf(mycolor), 10, 10);
```

In order to draw this value to the graphics area of the window, the integer value is converted to a string and then drawn with the **drawString()** member function.

Using getRGB()

This member function gets the RGB value of the specified color. The returned information is represented in the following manner:

bits 31 – 24	are set to 0 x FF
bits 23 – 16	are the red component
bits 15 – 8	are the green component
bits 7 – 0	are the blue component

The **getRGB()** member function returns an integer value.

Using HSBtoRGB()

This member function returns a RGB value based on the RGB color model for the HSB (hue, saturation, and brightness) values specified. The syntax for the member function is as follows:

```
int HSBtoRGB(float hue, float saturation, float brightness);
```

This member function returns an integer value. Here is a small portion of code to illustrate this member function.

```
int mycolor;
mycolor=(Color.HSBtoRGB((float) 0.7, (float) 0.35, (float) 1.0));
g.setColor(Color.black);
g.drawString(String.valueOf(mycolor), 10, 10);
```

The integer value, because it will be reported as a decimal, will be the complement. In this example, the value is -4741633. If you convert to hexadecimal and use the following scheme, you will be able to extract the RGB values:

bits	31 – 24	are set to 0xFF
bits	23 – 16	are the red component
bits	15 – 8	are the green component
bits	7 – 0	are the blue component

The red component is 0xB7, or 183 decimal. The green component is 0xA5, or 165 decimal. The blue component is 0xFE, or 254 decimal.

Using RGBtoHSB()

This member function returns a HSB (hue, saturation, and brightness) value for the RGB values given. The syntax for the member function is as follows:

```
float[] RGBtoHSB(int r, int g, int b, float[] hsbvals);
```

Here *r*, *g*, and *b* are the integer values for the red, green, and blue values, ranging from 0 to 255 each. The *hsbvals* is an array of type **float** used to return the HSB values.

Using toString()

This member function is used to return the specified color's RGB values as a string of formatted values. In the following portion of code, a new Color object is created. The lightBlue color information is processed by **toString()** and drawn to the window with the help of the **drawString()** member function.

```
Color lightBlue = new Color(66, 127, 255);
g.drawString(lightBlue.toString(), 10, 10);
```

The format for the output will be: r = 66 b = 127 g = 255.

DESIGNING A SIMPLE APPLICATION

The applications presented earlier in this chapter, and the Rainbow application presented in the next section, can be built with the Visual J++ Applet Expert. For a step-by-step approach for developing Java applications with the Microsoft J++ compiler, refer to Chapter 7.

The code for the Rainbow application, which follows, can be entered, compiled, and executed as a standalone application. If you encounter errors during the compile or run process that are not related to a typing error, you have probably forgotten one of the steps detailed in Chapter 7.

THE RAINBOW APPLICATION

The Rainbow application presented in this section is a straightforward graphics application that illustrates the use of Java's graphics and color capabilities. While this example was kept intentionally simple, there are design considerations that should be taken into account before coding begins. Study the code in the following listing.

```
import java.applet.*;
import java.awt.*;
import RainbowFrame;

public class Rainbow extends Applet
{
  // STANDALONE APPLICATION SUPPORT:
```

```
//   m_fStandAlone will be set to true if applet is run
//   standalone
//--------------------------------------------------------------
boolean m_fStandAlone = false;

public static void main(String args[])
{
  RainbowFrame frame = new RainbowFrame("Rainbow");

  // Must show Frame before we size it so insets() will
  // return valid values
  //------------------------------------------------------------
  frame.show();
  frame.resize(frame.insets().left+frame.insets().right+640,
         frame.insets().top  + frame.insets().bottom + 480);

  Rainbow applet_Rainbow = new Rainbow();

  frame.add("Center", applet_Rainbow);
  applet_Rainbow.m_fStandAlone = true;
  applet_Rainbow.init();
  applet_Rainbow.start();
}

public Rainbow()
{
}

public void finalize()
{
}

public String getAppletInfo()
{
  return "Name: Rainbow\r\n" +
         "Author: Chris H. Pappas and William H. Murray\r\n"+
         "Created with Microsoft Visual J++";
}
```

```
    public void init()
    {
      resize(640, 480);
    }

    public void destroy()
    {
    }

    public void paint(Graphics g)
    {
      g.setColor(Color.red);
      g.fillArc(80, 0, 480, 479, 0, 180);

      g.setColor(Color.green);
      g.fillArc(140, 60, 360, 359, 0, 180);

      g.setColor(Color.blue);
      g.fillArc(200, 120, 240, 239, 0, 180);

      g.setColor(Color.yellow);
      g.fillArc(260, 180, 120, 119, 0, 180);
    }

    public void start()
    {
    }

    public void stop()
    {
    }

}
```

The following listing is produced by the J++ Applet Wizard in order to support standalone applications.

```
import java.awt.*;

class RainbowFrame extends Frame
```

```
{
  public RainbowFrame(String str)
  {
    super (str);
  }

  public void finalize()
  {
  }

  public boolean handleEvent(Event evt)
  {
    switch (evt.id)
    {
      case Event.WINDOW_DESTROY:
        dispose();
        System.exit(0);
        return true;

      default:
        return super.handleEvent(evt);
    }
  }
}
```

This application calls the **fillArc()** member function four times, each time changing the fill color with the **setColor()** member function to create a rainbow effect on the screen. By this time, you should have a good understanding of how both of these functions work. The challenge here is how the values for the **fillArc()** function are determined. Remember that the Java coordinate system for graphics starts with the origin in the upper-left corner of the window. Positive increases proceed to the right and downward.

The rainbow image was designed for a VGA screen that measures 640 x 480 pixels. The **fillArc()** function has four parameters. The first two parameters represent the coordinates of the upper-left corner of an imaginary rectangle that bounds the shape. The second two parameters represent the width and height of the bounding rectangle.

To best illustrate how all coordinate values were determined, four separate figures are used. The first figure is for the largest arc. The last figure is for the smallest arc. Examine Figures 9.5–9.8 and make sure you understand how the values used for the **fillArc()** parameters were determined.

If you understand how these values were determined, you are well on your way to creating the more complicated graphics applications presented in future chapters. When you execute this application, the rainbow image will be similar to that shown in Figure 9.9.

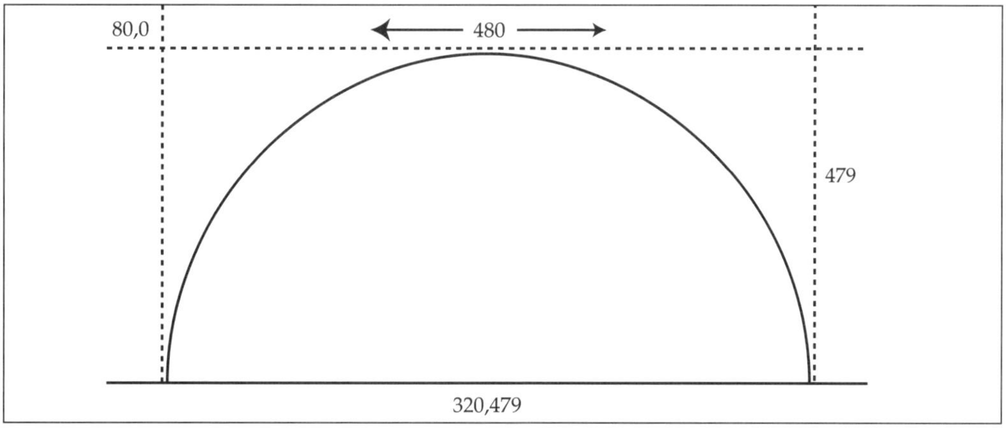

Figure 9.5: The red arc uses these values.

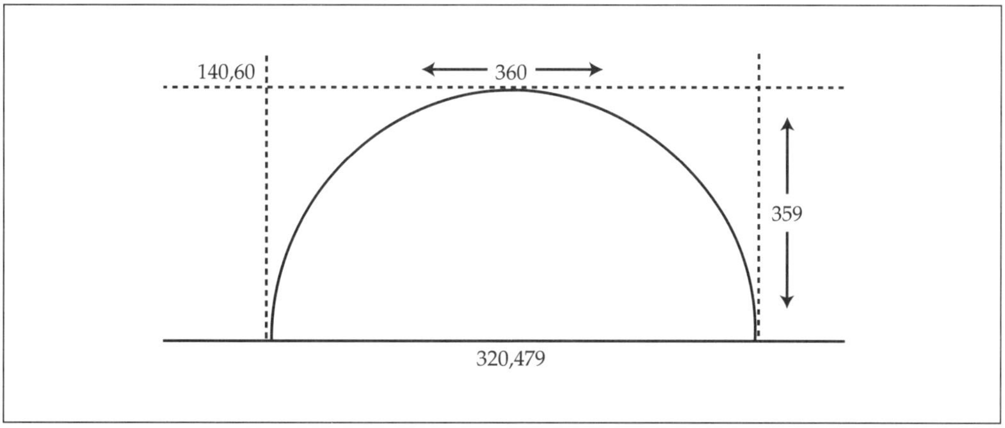

Figure 9.6: The green arc uses these values.

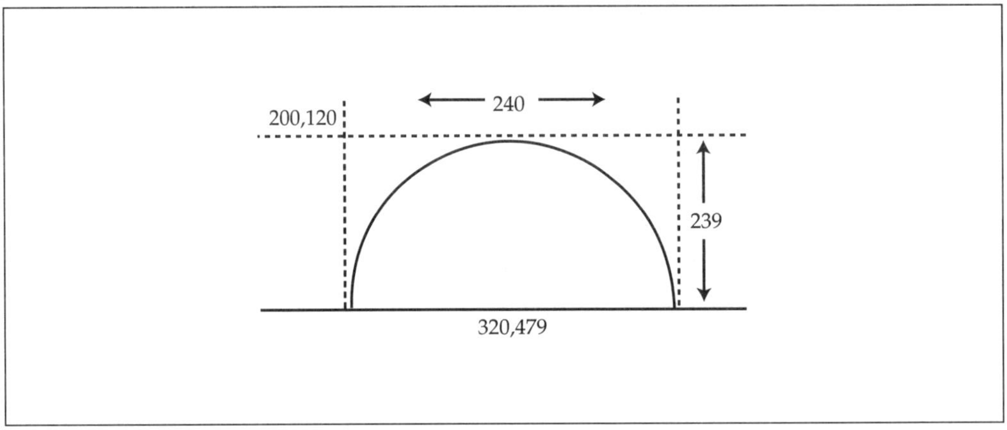

Figure 9.7: The blue arc uses these values.

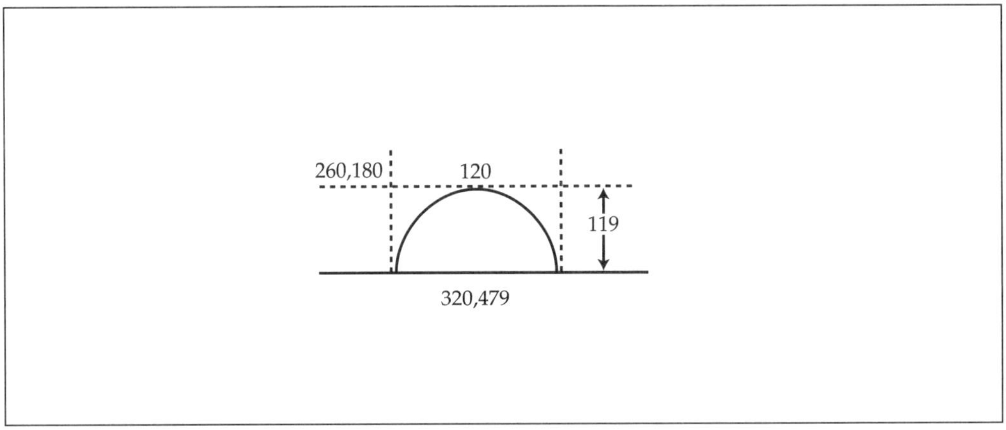

Figure 9.8: The yellow arc uses these values.

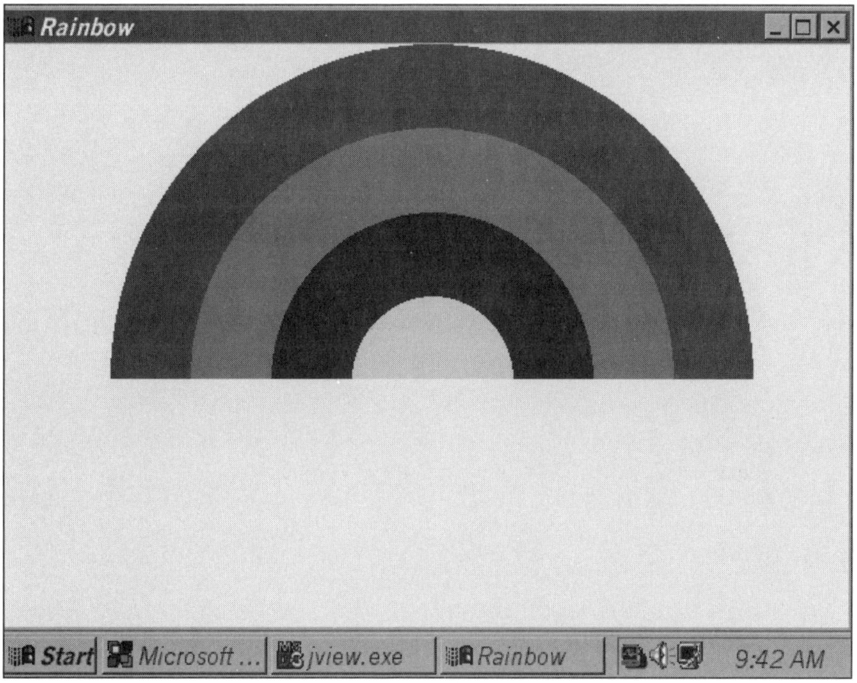

Figure 9.9: The Rainbow application draws this image to a VGA screen.

COMING TO TERMS

Custom palette—Java allows the programmer to define a custom palette of colors by mixing color combinations. Over 16 million colors are possible.

HSB—Stands for hue, saturation, and brightness color qualities. In various Java member functions, these quantities are often specified within the range of 0.0 to 1.0.

RGB—Stands for red, green, and blue color components. In various Java member functions, a green color would be specified as (0, 255, 0) or as (0.0, 1.0, 0.0).

Stock palette—The stock palette for Java contains thirteen predefined colors that can be used to draw and fill graphics objects.

Chapter 10

COMBINING COLOR AND GRAPHICS TOOLS

The previous two chapters experiment with various graphics drawing primitives and color palettes. This chapter shows how to weave many of these concepts into simple yet impressive Java applications and applets. Additional features covered in this chapter are mouse and image control.

The applications are divided into several groups. The bar chart application illustrates how to take an array of integer data points and automatically draw and scale a bar chart. Each bar is filled with a different color. The pie chart application shows how to draw and scale a pie chart with similar data. You can produce a closed pie chart regardless of the pie chart data. For a more refined bar and pie chart application, see Chapter 15.

The sketching application is simple but unique. It demonstrates a simple technique for drawing in the window with your mouse. Push a mouse button to draw, release the mouse button, and move to a new spot on the canvas. To complete this chapter, two image-manipulating applets are developed. The first applet shows how easy it is to incorporate a graphics image with a .jpg or .gif file format. The second applet scales the image to the window. Image manipulations form the basis of our animation examples in Chapter 16.

CREATING A SIMPLE BAR CHART

The bar chart application is a straightforward adaptation of the charting concepts presented in the previous two chapters. Examine the following listing and identify the various graphics primitives that you've already used.

```
import java.applet.*;
import java.awt.*;
import BarChartFrame;

public class BarChart extends Applet
{
  // STANDALONE APPLICATION SUPPORT:
  //   m_fStandAlone will be set to true if applet is run
  //   standalone
  //--------------------------------------------------------------
  boolean m_fStandAlone = false;

  public static void main(String args[])
  {
    BarChartFrame frame = new BarChartFrame("BarChart");

    // Must show Frame before we size it so insets() will
    // return valid values
    //------------------------------------------------------------
    frame.show();
    frame.resize(frame.insets().left+frame.insets().right+640,
           frame.insets().top  + frame.insets().bottom + 480);

    BarChart applet_BarChart = new BarChart();

    frame.add("Center", applet_BarChart);
    applet_BarChart.m_fStandAlone = true;
    applet_BarChart.init();
    applet_BarChart.start();
  }

  public BarChart()
  {
  }
```

```
public void finalize()
{
}

public String getAppletInfo()
{
  return "Name: BarChart\r\n" +
         "Author: Chris H. Pappas and William H. Murray\r\n"+
         "Created with Microsoft Visual J++";
}

public void init()
{
  resize(640, 480);
}

public void destroy()
{
}

public void paint(Graphics g)
{
  int height[] = {100, 250, 225, 80, 90};
  int numBars = 5;                      // number of bars
                                        // (1 to 11 max)

  int newstart = 2;                     // start position
  int width = 400 / numBars;            // width of a bar
  Color barColor[] =    {Color.red,     // bar colors
                         Color.blue,
                         Color.yellow,
                         Color.green,
                         Color.cyan,
                         Color.magenta,
                         Color.orange,
                         Color.pink,
                         Color.gray,
                         Color.darkGray,
```

```
                           Color.black};

    // draw coordinate axes
    g.translate(99, 379);              // move origin
    g.drawLine(0, -329, 0, 0);         // vert. axis
    g.drawLine(0, 0, 429, 0);          // horz. axis

    // draw and fill bars
    for (int i = 0; i < numBars; i++) {
      g.setColor(barColor[i]);         // set fill color
      g.fillRect  (newstart,           // draw a bar
                   -height[i],
                   width,
                   height[i] - 1);
      newstart += 2 + width;           // set new position
    }
  }

  public void start()
  {
  }

  public void stop()
  {
  }

}
```

The following file is generated by the Microsoft Visual J++ compiler for support of standalone applications.

```
import java.awt.*;

class BarChartFrame extends Frame
{
  public BarChartFrame(String str)
  {
    super (str);
  }

  public void finalize()
```

```
    {
    }

    public boolean handleEvent(Event evt)
    {
      switch (evt.id)
      {
        case Event.WINDOW_DESTROY:
          dispose();
          System.exit(0);
          return true;

        default:
          return super.handleEvent(evt);
      }
    }
}
```

This application charts data in the vertical range from 0 to approximately 329. Data points are entered into the *height[]* array. No error checking is provided. These values directly represent the height of each individual bar chart bar. The number of bars is limited to eleven, before the bar chart colors begin to repeat themselves. As the number of bars increases, the width of each individual bar decreases. The bar chart is always the same total width, regardless of the number of bars plotted. The width of each bar is calculated and stored in the variable *width*. Fill colors are selected sequentially from the *barColor[]* array. This array is filled with eleven Java stock palette colors. Naturally, you could extend the array's size by specifying new color combinations with the techniques covered in the previous chapter.

Three lines of code are all that are required to draw an x- and y-axis, as you can see from the following partial listing.

```
// draw coordinate axes
g.translate(99, 379);        // move origin
g.drawLine(0, -329, 0, 0);   // vert. axis
g.drawLine(0, 0, 429, 0);    // horz. axis
```

But, wait! What is **translate()** doing here? The **translate()** member function is used to change the bar chart's origin to 99,379. This means that the lower-left corner of the bar chart is now represented as 0,0!

This spacing provides a margin on the left and bottom edges of the chart.

A **for** loop will help you select color values and plot the individual bars, as you can see in the following portion of code.

```
// draw and fill bars
for (int i = 0; i < numBars; i++) {
  g.setColor(barColor[i]);          // set fill color
  g.fillRect(newstart,              // draw a bar
             -height[i],
             width,
             height[i] - 1);
  newstart += 2 + width;            // set new position
}
```

Color values are selected starting with *barColor[0]* and proceeding to *barColor[numBars-1]*. The **fillRect()** member function draws the filled bar in the proper color. The values for **fillRect()** are obtained sequentially from the *height[]* array. The variable *newstart* is used to represent the starting position of each new bar. You might notice that the new start value is the accumulated width of all previously plotted bars + 2. This allows a small space between each bar. If you don't want the space, just remove the 2 from the equation. The negative sign is used to flip the positive data value. Remember, even though the origin was moved, the positive y direction is still down.

If you enter this application, you should obtain results similar to those displayed in Figure 10.1.

CREATING A SIMPLE PIE CHART

The bar chart in the previous application is a simple chart to create. The pie chart, discussed in this section, adds a few twists to your programming. First, in the bar chart application, the height of one bar is unrelated to the height of another bar. Second, the heights in the data array can easily be mistyped, sending the plotted bar right off of the screen.

In the pie chart example, you always draw a complete pie. Data values are scaled so that they are proportional to each other and always produce a closed pie chart. This is easier to do than you might initially suspect.

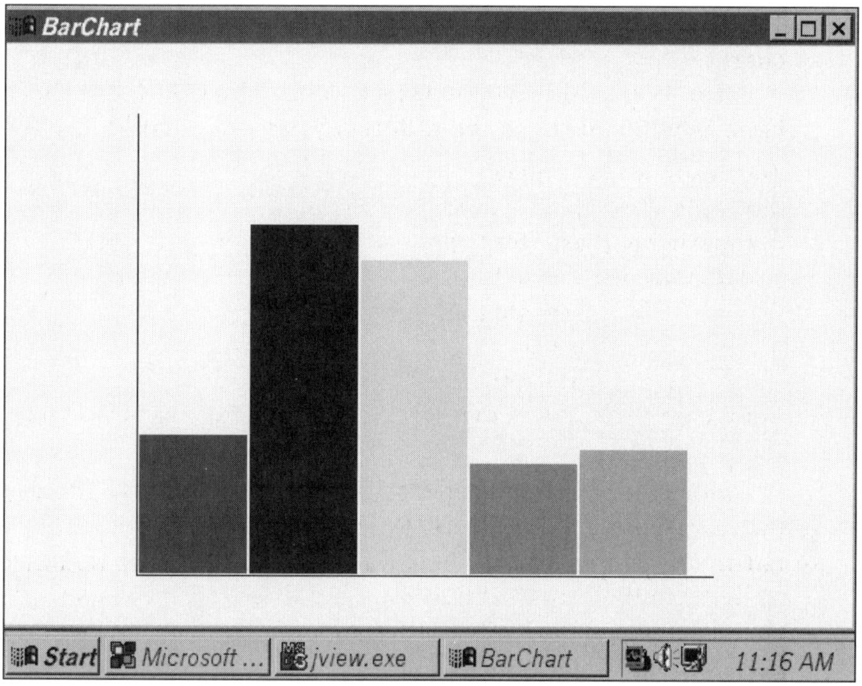

Figure 10.1: A simple bar chart produced by the BarChart application.

Examine the following listing for the pie chart application and note how many lines of code are similar to the bar chart application.

```
import java.applet.*;
import java.awt.*;
import PieChartFrame;

public class PieChart extends Applet
{
  // STANDALONE APPLICATION SUPPORT:
  //   m_fStandAlone will be set to true if applet is run
  //   standalone
  //-----------------------------------------------------------
  boolean m_fStandAlone = false;

  public static void main(String args[])
  {
    PieChartFrame frame = new PieChartFrame("PieChart");
```

```
    // Must show Frame before we size it so insets() will
    // return valid values
    //----------------------------------------------------------
    frame.show();
    frame.resize(frame.insets().left+frame.insets().right+640,
           frame.insets().top  + frame.insets().bottom + 480);

    PieChart applet_PieChart = new PieChart();

    frame.add("Center", applet_PieChart);
    applet_PieChart.m_fStandAlone = true;
    applet_PieChart.init();
    applet_PieChart.start();
  }

  public PieChart()
  {
  }

  public void finalize()
  {
  }

  public String getAppletInfo()
  {
    return "Name: PieChart\r\n" +
           "Author: Chris H. Pappas and William H. Murray\r\n"+
           "Created with Microsoft Visual J++";
  }

  public void init()
  {
    resize(640, 480);
  }

  public void destroy()
  {
  }

  public void paint(Graphics g)
```

```
{
  int wedgeSize[] = {100, 250, 225, 80, 90};
  int numWedges = 5;                      // number of wedges
                                         // (1 to 11 max)
  int wedgeAngle[] = {0, 0, 0, 0, 0};
  int totalWedge = 0;
  int startAngle = 0;
  int sweepAngle = 0;
  Color sliceColor[] =   {Color.red,    // pie colors
                          Color.blue,
                          Color.yellow,
                          Color.green,
                          Color.cyan,
                          Color.magenta,
                          Color.orange,
                          Color.pink,
                          Color.gray,
                          Color.darkGray,
                          Color.black};

  g.translate(170, 90);                  // move origin

  for (int i = 0; i < numWedges; i++)
    totalWedge += wedgeSize[i];

  for (int i = 0; i < numWedges; i++)
    wedgeAngle[i] = (wedgeSize[i] * 363) / totalWedge;

  sweepAngle = wedgeAngle[0];

  // draw and fill pie slices
  for (int i = 0; i < numWedges; ++i) {
    g.setColor(sliceColor[i]);          // set fill color
    g.fillArc(0, 0, 300, 300,
              startAngle, sweepAngle);
    startAngle += wedgeAngle[i];
    sweepAngle = wedgeAngle[i+1];
  }
}
```

```
  public void start()
  {
  }

  public void stop()
  {
  }

}
```

The Microsoft Visual J++ Applet Wizard adds the following file to the project in order to support standalone applications.

```
import java.awt.*;

class PieChartFrame extends Frame
{
  public PieChartFrame(String str)
  {
    super (str);
  }

  public void finalize()
  {
  }

  public boolean handleEvent(Event evt)
  {
    switch (evt.id)
    {
      case Event.WINDOW_DESTROY:
        dispose();
        System.exit(0);
        return true;

      default:
        return super.handleEvent(evt);
    }
  }
}
```

The data array *wedgeSize[]* contains the identical data used in the bar chart. Notice that the array of colors for the pie slices is similar to that for the bar chart's array. Here, *sliceColor[]* contains the same eleven colors from Java's stock palette. The *wedgeAngle[]* array is used to hold angle values for each pie slice's angular sweep.

The game plan is simple. Add up all individual data values in *wedgeSize[]*, obtain a total, and save it in a variable named *totalWedge*. To calculate individual *wedgeAngle[]* values, divide each *wedgeSize[]* value by *totalWedge* and multiply by 363 degrees. (Yes, there are 360 degrees in a complete circle! The code cheats a little, the reason for which will be explained shortly.) The individual values stored in *wedgeSize[]* represent the original data values scaled to fit into a complete circle (pie).

The origin is moved to (170,90) in order to approximately center the pie chart on a VGA screen. The charting begins with the use of a **for** loop, once again.

```
// draw and fill pie slices
for (int i = 0; i < numWedges; ++i) {
  g.setColor(sliceColor[i]);            // set fill color
  g.fillArc(0, 0, 300, 300,
            startAngle, sweepAngle);
  startAngle += wedgeAngle[i];
  sweepAngle = wedgeAngle[i+1];
}
```

As explained in Chapter 8, the first two parameters in the **fillArc()** member function represent the coordinates for the center point of the arc. The values used here are (0,0) because the origin was moved. The next two parameters represent the width and height of the bounding rectangle for this member function. The values are identical in order to produce a round pie chart. The final two parameters are used to specify the start angle for the arc and the number of degrees degrees that are actually transversed. Remember, unlike Windows GDI graphics functions, these values are expressed in degrees.

The variable *startAngle* is initialized to 0. Plotting takes place in the counterclockwise direction. The extent of the sweep, *sweepAngle*, is obtained for the first slice from the first value stored in the *wedgeAngle[]* array. Then notice what happens. *startAngle* is increased by the first *wedgeAngle[]* value, which represents the finishing position for the first pie slice.

The process repeats itself until all slices have been drawn. The last slice touches the first slice, closing the pie shape. Well, not exactly. Here is the problem and the answer to why 363 was used instead of

360 degrees. There is a problem with round-off error in making calculations. You're saving integer values when you make that calculation, but the results are not always integer values. The results are rounded up or down. This round-off error tends to make the pie chart just miss closing if 360 is used in the equation. By using 363, you take the chance of distorting the figure just a bit, but the technique works fine for this simple example. A better technique is used for the professional-quality pie chart in Chapter 15.

If you execute this application, you should see a pie chart similar to that shown in Figure 10.2.

WORKING WITH THE MOUSE

In the next application, we'll use the mouse in a sketching application that will allow you to doodle on the screen. Mouse events are handled

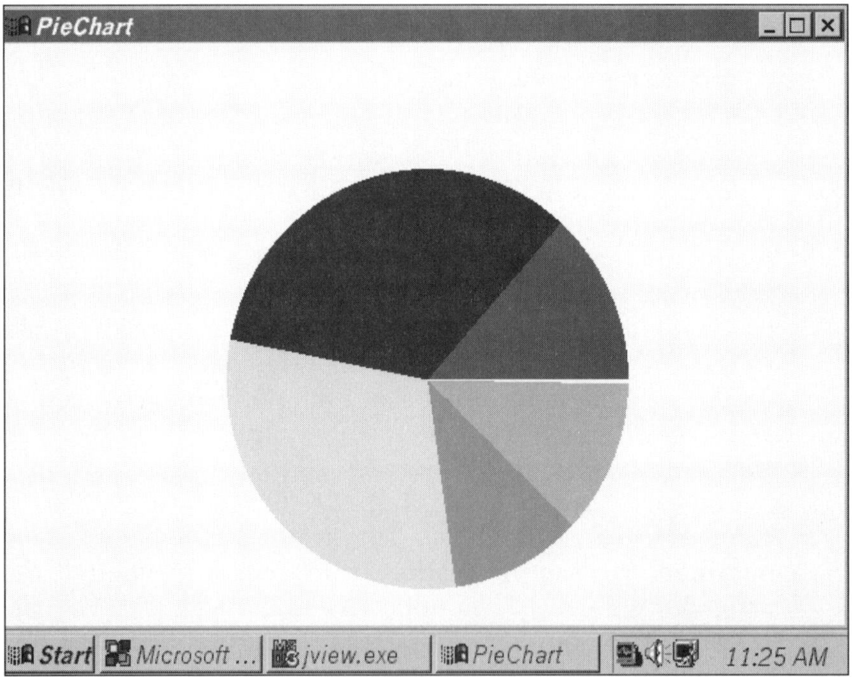

Figure 10.2: The pie chart drawn with the PieChart application.

by a half-dozen methods or member functions. Before continuing, let's look at the syntax for using each of these mouse member functions.

Working with Mouse Events

As you study the member functions in this section, you will notice that all six use similar arguments. The parameter *evt* is an instance of **Event.** The **Event** class provides information on an event's occurrence. This log information tells where and when the event took place. The *x* and *y* parameters provide coordinate information on the mouse's current location.

The **mouseDown()** member function signals a mouse button event when any mouse button is depressed. The syntax is:

```
mouseDown(Event evt, int x, int y);
```

The **mouseDrag()** member function signals an event when the mouse is dragged while a mouse button is depressed. The syntax is:

```
mouseDrag(Event evt, int x, int y);
```

The **mouseEnter()** member function signals an event when the mouse pointer is moved into an application or applet. The syntax is:

```
mouseEnter(Event evt, int x, int y);
```

The **mouseExit()** member function signals an event when the mouse pointer is moved outside of an application or applet. The syntax is:

```
mouseExit(Event evt, int x, int y);
```

The **mouseMove()** member function signals an event when the mouse is moved. The syntax is:

```
mouseMove(Event evt, int x, int y);
```

The **mouseUp()** member function signals an event when a depressed mouse button is released. The syntax is:

```
mouseUp(Event evt, int x, int y)
```

The next section includes a simple application that uses several of these member functions.

Creating an Application Using the Mouse

The Mouse-A-Sketch application is a simple sketching application that lets the user draw in the window with the mouse. The drawing color and window size are set before drawing starts. Examine the following listing and find where the **mouseDown()** and **mouseDrag()** member functions are used.

Remember that when you use the Microsoft Visual J++ Applet Wizard to create this application, you'll need to request mouse support for the **mouseDown()** and **mouseDrag()** methods in step 3 of 5.

```
import java.applet.*;
import java.awt.*;
import SketchFrame;

public class Sketch extends Applet
{
  // STANDALONE APPLICATION SUPPORT:
  //    m_fStandAlone will be set to true if applet is run
  //    standalone
  //------------------------------------------------------------
  boolean m_fStandAlone = false;

  Point newPoint, oldPoint;

  public static void main(String args[])
  {
    SketchFrame frame = new SketchFrame("Sketch");

    // Must show Frame before we size it so insets() will
    // return valid values
    //----------------------------------------------------------
    frame.show();
    frame.resize(frame.insets().left+frame.insets().right+640,
           frame.insets().top  + frame.insets().bottom + 480);

    Sketch applet_Sketch = new Sketch();

    frame.add("Center", applet_Sketch);
    applet_Sketch.m_fStandAlone = true;
    applet_Sketch.init();
    applet_Sketch.start();
  }

  public Sketch()
  {
```

```
    }

    public void finalize()
    {
    }

    public String getAppletInfo()
    {
      return "Name: Sketch\r\n" +
             "Author: Chris H. Pappas and William H. Murray\r\n"+
             "Created with Microsoft Visual J++";
    }

    public void init()
    {
      resize(640, 480);
    }

    public void destroy()
    {
    }

    public void update(Graphics g)
    {
      paint(g);
    }

    public void paint(Graphics g)
    {
      g.setColor(Color.blue);
      g.drawLine(oldPoint.x, oldPoint.y, newPoint.x,
                 newPoint.y);
    }

    public void start()
    {
    }

    public void stop()
    {
```

```
  }

  public boolean mouseDown(Event evt, int x, int y)
  {
    newPoint = new Point(x, y);
    return true;
  }

  public boolean mouseUp(Event evt, int x, int y)
  {
    return true;
  }

  public boolean mouseDrag(Event evt, int x, int y)
  {
    oldPoint = newPoint;
    newPoint = new Point(x, y);
    repaint();
    return true;
  }

  public boolean mouseMove(Event evt, int x, int y)
  {
    return true;
  }

}
```

The Microsoft Visual J++ Applet Wizard adds the following file to the project in order to support standalone applications.

```
import java.awt.*;

class SketchFrame extends Frame
{
  public SketchFrame(String str)
  {
    super (str);
  }

  public void finalize()
  {
  }
```

```
  public boolean handleEvent(Event evt)
  {
    switch (evt.id)
    {
      case Event.WINDOW_DESTROY:
        dispose();
        System.exit(0);
        return true;

      default:
        return super.handleEvent(evt);
    }
  }
}
```

The **mouseDown()** method is used in this application to signal when a mouse button is depressed. This marks the beginning point of a doodle on the screen. This member function is used to return a **Point()** value, the x and y coordinates, to variable *newPoint.*

As the mouse is moved, with a mouse button depressed, new x and y coordinate values must be returned. The **mouseDrag()** method lets you obtain this information. A previously obtained coordinate value, currently held in *newPoint,* is saved in *oldPoint.*

```
oldPoint = newPoint;
```

Now, a new current point is obtained with the following line of code:

```
newPoint = new Point(x, y);
```

Together, *oldPoint* and *newPoint* give you the information needed to draw a line segment. The line segment will be short because the application is continuously checking mouse movement, so even small changes in the mouse's position will generate new values for *oldPoint* and *newPoint.*

Each time a new pair of points is generated, it is necessary to use the **paint()** method to draw the new line segment in the window. This is as simple as calling **repaint()** from within **mouseDrag()**. Now, you can draw the line in any color you choose.

```
g.setColor(Color.blue);
g.drawLine(oldPoint.x, oldPoint.y, newPoint.x,
         newPoint.y);
```

If you stopped here, the results would not be very satisfactory. Each new line segment would request a **repaint()**, which in turn would use the **update()** method to erase and draw on a cleared screen. You would see a series of flashing short line segments as you moved the mouse across the screen. To complete this application, what you need to do is to override the **update()** method so that it does not clear the screen when handling a request for a screen update. For this purpose, you use the following method:

```
public void update(Graphics g)
{
  paint(g);
}
```

Now you can sketch to your heart's content, as you can see in Figure 10.3.

Note: Unlike Windows API functions, which allow the pen width to be set, Java currently allows only a one-pixel width for the pen.

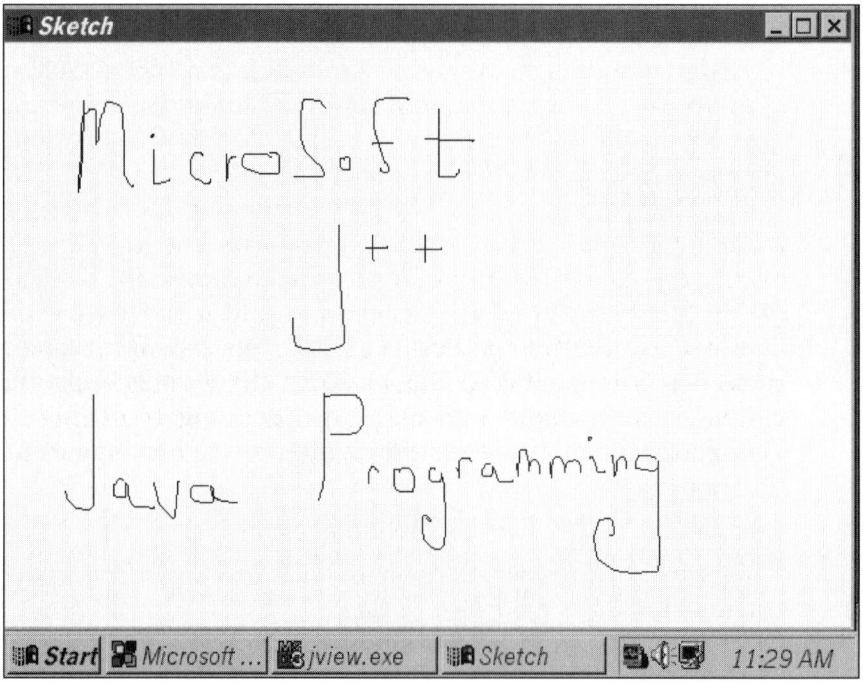

Figure 10.3: Doodling in a window is now possible with the Mouse-A-Sketch sketching application.

Note: Unlike Windows API functions, which allow the user to detect which mouse button triggered an event, Java cannot currently distinguish between mouse buttons.

Chapters 13 and 14 explain how to provide menu and dialog box selections. You might want to return to this application when you are armed with that information and provide the user with a choice of pen colors.

BRINGING IMAGE CAPABILITIES INTO YOUR APPLETS

In Windows, information is often placed in the client area of a window by issuing a series of Windows GDI graphics function calls or moving a bitmapped image from memory to a specific screen area. Java allows the same type of action. Under Windows, the native image format is a bitmapped file with a .bmp file extension. As you know, other types of image formats exist. Currently, Java will allow graphics formats with .jpg and .gif file extensions.

This section looks at two applets, Image1 and Image2, that you can use to experiment with previously saved image files.

Getting Images

In Java, there are basically two key member functions for getting and drawing images. Traditional coding techniques are then applied to manipulate these images. For example, adding animation to a project requires essentially the same code whether you are programming in Windows or Java. This section examines how images are obtained.

Images are obtained through the **getImage()** member function. There are two variations of **getImage()**. Let's look at the syntax for the first one:

```
public abstract Image getImage(URL url);
```

This version returns an image that obtains pixel data from the given Universal Resource Locator (URL).

The syntax for the second variation is:

```
public abstract Image getImage(String filename);
```

The version returns an image that obtains pixel data from the given file. Currently, the file format must be a file saved as a .jpg or .gif file.

The URL is typically an address, such as:

```
"http://www.thelocation.com/image/car.jpg"
```

If a program uses the URL, it might appear in this format:

```
Image output;

output = getImage("http://www.thelocation.com/image/car.jpg");
```

Hard wiring addresses sometimes make an application or applet inflexible. Java provides two methods for obtaining URL information, without the need of a specific string. If **getDocumentBase()** is used, a URL is returned with the directory containing the HTML file, for this applet. If **getCodeBase()** is used, directory information is also returned. In this case, however, the applet and the HTML can be in different directories.

For example, if the image and applet files are located in the same directory as the HTML files, the following syntax can be used:

```
Image output;

output = getImage(getDocumentBase(), "car.jpg");
```

You might want to save images in a subdirectory, separate from your applet and HTML file. This seems to be a standard practice for Java programmers and one used in many Microsoft Visual J++ examples. In this case, you might prefer this method:

```
Image output;

output = getImage(getBaseCode(), "image/car.jpg");
```

If Java cannot load the given file, a **NULL** is returned. You will be looking at a blank screen, with no other error messages, unless your application signals you when this condition occurs.

Drawing Images

Once an image is obtained with **getImage()**, it can be drawn on the screen. There are four variations of the **drawImage()** member function. Here is the syntax for the first variation:

```
public abstract boolean drawImage(Image img, int x, int y,
                                  ImageObserver observer);
```

Here, the image, specified by *img*, is drawn starting at the given *x,y* coordinate location. The *observer* parameter returns information indicating if the image is complete.

The second variation expands the capabilities of the previous member function:

```
public abstract boolean drawImage(Image img, int x, int y,
                                  int width, int height,
                                  ImageObserver observer);
```

This member function lets the image be scaled to fit within the given rectangle. Here *x,y* mark the beginning of the rectangle and *width* and *height* the breadth of the rectangle. All other parameters are similar to the first variation.

Note: The width and height parameters are not the endpoints of the rectangle, as they are when you specify rectangles in Windows. If your application needs endpoints for some reason, they will have to be calculated by algebraically adding the x,y starting point values to the appropriate width or height values.

The remaining two variations are similar to the first two already discussed. These member functions allow a solid background color to be specified during the call to **drawImage()**. Here is the syntax for the third variation:

```
public abstract boolean drawImage(Image img, int x, int y,
                                  Color bgcolor,
                                  ImageObserver observer);
```

Here is the syntax for the fourth variation:

```
public abstract boolean drawImage(Image img, int x, int y,
                                  int width, int height,
                                  Color bgcolor,
                                  ImageObserver observer);
```

All parameters except the *color* parameter are similar to the first two variations. In both of these member functions, *bgcolor* is of type **Color**. Stock or custom colors can be specified.

The following sections show how simple images can be manipulated with two simple applets.

The First Applet Example

The first applet, Image1, loads a small JPEG image of a GG-1 engine to the window. The code is straightforward, as you can see in the following listing.

```
import java.applet.*;
import java.awt.*;
```

```
public class Image1 extends Applet
{

  Image output;

  public Image1()
  {
  }

  public void finalize()
  {
  }

  public String getAppletInfo()
  {
    return "Name: Image1\r\n" +
           "Author: Chris H. Pappas and William H. Murray\r\n"+
           "Created with Microsoft Visual J++";
  }

  public void init()
  {
    resize(640, 480);
    output = getImage(getCodeBase(), "Train.jpg");
  }

  public void destroy()
  {
  }

  public void paint(Graphics g)
  {
    g.drawImage(output, 10, 10, this);
  }

  public void start()
  {
  }

  public void stop()
  {
```

```
    }

}
```

This project has created an applet. The Microsoft Visual J++ Applet Wizard supplies the following HTML file to support the applet.

```
<html>
<head>
<title>Image1</title>
</head>
<body>
<hr>
<applet
    code=Image1.class
    width=640
    height=480 >
</applet>
<hr>
<a href="Image1.java">The source.</a>
</body>
</html>
```

The image is drawn, starting at a coordinate position of (10,10) in the window. The size of the initial applet screen is controlled by the HTML file.

The version of the **drawImage()** member function that is used here draws the portion of the image that fits within the window. In this case, the window is large enough to accommodate the whole image of the train, as you can see in Figure 10.4.

Note: The GG-1 was an electric engine used by the Pennsylvania Railroad. It saw peak service in the 1940s, pulling passenger trains from Washington, D.C., to New York City.

The Second Applet Example

The second applet, Image2, loads a .gif image to the window. This applet used the second variation of the **drawImage()** member function. The code is similar to the previous listing.

```
import java.applet.*;

import java.awt.*;
```

Figure 10.4: The mighty GG-1 thunders out of the clouds in this Java applet.

```
public class Image2 extends Applet
{

  Image output;

  public Image2()
  {
  }

  public void finalize()
  {
  }

  public String getAppletInfo()
  {
    return "Name: Image2\r\n" +
```

```
            "Author: Chris H. Pappas and William H. Murray\r\n"+
            "Created with Microsoft Visual J++";
    }

    public void init()
    {
      resize(640, 480);
      output = getImage(getCodeBase(), "Object.gif");
    }

    public void destroy()
    {
    }

    public void paint(Graphics g)
    {
      int objwidth = output.getWidth(this);
      int objheight = output.getHeight(this);
      g.drawImage(output, 0, 0, objwidth,
                  objheight, this);
    }

    public void start()
    {
    }

    public void stop()
    {
    }

}
```

The trick used here stretches or shrinks the image to fit the window. The width and height of the image are obtained with **getWidth()** and **getHeight()**. They are then used as the *width* and *height* parameters in the **drawImage()** member function.

The image is drawn, starting at a coordinate position of (0,0) in the window. Again, an HTML file is used to support the applet.

```
<html>
<head>
<title>Image2</title>
```

```
</head>
<body>
<hr>
<applet
    code=Image2.class
    width=640
    height=480 >
</applet>
<hr>
<a href="Image2.java">The source.</a>
</body>
</html>
```

Run this applet, and you'll see a screen similar to that shown in Figure 10.5.

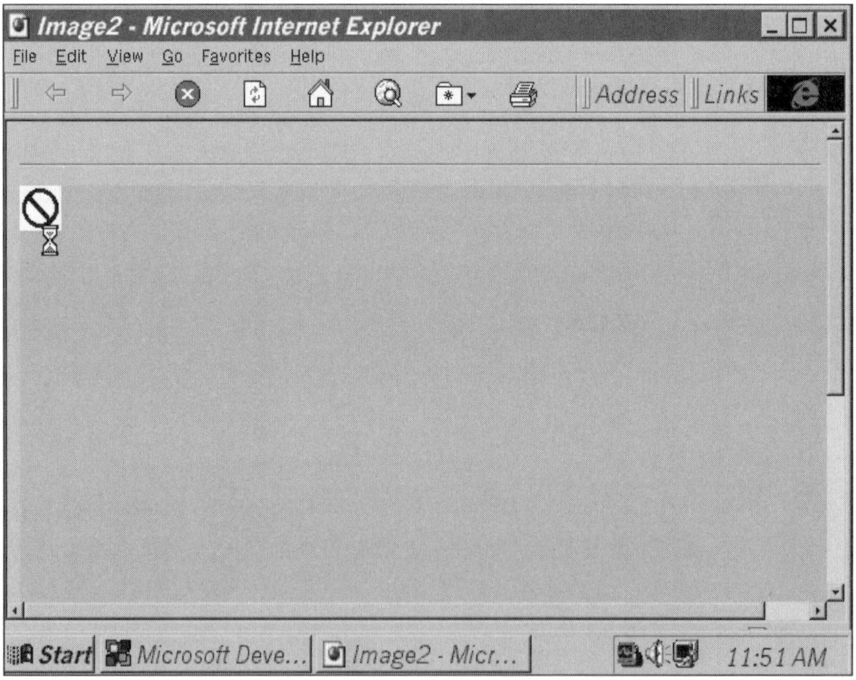

Figure 10.5: A reminder screen is borrowed for this Java applet.

COMING TO TERMS

AWT—Abstract Windowing Toolkit forms the pathway for communicating events to you or the applet. Mouse events use the AWT.

GUI—The Graphics User Interface forms the basis of communications between graphics elements and the user. Both Windows and Java have a collection of GUI functions and member functions.

images—A wide variety of image formats are available. For example, bitmap (.bmp) and JPEG images are very popular. Java currently supports JPEG and GIF image formats. These have .jpg and .gif file extensions.

UI—The user interface forms the basis of communications between programming elements and the user. Mouse and keyboard events might be considered UI components.

URL—The Universal Resource Locator helps identify the path to files.

Chapter 11

ADDING SOUND RESOURCES

You can add sound to your applets through Java's **play()** and **getAudioClip()** methods. The only restriction is that the files must be Sun's formatted audio clips. These are sound clips that end with an .au file extension.

You can download a large variety of audio samples from the World Wide Web. To find samples, use the YAHOO search engine and search for two words: **sound au.** You'll find everything from simple sound effects to complete speeches and music scores.

This chapter investigates three simple applets and shows how they make use of Java's sound capabilities. You'll find that adding sound capabilities is a very simple process.

METHODS USED FOR SOUND

There are two important methods for adding sound to applets. The first member function or method is **getAudioClip()**. This function is available in two versions:

```
AudioClip getAudioClip(URL url);
```

Here the URL (Universal Resource Locator) locates and loads the audio clip:

```
AudioClip getAudioClip(URL url, String name);
```

In this version, the URL functions as it did in the first version. However, it is now possible to use a string to specify a pathname and filename. These two formats should look familiar. These formats are identical to the formats used to locate and obtain images, used in the previous chapter.

The **getDocumentBase()** or **getCodeBase()** member functions can be used to obtain the URL information, as they were in the previous chapter. Typically, sound information is obtained with code similar to that in the following sequence:

```
AudioClip soundclip;
      .
      .
      .
soundclip = getAudioClip(getCodeBase(), "audio/testclip.au");
```

Here the sound clip is loaded into an instance of the AudioClip class, *soundclip*. The file, testclip.au, is located in the audio subdirectory located off of the parent directory that contains the applet. If the sound clip isn't located, a **NULL** is returned. The application will operate; you just won't hear any sound.

Once the sound clip is obtained, it can be played, stopped, and repeated. To play the sound clip, the **play()** method is used.

If you are using the previous sequence of code to locate the sound clip, the **play()** method can be called without passing any parameters:

```
soundclip.play();
```

If the sound clip is long and you want to stop playing it at any time, the **stop()** method can be used. Again, no parameters are needed:

```
soundclip.stop();
```

Likewise, a sound clip can be played repeatedly with the use of the **loop()** method:

```
soundclip.loop();
```

The remainder of this chapter investigates the use of these member functions in three simple applets. Adding sound gives your Java applets a new dimension—a dimension that adds a professional touch to your work.

PLAYING A SOUND CLIP

The following applet, Sound1, illustrates just how easy it is to add sound to an applet. The Microsoft Visual J++ compiler generated the basic code. The additional lines required to add a sound clip to the applet are bolded.

```
import java.applet.*;
import java.awt.*;
import java.applet.AudioClip;

public class Sound1 extends Applet
{

  AudioClip soundclip;

  public Sound1()
  {
  }

  public void finalize()
  {
  }

  public String getAppletInfo()
  {
    return "Name: Sound1\r\n" +
           "Author: Chris H. Pappas and William H. Murray\r\n"+
           "Created with Microsoft Visual J++";
  }

  public void init()
  {
    resize(640, 480);
    soundclip = getAudioClip(getCodeBase(),
                             "audio/testclip.au");
  }

  public void destroy()
```

```
  {
  }

  public void paint(Graphics g)
  {
    g.drawString("Listen to the sound clip...",
                 20, 20);
    soundclip.play();
  }

  public void start()
  {
  }

  public void stop()
  {
  }

}
```

Execute this example as an applet. The following HTML file was generated by Microsoft's Visual J++ compiler, too.

```
<html>
<head>
<title>Sound1</title>
</head>
<body>
<hr>
<applet
    code=Sound1.class
    width=640
    height=480 >
</applet>
<hr>
<a href="Sound1.java">The source.</a>
</body>
</html>
```

This is really a very simple applet. Start the applet and hear the sound. If you're using the applet and sound resource from the optional diskette, you might be surprised when you hear the audio clip. Give it a try!

STARTING AND STOPPING SOUNDS

The previous applet was rather limited. It played a sound clip when the applet was started, but that was it. You can expand the sound capabilities of an applet by adding some techniques covered in the previous chapter.

In the following applet, a sound clip is played any time a mouse button is depressed. The sound clip continues to play until the mouse button is released. Want to hear the sound clip again? Just depress the mouse button to start the sound clip at the beginning. The code that relates directly to producing sound in the following applet is bolded.

```
import java.applet.*;
import java.awt.*;
import java.applet.AudioClip;

public class MouseSnd extends Applet
{

  AudioClip mouseclip;

  public MouseSnd()
  {
  }

  public void finalize()
  {
  }

  public String getAppletInfo()
  {
    return "Name: MouseSnd\r\n" +
           "Author: Chris H. Pappas and William H. Murray\r\n"+
           "Created with Microsoft Visual J++";
  }

  public void init()
  {
    resize(640, 480);
    mouseclip = getAudioClip(getCodeBase(),
                                      "audio/mouseclip.au");
```

```
    }

    public void destroy()
    {
    }

    public void paint(Graphics g)
    {
      g.drawString("Click button to play...", 20, 20);
      g.drawString("Release to stop play...", 20, 40);
    }

    public void start()
    {
    }

    public void stop()
    {
    }

    public boolean mouseDown(Event evt, int x, int y)
    {
      mouseclip.play();
      return true;
    }

    public boolean mouseUp(Event evt, int x, int y)
    {
      mouseclip.stop();
      return true;
    }

}
```

That's all there is to it. Microsoft's Visual J++ compiler created the following HTML file for this applet.

```
<html>
<head>
<title>MouseSnd</title>
</head>
<body>
```

```
<hr>
<applet
    code=MouseSnd.class
    width=640
    height=480 >
</applet>
<hr>
<a href="MouseSnd.java">The source.</a>
</body>
</html>
```

This applet illustrates how the user can control sound resources with just the click of a mouse button. The final example uses the mouse once again and expands your control of sound resources even more.

A SKETCHING APPLET WITH SOUND PROMPTS

The previous chapter created a sketching application that allows the user to doodle in the window. Lines are drawn when a mouse button is depressed.

In the following applet, the sketching application has been modified to include audio prompts. One audio prompt sounds when the mouse button is depressed, signaling the user that drawing is about to commence. Another audio prompt sounds when the mouse button is released, signaling the user that that line segment is complete. Only the code relating to the sound resource is highlighted in the following listing.

```
import java.applet.*;
import java.awt.*;
import java.applet.AudioClip;

public class SketSnd extends Applet
{

  AudioClip sketclip1;
  AudioClip sketclip2;
  Point newPoint, oldPoint;

  public SketSnd()
  {
```

```
}

public void finalize()
{
}

public String getAppletInfo()
{
  return "Name: SketSnd\r\n" +
         "Author: Chris H. Pappas and William H. Murray\r\n"+
         "Created with Microsoft Visual J++";
}

public void init()
{
  resize(640, 480);
  sketclip1 = getAudioClip(getCodeBase(),
                          "audio/sndclip1.au");
  sketclip2 = getAudioClip(getCodeBase(),
                          "audio/sndclip2.au");
}

public void destroy()
{
}

public void update(Graphics graphic)
{
  paint(graphic);
}

public void paint(Graphics g)
{
  g.setColor(Color.blue);
  g.drawLine(oldPoint.x, oldPoint.y,
             newPoint.x, newPoint.y);
}

public void start()
{
```

```
    }

    public void stop()
    {
    }

    public boolean mouseDown(Event evt, int x, int y)
    {
      newPoint = new Point(x, y);
      sketclip1.play();

      return true;
    }

    public boolean mouseUp(Event evt, int x, int y)
    {
      sketclip2.play();
      return true;
    }

    public boolean mouseDrag(Event event, int x, int y)
    {
      oldPoint = newPoint;
      newPoint = new Point(x, y);
      repaint();
      return true;
    }

}
```

Now the sketching application is complete with audio prompts. Here is the default HTML file created by the Microsoft Visual J++ compiler for this applet.

```
<html>
<head>
<title>SketSnd</title>
</head>
<body>
<hr>
<applet
    code=SketSnd.class
```

```
    width=640
    height=480 >
</applet>
<hr>
<a href="SketSnd.java">The source.</a>
</body>
</html>
```

As you have learned, sound resources are easy to add to your applets. As you develop more involved applets, keep in mind that too much of a good thing can be boring. Use sound resources wisely.

COMING TO TERMS

AU—Sun's audio format for sound resources. Literally thousands of these sound resource files can be found on the World Wide Web.

Chapter 12

ADDING FONT RESOURCES

A variety of different fonts can greatly enhance text in your applications and applets. Fonts have properties. These properties include the ability to size characters and to turn bold and italic characteristics on or off. Strings can then be drawn to the screen with the new fonts in any color you desire. Color selections are discussed in Chapter 9.

If you program in C or C++ for Windows, you will find that Java doesn't have quite as much flexibility as the Windows GDI functions allow. For example, Java currently does not provide control over a font's orientation or escapement—the rotation of strings or characters. The ability to manipulate orientation or escapement is great for printing vertical axis labels in charts and graphs. Also missing is the ability to use Windows TrueType fonts. Java currently provides a rather limited collection of fonts.

With all of that aside, there are a great number of things you can do with font resources to enhance your Java projects. This chapter examines a number of these features, and font resources will be used throughout the remaining chapters of the book.

FONT METHODS

This section focuses on the member functions (methods) described in Java's Font class. References are also made, however, to the Java Toolkit and FontMetrics classes. Member functions from these two classes are explained as they are used. Table 12.1 shows an abbreviated list of the member functions that appear in the Font class.

The Font class lets you create font objects. These objects are specified by a name, style, and point size. Font names currently available to Java include Helvetica, Dialog, TimesRoman, Symbol, and Courier. As mentioned earlier, you do not have access to Windows TrueType fonts. Font styles include PLAIN, BOLD, and ITALIC. A bold italic font can be created, too, by logically oring the BOLD and ITALIC styles together. Point size is a number. An 8-point font is very small, and a 12-point font is very common for applications and applets. A 72-point

Table 12.1: Font Class Methods

Method	*Return Type*	*Parameters*	*Description*
Font()	Font	String name, int style, int size	Creates a new font
getFamily()	String		Gets platform family name of font
getName()	String		Gets logical name of font
getStyle()	int		Gets the style of the font
getSize()	int		Gets the size of the font
isPlain()	boolean		true when font is plain
isBold()	boolean		true when font is bold
isItalic()	boolean		true when font is italic
getFont()	static	string nm or String nm, Font font	Gets a font from the system properties list
hashcode()	int		Returns a hash code for the font
equals()	boolean	Object obj	Compares this object to given object; true when both are the same
toString()	String		Converts object to a string

font is very large. An application that might use a very large font would be a count-down timer that would show only a few digits on the whole screen.

Creating a new font is easy. Only the following sequence of code is required:

```
Font newfont;
    .
    .
    .
newfont = new Font("Courier", Font.PLAIN, 12);
graphic.setFont(newfont);
    .
    .
    .
```

As you can see, a 12-point plain Courier font will be requested. Java will supply the font that is closest to your specifications. If a 12-point font isn't available, the closest point size is provided.

Note: Remember that while it is possible to manipulate many of Java's font characteristics, you cannot directly rotate characters or strings in Java as you can in Windows. If you need to print a vertical label, for example, you will have to parse a string of characters, printing them one at a time in a vertical column.

GETTING A LIST OF FONTS

Many projects, including graphics applications such as the bar and pie chart applications in Chapter 10, require a variety of fonts. If you do not know which fonts are available on your system, the **getFontList()** member function can be used to obtain the information. The **getFontList()** member function is described in the Toolkit class.

The syntax for this member function is:

```
String[] getFontList();
```

When calling **getFontList()**, you should use the following sequence of code:

```
import java.awt.Toolkit
    .
    .
    .
```

```
Toolkit tk;
    .
    .
    .
tk = getToolkit();
mystring = tk.getFontList();
```

Other than that, the use of the member function is quite simple. In the following application, created with the Microsoft Visual J++ compiler, those lines of code are bolded.

```
import java.applet.*;
import java.awt.*;
import Font1Frame;

public class Font1 extends Applet
{
  // STANDALONE APPLICATION SUPPORT:
  //    m_fStandAlone will be set to true if applet is run
  //    standalone
  //--------------------------------------------------------------
  boolean m_fStandAlone = false;
  Toolkit tk;
  String[] mystring;

  public static void main(String args[])
  {
    Font1Frame frame = new Font1Frame("Font1");

    // Must show Frame before we size it so insets() will
    // return valid values
    //-----------------------------------------------------------
    frame.show();
    frame.resize(frame.insets().left+frame.insets().right+640,
           frame.insets().top  + frame.insets().bottom + 480);

    Font1 applet_Font1 = new Font1();

    frame.add("Center", applet_Font1);
    applet_Font1.m_fStandAlone = true;
    applet_Font1.init();
    applet_Font1.start();
```

```
}

public Font1()
{
}

public void finalize()
{
}

public String getAppletInfo()
{
  return "Name: Font1\r\n" +
         "Author: Chris H. Pappas and William H. Murray\r\n"+
         "Created with Microsoft Visual J++";
}

public void init()
{
  resize(640, 480);

}

public void destroy()
{
}

public void paint(Graphics g)
{
  tk = getToolkit();
  mystring = tk.getFontList();

  for (int i = 0; i < 10; i++) {
    g.drawString(mystring[i], 0, 30 * (i + 1));
  }
}

public void start()
{
}
```

```
  public void stop()
  {
  }

}
```

The following listing, generated by the Microsoft Visual J++ compiler, provides support for standalone applications.

```
import java.awt.*;

class Font1Frame extends Frame
{
  public Font1Frame(String str)
  {
    super (str);
  }

  public void finalize()
  {
  }

  public boolean handleEvent(Event evt)
  {
    switch (evt.id)
    {
      case Event.WINDOW_DESTROY:
        dispose();
        System.exit(0);
        return true;

      default:
        return super.handleEvent(evt);
    }
  }
}
```

For our installation, the **getFontList()** member function returns a font list that includes Courier, Dialog, Helvetica, TimesRoman, and Symbol fonts. Figure 12.1 shows the output sent to the screen.

Figure 12.1: The getFontList( ) member function returns a list of available fonts.

FONT SIZES

Many projects require different size fonts from the same font family. For example, a project might need a 28-point Courier font for a title and a 12-point font for labels. Font size is a property that is very easy to alter.

In the following application, a string is drawn several times in the window as the point size is increased. As you study the listing, notice that the font's point size is set with the use of the **Font()** member function. This member function, described earlier in this chapter, is part of Java's Font class.

```
import java.applet.*;
import java.awt.*;
import Font2Frame;
```

```
public class Font2 extends Applet
{
  // STANDALONE APPLICATION SUPPORT:
  //   m_fStandAlone will be set to true if applet is run
  //   standalone
  //--------------------------------------------------------------
  boolean m_fStandAlone = false;
  Font newfont;

  public static void main(String args[])
  {
    Font2Frame frame = new Font2Frame("Font2");

    // Must show Frame before we size it so insets() will
    // return valid values
    //------------------------------------------------------------
    frame.show();
    frame.resize(frame.insets().left+frame.insets().right+640,
           frame.insets().top  + frame.insets().bottom + 480);

    Font2 applet_Font2 = new Font2();

    frame.add("Center", applet_Font2);
    applet_Font2.m_fStandAlone = true;
    applet_Font2.init();
    applet_Font2.start();
  }

  public Font2()
  {
  }

  public void finalize()
  {
  }

  public String getAppletInfo()
  {
    return "Name: Font2\r\n" +
           "Author: Chris H. Pappas and William H. Murray\r\n"+
```

```
            "Created with Microsoft Visual J++";
  }

  public void init()
  {
    resize(640, 480);
  }

  public void destroy()
  {
  }

  public void paint(Graphics g)
  {
    // A Courier font is sized
    for (int i = 1; i < 11; i++) {
    newfont = new Font("Courier", Font.PLAIN, (i * 5));
    g.setFont(newfont);
    g.drawString("Sizing a Courier font",
                 0, 10 + (i * 40));
    }
  }

  public void start()
  {
  }

  public void stop()
  {
  }

}
```

The following listing, generated by the Microsoft Visual J++ compiler, provides support for standalone applications.

```
import java.awt.*;

class Font2Frame extends Frame
{
  public Font2Frame(String str)
  {
```

```
    super (str);
  }

  public void finalize()
  {
  }

  public boolean handleEvent(Event evt)
  {
    switch (evt.id)
    {
      case Event.WINDOW_DESTROY:
        dispose();
        System.exit(0);
        return true;

      default:
        return super.handleEvent(evt);
    }
  }
}
```

The **Font()** member function is included in a loop. Each pass through the loop requests a larger font. The size varies from 5 points to 50 points. Figure 12.2 illustrates these various font sizes.

When a font size is requested, the closest match to the requested size will be returned. For example, if you request a 14-point and 15-point font size, it is possible that only a 14-point size is available. If that is the case, both requests will be filled with a 14-point font size.

Note: Windows programmers often make use of a very scaleable font type called a TrueType font. TrueType fonts are not available for Java programmers at this time.

FONT PROPERTIES

Font families are often made up of plain, bold, italic, and bold-italic components. These terms, along with point size, are considered font properties. In the following example you'll see how font properties can be changed. Font properties were described earlier in this chapter.

Study the following listing and find the properties PLAIN, ITALIC, BOLD, and ITALIC + BOLD.

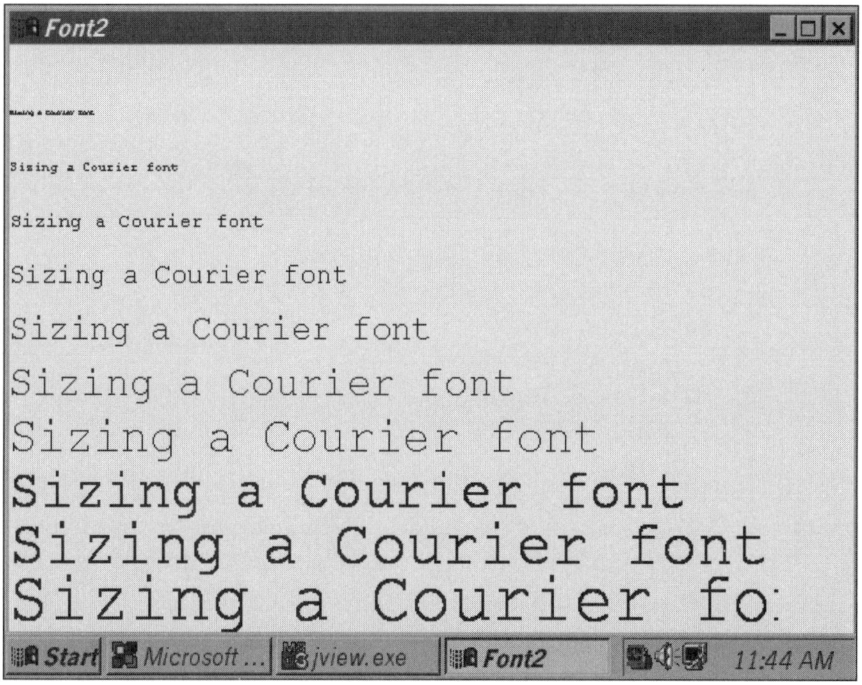

Figure 12.2: Using the Font() member function to experiment with font sizes.

```
import java.applet.*;
import java.awt.*;
import Font3Frame;

public class Font3 extends Applet
{
  // STANDALONE APPLICATION SUPPORT:
  //    m_fStandAlone will be set to true if applet is run
  //    standalone
  //--------------------------------------------------------------
  boolean m_fStandAlone = false;
  Font newfont;

  public static void main(String args[])
  {
    Font3Frame frame = new Font3Frame("Font3");

    // Must show Frame before we size it so insets() will
    // return valid values
```

```
  //---------------------------------------------------------------
  frame.show();
  frame.resize(frame.insets().left+frame.insets().right+640,
         frame.insets().top  + frame.insets().bottom + 480);

  Font3 applet_Font3 = new Font3();

  frame.add("Center", applet_Font3);
  applet_Font3.m_fStandAlone = true;
  applet_Font3.init();
  applet_Font3.start();
}

public Font3()
{
}

public void finalize()
{
}

public String getAppletInfo()
{
  return "Name: Font3\r\n" +
         "Author: Chris H. Pappas and William H. Murray\r\n"+
         "Created with Microsoft Visual J++";
}

public void init()
{
  resize(640, 480);

}

public void destroy()
{
}

public void paint(Graphics g)
{
```

```
        // Helvetica Font Properties
        newfont = new Font("Helvetica", Font.PLAIN, 30);
        g.setFont(newfont);
        g.drawString("Helvetica 30pt", 0, 50);

        newfont = new Font("Helvetica", Font.ITALIC, 30);
        g.setFont(newfont);
        g.drawString("Helvetica 30pt italic", 0, 150);

        newfont = new Font("Helvetica", Font.BOLD, 30);
        g.setFont(newfont);
        g.drawString("Helvetica 30pt BOLD", 0, 250);

        newfont = new Font("Helvetica",
                           Font.ITALIC + Font.BOLD, 30);
        g.setFont(newfont);
        g.drawString("Helvetica 30pt BOLD italic",
                     0, 350);
      }

      public void start()
      {
      }

      public void stop()
      {
      }

    }
```

The following listing, generated by the Microsoft Visual J++ compiler, provides support for standalone applications.

```
import java.awt.*;

class Font3Frame extends Frame
{
  public Font3Frame(String str)
  {
    super (str);
  }
```

```
  public void finalize()
  {
  }

  public boolean handleEvent(Event evt)
  {
    switch (evt.id)
    {
      case Event.WINDOW_DESTROY:
        dispose();
        System.exit(0);
        return true;

      default:
        return super.handleEvent(evt);
    }
  }
}
```

This application makes continued use of the **Font()** member function described earlier in this chapter. All of the strings are printed with a 30-point Helvetica font. As you can see from Figure 12.3, the application sequences from plain to italic plus bold.

USING FONTMETRICS()

The FontMetrics class provides a number of member functions (methods) for obtaining detailed information about a font family. Table 12.2 lists the individual member functions for this class.

The font information returned by these various methods can be obtained individually, or in a string format by using the **toString()** member function. The **toString()** member function is overridden in FontMetrics to provide this information.

The following application illustrates the use of the **toString()** member function to obtain information about a bold italic Helvetica 14-point font. If you are not prepared to parse the string of information, set your screen parameters so that you can display a large number of horizontal characters.

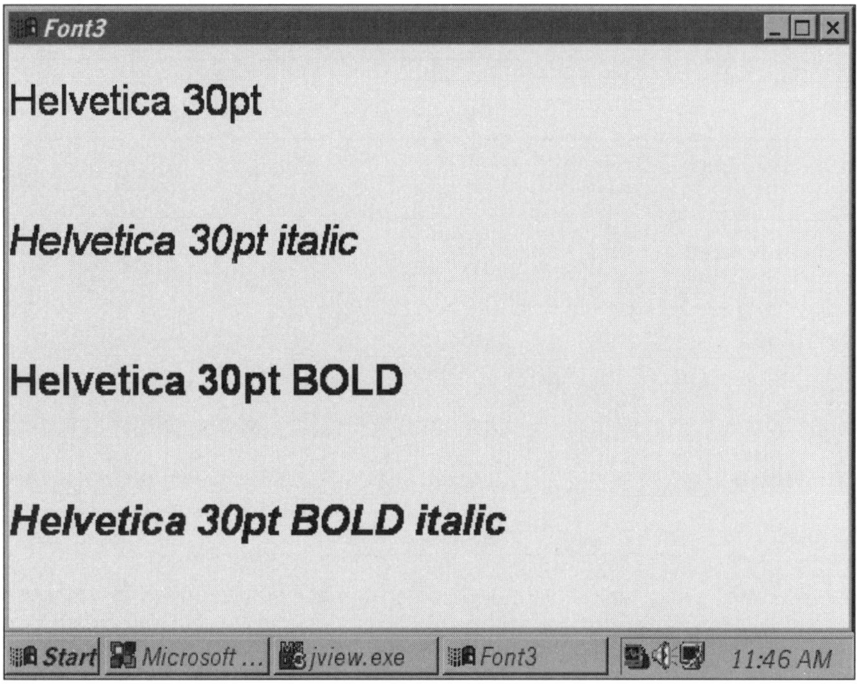

Figure 12.3: Font properties such as PLAIN, ITALIC, and BOLD can be used to create fonts for every purpose.

Table 12.2: Font Metrics Class Methods

Method	*Return Type*	*Parameters*	*Description*
getFont()	Font		Obtains the current font
getLeading()	int		Obtains leading or line space
getAscent()	int		Obtains ascent distance from font's baseline to top of character
getDescent()	int		Obtains descent distance from font's baseline to bottom of character
getHeight()	int		Obtains ascent + descent + leading
getMaxAscent()	int		Obtains the maximum ascent in the font

Continued

Table 12.2: Font Metrics Class Methods *Continued*

Method	*Return Type*	*Parameters*	*Description*
getMaxDescent()	int		Obtains the maximum descent in the font
getMaxAdvance()	int		Obtains maximum advance width in the font
charWidth()	int	int ch or char ch	Obtains the width of the given character
stringWidth()	int	String str	Obtains the width of the given string
charsWidth()	int	char data[], int off, int len	Obtains the width of the given character array
bytesWidth()	int	byte data[], int off, int len	Obtains width of given array of bytes
getWidths()	int[]		Obtains widths for first 256 characters
toString()	String		FontMetric values for font returned as string

```
import java.applet.*;
import java.awt.*;
import Font4Frame;

public class Font4 extends Applet
{
  // STANDALONE APPLICATION SUPPORT:
  //    m_fStandAlone will be set to true if applet is run
  //    standalone
  //-------------------------------------------------------------
  boolean m_fStandAlone = false;
  Font newfont;
  FontMetrics fm;

  public static void main(String args[])
```

```
{
  Font4Frame frame = new Font4Frame("Font4");

  // Must show Frame before we size it so insets() will
  // return valid values
  //----------------------------------------------------------
  frame.show();
  frame.resize(frame.insets().left+frame.insets().right+640,
         frame.insets().top  + frame.insets().bottom + 480);

  Font4 applet_Font4 = new Font4();

  frame.add("Center", applet_Font4);
  applet_Font4.m_fStandAlone = true;
  applet_Font4.init();
  applet_Font4.start();
}

public Font4()
{
}

public void finalize()
{
}

public String getAppletInfo()
{
  return "Name: Font4\r\n" +
         "Author: Chris H. Pappas and William H. Murray\r\n"+
         "Created with Microsoft Visual J++";
}

public void init()
{
  resize(640, 480);
}

public void destroy()
{
}
```

```
  public void paint(Graphics g)
  {
    String mystring;

    newfont = new Font("Helvetica",
                       Font.ITALIC + Font.BOLD, 14);
    g.setFont(newfont);

    fm = g.getFontMetrics();
    mystring = fm.toString();
    g.drawString(mystring, 0, 300);
  }

  public void start()
  {
  }

  public void stop()
  {
  }

}
```

The following listing, generated by the Microsoft Visual J++ compiler, provides support for standalone applications.

```
import java.awt.*;

class Font4Frame extends Frame
{
  public Font4Frame(String str)
  {
    super (str);
  }

  public void finalize()
  {
  }

  public boolean handleEvent(Event evt)
  {
    switch (evt.id)
```

```
        {
          case Event.WINDOW_DESTROY:
            dispose();
            System.exit(0);
            return true;

          default:
            return super.handleEvent(evt);
        }
      }
    }
```

You can see that the use of the function is very straightforward. FontMetric information is very useful when you are designing applications that, for example, center strings of characters in a line.

Figure 12.4 shows the results of the information returned in this application.

A CHART WITH LABELS

In Chapter 10, a bar chart application was developed. This application illustrated several concepts used in making a chart application, but it did not have any labels! This section explains how to put font information to a practical use.

The following listing is a modified version of the bar chart application presented in Chapter 10. The bolded lines represent the portions of code added to allow a title, vertical and horizontal axis labels, and the creation of a legend. You might want to compare this code with the bar chart application in Chapter 10.

```
import java.applet.*;
import java.awt.*;
import Font5Frame;

public class Font5 extends Applet
{
  // STANDALONE APPLICATION SUPPORT:
  //   m_fStandAlone will be set to true if applet is run
  //   standalone
  //-------------------------------
  boolean m_fStandAlone = false;
```

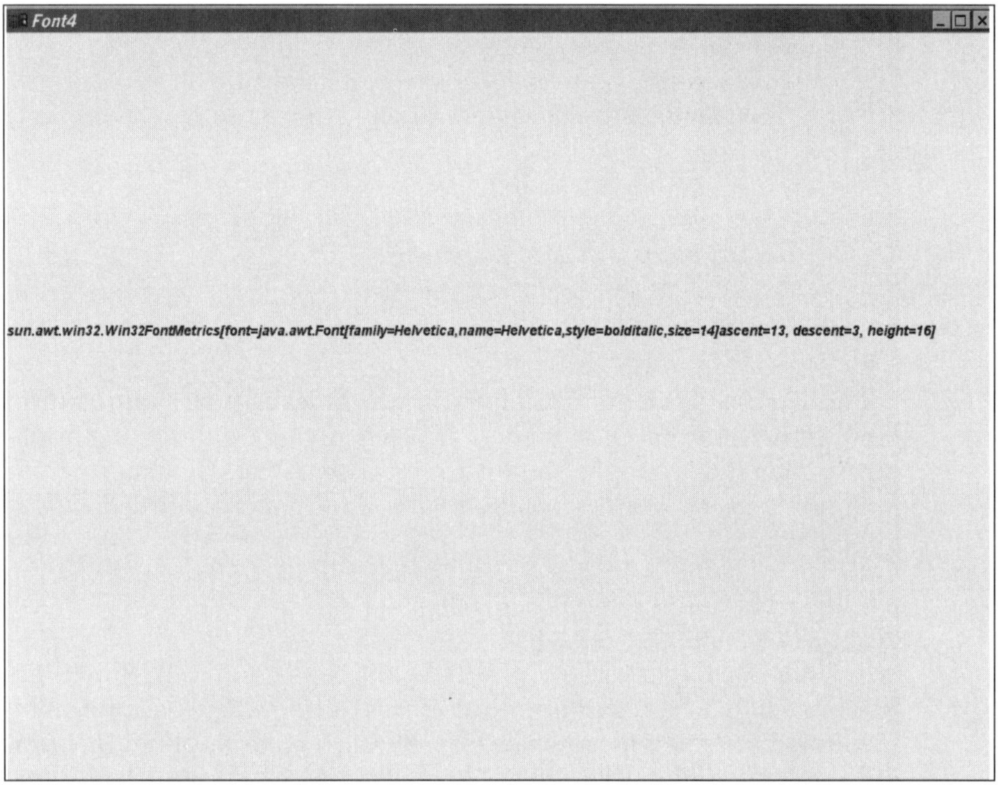

Figure 12.4: FontMetric information can be returned by member functions in the FontMetrics class.

```
Font titlefont, labelfont, legendfont;
FontMetrics fm;

public static void main(String args[])
{
  Font5Frame frame = new Font5Frame("Font5");

  // Must show Frame before we size it so insets() will
  // return valid values
```

```
    //-----------------------------------------------------------
    frame.show();
    frame.resize(frame.insets().left+frame.insets().right+640,
           frame.insets().top  + frame.insets().bottom + 480);

    Font5 applet_Font5 = new Font5();

    frame.add("Center", applet_Font5);
    applet_Font5.m_fStandAlone = true;
    applet_Font5.init();
    applet_Font5.start();
  }

  public Font5()
  {
  }

  public void finalize()
  {
  }

  public String getAppletInfo()
  {
    return "Name: Font5\r\n" +
           "Author: Chris H. Pappas and William H. Murray\r\n" +
           "Created with Microsoft Visual J++";
  }

  public void init()
  {
    resize(640, 480);
  }

  public void destroy()
  {
  }

  public void paint(Graphics g)
```

```
{
  int height[] = {300, 50, 225, 180, 75};
  int numBars = 5;                        // number of bars
                                           // (1 to 11 max)
  String charttitle = "Profit Margin"; // title
  String vertlabel =  "$$$";            // vertical label
  String horzlabel =  "Months";         // horizontal label
  String[] legend = { "January",        // legend labels
                      "February",
                      "March",
                      "April",
                      "May",
                      "June",
                      "July",
                      "August",
                      "September",
                      "October",
                      "November",
                      "December" };

  int newstart = 2;                      // start position
  int width = 300 / numBars;             // width of a bar
  Color barColor[] = {Color.red,         // bar colors
                     Color.blue,
                     Color.yellow,
                     Color.green,
                     Color.cyan,
                     Color.magenta,
                     Color.orange,
                     Color.pink,
                     Color.gray,
                     Color.darkGray,
                     Color.black};

  // create fonts
  titlefont = new Font("TimesRoman", Font.BOLD, 36);
  labelfont = new Font("TimesRoman", Font.PLAIN, 14);
  legendfont = new Font("TimesRoman", Font.ITALIC, 10);
```

```
// draw coordinate axes
g.translate(99, 379);              // move origin
g.drawLine(0, -329, 0, 0);         // vert. axis
g.drawLine(0, 0, 329, 0);          // horz. axis

// draw and center chart title
g.setFont(titlefont);
fm = getFontMetrics(titlefont);
g.drawString(charttitle,
             165 - (fm.stringWidth(charttitle)/2),
             -340);

// draw vertical label and center horizontal label
g.setFont(labelfont);
fm = getFontMetrics(labelfont);
g.drawString(vertlabel,
             -10 - fm.stringWidth(vertlabel),
             -150);
g.drawString(horzlabel,
             165 - (fm.stringWidth(horzlabel)/2),
             40);

// draw and fill bars
for (int i = 0; i < numBars; i++) {
  g.setColor(barColor[i]);         // set fill color
  g.fillRect(newstart,             // draw a bar
             -height[i],
             width,
             height[i] - 1);
  newstart += 2 + width;           // set new position
}

// draw, fill and label chart legend
g.setFont(legendfont);
for (int i = 0; i < numBars; i++) {
  g.setColor(barColor[i]);         // set fill color
  g.fillRect(360, -300 + (i * 30), 15, 15);

  // first bar will be for March
```

```
        g.setColor(Color.black);          // set font color
        g.drawString(legend[i + 2], 380,
                      -290 + (i * 30));
      }
    }

    public void start()
    {
    }

    public void stop()
    {
    }

}
```

The following listing, generated by the Microsoft Visual J++ compiler, provides support for standalone applications.

```
import java.awt.*;

class Font5Frame extends Frame
{
  public Font5Frame(String str)
  {
    super (str);
  }

  public void finalize()
  {
  }

  public boolean handleEvent(Event evt)
  {
    switch (evt.id)
    {
      case Event.WINDOW_DESTROY:
        dispose();
        System.exit(0);
        return true;
```

```
        default:
          return super.handleEvent(evt);
      }
    }
  }
```

Examine the second portion of bolded code in the first file of the previous listing. The chart label, axis labels, and legend labels are included in this portion of code. For this application, each bar value represents data on a particular month. The months can be accessed sequentially, as is done in this application, or one at a time.

Next, three TimesRoman fonts are created with the following portion of code.

```
// create fonts
titlefont = new Font("TimesRoman", Font.BOLD, 36);
labelfont = new Font("TimesRoman", Font.PLAIN, 14);
legendfont = new Font("TimesRoman", Font.ITALIC, 10);
```

The chart title and axis labels are drawn next. For example, the title can be drawn and centered in the window with the following portion of code.

```
// draw and center chart title
g.setFont(titlefont);
fm = getFontMetrics(titlefont);
g.drawString(charttitle,
             165 - (fm.stringWidth(charttitle)/2),
             -340);
```

The value 165 represents the center of the bar chart proper. To center a line of text, the application needs to move to the left of this center by one-half the width of the string being used for the chart title. Ah, FontMetrics to the rescue. Here the **stringWidth()** member function is used to obtain information on the width of the string. This process must be used because proportional fonts, such as TimesRoman, will not produce equal string widths for strings made up of various characters. This is because, for example, an "i" in TimesRoman is not as wide as a "w".

A good bar chart application will let you identify individual bar values. Here the developer has a choice. The bar value can be drawn within the bar proper, under the bar, above the bar, or in a legend. The first option is not a good choice because the bar value can be very small, not allowing for the bar value to be drawn correctly. If drawn under the bar, the label can interfere with the horizontal axis label or, if it is long enough, run into a neighboring label. Drawing above the bar presents its own set of programming problems as the bar heights vary up and down. The best choice is to draw a legend to the right of the bar chart itself. The user can identify which legend label goes with a bar because a small rectangle of the proper bar's color is drawn in the legend table, too.

Here is the portion of code that creates the legend for this application.

```
// draw, fill and label chart legend
g.setFont(legendfont);
for (int i = 0; i < numBars; i++) {
  g.setColor(barColor[i]);                    // set fill color
  g.fillRect(360, -300 + (i * 30), 15, 15);

  // first bar will be for March
  g.setColor(Color.black);                    // set font color
  g.drawString(legend[i + 2], 380,
               -290 + (i * 30));
}
```

As you can see, there is no secret to creating a legend. The rectangle is drawn in the proper color and the legend label is drawn to its right. A new location is selected, and the next group is drawn.

Examine Figure 12.5, however, and see what a legend adds to the value of a bar chart application.

COMING TO TERMS

fixed—A fixed font, like Courier, means that all characters occupy the same cell width. An "i" takes up just as much space as a "w". The earliest versions of Windows used fixed fonts.

font name—A font name refers to the name associated with the font. Currently, Helvetica, Dialog, TimesRoman, Symbol, and Courier are available with the resources provided by Microsoft.

point size—Font size is measured in points. A 12-point font is very common. The larger the point size is, the larger the font.

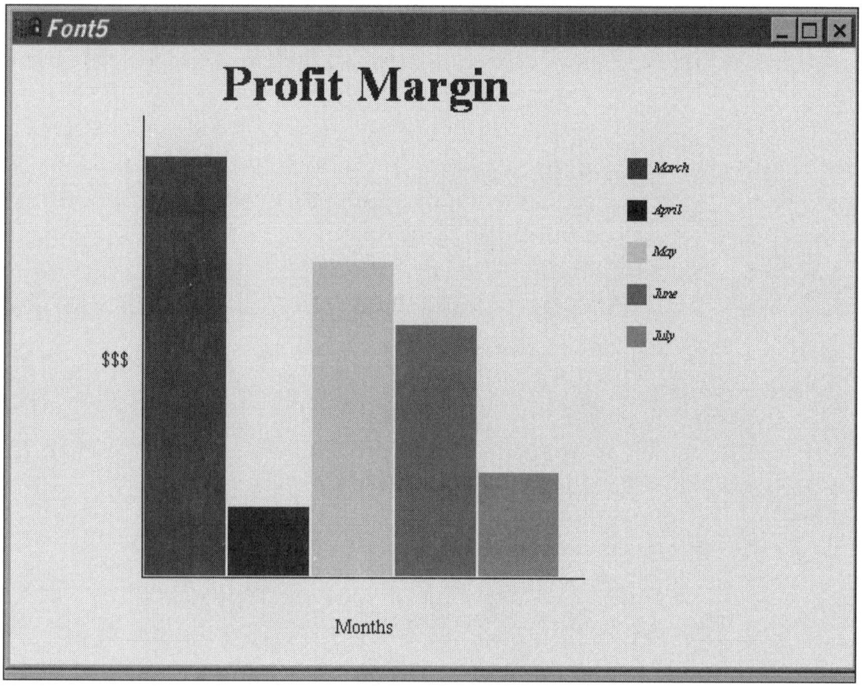

Figure 12.5: Adding a title, axis labels, and labels to a bar chart application.

proportional—A proportional font, like Helvetica or TimesRoman, provides a proportional amount of space for each character. Thus, an "i" requires less horizontal width than a "w". Windows now uses proportional fonts.

style—Font style refers to whether the font is normal, bold, italic, or a combination of the three.

Chapter 13

THE ABSTRACT WINDOW TOOLKIT AND MENU RESOURCES

The Microsoft Windows Graphical User Interface (GUI) provides a consistent appearance to all Windows applications. You are familiar with the design of standard Windows 95 and Windows NT windows, which include a title bar, client area, borders, and various system buttons. These windows can also include a menu bar, scroll bars, and a variety of different window styles. Users have come to depend on the familiar Windows GUI.

There are two basic methods of creating these components that are available to the Microsoft Visual J++ developer. One method involves the use of the Abstract Window Toolkit (AWT) available to all Java programmers. The second method lets you use the resource toolkit provided with the Microsoft C++ and J++ compilers. This resource toolkit, working in conjunction with the AWT, makes the addition of controls almost effortless.

The AWT gives Java programmers the ability to create applets and applications within a graphical user interface that provides programming components similar to those provided to Microsoft Windows programmers. A Java programmer can create canvases, panels, frames, menus, and even objects that look like standard Windows dialog boxes. Additionally, controls such as scrollbars, check boxes, radiobuttons, and text fields can be used in any Java project. The addition of controls, using the raw AWT, however, is often time consuming and difficult.

If you use the Microsoft resource toolkit to develop menus and dialog boxes for Windows projects, you know how easy it is to add resources to your projects. Microsoft lets you use the same toolkit to develop resources for Java. The only difference is that the final resource file must be converted to one acceptable by Java. This task is achieved from the **Tools** menu in the J++ compiler. If you select the **Java Resource Wizard** command, the conversion process is almost automatic. The Wizard will convert a compiled resource file (.res file extension) to a Java resource file (*Java* file extension). There are some limitations that will be mentioned in the next chapter.

This chapter covers many aspects of the AWT including how to use it to control the Java environment and then build applets and applications with various layout features and menus to demonstrate AWT features. In addition, the chapter covers how to create a simple menu with the Microsoft resource toolkit, convert it with the Java Resource Wizard, and incorporate the code into your Java project.

Chapter 14 explains how to use the AWT and the resource toolkit to produce dialog boxes with a variety of controls.

AWT: FROM THE BEGINNING

You have been working with various pieces of the AWT since the beginning of this book. Have you noticed that the following line of code is added to each applet or application you developed with the Microsoft J++ compiler?

```
import java.awt.*;
```

This line of code allowed you to access all of the classes provided in the AWT package. These classes hold all of the graphical functions and procedures you need when you are working in the GUI. For example, you have already used the Color.class, Font.class, Frame.class, Graphics.class, and Image.class in earlier programming examples. If you were certain that your applet or application only needed access to a few specific classes, code size could be reduced by using statements such as the following:

```
import java.awt.Font;
import java.awt.Graphics;
```

You can examine the contents of these classes by looking at files such as Font.java and Graphics.java. If you performed a default installation of your Microsoft J++ compiler, these files can probably be found at:

```
c:\msdev\classes\java\awt
```

These ASCII files can be examined with almost any editor. For example, if you want to examine the contents of the Font class, you would bring the *font.java* file into the editor.

WHY NOW?

You might very well be asking the question, "If we've already done so much work with the AWT, why are the details of the AWT that are related to a windowing environment now being discussed"? That's a good question that has a fairly simple answer. The Microsoft J++ Java Applet Wizard creates a default applet or application that is simple enough to let you experiment with many Java components. All GUI environments provide font, graphics functions, text capabilities, and so on. By keeping the AWT overhead as simple as possible, the Microsoft J++ Java Applet Wizard lets you focus on those aspects of the Java language.

Now, as you begin to approach the task of creating interactive Java applets and applications, more horsepower will be required from the AWT.

WHAT IS SEEN AND USED IN JAVA

The Microsoft J++ Java Applet Wizard has provided a launching ground for each applet or application developed in this book. This has helped keep each project consistent in appearance and, hopefully, made your task of learning the Java language that much simpler. If you have built your applets and applications with the techniques suggested throughout this book, much of your Java code can be used as either an applet or a standalone Java application.

Standalone Java applications require the creation of a frame. A frame is required if the application is to draw text or graphics on the screen. The Microsoft J++ Java Applet Wizard provides frame template code in a separate file. Here is an example of this code.

```
import java.awt.*;

class MuDm2Frame extends Frame
{
```

```
    public MuDm2Frame(String str)
   {
     super (str);
   }

   public boolean handleEvent(Event evt)
   {
     switch (evt.id)
     {
       case Event.WINDOW_DESTROY:
         dispose();
         System.exit(0);
         return true;

       default:
         return super.handleEvent(evt);
     }
   }
}
```

The previous code is not required if you are building just an applet. With applets, an applet viewer provides the default drawing surface and is specified in the HTML file. This file can also be generated by the Microsoft J++ Java Applet Wizard. Thus, if the parameters in the **reshape()** member function are changed in a frame, they will only affect standalone Java applications. If you want to achieve the same results with an applet, you will have to change the values provided in the HTML file.

The following discussion explains Java concepts that will allow you to gain more control over the environment in which you are working. Once you have mastered these concepts, you will be able to build applications and applets that can take on the appearance of a regular Microsoft Windows program, if you desire, and give your project true interactive capabilities.

Component Class

The Component class is an abstract class that encapsulates all of the components of the visual interface. On a smaller scale, this Java class is nearly the equivalent of the Microsoft Foundation Class (MFC) library for C++ Windows programmers. All other classes for the visual interface are derived from the abstract Component class.

```
Hierarchy:

Abstract Component Class -
```

Note: The term component *is used frequently in Java to refer to User Interface (UI) components such as buttons, check boxes, and so on. While these UI components are part of the hierarchy of the Component class, they are not abstract Component classes in their own right. We prefer to call them* controls, *as is done in Windows.*

Container Class

The Container class is an abstract class derived from the Component class. Other classes are, in turn, derived from the Container class, such as the Panel class, Frame class, and Dialog class.

```
Hierarchy:

Abstract Component Class -
  Abstract Container Class
```

Panel Class

The Panel class is derived from the Container class and is used to produce a generic container. An applet, for example, may use several panels, created with the Panel class. These panels can then contain several canvases, additional panels, and so on. Panels typically contain multiple UI components or controls.

```
Hierarchy:

Abstract Component Class -
  Abstract Container Class
    Panel Class
```

Panels can contain additional panels. Frames, too, can contain multiple panels. The following portion of code illustrates how two panels can be added to a frame.

```
Class MyFrame extends Frame
MyFrame(String title) {
  super("Multiple panels in a frame");
```

```
   setLayout(new BorderLayout());
   Panel PanelEast = new Panel();
   Panel PanelWest = new Panel();
   add("East", PanelEast);
   add("West", PanelWest);
    .
    .
    .
}
```

The created panels are placed on the right-hand edge (East) and left-hand edge (West) of the frame, by the layout manager. The use of the AWT's layout manager is discussed in this chapter.

Frame Class

A Frame class is derived from the Window class that is in turn derived from the abstract Container Class. Frames are similar to panels, but are Windows in their own right. A frame is considered a top-level window containing, at a minimum, a title. Frames are provided with a default layout. This layout is a BorderLayout. The concept of layouts will be explained shortly. Frames can be created, moved, resized, and have menu bars just like Windows programs. Frames, like panels, can hold UI components such as buttons, check boxes, and so on.

```
Hierarchy:

Abstract Component Class -
  Abstract Container Class
    Window Class
      Frame Class
```

New or additional frames can be created easily. Here is a small portion of code that adds a new frame to an applet or application.

```
// initialize upon entry
Public void init()
{
    .
    .
    .
  Frame myframe = new Frame("An additional frame");
```

```
  myframe.resize(100, 200);
  myframe.show();
    .
    .
    .
}
```

This portion of code creates a new frame, identified as *myframe*, sized to 100 by 200 pixels. The **show()** member function is used to make the frame visible.

Canvas Class

The Canvas class is derived from the abstract Component class and provides a drawing surface for other UI components or controls. Panels and frames can contain multiple canvases.

```
Hierarchy:

Abstract Component Class -
  Canvas Class
```

New or additional canvases are easy to create and add to an applet or application. Here is a small portion of code that creates a new canvas.

```
NewCanvas newcanvas;
    .
    .
    .
class NewCanvas extends Canvas {
  public void paint(Graphics graphic) {
    graphic.fillOval(50, 50, 100, 100);
  }
}
```

This portion of code extends the Canvas class to create a new canvas. The new canvas uses **paint()** to draw a filled oval shape on the canvas.

UI Components

User Interface (UI) components include check boxes, buttons, menus, dialog boxes, and so on.

Note: Remember that under Microsoft Windows, these same types of items are called controls.

```
Hierarchy:

Abstract Component Class -
  Button, Check Box, Choice Menu Classes, and so on.
```

The following portion of code illustrates how two buttons can be added and modified slightly.

```
// initialize upon entry
Public void init()
{
   .
   .
   .
  Button On = new Button("Turn machinery on");
  Button Off = new Button("Turn machinery off");
  add(On);
  add(Off);
  On.reshape(20, 20, 40, 40);
   .
   .
   .
}
```

Most UI components, with the exception of menus, which are covered in this chapter, are discussed in detail in Chapter 14.

AWT LAYOUTS

Java was designed to create applets and applications that operate across many platforms. Java applets and applications are unlike Microsoft Windows applications. Windows applications operate with the benefit of a whole operating system designed to specific specifications. Java applets and applications must exist across many operating systems and platforms. That leads to an immediate problem. For example, Windows handles the hardware interfacing that resolves differences between EGA, VGA, and SVGA screen resolutions. Therefore, if you draw a round oval in the upper corner of a SVGA screen, it will still be a round circle on an EGA screen. Java doesn't have that total degree of luxury.

You could design full-screen Java applets or applications on an SVGA screen that would be a total disaster if run on a VGA screen. The Java solution to the problem is to employ a *layout manager* to aid in the resolution of these types of problems. The layout manager does not resolve problems in the manner in which you probably think it might. It resolves problems by constraining the types of layouts you are allowed to use. Initially, this will sound like a design nightmare, especially if you are a Windows programmer. You'll find, however, that things will work rather smoothly.

A layout manager manages the placement of components within a panel. Because multiple panels are permissible in a Java applet or application, so are multiple layout managers. Because multiple panels and layout managers are possible, it is almost always possible to design your screens exactly the way you wish them to appear. There are five basic styles used as layout managers: BorderLayout, CardLayout, FlowLayout, GridLayout, and GridBagLayout. Insets, while not a style of layout manager, are often discussed here because they provide component spacing within the panel.

Note: Remember that your Microsoft J++ compiler provides an alternative method for designing menu and dialog resources. The C++ or J++ resource toolkit can be used in conjunction with the Microsoft J++ Java Resource Wizard to aid in the design of these components. The resource editor is introduced later in this chapter.

BorderLayout Class

The BorderLayout class provides four fixed areas around the edges of a panel, labeled North, West, South, and East. A fifth central area varies in size with the panel and is designated as Center. Figure 13.1 shows a border layout, with all five areas marked.

The following code shows an example of how the BorderLayout can be used to position four buttons. The four buttons are located on the top, bottom, and side borders of the screen.

```
import java.applet.*;
import java.awt.*;
import BorderFrame;

public class Border extends Applet
{
```

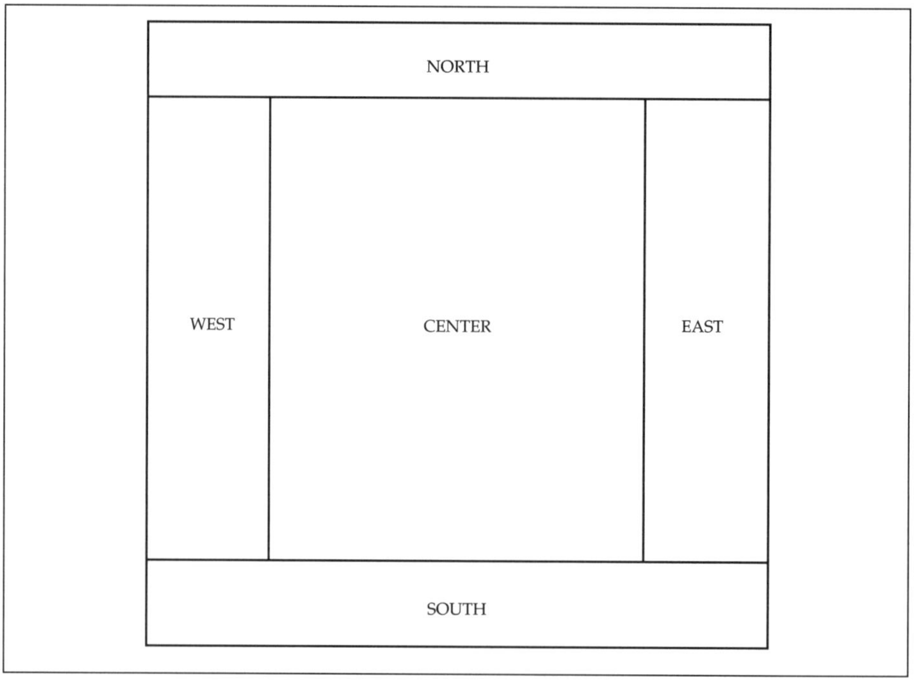

Figure 13.1: The BorderLayout class provides four fixed areas and one variable area for designating the layout of a panel.

```
  // STANDALONE APPLICATION SUPPORT:
  //   m_fStandAlone will be set to true if applet is run
  //   standalone
  //--------------------------------------------------------
boolean m_fStandAlone = false;

  public static void main(String args[])
  {
    BorderFrame frame = new BorderFrame("Border");

    // Must show Frame before we size it so insets() will
    // return valid values
    //------------------------------------------------------
    frame.show();
    frame.resize(frame.insets().left+frame.insets().right+640,
           frame.insets().top  + frame.insets().bottom + 480);

    Border applet_Border = new Border();
```

```
    frame.add("Center", applet_Border);
    applet_Border.m_fStandAlone = true;
    applet_Border.init();
    applet_Border.start();
  }

  public Border()
  {
  }

  public String getAppletInfo()
  {
    return "Name: Border\r\n" +
           "Author: Chris H. Pappas and William H.
Murray\r\n"+
           "Created with Microsoft Visual J++";
  }

  public void init()
  {
    resize(640, 480);

    setLayout(new BorderLayout());
    add("West", new Button("Left Button"));
    add("East", new Button("Right Button"));
    add("North", new Button("Top Button"));
    add("South", new Button("Bottom Button"));
  }

  public boolean action(Event event, Object object)
  {
    if (event.target instanceof Button) {
      newColor();
      return true;
    } else
    return false;
  }

  void newColor()
```

```
  {
    setBackground(Color.yellow);
    this.repaint();
  }

  public void destroy()
  {
  }

  public void paint(Graphics g)
  {
  }

  public void start()
  {
  }

  public void stop()
  {
  }

}
```

The Microsoft J++ compiler also provides the necessary code to support the frame required by standalone applications.

```
import java.awt.*;

class BorderFrame extends Frame
{
  public BorderFrame(String str)
  {
    super (str);
  }

  public boolean handleEvent(Event evt)
  {
    switch (evt.id)
    {
      case Event.WINDOW_DESTROY:
        dispose();
        System.exit(0);
        return true;
```

```
        default:
          return super.handleEvent(evt);
      }
    }
}
```

The code is functional. Run the application, resize the window, then push on any of the four buttons and the central portion of the window will turn yellow. There is only a small portion of code required to implement the border layout, as you can see in the following partial listing:

```
setLayout(new BorderLayout());
add("West", new Button("Left Button"));
add("East", new Button("Right Button"));
add("North", new Button("Top Button"));
add("South", new Button("Bottom Button"));
```

The layout is set with a call to the **setLayout()** member function, and then each button is added with a call to the **add()** member function. Figure 13.2 shows the output from this application.

To make the buttons functional, a technique for interfacing with them is required. In this and the remaining examples in this section, a very simple event handler is used. Later in this chapter, event handling is discussed in more detail.

If you want to have a gap placed between each button, specify the gap in pixels, as shown here:

```
setLayout(new BorderLayout(20, 15));
```

In this case, a gap of 20 pixels is placed between horizontal boundaries and 15 pixels between vertical boundaries.

CardLayout Class

The CardLayout class is unique in the sense that not all areas are visible to the user at the same time. Card layouts usually involve the use of multiple panels that are displayed one at a time, like the top card in a deck of cards. Figure 13.3 shows the concept of a card layout. Only the top area is visible to the user.

The following code shows an example of how the CardLayout can be used to position a new button on each of three panels. The buttons are placed on the top-center portion of each panel.

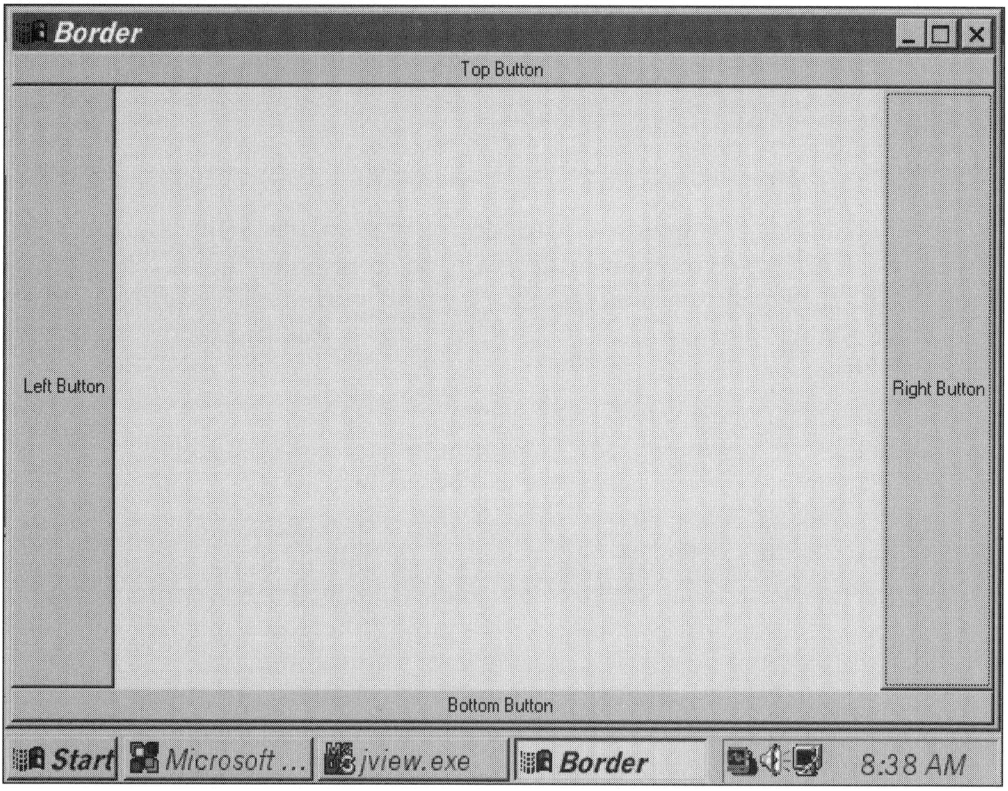

Figure 13.2: The BorderLayout class is used to place four buttons.

```
import java.applet.*;
import java.awt.*;
import CardFrame;

public class Card extends Applet
{
  // STANDALONE APPLICATION SUPPORT:
  //    m_fStandAlone will be set to true if applet is run
  //    standalone
  //--------------------------------------------------------------
  boolean m_fStandAlone = false;

  public static void main(String args[])
  {
    CardFrame frame = new CardFrame("Card");
```

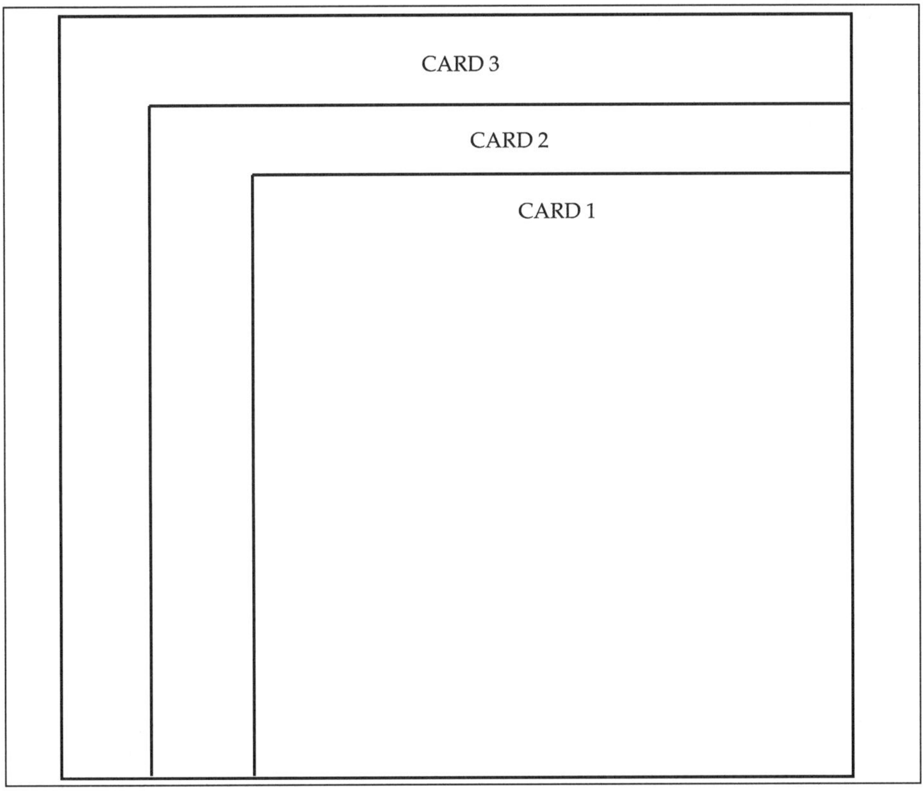

Figure 13.3: The CardLayout class makes only the top area visible.

```
    // Must show Frame before we size it so insets() will
    // return valid values
    //----------------------------------------------------------
frame.show();
    frame.resize(frame.insets().left+frame.insets().right+640,
            frame.insets().top  + frame.insets().bottom + 480);

    Card applet_Card = new Card();

    frame.add("Center", applet_Card);
    applet_Card.m_fStandAlone = true;
    applet_Card.init();
    applet_Card.start();
  }
```

```
public Card()
{
}

public String getAppletInfo()
{
  return "Name: Card\r\n" +
         "Author:Chris H. Pappas and William H. Murray\r\n"+
         "Created with Microsoft Visual J++";
}

public void init()
{
  resize(640, 480);

  CardLayout mycard = new CardLayout();
  setLayout(mycard);

  Panel one = new Panel();
  add("1", one);
  Panel two = new Panel();
  add("2", two);
  Panel three = new Panel();
  add("3", three);

  one.add(new Button("First Button"));
  two.add(new Button("Second Button"));
  three.add(new Button("Third Button"));

  // shows third panel
  mycard.show(this, "3");
}

public void destroy()
{
}

public void paint(Graphics g)
{
```

```
    }

    public void start()
    {
    }

    public void stop()
    {
    }

}
```

The Microsoft J++ compiler also provides the necessary code to support the frame required by standalone applications.

```
import java.awt.*;

class CardFrame extends Frame
{
  public CardFrame(String str)
  {
    super (str);
  }

  public boolean handleEvent(Event evt)
  {
    switch (evt.id)
    {
      case Event.WINDOW_DESTROY:
        dispose();
        System.exit(0);
        return true;

      default:
        return super.handleEvent(evt);
    }
  }
}
```

One new button is installed at the top center of each of three panels. There is only a small portion of code required to implement the card layout, as you can see in the following partial listing:

```
CardLayout mycard = new CardLayout();
setLayout(mycard);
```

The layout is set with a call to the **setLayout()** member function. It is then necessary to create each of the three panels, as shown in the following partial listing:

```
Panel one = new Panel();
add("1", one);
Panel two = new Panel();
add("2", two);
Panel three = new Panel();
add("3", three);
```

The panels are added with a call to the **add()** member function. Finally, the three buttons are created and added to the named panel with the following code:

```
one.add(new Button("First Button"));
two.add(new Button("Second Button"));
three.add(new Button("Third Button"));
```

Only one "card" or panel is visible at a time. The following portion of code makes the third panel visible:

```
// shows third panel
mycard.show(this, "3");
```

Figure 13.4 shows the output from this application.

Other panels can be viewed with the **show()** member function or other member functions, such as **last()**, provided in the CardLayout class.

FlowLayout Class

The FlowLayout class adds UI components (controls) to a panel in consecutive order. UI components are added to the first row, until it is filled. Additional UI components are then added to the second row, and so on. Alignment can be designated as LEFT, CENTER, or RIGHT. Gaps can also be set vertically or horizontally between UI components by specifying the number of pixels in the gap. Figure 13.5 shows a flow layout with three buttons centered in the first row.

The following code shows an example of how the class can be used to position three buttons. The three buttons are centered along the top portion of the window, by default.

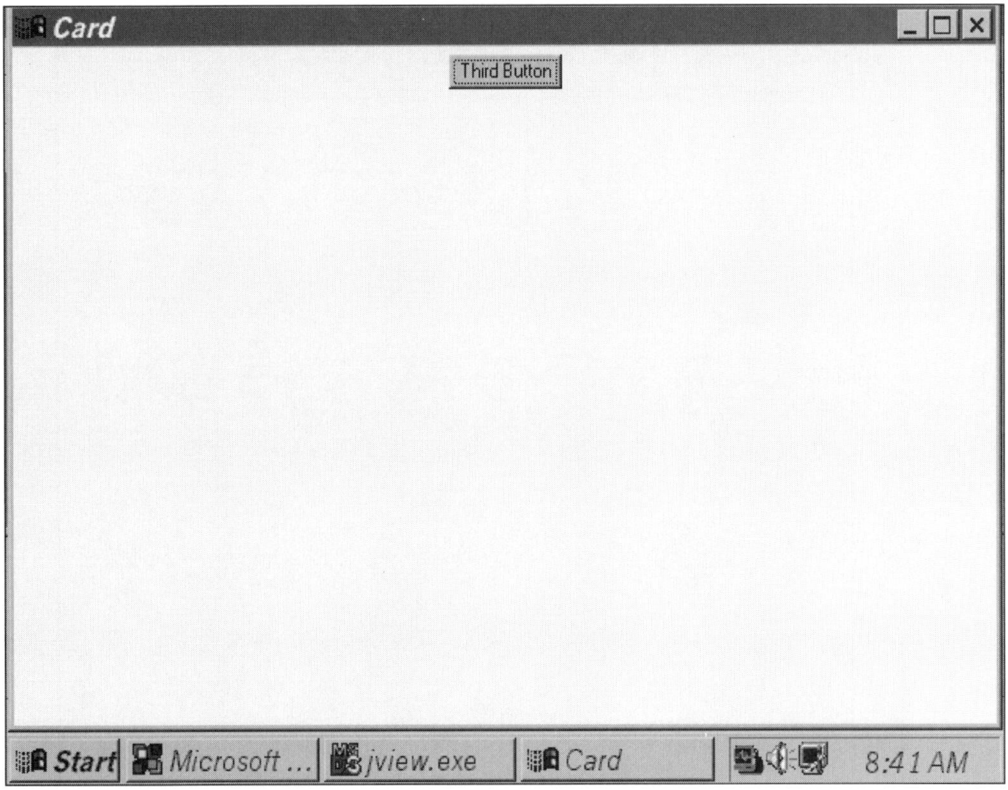

Figure 13.4: The CardLayout class places three buttons, each on a separate panel.

```
import java.applet.*;
import java.awt.*;
import FlowFrame;

public class Flow extends Applet
{
  // STANDALONE APPLICATION SUPPORT:
  //    m_fStandAlone will be set to true if applet is run
  //    standalone
  //--------------------------------------------------------------
  boolean m_fStandAlone = false;

  public static void main(String args[])
  {
```

Figure 13.5: The FlowLayout class allows UI components to be added row by row.

```
FlowFrame frame = new FlowFrame("Flow");

// Must show Frame before we size it so insets() will
// return valid values
//-----------------------------------------------------------
frame.show();
frame.resize(frame.insets().left+frame.insets().right+640,
        frame.insets().top  + frame.insets().bottom + 480);

Flow applet_Flow = new Flow();

frame.add("Center", applet_Flow);
applet_Flow.m_fStandAlone = true;
applet_Flow.init();
applet_Flow.start();
```

```
}

public Flow()
{
}

public String getAppletInfo()
{
  return "Name: Flow\r\n" +
         "Author: Chris H. Pappas and William H. Murray\r\n"+
         "Created with Microsoft Visual J++";
}


public void init()
{
  resize(640, 480);

  setLayout(new FlowLayout());
  add(new Button("First Button"));
  add(new Button("Second Button"));
  add(new Button("Third Button"));
}

  public boolean action(Event event, Object object)
{
  if (event.target instanceof Button) {
    newColor();
    return true;
  } else
  return false;
}

void newColor()
{
  setBackground(Color.yellow);
  this.repaint();
}

public void destroy()
{
```

```
  }

  public void paint(Graphics g)
  {
  }

  public void start()
  {
  }

  public void stop()
  {
  }

}
```

The Microsoft J++ compiler also provides the necessary code to support the frame required by standalone applications.

```
import java.awt.*;

class FlowFrame extends Frame
{
  public FlowFrame(String str)
  {
    super (str);
  }

  public boolean handleEvent(Event evt)
  {
    switch (evt.id)
    {
      case Event.WINDOW_DESTROY:
        dispose();
        System.exit(0);
        return true;

      default:
        return super.handleEvent(evt);
    }
  }
}
```

This code is functional. Click on any of the three buttons and the remaining portion of the window will turn yellow. There is only a small piece of code required to implement the flow layout.

```
// initialize
public void init()
{
  setLayout(new FlowLayout());
  add(new Button("First Button"));
  add(new Button("Second Button"));
  add(new Button("Third Button"));
}
```

The layout is set with a call to the **setLayout()** member function, and then each button is added with a call to the **add()** member function. Figure 13.6 shows the output from this application.

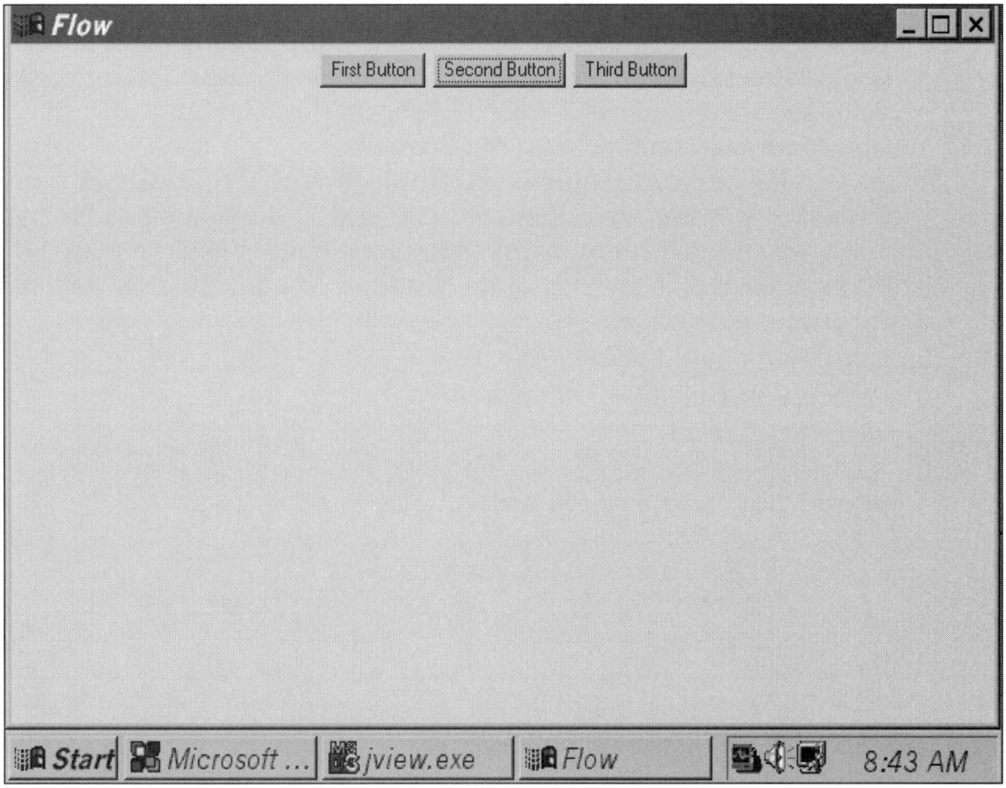

Figure 13.6: The FlowLayout class is used to place and center three buttons.

The simple event handler, used earlier, is used to intercept the button events.

If you want to change text alignment or place a gap between buttons, any of the following variations are acceptable for the flow layout.

```
setLayout(new FlowLayout());                        // Centered
setLayout(new FlowLayout(FlowLayout.LEFT));   // Left Just.
setLayout(new FlowLayout(FlowLayout.RIGHT)); // Right Just.
setLayout(new FlowLayout(FlowLayout.LEFT), 20, 15); // Gap
```

In the final case, a gap of 20 pixels is placed between horizontal boundaries and 15 pixels between vertical boundaries of any UI components.

GridLayout Class

The GridLayout class allows a portion of a panel to be partitioned into cells, designated by rows and columns. UI components are added to a cell, sequentially from left to right and then top to bottom, each time the **add()** member function (method) is invoked. Gaps between cells can be specified in pixels. Figure 13.7 shows a grid layout with a small gap between row and column components.

The following code shows an example of how the GridLayout can be used to position three buttons. The grid is designated as having four rows and one column. Thus, the three buttons will be placed in this grid starting at the top of the window. The fourth grid position will not have a button.

```
import java.applet.*;
import java.awt.*;
import GridFrame;

public class Grid extends Applet
{
  // STANDALONE APPLICATION SUPPORT:
  //    m_fStandAlone will be set to true if applet is run
  //    standalone
  //--------------------------------------------------------------
  boolean m_fStandAlone = false;

  public static void main(String args[])
  {
```

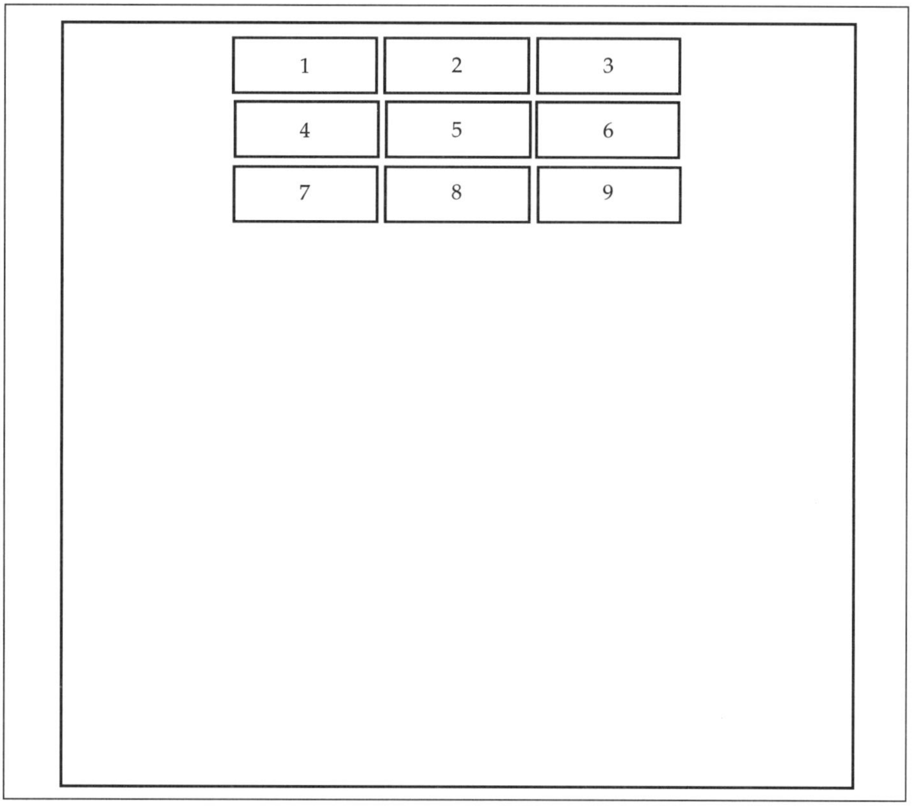

Figure 13.7: The GridLayout class allows UI components to be added to cells specified by row and column.

```
GridFrame frame = new GridFrame("Grid");

// Must show Frame before we size it so insets() will
// return valid values
//----------------------------------------------------------
frame.show();
frame.resize(frame.insets().left+frame.insets().right+640,
        frame.insets().top  + frame.insets().bottom + 480);

Grid applet_Grid = new Grid();

frame.add("Center", applet_Grid);
applet_Grid.m_fStandAlone = true;
applet_Grid.init();
```

```
  applet_Grid.start();
}

public Grid()
{
}

public String getAppletInfo()
{
  return "Name: Grid\r\n" +
         "Author: Chris H. Pappas and William H. Murray\r\n"+
         "Created with Microsoft Visual J++";
}

public void init()
{
  resize(640, 480);

  setLayout(new GridLayout(4, 1, 20, 20));
  add(new Button("Top Button"));
  add(new Button("Middle Button"));
  add(new Button("Bottom Button"));
}

public boolean action(Event event, Object object)
{
  if (event.target instanceof Button) {
    newColor();
    return true;
  } else
  return false;
}

void newColor()
{
  setBackground(Color.yellow);
  this.repaint();
}

public void destroy()
{
```

```
    }

    public void paint(Graphics g)
    {
    }

    public void start()
    {
    }

    public void stop()
    {
    }

}
```

The Microsoft J++ compiler also provides the necessary code to support the frame required by standalone applications.

```
import java.awt.*;

class GridFrame extends Frame
{
  public GridFrame(String str)
  {
    super (str);
  }

  public boolean handleEvent(Event evt)
  {
    switch (evt.id)
    {
      case Event.WINDOW_DESTROY:
        dispose();
        System.exit(0);
        return true;

      default:
        return super.handleEvent(evt);
    }
  }
}
```

This application is functional. Start the application, resize the window, click any of the three buttons, and the bottom portion of the window will turn yellow. There is only a small portion of code required to implement the grid layout.

```
public void init()
{
  setLayout(new GridLayout(4, 1, 20, 20));
  add(new Button("Top Button"));
  add(new Button("Middle Button"));
  add(new Button("Bottom Button"));
}
```

The layout is set with a call to the **setLayout()** member function, and then each button is added with a call to the **add()** member function. Again, the first parameter specified in the **GridLayout()** call represents the number of rows in the grid. The second number is the number of columns. The remaining two numbers, which are optional, represent the gap between UI components. Figure 13.8 shows the output from this application.

The event handler used in earlier examples is used to intercept the button events.

GridBagLayout Class

The GridBagLayout class is actually a variation on the GridLayout class. The GridBagLayout class operates in a similar manner to the GridLayout class, but offers the additional capability of specifying the format used in each cell. Formatting for this class is achieved with the help of the GridBagConstraints class.

Figure 13.9 shows a grid bag layout with each cell formatted differently.

The following code shows an example of how the GridBagLayout can be used to format and position three buttons. The buttons will be placed horizontally. The width of each button will vary because each is assigned a different weight.

```
import java.applet.*;
import java.awt.*;
import GridBagFrame;

public class GridBag extends Applet
```

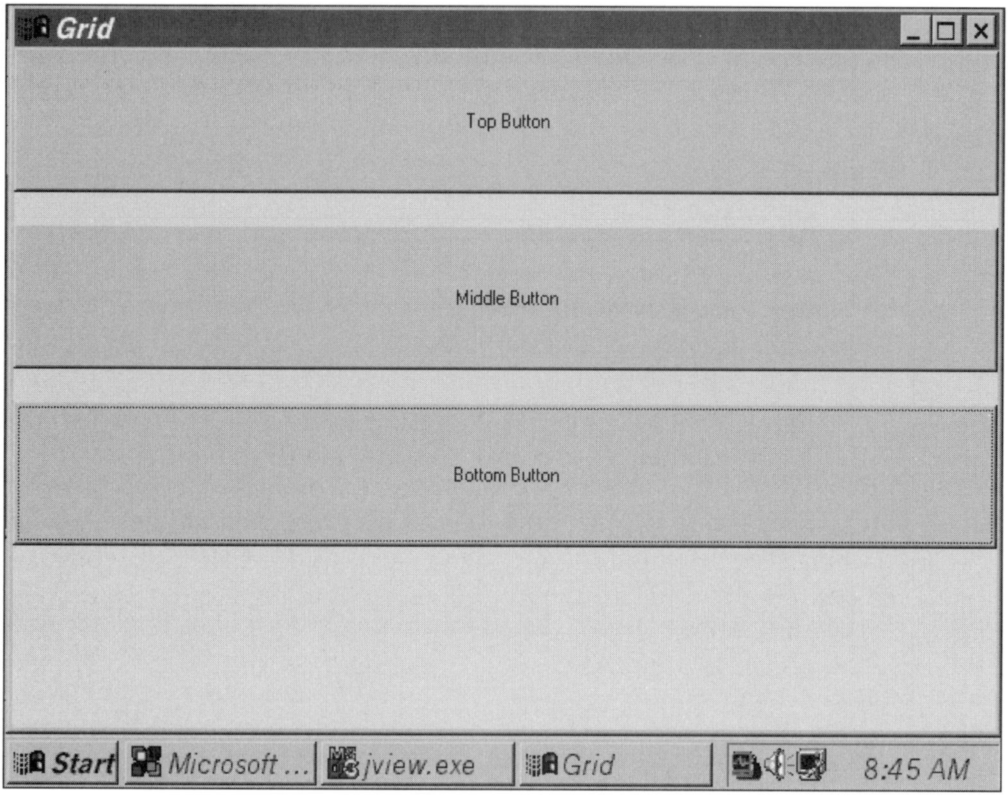

Figure 13.8: The GridLayout class is used to place three buttons, one on top of the other.

```
{
  // STANDALONE APPLICATION SUPPORT:
  //    m_fStandAlone will be set to true if applet is run
  //    standalone
  //----------------------------------------------------------------
  boolean m_fStandAlone = false;
  Button But1, But2, But3;

  public static void main(String args[])
  {
    GridBagFrame frame = new GridBagFrame("GridBag");

    // Must show Frame before we size it so insets() will
```

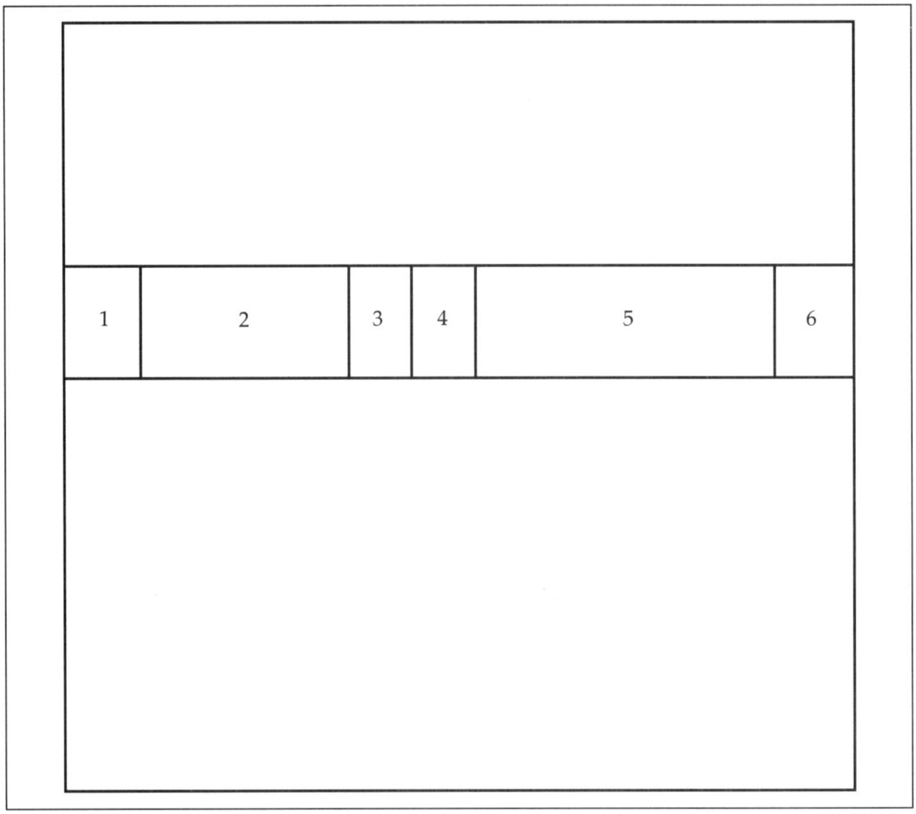

Figure 13.9: The GridBagLayout class in conjunction with the GridBagConstraints class allows individual cells to be formatted differently.

```
// return valid values
//--------------------------------------------------------------
frame.show();
frame.resize(frame.insets().left+frame.insets().right+640,
       frame.insets().top  + frame.insets().bottom + 480);

GridBag applet_GridBag = new GridBag();

frame.add("Center", applet_GridBag);
applet_GridBag.m_fStandAlone = true;
applet_GridBag.init();
applet_GridBag.start();
```

```
    }

    public GridBag()
    {
    }

    public String getAppletInfo()
    {
      return "Name: GridBag\r\n" +
             "Author: Chris H. Pappas and William H. Murray\r\n"+
             "Created with Microsoft Visual J++";
    }

    public void init()
    {
      GridBagLayout gridbag = new GridBagLayout();
      GridBagConstraints cts = new GridBagConstraints();

      setLayout(gridbag);
      cts.fill = GridBagConstraints.BOTH;

      cts.weightx = 0.0;
      But1 = new Button("Button #1");
      gridbag.setConstraints(But1, cts);
      add(But1);

      cts.weightx = 1.0;
      But2 = new Button("Button #2");
      gridbag.setConstraints(But2, cts);
      add(But2);

      cts.weightx = 2.0;
      But3 = new Button("Button #3");
      gridbag.setConstraints(But3, cts);
      add(But3);

      resize(640, 480);
    }
```

```
  public boolean action(Event event, Object object)
  {
    if (event.target instanceof Button) {
      newColor();
      return true;
    } else
    return false;
  }

  void newColor()
  {
    setBackground(Color.yellow);
    this.repaint();
  }

  public void destroy()
  {
  }

  public void paint(Graphics g)
  {
  }

  public void start()
  {
  }

  public void stop()
  {
  }

}
```

The Microsoft J++ compiler also provides the necessary code to support the frame required by standalone applications.

```
import java.awt.*;

class GridBagFrame extends Frame
{
  public GridBagFrame(String str)
```

```
    {
      super (str);
    }

    public boolean handleEvent(Event evt)
    {
      switch (evt.id)
      {
        case Event.WINDOW_DESTROY:
          dispose();
          System.exit(0);
          return true;

        default:
          return super.handleEvent(evt);
      }
    }
}
```

This application is functional. Start the application, resize the window, click any of the three buttons, and the remaining portion of the window will turn yellow. The new layout and required constraints are implemented with the following code.

```
public void init()
{
  GridBagLayout gridbag = new GridBagLayout();
  GridBagConstraints cts = new GridBagConstraints();

  setLayout(gridbag);
  cts.fill = GridBagConstraints.BOTH;
```

The GridBagConstraints class *fill* parameter, *cts.fill* in this example, is used to determine how a component will fill a display area when the component's display area is larger than the component's requested size. Valid values include NONE, BOTH, HORIZONTAL, and VERTICAL.

The *anchor* parameter, not used in this example, is used to determine how a component will be placed in a display area when the component is smaller than the display area. Valid values include CENTER, NORTH, NORTHEAST, EAST, SOUTHEAST, SOUTH, SOUTHWEST, WEST, and NORTHWEST.

As the buttons are added horizontally, the weight constraint for each button is varied. This changes the horizontal cell width so that each button is proportionally larger.

```
cts.weightx = 0.0;
But1 = new Button("Button #1");
gridbag.setConstraints(But1, cts);
add(But1);
 .
 .
 .
cts.weightx = 1.0;
 .
 .
 .
cts.weightx = 2.0;
```

The *weight* parameter, *cts.weightx* in this example, is used to specify a resizing weight. Default values of zero are used for unspecified values of *weightx* and *weighty*. If either value is unspecified, components are centered. Determine how a component will fill a display area when the component's display area is larger than the component's requested size. Valid values include NONE, BOTH, HORIZONTAL, and VERTICAL.

Additional parameters can be studied by close examination of the GridBagLayout and GridBagConstraints classes. Figure 13.10 shows how the *fill* and *weight* parameters affect this example, when placing buttons.

The event handler used in earlier examples is used to intercept the button events, and color the window when any of the buttons is pushed.

Insets

Insets can be used to provide a border-like effect around a group of controls. First, select the layout desired, and then override the **insets()** method. Figure 13.11 shows three buttons with insets and gaps included.

The height and width of the inset is specified in pixels. For example, the following portion of code will provide a left and right inset of 20 pixels and a top and bottom inset of 15 pixels.

```
Public Insets insets()
{
```

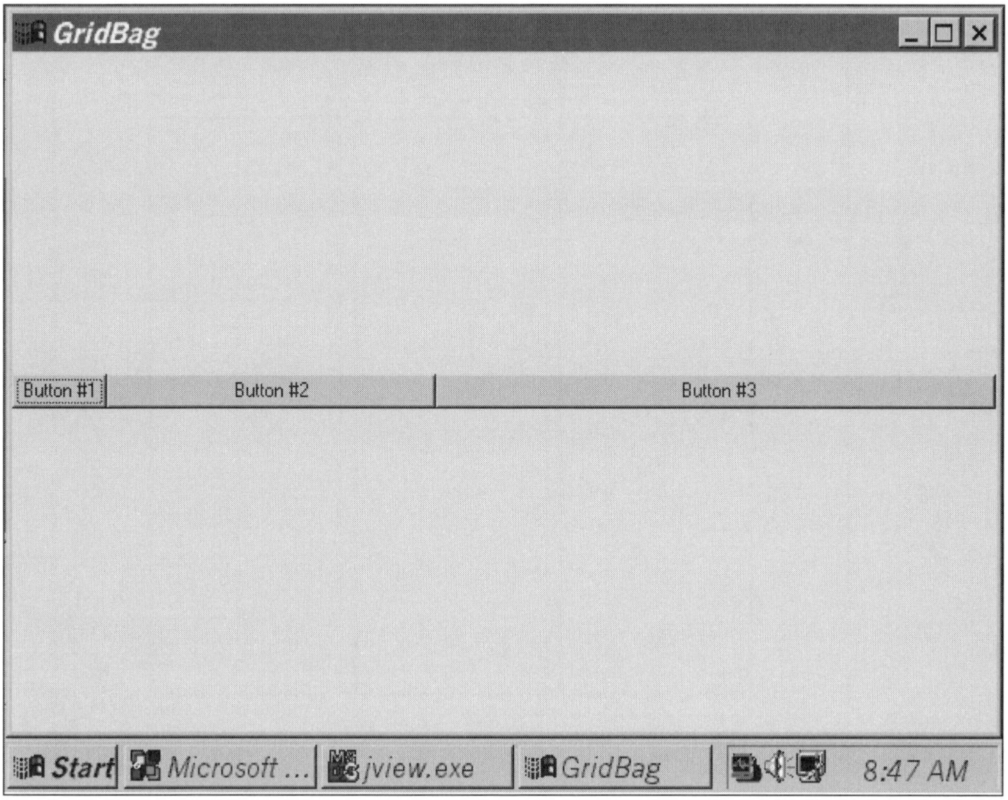

Figure 13.10: The GridBagLayout() is used to add three different width buttons to the window.

```
  return new Insets(20, 15, 20, 15);
}
```

EVENTS

Many of the examples used to illustrate various layouts have used a simple event handler to process button information. Every UI component, or control, must interface with the application or applet to be useful. This section examines two techniques for processing returned by UI components. The examples in this section focus on buttons, but other UI components can be handled in the same manner. Chapter 14 includes additional examples dealing with UI components and their associated events.

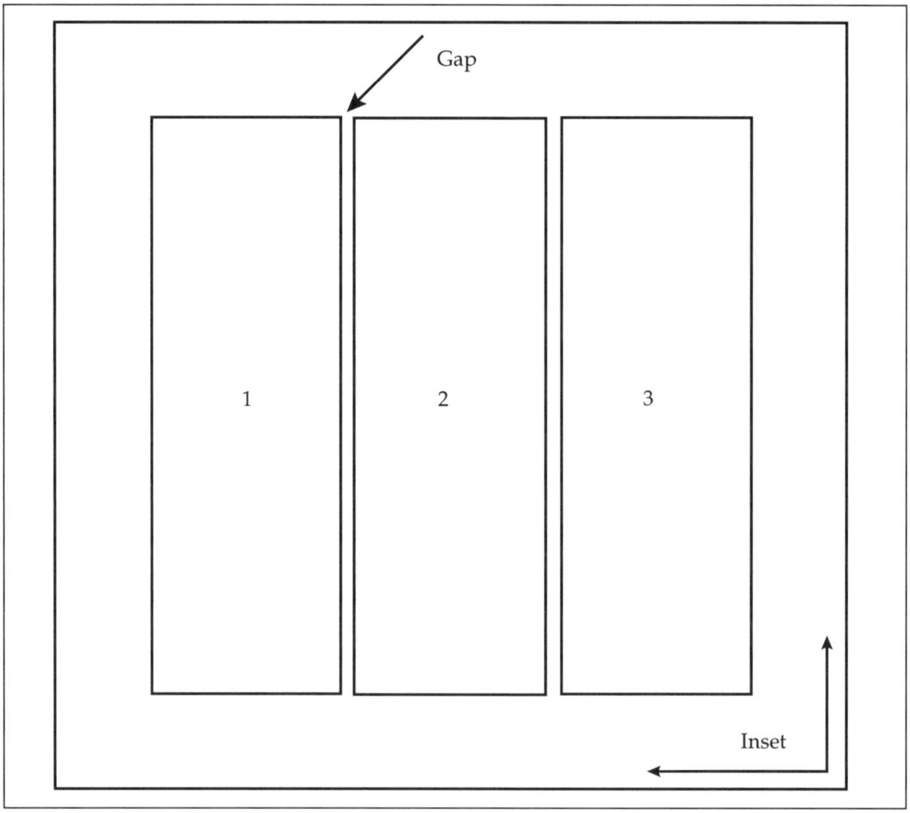

Figure 13.11: Insets can provide a border effect around a group of UI components.

The action() Method

The **action()** member function provides one of the simplest techniques for interfacing an application or applet to UI component events. One form for the **action()** member function is:

```
public boolean action(Event event, Object object)
{
  if(event.target instanceof UI_component)
  {
    .
    .
    .
```

```
    return true;
  } else
  return false;
}
```

The **if()** statement will test the event against the object that generated the event by examining the instance variable. For example, if the *UI_component* was BUTTON and a button had been pushed, the **if()** statement would have been true. Additional UI components are examined in the next chapter.

Thus, for the simple layout examples that tested to see if any button had been pushed, the **action()** member function's code took the following form:

```
public boolean action(Event event, Object object)
{
  if (event.target instanceof Button) {
    newColor();
    return true;
  } else
  return false;
}
```

Here, the only concern is if a button had been pushed, but not which button. How could you determine if a particular button had been pushed?

That can be done by casting the *object* to a String and comparing it to the actual button name. For example in the flow layout application:

```
if((String)object.equals("First Button"))
{
    .
    .
    .
} else
if((String)object.equals("Second Button"))
    .
    .
    .
```

You'll see a variation of this technique in the menu bar example that follows shortly.

The handleEvent() Method

The **handleEvent()** member function provides another simple technique for interfacing an application or applet to UI component events. The most popular form for the **handleEvent()** member function involves the use of a **switch-case** statement. Windows programmers are very familiar with **switch-case** statements because they are used frequently when processing menu and dialog box information. The flow layout example could process the first two buttons in the following manner.

```
public boolean handleEvent(Event event)
{
  switch(event.id)
  {
    case Event.ACTION_EVENT:
    {
      if (event.object == "First Button") {
        .
        .
        .
        return true;
      } else
      if (event.object == "Second Button") {
        .
        .
        .
        return true;
      } else
        return false;
    }
    default:
      return false;
  }
}
```

You will, no doubt, choose one style to use when writing event handlers. There is no major advantage of one over the other. We prefer the use of the **action()** member function, because of the simplicity of the coding.

CREATING A MENU USING THE AWT

The GUI Windows interface has become popular because correctly written applications take on a consistent look and feel. We all know, for example, what to expect when we click the mouse on the **File** menu in a word processing, spreadsheet, or database application.

One of the important reasons for developing a good understanding of Java's AWT is so that your Java applications and applets can have the same consistent look and feel. The previous sections covered panels, frames, layouts, and placement of UI components (controls). You have even learned how to interact with these components. What's the point? You are now on the verge of being able to create applications and applets that are interactive. The first step toward creating interactive applications and applets is to provide menu capabilities, similar to those of Microsoft Windows.

The Menu1 project, shown in the next listing, is one of the simplest menu techniques possible. Here a menu will allow the user to select one of three shape sizes. When the shape size is selected, the new shape will be drawn in the window.

Examine the following listing. Notice, too, that an event handler has been included to process the information returned when a menu selection is made.

```
import java.applet.*;
import java.awt.*;
import Menu1Frame;

public class Menu1 extends Applet
{
  // STANDALONE APPLICATION SUPPORT:
  //   m_fStandAlone will be set to true if applet is run
  //   standalone
  //------------------------------------------------------------
  boolean m_fStandAlone = false;
  int index;

  public static void main(String args[])
  {
    Menu1Frame frame = new Menu1Frame("Menu1");
```

```
    // Must show Frame before we size it so insets() will
    // return valid values
    //----------------------------------------------------------
    frame.show();
    frame.resize(frame.insets().left+frame.insets().right+640,
           frame.insets().top  + frame.insets().bottom + 480);

    Menu1 applet_Menu1 = new Menu1();

    frame.add("Center", applet_Menu1);
    applet_Menu1.m_fStandAlone = true;
    applet_Menu1.init();
    applet_Menu1.start();
  }

  public Menu1()
  {
  }

  public String getAppletInfo()
  {
    return "Name: Menu1\r\n" +
           "Author: Chris H. Pappas and William H. Murray\r\n"+
           "Created with Microsoft Visual J++";
  }


  public void init()
  {
    resize(640, 480);

    Choice menuchoice = new Choice();

    menuchoice.addItem("small");
    menuchoice.addItem("Medium");
    menuchoice.addItem("LARGE");
    add(menuchoice);
  }

  // prepare to intercept menu item
```

```
public boolean action(Event event, Object arg)
{
  switch (event.id)
  {
    case Event.ACTION_EVENT: {
      if (event.arg == "small") {
        index = 0;
      } else
      if (event.arg == "Medium") {
        index = 1;
      } else
      if (event.arg == "LARGE") {
        index = 2;
      } else {
        repaint();
        return false;
      }
    }
    default:
      repaint();
      return true;
  }
}

public void destroy()
{
}

public void paint(Graphics g)
{
  if (index == 0) {
    g.fillOval(50, 50, 100, 100);
  } else
  if (index == 1) {
    g.fillOval(50, 50, 200, 200);
  } else
  if (index == 2) {
    g.fillOval(50, 50, 300, 300);
  } else
    g.drawString("This event never happened",
```

```
                    10, 10);
  }

  public void start()
  {
  }

  public void stop()
  {
  }

}
```

The Microsoft J++ compiler also provides the necessary code to support the frame required by standalone applications.

```
import java.awt.*;

class Menu1Frame extends Frame
{
  public Menu1Frame(String str)
  {
    super (str);
  }

  public boolean handleEvent(Event evt)
  {
    switch (evt.id)
    {
      case Event.WINDOW_DESTROY:
        dispose();
        System.exit(0);
        return true;

      default:
        return super.handleEvent(evt);
    }
  }
}
```

The main portion of code implements a choice list. A choice list is created by using the Choice class. A choice list consists of a number of menu items. The currently selected item appears in a small window. When that window is clicked with the mouse, all of the remaining choices become visible. New items, from the list, can be selected just as in Microsoft Windows.

In the previous listing, the choice list is named *menuchoice*. Menu items are added to the menu with the **addItem()** member function. Figure 13.12 shows the default choice list, and the figure corresponding to that menu item.

Figure 13.13 shows the whole choice list for this example.

The menu was placed without the use of a layout. If the grid layout, from an earlier example is used, the choice list will be added in the fourth row, as specified in the following partial listing.

```
// initialize
public void init()
```

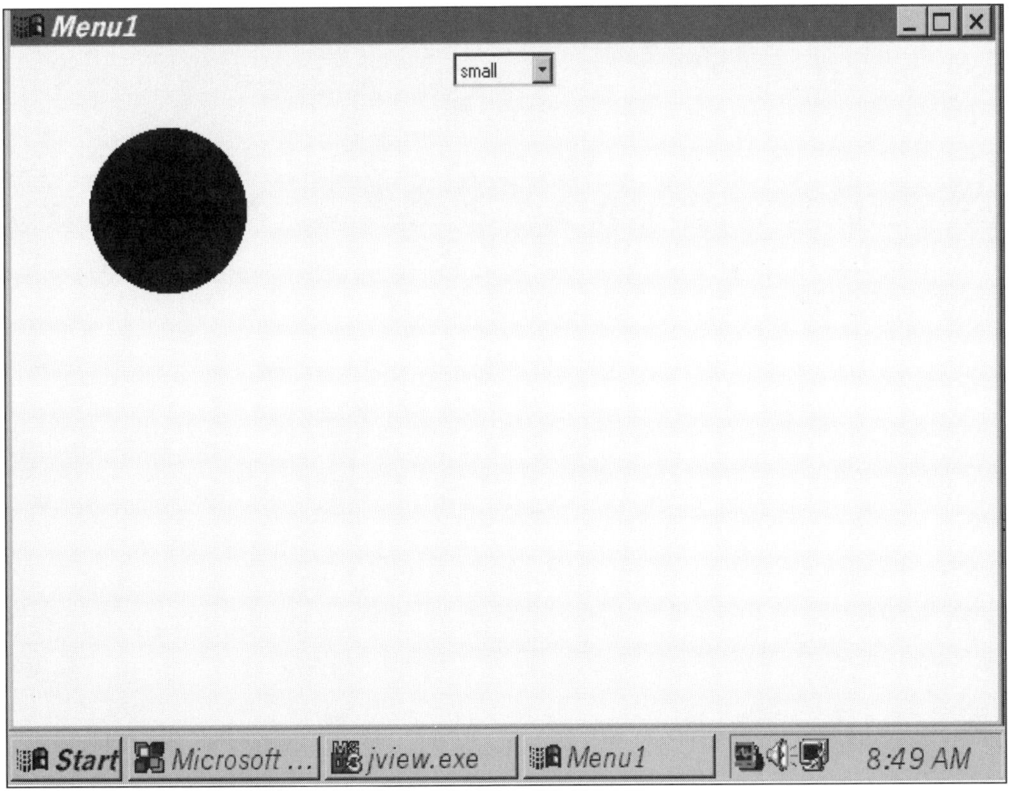

Figure 13.12: The first item in the choice list serves as the initial menu value.

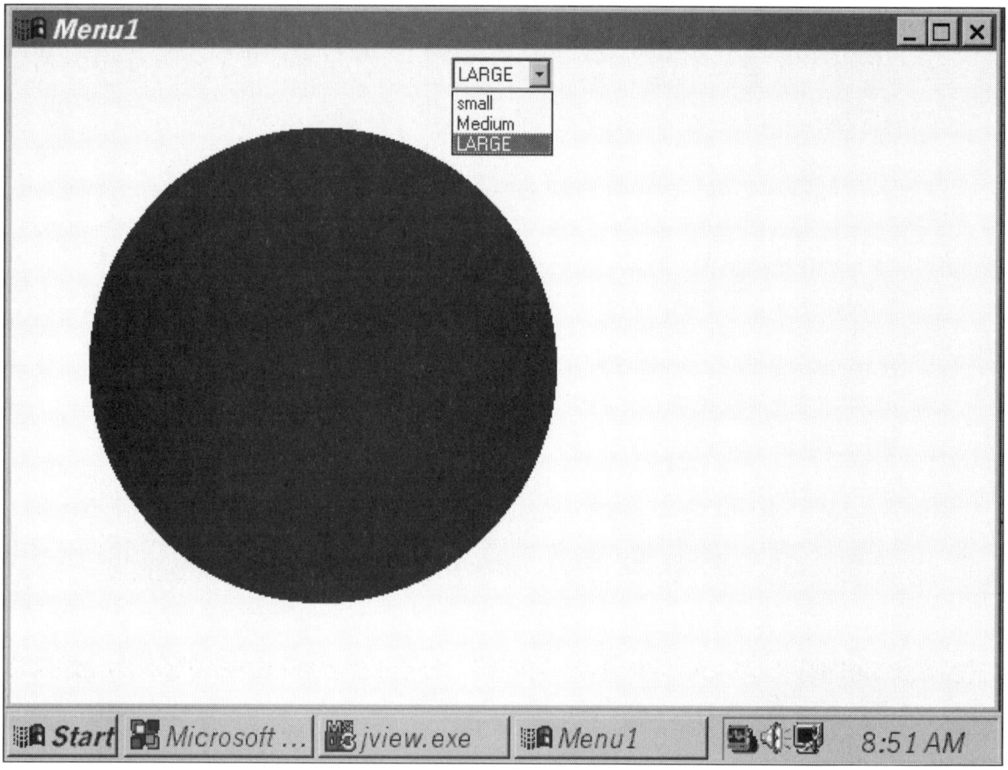

Figure 13.13: The whole choice list for this example includes three size options.

```
{
  setLayout(new GridLayout(4, 1, 20, 20));
  add(new Button("Top Button"));
  add(new Button("Middle Button"));
  add(new Button("Bottom Button"));

  Choice menuchoice = new Choice();
  menuchoice.addItem("small");
  menuchoice.addItem("Medium");
  menuchoice.addItem("LARGE");
  add(menuchoice);
}
```

Compare Figure 13.14 to Figure 13.8. With layouts, you will have control over the placement of all UI components, even choice lists!

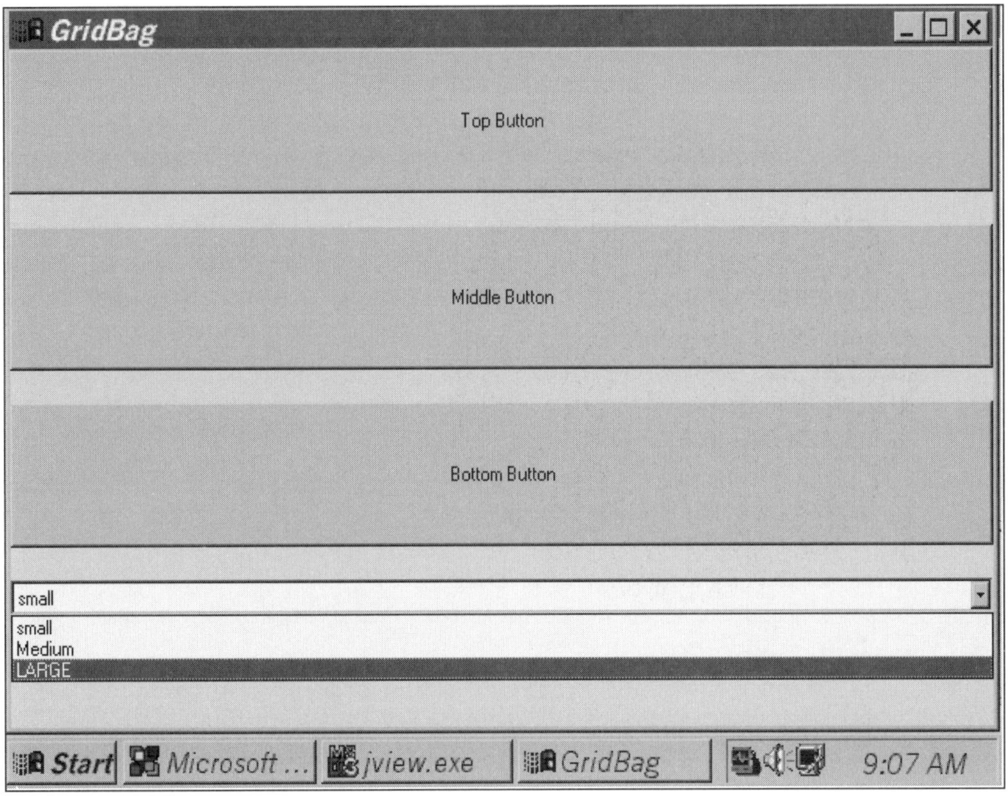

Figure 13.14: The choice list (menu) is added on the fourth row of the grid as specified in the gridLayout class.

But wait! The menus you are most familiar with, from Microsoft Windows, have a menu contained in a menu bar. When the menu name is clicked, the menu pops up. You'll see how to add a menu bar and menu with the help of the resource toolkit, in the next example.

CREATING A MENU USING THE RESOURCE TOOLKIT

Menu bars give your application or applet an appearance that closely matches Microsoft Windows applications.

The Frame class produces the window that is most closely associated with a Microsoft Windows window. The Window class, which is similar to a panel, can also produce a top-level window. Both of these classes serve as the base for adding menu bars to applications and applets. To add a menu bar, it is necessary to create a frame.

In the following listing, three classes help add the menu bar to this application. Each is shown in a bolded font. You know that the **action()** member function is responsible for processing the menu item selection events. A new canvas, *newcanvas*, is created from the Canvas class to allow drawing to occur in the new frame. That leaves the class *MyFrame* as the class that actually implements the menu bar. Examine the complete listing below, and note each of these portions of code.

```
import java.applet.*;
import java.awt.*;
import Menu2Frame;
import Menu2Res;

public class Menu2 extends Applet
{
  // STANDALONE APPLICATION SUPPORT:
  //   m_fStandAlone will be set to true if applet is run
  //   standalone
  //--------------------------------------------------------------
  boolean m_fStandAlone = false;
  static int index;

  public static void main(String args[])
  {
    Menu2Frame frame = new Menu2Frame("Menu2");

    // Must show Frame before we size it so insets() will
    // return valid values
    //------------------------------------------------------------
    frame.show();
    frame.resize(frame.insets().left+frame.insets().right+640,
           frame.insets().top  + frame.insets().bottom + 480);

    Menu2 applet_Menu2 = new Menu2();

    frame.add("Center", applet_Menu2);
    applet_Menu2.m_fStandAlone = true;
    applet_Menu2.init();
    applet_Menu2.start();
```

```
    }

    public Menu2()
    {
    }

    public String getAppletInfo()
    {
      return "Name: Menu2\r\n" +
             "Author: Chris H. Pappas and William H. Murray\r\n"+
             "Created with Microsoft Visual J++";
    }


    public void init()
    {
      resize(640, 480);
      new MyFrame("");
    }

    public void destroy()
    {
    }

    public void paint(Graphics g)
    {
    }

    public void start()
    {
    }

    public void stop()
    {
    }

  }

  class MyFrame extends Frame
  {
```

```
    NewCanvas newcanvas;
    MyFrame(String title) {
      super("Simple Menu Bar");
      add("Center", newcanvas = new NewCanvas());
      reshape(0, 0, 639, 479);

      // allows new menu bar & menu items
      // from resource file to be displayed
      Menu2Res myMenu = new Menu2Res(super);
      myMenu.CreateMenu();

      show();
    }

    public boolean action(Event event, Object object) {
      if(object.equals("small")) {
        Menu2.index = 0;
        newcanvas.repaint();
        return true;
      } else
      if(object.equals("Medium")) {
        Menu2.index = 1;
        newcanvas.repaint();
        return true;
      } else
      if(object.equals("LARGE")) {
        Menu2.index = 2;
        newcanvas.repaint();
        return true;
      } else
      if(object.equals("Close")) {
        System.exit(0);
      } else
        return false;
      return true;
    }
  }

  class NewCanvas extends Canvas {
```

```
  public void paint(Graphics g) {
    if (Menu2.index == 0) {
      g.fillOval(50, 50, 100, 100);
    } else
    if (Menu2.index == 1) {
      g.fillOval(50, 50, 200, 200);
    } else
    if (Menu2.index == 2) {
      g.fillOval(50, 50, 300, 300);
    } else
      g.drawString("This event never happened",
                   10, 10);
  }
}
```

The Microsoft J++ compiler also provides the necessary code to support the frame required by standalone applications.

```
import java.awt.*;

class Menu2Frame extends Frame
{
  public Menu2Frame(String str)
  {
    super (str);
  }

  public boolean handleEvent(Event evt)
  {
    switch (evt.id)
    {
      case Event.WINDOW_DESTROY:
        dispose();
        System.exit(0);
        return true;

      default:
        return super.handleEvent(evt);
    }
  }
}
```

A resource file, containing the menu, was generated by the resource toolkit and converted into a Java resource with the help of the Java Resource Wizard. Here is that file:

```
//------------------------------------------------------------
// Menu2Res.java:
//     Implementation for menu creation class Menu2Res
//
//------------------------------------------------------------
import java.awt.*;

public class Menu2Res
{
  Frame    m_Frame         = null;
  boolean m_fInitialized = false;

  // MenuBar definitions
  //------------------------------------------------------------
  MenuBar mb;

  // Menu and Menu item definitions
  //------------------------------------------------------------
  Menu m1;  // Size
  MenuItem m2;  // small
  MenuItem m3;  // Medium
  MenuItem m4;  // LARGE
  MenuItem m5;  // Separator
  MenuItem m6;  // Close

  // Constructor
  //------------------------------------------------------------
  public Menu2Res (Frame frame)
  {
    m_Frame = frame;
  }

  // Initialization.
  //------------------------------------------------------------
  public boolean CreateMenu()
  {
    // Can only init controls once
    //---------------------------------------------------------
```

```
      if (m_fInitialized || m_Frame == null)
        return false;

      // Create menubar and attach to the frame
      //-----------------------------------------------------------
      mb = new MenuBar();
      m_Frame.setMenuBar(mb);

      // Create menu and menu items and assign to menubar
      //-----------------------------------------------------------
      m1 = new Menu("Size");
      mb.add(m1);
        m2 = new MenuItem("small");
        m1.add(m2);
        m3 = new MenuItem("Medium");
        m1.add(m3);
        m4 = new MenuItem("LARGE");
        m1.add(m4);
        m5 = new MenuItem("-");
        m1.add(m5);
        m6 = new MenuItem("Close");
        m1.add(m6);

      m_fInitialized = true;
      return true;
    }
}
```

The code used in the *MyFrame* class establishes a new canvas and new frame. It is here that we also gain access to the menu bar and menu resources described in Menu2Res.java. Examine the following portion of code to see how this is accomplished.

```
class MyFrame extends Frame
{
  NewCanvas newcanvas;
  MyFrame(String title) {
    super("Simple Menu Bar");
    add("Center", newcanvas = new NewCanvas());
    reshape(0, 0, 639, 479);

    // allows new menu bar & menu items
```

```
    // from resource file to be displayed
    Menu2Res myMenu = new Menu2Res(super);
    myMenu.CreateMenu();

    show();
}
```

The new canvas is created with the *NewCanvas* class. The new frame, *MyFrame*, uses **super()** to allow this class to communicate with the constructor of the parent class. This statement allows objects to be drawn on the new canvas.

myMenu represents the menu bar and menu used for this application. To create the menu bar and menu, call **CreateMenu()**, which is a member function of the Menu2Res class. That was the class created by the Java Resource Wizard.

The new menu bar and menu are placed in the new frame. A menu, named *size*, is placed on the menu bar with the **Menu()** member function. Individual menu items are identified with the **MenuItem()** member function and added to the menu bar with the **add()** member function. Once all of the items are created, the menu bar is added with a call to the **add()** member function. The **show()** member function makes the menu bar and menu visible.

The remainder of the code used in this application is similar to code discussed in the previous example in this chapter. Figure 13.15 shows a sample screen with the pop-up menu extended.

Chapter 14 extends the concepts covered here by introducing additional UI components (controls), menus, and dialog boxes.

COMING TO TERMS

AWT—The Abstract Window Toolkit gives Java programmers the ability to create applets and applications within a graphical user interface.

canvas—A canvas provides a drawing surface for other UI components or controls. Panels and frames can contain multiple canvases.

component—In the strictest sense, the Component class is an abstract class that encapsulates all of the components of the GUI visual interface.

container—Another abstract class from which other classes are derived. These include the Panel class, Frame class, Dialog class, and so on.

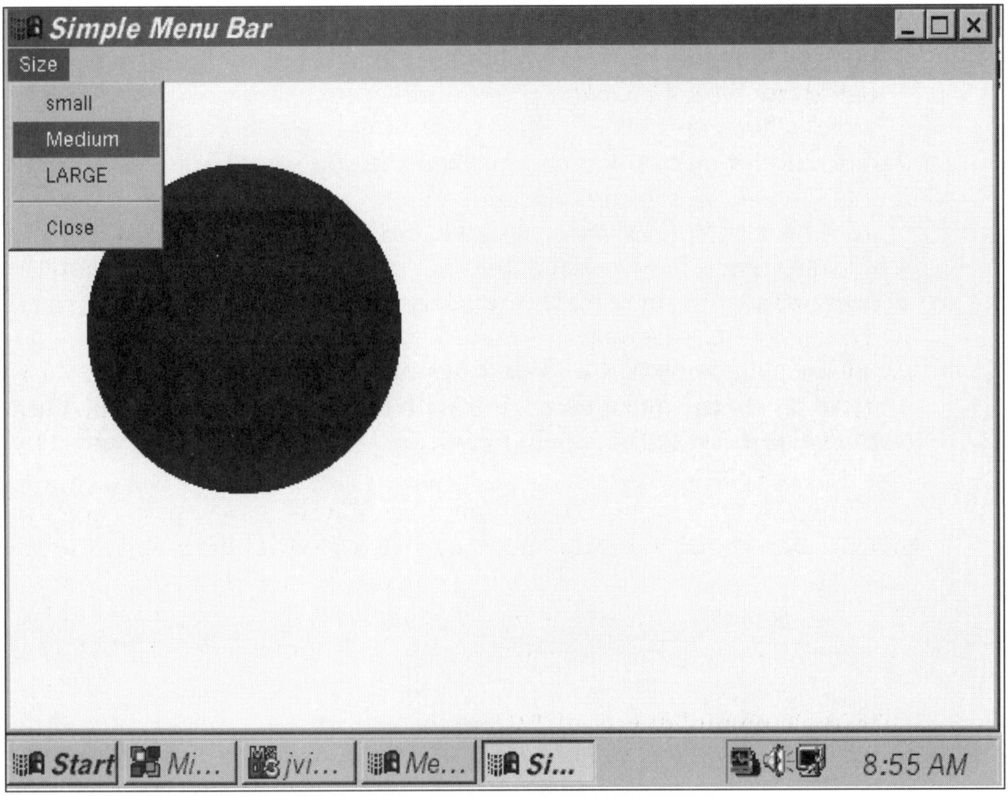

Figure 13.15: A simple menu bar and menu are created in this Java project.

event—In the context of this chapter, an event is a notification by a UI component that some action has taken place. Applications and applets must provide event handlers in order to process information between applications, applets, and UI components.

frame—Frames are considered windows in their own right. A frame typically has a title, sizing buttons, and menu bar.

gap—Refers to the space provided between UI components in various layout configurations. Usually specified in pixels.

GUI—A graphical user interface provides an environment that supports graphical elements such as font, graphics functions, and text capabilities.

inset—Refers to the space that can be used for a border around a group of UI components in a specific layout situation.

layout—How UI components are placed within a panel or frame. Predefined layouts prevent problems with screen configurations when moving from one hardware platform to another.

panel—The Panel class is used to produce a generic container for an application or applet. Panels can then contain several canvases, additional panels, UI components, and so on.

resource toolkit—A graphical toolkit provided by Microsoft C++ and J++ compilers. This toolkit allows the graphical design and layout of resources, such as menus, dialog boxes, and so on.

UI component—These items include buttons, check boxes, and so on. They are called controls by Windows programmers.

window—Similar to a panel, but with the added ability of creating a top-level window.

Chapter 14

ADDING DIALOG BOX RESOURCES

The previous chapter covered the Abstract Windowing Toolkit (AWT) from a macro perspective. This perspective lets you view the components in the AWT in terms of large-scale components such as panels, frames, layouts, and menus. This chapter concentrates on items such as buttons, check boxes, labels, and dialog boxes.

The individual UI components, described in this chapter, are called *controls* by Windows programmers. That name is used through the rest of this book to avoid confusion with Java's abstract Component class, which was also discussed in the previous chapter.

Much of the work in the last chapter focused on how to control the Java screen and produce menus similar to those used in Windows applications. Recall that it is Windows' consistent appearance and operation that have made it so successful. This chapter continues the study of controls with that thought in mind. In Windows programs, controls are most frequently found in dialog boxes. The chapter examines individual controls and then investigates how they can be used to create effective dialog boxes for data entry and thus truly interactive applications and applets.

Dialog boxes will give your projects a consistent look and operation, similar to their Windows counterparts. You can specify dialog boxes directly in your Java code or bring those dialog box resources into your applications from external sources. By using the Microsoft Resource Toolkit and the Java Resource Wizard, you'll be able to design and convert a graphical version of your dialog box directly to Java code.

BUTTONS

Buttons are the only control discussed in Chapter 13. As a matter of fact, they were used in most of the examples. Why? Buttons are one of the easiest controls to implement. A control similar to this is often referred to as a pushbutton by Windows programmers. The following portion of code was extracted from an application discussed in the previous chapter.

```
// initialize
  public void init()
  {
    setLayout(new FlowLayout());
    add(new Button("First Button"));
    add(new Button("Second Button"));
    add(new Button("Third Button"));
  }
```

In this listing, three buttons are added by using the Button class, as you can see from the bolded text. When a user clicks the mouse on a button, the button is activated and generates an event. You learned how to intercept these events in the previous chapter, too. The **getLabel()** and **setLabel()** member functions are available in this class for manipulating button labels. Figure 14.1 shows the placement of several buttons.

The **reshape()** method can be used to change the size of the button control once it is created.

CHECKBOXES AND RADIOBUTTONS

In Windows, there are two closely associated controls: Checkboxes and Radio Buttons. Under Windows, multiple items in a group can be checked. Radio buttons, however, only permit one item in a group to be selected.

Java uses two forms of Checkboxes. One form behaves like a Windows Checkbox and the other like a Windows Radio button. Java

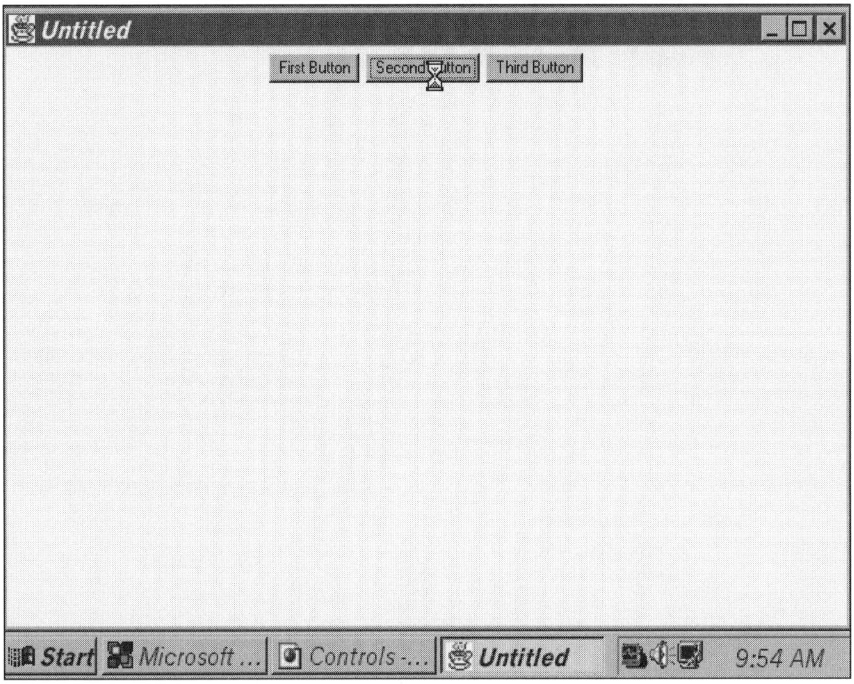

Figure 14.1: Buttons are easy to implement. Layout managers can determine a button's placement.

uses a small rectangle symbol for the true check box form. However, instead of an "x", a small check symbol is used within the rectangle to indicate selected items. When being used as a Radio button, a small circle symbol is used with a central dot to indicated a selected item. These appear just like Windows check boxes and radio buttons, otherwise. In the first check box form, called a nonexclusive Checkbox, the check box functions like a normal Windows Checkbox where multiple items can be selected at the same time. The other form of Java Checkbox, called an exclusive Checkbox, functions more like Windows Radio buttons, where only a single selection is permitted.

Several nonexclusive check box items are added with the following code. Here multiple items can be checked.

```
// initialize
  public void init()
  {
    setLayout(new FlowLayout());
    add(new Checkbox("Background"));
```

```
    add(new Checkbox("Foreground"));
    add(new Checkbox("New Font"));
}
```

Figure 14.2 shows the placement of several check boxes.

An exclusive check box list can be created with the following portion of code. Here only one item in the group can be selected.

```
// initialize
public void init()
{
  setLayout(new GridLayout(4, 1, 20, 20));
  CheckboxGroup cbgroup = new CheckboxGroup();

  add(new Checkbox("Times Roman Font", cbgroup, false));
  add(new Checkbox("Courier Font", cbgroup, true));
  add(new Checkbox("System Font", cbgroup, false));
}
```

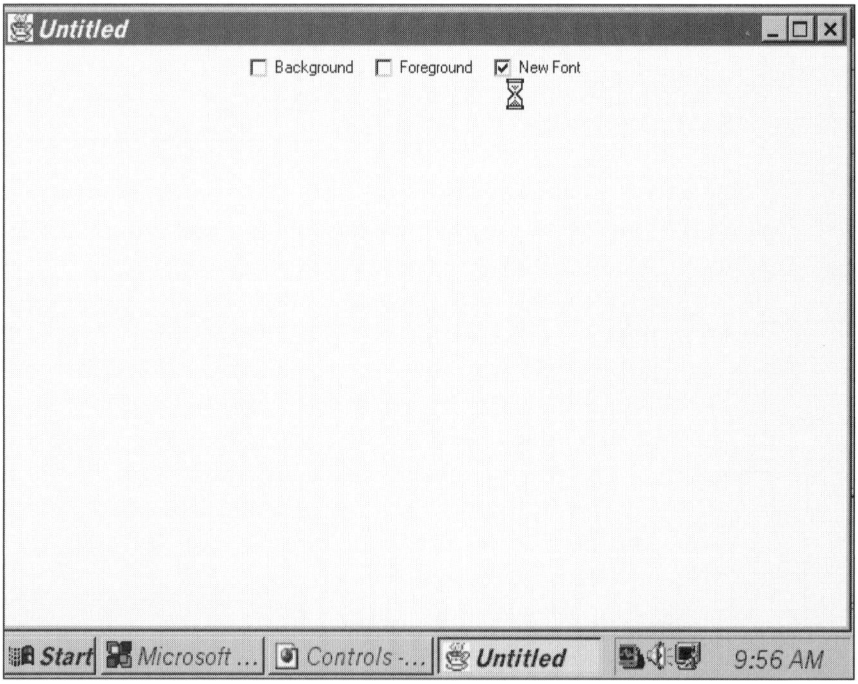

Figure 14.2: Multiple selections can be checked with the nonexclusive form of the Checkbox control.

Figure 14.3 shows several exclusive check box items that form radio controls.

In the previous example, the second item will appear checked when the check box group is drawn.

The **getLabel()**, **getState()**, **setState(boolean)**, **setCheckboxGroup()** and **setLabel(String)** member functions are available for this class. The **getState()** and **setState()** member functions let you get or toggle whether a check box item is selected.

Checkbox controls usually do not generate events on their own, so you will not normally use an event handler with check boxes. They are typically used to set features for some other event, such as a color or font selection. When used in a dialog box, for example, they set features that are intercepted when an Okay button is clicked to close the dialog box.

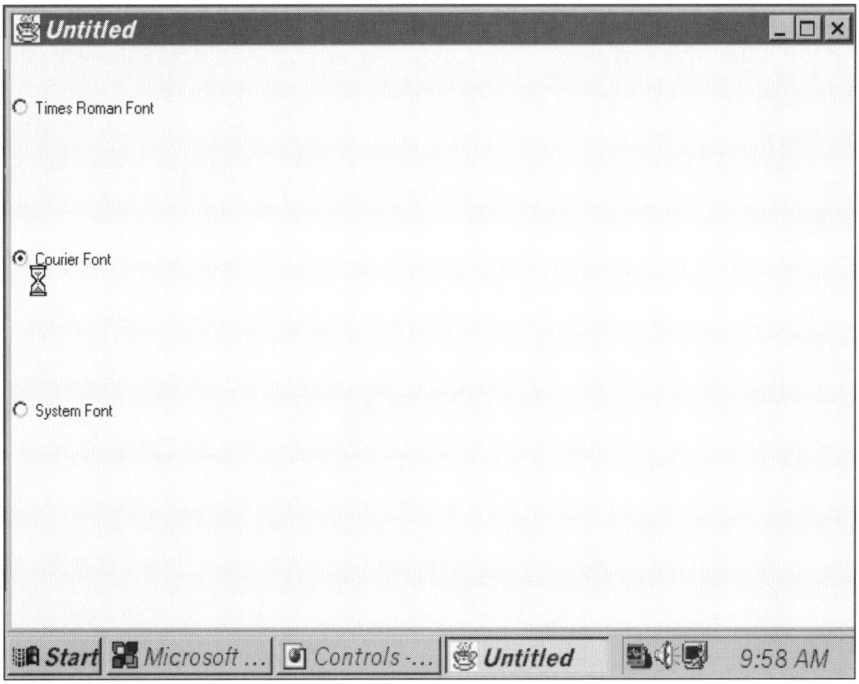

Figure 14.3: Only single selections can be selected with the exclusive form of Checkbox control.

SCROLLBARS

The Scrollbar class allows individual scroll bars to be drawn and managed easily in a Java application or applet. It is also possible to simulate the action of a slide control with the Scrollbar class. Scrollbars and Slide controls have up-down or left-right arrows, a slider (thumb), and a range of motion that the slider can be moved through. Figure 14.4 shows a vertical scrollbar and a simulated horizontal Slide control.

The syntax for creating a scrollbar can take on any of the following three forms. These constructors are described as follows:

```
Scrollbar();
Scrollbar(int orientation);
Scrollbar(int orientation, int initial_value, int thumb_size,
        int minimum, int maximum);
```

The first form creates a vertical scrollbar with a default thumb size. The initial minimum and maximum values are set to 0. The second form allows the orientation to be set. HORIZONTAL or VERTICAL can be used. The third form gives the greatest control over the appearance of a scrollbar. Orientation is specified in the same manner as it is for the second form. The second parameter gives the initial thumb

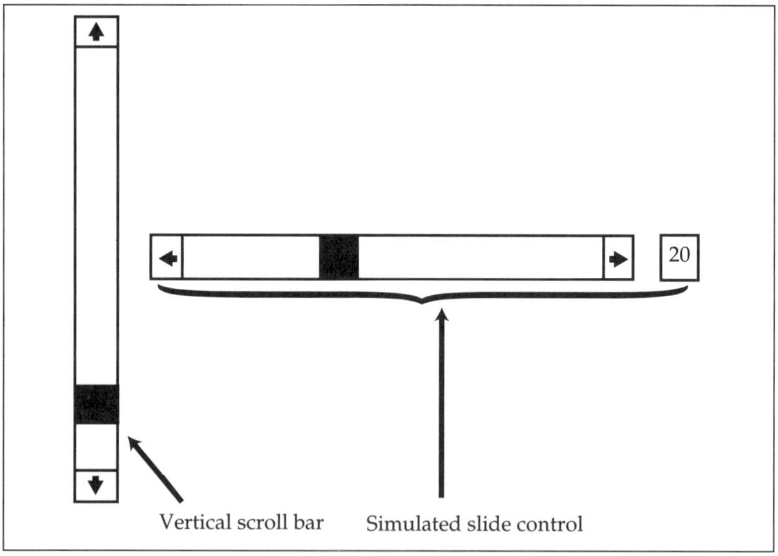

Figure 14.4: Scroll bars can be vertical or horizontal. When used in conjunction with a label control, their combined action simulates a slide control.

position. The third parameter gives the thumb size. Larger values are used to represent the need for less overall scrolling. Small values are used to indicate a large amount of scrolling. The final two parameters specify the minimum and maximum extents of the scroll as the thumb position is moved from top to bottom or left to right.

The placement of Scrollbar controls and slide controls is dependent on the layout manager selected. Various layout managers are discussed in Chapter 13.

In the following application, a vertical and horizontal scrollbar are created. They are placed with the border layout manager. The vertical scrollbar simulates a slide control, reporting the current scroll position to the screen. Examine the bolded portions of code in the following listing.

```
import java.applet.*;
import java.awt.*;
import ScrollFrame;

public class Scroll extends Applet
{
  // STANDALONE APPLICATION SUPPORT:
  //    m_fStandAlone will be set to true if applet is run
  //    standalone
  //--------------------------------------------------------------
  boolean m_fStandAlone = false;
  Label myinit;
  Scrollbar VScroll, HScroll;
  int vert, horz;

  public static void main(String args[])
  {
    ScrollFrame frame = new ScrollFrame("Scroll");

    // Must show Frame before we size it so insets() will
    // return valid values
    //----------------------------------------------------------
    frame.show();
    frame.resize(frame.insets().left+frame.insets().right+640,
           frame.insets().top  + frame.insets().bottom + 480);

    Scroll applet_Scroll = new Scroll();
```

```
    frame.add("Center", applet_Scroll);
    applet_Scroll.m_fStandAlone = true;
    applet_Scroll.init();
    applet_Scroll.start();
  }

  public Scroll()
  {
  }

  public String getAppletInfo()
  {
    return "Name: Scroll\r\n" +
           "Author: Chris H. Pappas and William H. Murray\r\n" +
           "Created with Microsoft Visual J++";
  }

  public void init()
  {
    resize(640, 480);
    setLayout(new BorderLayout());
    myinit = new Label("20");
    add("North", myinit);

    VScroll = new Scrollbar(Scrollbar.VERTICAL, 20,
                            1, 0, 400);
    add("West", VScroll);

    HScroll = new Scrollbar(Scrollbar.HORIZONTAL, 20,
                            1, 0, 400);
    add("South", HScroll);

    show();
  }

  public boolean handleEvent(Event event)
  {
    String newVvalue, newHvalue;
    if (event.target == VScroll ||
        event.target == HScroll) {
      vert = VScroll.getValue();
```

```
      horz = HScroll.getValue();
      newVvalue = String.valueOf(vert);
      myinit.setText(newVvalue);

      repaint();
      return true;
    } else
    return false;
  }

  public void destroy()
  {
  }

  public void paint(Graphics g)
  {
    g.fillOval(160 - horz, 120 - vert, 200, 300);
  }

  public void start()
  {
  }

  public void stop()
  {
  }

}
```

The ScrollFrame.java file is created by the Microsoft J++ compiler to support a standalone application. That file is shown in the following listing.

```
import java.awt.*;

class ScrollFrame extends Frame
{
  public ScrollFrame(String str)
  {
    super (str);
  }

  public boolean handleEvent(Event evt)
```

```
  {
    switch (evt.id)
    {
      case Event.WINDOW_DESTROY:
        dispose();
        System.exit(0);
        return true;

      default:
        return super.handleEvent(evt);
    }
  }
}
```

A slide control is simulated with a combination of a label control and a scrollbar control. Examine the following portion of code and note where both are created. Remember, too, that with a border layout, controls can be placed on any border of the screen.

```
public void init()
{
  setLayout(new BorderLayout());
  myinit = new Label("20");
  add("North", myinit);

  VScroll = new Scrollbar(Scrollbar.VERTICAL, 20,
                          1, 0, 400);
  add("West", VScroll);

  HScroll = new Scrollbar(Scrollbar.HORIZONTAL, 20,
                          1, 0, 400);
  add("South", HScroll);

  show();
}
```

The message handler is similar to examples discussed in Chapter 13. Note, however, in the following portion of code that the current thumb position for the vertical scrollbar is retrieved with a call to **getValue()** and then used to set the value shown in the label control with the **setText()** member function.

```
public boolean handleEvent(Event event)
{
```

```
  String newVvalue, newHvalue;
  if (event.target == VScroll ||
      event.target == HScroll) {
    vert = VScroll.getValue();
    horz = HScroll.getValue();
    newVvalue = String.valueOf(vert);
    myinit.setText(newVvalue);

    repaint();
    return true;
  } else
  return false;
}
```

The scrollbars can now be used to scroll a text document, an image retrieved from a file, or a simple graphics shape. This example uses the scrollbar information to allow scrolling an oval shape.

```
public void paint(Graphics g)
{
  g.fillOval(160 - horz, 120 - vert, 200, 300);
}
```

Figure 14.5 shows the scroll bar code during execution.

Here is one final interesting note: if you resize the window, Java will resize both scrollbars accordingly.

LISTS

A list control manages a list of items added by the programmer. If the list control is created in an exclusive form, the user will only be able to select one item from the list. If the list control is created in a nonexclusive form, multiple items in the list can be selected. Recall that Checkbox controls provided similar forms.

If the number of items in a list control exceeds the size of the List control, Java will automatically add and manage a vertical scrollbar for the List control. The List class provides two forms via the following constructors:

```
List();
List(int number, boolean value);
```

The first constructor creates a List control that operates in the exclusive form, allowing only one selection from the list. The second

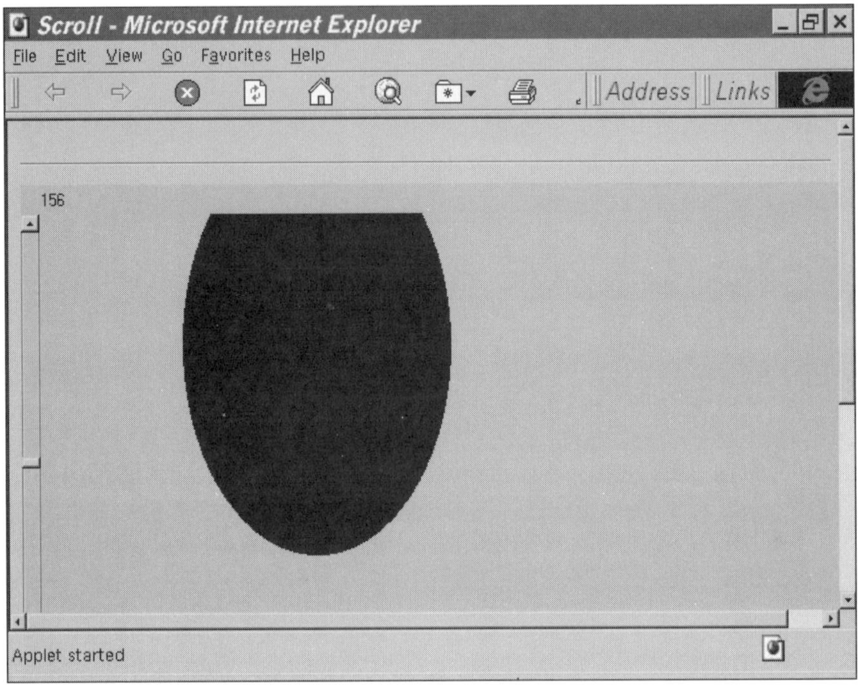

Figure 14.5: Two scrollbars are used to scroll about a graphics figure. The vertical scrollbar simulates a slide control.

constructor allows the number of items to be displayed to be specified as the first parameter, and whether the List control will operate in exclusive or nonexclusive form to be specified by the second parameter. If the second parameter is false, the List control operates in exclusive form. If true, multiple items can be selected from the list.

Here is a small portion of code that will implement two List controls. The first List control displays two items in the list and allows the user to select one item at a time. The second List control displays three items in the list and allows the user to make multiple selections at the same time. Remember that the layout manager selected will often determine the limits of what is visible on the screen.

```
public void init()
{
  setLayout(new FlowLayout(FlowLayout.CENTER, 20, 20));

  List res_list = new List(2, false);
  res_list.addItem("640 x 480");
```

```
    res_list.addItem("800 x 600");
    res_list.addItem("1024 x 768");
    res_list.addItem("1024 x 1024");

    List font_char = new List(3, true);
    font_char.addItem("bold");
    font_char.addItem("italic");
    font_char.addItem("redline");
    font_char.addItem("underscore the whole line");

    add(res_list);
    add(font_char);
}
```

Figure 14.6 shows the two list controls created in this example.

Additional member functions such as **countItems()**, **getItem()**, **getSelectedItem()**, and **select()** give this control added flexibility. For

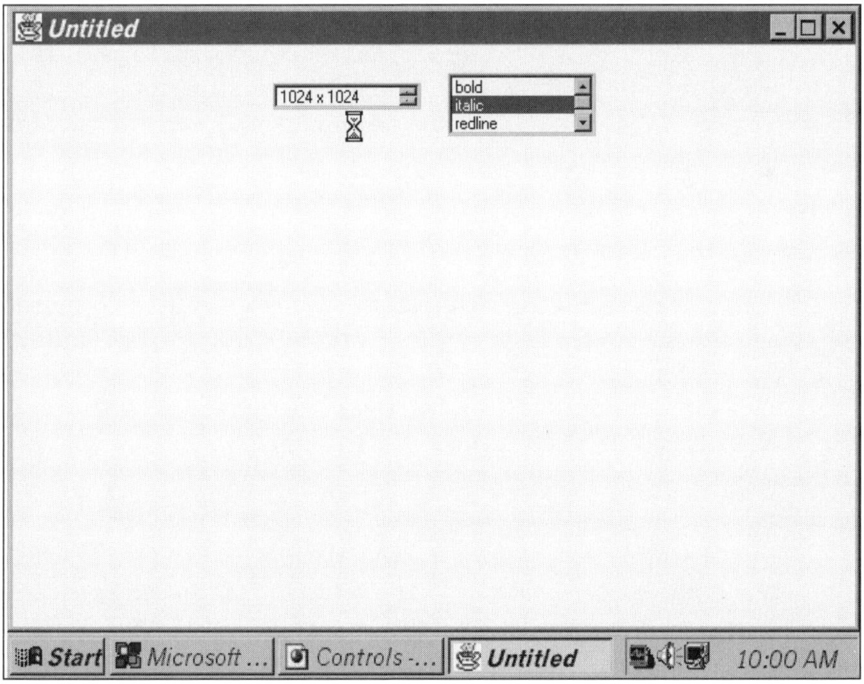

Figure 14.6: List controls allow single and/or multiple selection of list items.

example, **countItems()** can be used to return the number of items in a list. Examine this class to investigate other member functions.

TEXT AREAS

A Text Area control manages text in an area of the screen. A Text Area control is created by the TextArea class. This class manages the text area and provides and activates scrollbars when needed.

```
// initialize
public void init()
{
  String mystring = "      Text can be entered in a "+
                    "text area from a simple string, "+
                    "like this example or from a "+
                    "file.\n"+
                    "      The TextArea() class will "+
                    "automatically add and manage\n"+
                    "scroll bars where necessary.\n"+
                    "      This example has an active "+
                    "horizontal scroll bar.  There is "+
                    "not sufficient text to\n"+
                    "activate a vertical scroll bar.\n";

  TextArea text = new TextArea(mystring, 20, 20);
  add(text);
}
```

In this code, the TextArea class creates a text area 20 characters wide and 20 characters high within the frame. Figure 14.7 shows a sample output for this code.

There are actually four variations for creating text areas with this class, based on the supplied constructors.

```
TextArea();
TextArea(String mystring);
TextArea(int width, int height);
TextArea(String mystring, int width, int height);
```

The first form creates a text area without text with no width or height. This information, it is assumed, will be supplied at a later time. The second form creates a text area with the supplied string information, but still with no preset width or height. The third form creates a

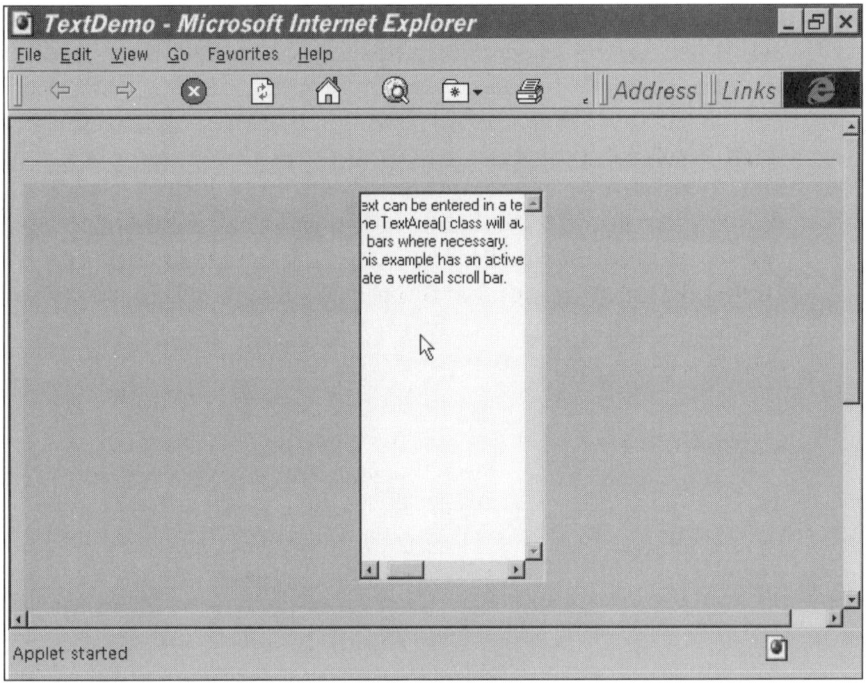

Figure 14.7: The TextArea class provides and activates scrollbars to help manage text on the screen.

text area with a predefined size, but with no initial string information. The final form creates a text area with initial string information and a predefined size.

When the TextArea class is used in conjunction with a layout manager, the layout manager will affect what you see in the layout area.

The TextArea class provides additional methods, such as **getColumns()**, **getRows()**, **insertText(String mystring)**, and **replaceText(String mystring, int newwidth, int newheight)**. These member functions provide additional flexibility and make this control ideal for managing and displaying large amounts of text on the screen.

LABELS AND TEXT FIELDS

Labels and text fields are frequently used together. The Label class lets you draw single-line string labels anywhere in the panel. It is one of the simplest controls available to the Java programmer because an event handler is never required in its implementation. Labels are frequently used to tag other controls, such as those produced by the TextField class. When labels are used in conjunction with text fields, the basic data entry component used in most dialog boxes is created.

Text fields are very similar to Windows Edit controls. They allow the user to enter string information from the keyboard. This information is usually limited to one line. The string information can be converted by the programmer to other data types. For example, 34.14, can be accepted and used as a string of characters or converted to the real number 34.14 with the appropriate routines.

Labels

The Label class provides three forms of constructors that allow the programmer more flexibility in label entry and alignment.

```
Label();
Label(String mystring);
Label(String mystring, int myalignment);
```

By default, labels are aligned on the left. The first form creates an empty label. The second form creates a label with an initial string. This default string can be changed at a later date with the **setText()** method. The third form adds an alignment option. Label alignments include CENTER, LEFT, and RIGHT. RIGHT justification is often used when a label is placed to the left of a text field.

The Label class also provides additional member functions that provide additional flexibility for this class. These member functions include **getAlignment()**, **getText()**, **setAlignment()**, and **setText(String newstring)**. Additionally, labels are printed in the current font and current color. The **reshape()** method can also be used to change the size of the label control.

Text Fields

The TextField class provides four forms of constructors that allow variations in the manner in which these controls are created.

```
TextField();
TextField(int newwidth);
TextField(String mystring);
TextField(String mystring, int newwidth);
```

If no additional parameters are specified, an empty text field will be created. The *newwidth* parameter allows the number of characters, for the text field, to be set. The *mystring* parameter allows an initial string to be specified as the default.

The **getText()** and **setText(String newstring)** member functions give this class additional flexibility.

Additionally, in situations in which you do not want the typed information to appear in the text field, the **setEchoCharacter()** member function can be used. For example:

```
textfield.setEchoCharacter(" ");
```

In this case, each character that appears in the text field will be a blank. If used for password entry, an asterisk (*) could be substituted for the blank character.

A Label and Text Field Example

In the following portion of code, several Label and TextField controls are placed in the panel. As you examine the code, notice the order in which the controls are added with the **add()** member function.

```
// Initialize
public void init()
{
  Label name = new Label("User Name:",
                         Label.RIGHT);
  Label ss = new Label("Social Security Number:",
                       Label.RIGHT);
  Label id = new Label("Password:", Label.RIGHT);

  TextField namedata = new TextField(20);
  TextField ssdata = new TextField(10);
  TextField iddata = new TextField("********", 20);
  iddata.setEchoCharacter('*');

  add(name);
  add(namedata);
  add(ss);
  add(ssdata);
  add(id);
  add(iddata);
}
```

The order in which controls are added is important, as well as the initial size of the frame, because no layout method is used. This piece of code will correctly draw and place the various controls. However, since no event handler is provided, there is no way to process the information entered by the user. This example is useful because it forms the foundation for the most important data entry control available—the dialog box. Dialog boxes are covered in detail in the next section. Figure 14.8 shows a panel of label and text field controls.

DIALOG BOXES

As discussed in the previous chapter, menus are a simple way to interact with a Java application or applet. This section explores a more significant means of data entry: the dialog box. Though you can place Java controls directly into an application's main panel or frame, dialog

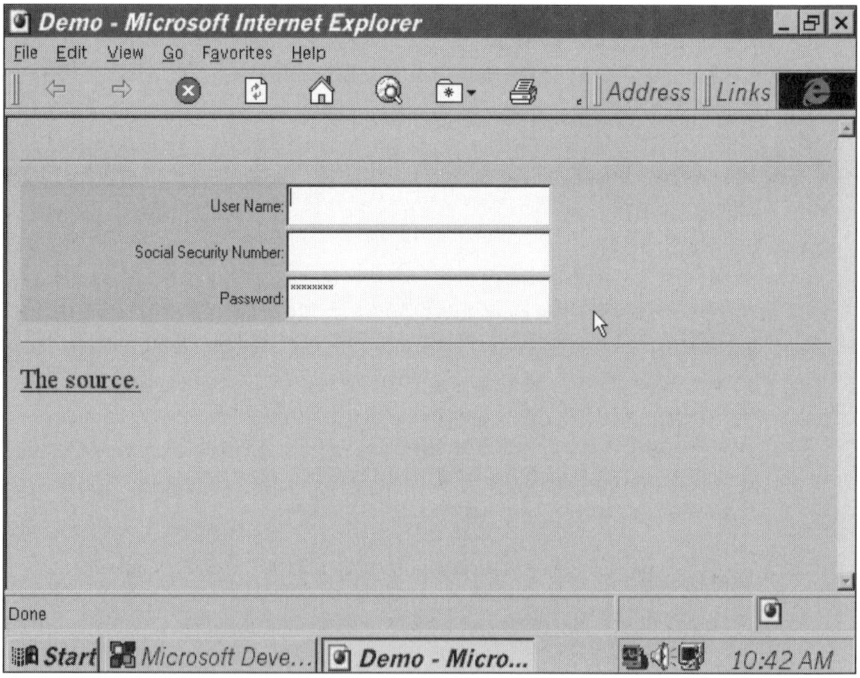

Figure 14.8: Careful alignment allows label controls and text field controls to form a data entry box that is the precursor to a dialog box.

boxes are a preferable data entry technique for maintaining consistency among all Java platforms.

Dialog boxes designed for Java can contain the same types of controls Windows dialog boxes contain. This includes buttons, check boxes, radiobuttons, labels, scrollbars, text fields, text areas, and so on. The dialog box gives the Java user true interactive communications with an application or applet while maintaining the consistent look and operation of the familiar Windows interface.

A dialog box is usually accessed as a menu item, in a normal Java menu. When selected as a menu item, the dialog box appears as a pop-up window to the user. To distinguish a dialog box entry from ordinary menu items, three dots or ellipsis (...) follow the dialog box menu item. Thus, when you view a menu and see three dots after a menu item, you know that a dialog box follows that selection.

Dialog boxes range in complexity from very simple to very complicated. **About** boxes are simple dialog boxes that require very little programming effort. They are used to inform the user about the application and usually contain the developer's name(s) and a copyright notice. On the other hand, dialog boxes used for data entry can be very complicated, take days to properly design, and require an extensive programming interface.

The remaining examples in this chapter illustrate simple **About** and data entry dialog boxes. The Dialog1 example shows how to create an **About** box. The Dialog2 example shows how to use a dialog box, in conjunction with several controls, to retrieve a title for some simple screen graphics. Dialog3 is used to show how numeric data can be entered in a dialog box and used directly in the application or applet. Dialog4 illustrates how to design a dialog box with the Resource Toolkit and bring that code into your Java application.

The dialog box concepts covered in the following sections are really put to work in the next chapter, Chapter 15, as you develop several professional-quality Java applications and applets.

Specifying Dialog Boxes Within Your Java Code

There are two basic methods of specifying dialog boxes for Java applications. The first technique, discussed in this section, allows you to use the AWT to design and place controls. The AWT and the layout manager allow controls to be manually placed in a dialog box. The process can be tedious, but placement is precise and portable from one system to another. The second technique, discussed in the next section, allows the use of the Resource Toolkit, a graphical design tool, to layout and place controls. The graphical file is then converted to a .java file with the Java Resource Wizard. Because of the portability issue with Java code, the second technique does have some limitations.

In this section the Dialog1, Dialog2, and Dialog3 examples are used to illustrate the first technique for incorporating dialog box resources.

Dialog1 **About** dialog boxes have the simplest style possible. They consist of several lines of text, usually created with a Label control. They usually contain a single Button control, labeled "Okay". Their sole purpose is not to collect data, but to inform the user regarding the application or applet they are using.

As you examine the following listing, you will notice many of the components that were present in the menu bar example from the previous chapter. This should not surprise you, because dialog boxes are typically accessed through a normal menu.

```
import java.applet.*;
import java.awt.*;
import Dialog1Frame;

public class Dialog1 extends Applet
{
  // STANDALONE APPLICATION SUPPORT:
  //    m_fStandAlone will be set to true if applet is run
  //    standalone
  //--------------------------------------------------------------
  boolean m_fStandAlone = false;

  public static void main(String args[])
  {
    Dialog1Frame frame = new Dialog1Frame("Dialog1");

    // Must show Frame before we size it so insets() will
    // return valid values
    //------------------------------------------------------------
    //frame.show();
    frame.resize(frame.insets().left+frame.insets().right+640,
          frame.insets().top  + frame.insets().bottom + 480);
```

```
    Dialog1 applet_Dialog1 = new Dialog1();

    frame.add("Center", applet_Dialog1);
    applet_Dialog1.m_fStandAlone = true;
    applet_Dialog1.init();
    applet_Dialog1.start();
  }

  public Dialog1()
  {
  }

  public String getAppletInfo()
  {
    return "Name: Dialog1\r\n" +
           "Author: Chris H. Pappas and William H. Murray\r\n"+
           "Created with Microsoft Visual J++";
  }

  public void init()
  {
    resize(640, 480);
    new MyFrame("");
  }

  public void destroy()
  {
  }

  public void paint(Graphics g)
  {
  }

  public void start()
  {
  }

  public void stop()
  {
  }
```

```
}

class MyFrame extends Frame
{
  NewCanvas newcanvas;
  Dialog AboutDialog;

  MyFrame(String title) {
    // Add a menu bar
    super("Simple Menu Bar");
    add("Center", newcanvas = new NewCanvas());
    reshape(0, 0, 639, 479);
    MenuBar menubar = new MenuBar();
    setMenuBar(menubar);

    // Add a menu and menu items
    Menu help = new Menu("Information");
    help.add(new MenuItem("About..."));
    help.add(new MenuItem("-"));
    help.add(new MenuItem("Close"));
    menubar.add(help);

    show();
  }

public boolean action(Event event, Object object) {
    String label = (String)object;
    if (event.target instanceof MenuItem) {
      if(label.equals("About...")) {
        Dialog aboutd = new AboutDialog(this);
        aboutd.show();
      } else
      if(label.equals("Close")) {
        System.exit(0);
      }
      return true;
    }
    else
      return false;
  }
}
```

```
class NewCanvas extends Canvas {
  public void paint(Graphics g) {
    // Draw a couple of shapes on canvas
    g.drawRect(50, 50, 100, 100);
    g.drawOval(200, 200, 200, 200);
  }
}

class AboutDialog extends Dialog {
  public AboutDialog(Frame parent) {
    super(parent, "About Dialog Box", true);

    Panel firstpanel = new Panel();
    firstpanel.setLayout(new GridLayout(4, 1, 10, 10));
    firstpanel.add(new Label("About Box Demo",
                             Label.CENTER));
    firstpanel.add(new Label("C. Pappas and W. Murray",
                             Label.CENTER));
    firstpanel.add(new Label("Copyright (c) 1996",
                             Label.CENTER));
    add("Center", firstpanel);

    Panel secondpanel = new Panel();
    secondpanel.add(new Button("Okay"));
    add("South", secondpanel);

    reshape(200, 200, 300, 200);
  }

  public boolean action(Event event, Object object) {
    String label = (String)object;
    if (event.target instanceof Button) {
      if(label.equals("Okay")) {
        dispose();
      }
      return true;
    } else
    return false;
  }
```

```
}
```

Because this application will be run as a standalone program, the Microsoft J++ compiler has created this additional file for support.

```
import java.awt.*;

class Dialog1Frame extends Frame
{
  public Dialog1Frame(String str)
  {
    super (str);
  }

  public boolean handleEvent(Event evt)
  {
    switch (evt.id)
    {
      case Event.WINDOW_DESTROY:
        dispose();
        System.exit(0);
        return true;

      default:
        return super.handleEvent(evt);
    }
  }
}
```

In this application, a menu bar requires a separate frame, so a new frame is created and displayed.

A new canvas is created for the drawing surface and resized to a VGA screen size. The menu bar is then added, as you can see in the following portion of code.

```
// Add a menu bar
super("Simple Menu Bar");
add("Center", newcanvas = new NewCanvas());
reshape(0, 0, 639, 479);
MenuBar menubar = new MenuBar();
setMenuBar(menubar);
```

The menu contains three menu items: an About... option, a menu bar break, and a Close option. The About... option opens an **About** dialog box, while the Close option closes the application.

```
// Add a menu and menu items
Menu help = new Menu("Information");
help.add(new MenuItem("About..."));
help.add(new MenuItem("-"));
help.add(new MenuItem("Close"));
menubar.add(help);
```

Recall from Chapter 13 that menu resources can be designed in the Resource Toolkit, converted with the Java Resource Wizard and then incorporated into your Java project code. In simple examples, we prefer to include the resource information in the Java source code, as shown in this example.

The Dialog class is used to create a new dialog box. There are two versions of constructors used by the Dialog class.

```
Dialog(Frame, boolean modal);
Dialog(Frame, String title, boolean modal);
```

The Frame parameter refers to the newly created frame for the application or applet. The *title*, if used, represents the string displayed within the title bar of the dialog box. The boolean *modal* value is used to determine if the dialog box must be closed before other screen action can take place. Modal dialog boxes are the most common dialog boxes used in both Java and Windows applications. A modeless dialog box is typically used when the user must constantly change a value or select a particular control while the application is in operation. For example, a CD player application lets you start, stop, and pause a playback. The user does not need to open a menu and make a dialog box selection for each choice. A boolean **true** marks the dialog box as a modal dialog box.

```
// Add an About DialogBox
AboutDialog = new Dialog(this, "About", true);
```

Designing a good-looking and functional dialog box can require a large investment in time. Windows programmers use the Resource Toolkit to graphically design dialog boxes and place controls. Java programmers can design dialog boxes the conventional way or use the Resource Toolkit and the Java Resource Wizard to convert their graphical designs to Java usable code. As mentioned earlier, the first three dialog box examples in this chapter create dialog boxes with the conventional method. When using conventional design, Java programmers rely on the layout manager to place Java controls.

In this example, a special class defines the dialog box resource. Here the **GridLayout()** class is used to place three labels. An Okay button is added to allow the user to leave the dialog box.

```
class AboutDialog extends Dialog {
  public AboutDialog(Frame parent) {
    super(parent, "About Dialog Box", true);

    Panel firstpanel = new Panel();
    firstpanel.setLayout(new GridLayout(3, 1, 10, 10));
    firstpanel.add(new Label("About Box Demo",
                             Label.CENTER));
    firstpanel.add(new Label("Chris Pappas and William Murray",
                             Label.CENTER));
    firstpanel.add(new Label("Copyright (c) 1996",
                             Label.CENTER));
    add("Center", firstpanel);

    Panel secondpanel = new Panel();
    secondpanel.add(new Button("Okay"));
    add("South", secondpanel);

    reshape(200, 200, 300, 200);
  }
```

Those three controls are added in a vertical fashion, with each label being centered on its given grid position. The button control is added at the bottom of the dialog box. As the dialog box becomes more complicated, the designer must make careful use of various layout managers.

Making a menu item selection or clicking on the button in the dialog box triggers an event that can be intercepted and processed by the application. The dialog box is placed on the screen, when the user selects the About... menu item. Examine the following portion of code:

```
if (event.target instanceof MenuItem) {
  if(label.equals("About...")) {
    Dialog aboutd = new AboutDialog(this);
    aboutd.show();
  } else
   .
   .
   .
```

When the user selects About..., the new dialog box is created. The **show()** member function displays the dialog box. This gives the effect of popping up a dialog box. The focus is now on the dialog box, and the user can make use of any controls placed within the dialog box area.

When the user has made selections in the dialog box, the dialog box must be destroyed. This is done with the following portion of code:

```
public boolean action(Event event, Object object) {
  String label = (String)object;
  if (event.target instanceof Button) {
    if(label.equals("Okay")) {
      dispose();
    }
   .
   .
   .
```

The dialog box is destroyed with a call to the **dispose()** member function. If the dialog box is modal, this is also the point at which dialog box information is transferred to the application or applet. If the dialog box is modeless, another technique must be used to continuously transfer dialog box information to the application while the dialog box remains opened.

To make this application fully functional, some simple graphics are drawn on the canvas. Figure 14.9 shows the dialog box and the canvas for this application.

As you continue to investigate dialog boxes in the remaining two examples, you will notice that the code has been kept as consistent as possible with this example. The code changes you will see for the dialog box are those required to add new functionality to the application or applet.

Dialog2 Dialog boxes are often used to allow the user to enter strings of text. These strings are then used as labels for charts, graphs, and other graphics presentations. The following dialog box example is patterned after the previous About box example. In this case, however, the dialog box has been expanded to include a label, text field control, and two buttons. The text field control lets the user enter a string that will later be used on the canvas as a label for the graphics image. Two buttons are included. One functions as a normal Okay button, while

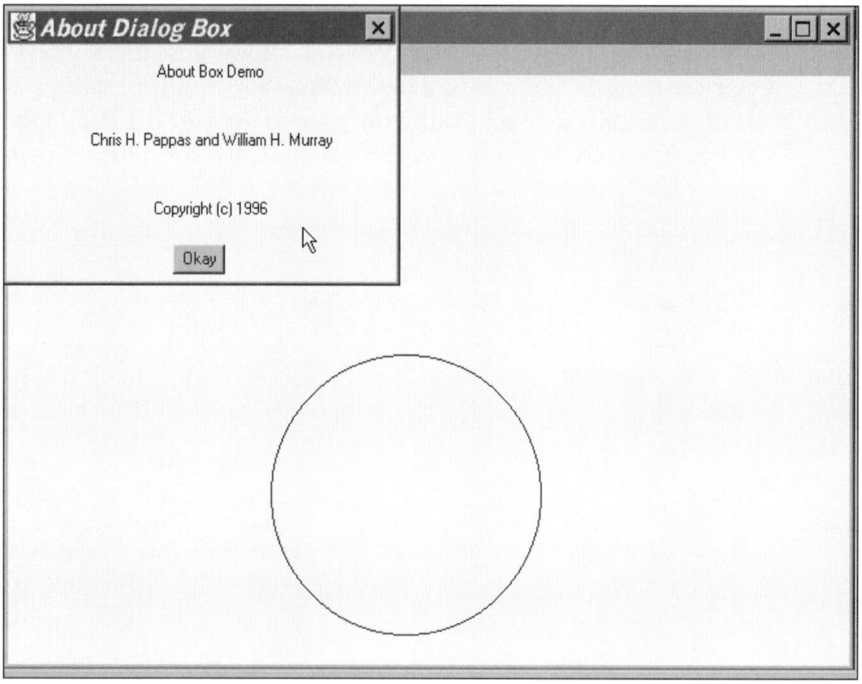

Figure 14.9: An About dialog box created for the Dialog1 example.

the other is a Cancel button. Cancel buttons are used to let users back out of dialog box changes that they have decided not to use.

Examine the following code listing. The items shown in a bold font are the portions of the example you should focus on. You'll notice that this code is patterned after the menu bar example in the previous chapter. A new dialog box has also been added.

```
import java.applet.*;
import java.awt.*;
import Dialog2Frame;

public class Dialog2 extends Applet
{
  // STANDALONE APPLICATION SUPPORT:
  //    m_fStandAlone will be set to true if applet is run
  //    standalone
  //--------------------------------------------------------------
  boolean m_fStandAlone = false;
```

```
public static void main(String args[])
{
  Dialog2Frame frame = new Dialog2Frame("Dialog2");

  // Must show Frame before we size it so insets() will
  // return valid values
  //----------------------------------------------------------
  //frame.show();
  frame.resize(frame.insets().left+frame.insets().right+640,
         frame.insets().top  + frame.insets().bottom + 480);

  Dialog2 applet_Dialog2 = new Dialog2();

  frame.add("Center", applet_Dialog2);
  applet_Dialog2.m_fStandAlone = true;
  applet_Dialog2.init();
  applet_Dialog2.start();
}

public Dialog2()
{
}

public String getAppletInfo()
{
  return "Name: Dialog2\r\n" +
         "Author: Chris H. Pappas and William H. Murray\r\n"+
         "Created with Microsoft Visual J++";
}

public void init()
{
  resize(640, 480);
  new MyFrame("");
}

public void destroy()
{
}
```

```
  public void paint(Graphics g)
  {
  }

  public void start()
  {
  }

  public void stop()
  {
  }

}

class MyFrame extends Frame
{
  NewCanvas newcanvas;
  Dialog TextDialog;
  static int index;
  static String mystring;

  MyFrame(String title) {
    // Add menu bar
    super("Menu Bar");
    add("Center", newcanvas = new NewCanvas());
    reshape(0, 0, 639, 479);
    MenuBar menubar = new MenuBar();
    setMenuBar(menubar);

    // Add Menu and Menu Items
    Menu size = new Menu("Size");
    size.add(new MenuItem("small"));
    size.add(new MenuItem("Medium"));
    size.add(new MenuItem("LARGE"));
    size.add(new MenuItem("-"));
    size.add(new MenuItem("Close"));
    menubar.add(size);

    Menu info = new Menu("Information");
    info.add(new MenuItem("Text..."));
    menubar.add(info);
```

```
      show();
    }

    // process menu selections
    public boolean action(Event event, Object object) {
      String label = (String)object;
      if (event.target instanceof MenuItem) {
        if(label.equals("small")) {
          index = 0;
        } else
        if(label.equals("Medium")) {
          index = 1;
        } else
        if(label.equals("LARGE")) {
          index = 2;
        } else
        // draw the dialog box and show
        if(label.equals("Text...")) {
          Dialog Textd = new TextDialog(this);
          Textd.show();
        } else
        if(label.equals("Close")) {
          System.exit(0);
        }
        newcanvas.repaint();
        return true;
      }
      else
        return false;
    }
  }

  class NewCanvas extends Canvas {
    public void paint(Graphics g) {
      // Draw graphics, draw entered string
      if (MyFrame.index == 0) {
        g.fillOval(50, 50, 100, 100);
      } else
      if (MyFrame.index == 1) {
```

```
      g.fillOval(50, 50, 200, 200);
    } else
    if (MyFrame.index == 2) {
      g.fillOval(50, 50, 300, 300);
    }
    g.drawString(MyFrame.mystring, 100, 400);
  }
}

// Information for dialog box creation
class TextDialog extends Dialog {
  public TextDialog(Frame parent) {
    super(parent, "Text Entry Dialog Box", true);

    Panel firstpanel = new Panel();
    firstpanel.setLayout(new GridLayout(2, 2, 10, 10));
    firstpanel.add(new Label("Enter Title:", Label.CENTER));
    NewText = new TextField(20);
    firstpanel.add(NewText);
    add("Center", firstpanel);

    Panel secondpanel = new Panel();
    secondpanel.add(new Button("Okay"));
    secondpanel.add(new Button("Cancel"));
    add("South", secondpanel);

    reshape(200, 200, 200, 125);
  }

  // process dialog box button events
  public boolean action(Event event, Object object) {
    String label = (String)object;
    if (event.target instanceof Button) {
      if(label.equals("Okay")) {
        // retrieve data from dialog box
        MyFrame.mystring = NewText.getText();
        dispose();
      }
      else
        if (label.equals("Cancel")) {
          dispose();
```

```
        }
        return true;
      } else
      return false;
    }

    TextField NewText;
}
```

Because this application will be run as a standalone program, the Microsoft J++ compiler has created this additional file for support.

```
import java.awt.*;

class Dialog2Frame extends Frame
{
  public Dialog2Frame(String str)
  {
    super (str);
  }

  public boolean handleEvent(Event evt)
  {
    switch (evt.id)
    {
      case Event.WINDOW_DESTROY:
        dispose();
        System.exit(0);
        return true;

      default:
        return super.handleEvent(evt);
    }
  }
}
```

The dialog box design will draw a label and text field, and then place both buttons at the bottom of the dialog box. As you design dialog boxes, you will probably have to experiment with layout managers and reshape the dialog box until it suits your design.

.

.

```
Panel firstpanel = new Panel();
firstpanel.setLayout(new GridLayout(2, 2, 10, 10));
firstpanel.add(new Label("Enter Title:", Label.CENTER));
NewText = new TextField(20);
firstpanel.add(NewText);
add("Center", firstpanel);

Panel secondpanel = new Panel();
secondpanel.add(new Button("Okay"));
secondpanel.add(new Button("Cancel"));
add("South", secondpanel);

reshape(200, 200, 200, 125);
   .
   .
   .
```

Apart from the fact that this dialog box contains more controls, the layout is not that much different from the **About** dialog box of the previous example. This dialog box does differ from the previous example in that it returns a string of text to the application or applet. Can you see where this takes place in the following portion of code?

```
if (event.target instanceof Button) {
  if(label.equals("Okay")) {
    // retrieve data from dialog box
    MyFrame.mystring = NewText.getText();
    dispose();
   .
   .
   .
TextField NewText;
```

The *mystring* variable was declared **static** so that its information could be shared with the graphics functions used in the new canvas. Here is the portion of code that draws the string of text on the new canvas.

```
   .
   .
   .
g.drawString(MyFrame.mystring, 100, 400);
```

Figure 14.10 shows the dialog box that allows text entry and the graphics on the canvas.

Dialog3 Often you'll want to use dialog boxes to enter numeric information. This information can then be used to make numeric calculations or draw pie, bar, and line charts. In the following example, two text fields are used to let the user enter integer values as strings. These string values are converted to integers and used to define the size of the graphics drawn to the canvas. Once again, pay particular attention to the bolded text because it represents the significant changes from the previous example.

```
import java.applet.*;
import java.awt.*;
import Dialog3Frame;
```

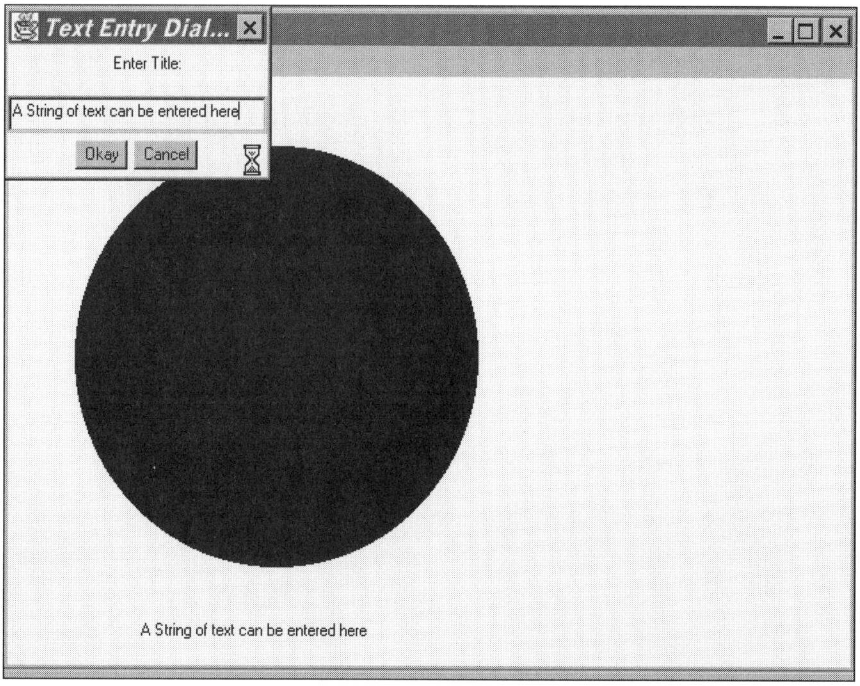

Figure 14.10: A dialog box that allows text entry is used in the Dialog2 example.

```
public class Dialog3 extends Applet
{
  // STANDALONE APPLICATION SUPPORT:
  //    m_fStandAlone will be set to true if applet is run
  //    standalone
  //--------------------------------------------------------------
  boolean m_fStandAlone = false;

  public static void main(String args[])
  {
    Dialog3Frame frame = new Dialog3Frame("Dialog3");

    // Must show Frame before we size it so insets() will
    // return valid values
    //------------------------------------------------------------
    //frame.show();
    frame.resize(frame.insets().left+frame.insets().right+640,
           frame.insets().top  + frame.insets().bottom + 480);

    Dialog3 applet_Dialog3 = new Dialog3();

    frame.add("Center", applet_Dialog3);
    applet_Dialog3.m_fStandAlone = true;
    applet_Dialog3.init();
    applet_Dialog3.start();
  }

  public Dialog3()
  {
  }

  public String getAppletInfo()
  {
    return "Name: Dialog3\r\n" +
           "Author: Chris H. Pappas and William H. Murray\r\n"+
           "Created with Microsoft Visual J++";
  }

  public void init()
  {
    resize(640, 480);
    new MyFrame("");
```

```
    }

    public void destroy()
    {
    }

    public void paint(Graphics g)
    {
    }

    public void start()
    {
    }

    public void stop()
    {
    }

}

class MyFrame extends Frame
{
  NewCanvas newcanvas;
  Dialog NumDialog;
  TextField NewNum1, NewNum2;
  static String mystring1, mystring2;

  MyFrame(String title) {
    // Add menu bar
    super("Simple Menu Bar");
    add("Center", newcanvas = new NewCanvas());
    reshape(0, 0, 639, 479);
    MenuBar menubar = new MenuBar();
    setMenuBar(menubar);

    Menu info = new Menu("Numbers");
    info.add(new MenuItem("Data..."));
    info.add(new MenuItem("-"));
    info.add(new MenuItem("Exit"));
    menubar.add(info);
```

```
    show();
  }

  public boolean action(Event event, Object object) {
    String label = (String)object;
    if (event.target instanceof MenuItem) {
      if(label.equals("Data...")) {
        Dialog Numd = new NumDialog(this);
        Numd.show();
      } else
      if(label.equals("Exit")) {
        System.exit(0);
      }
      newcanvas.repaint();
      return true;
    }
    else
      return false;
  }
}

class NewCanvas extends Canvas {
  public void paint(Graphics g) {
    int intx, inty;

    intx = Integer.parseInt(MyFrame.mystring1);
    inty = Integer.parseInt(MyFrame.mystring2);
    g.drawOval(50, 50, intx, inty);
  }
}

// Information for dialog box creation
class NumDialog extends Dialog {
  public NumDialog(Frame parent) {
    super(parent, "Numeric Entry Dialog Box", true);

    Panel firstpanel = new Panel();
    firstpanel.setLayout(new GridLayout(2, 2, 5, 5));
    firstpanel.add(new Label("Integer #1:", Label.CENTER));
    NewNum1 = new TextField(20);
    firstpanel.add(NewNum1);
```

```
    firstpanel.add(new Label("Integer #2:", Label.CENTER));
    NewNum2 = new TextField(20);
    firstpanel.add(NewNum2);
    add("Center", firstpanel);

    Panel secondpanel = new Panel();
    secondpanel.add(new Button("Okay"));
    secondpanel.add(new Button("Cancel"));
    add("South", secondpanel);

    reshape(200, 200, 300, 120);
  }

  // process dialog box button events
  public boolean action(Event event, Object object) {
    String label = (String)object;
    if (event.target instanceof Button) {
      if(label.equals("Okay")) {
        // retrieve data from dialog box
        MyFrame.mystring1 = NewNum1.getText();
        MyFrame.mystring2 = NewNum2.getText();
        dispose();
      }
      else
        if (label.equals("Cancel")) {
          dispose();
      }
      return true;
    } else
    return false;
  }

  TextField NewNum1, NewNum2;
}
```

Because this application will be run as a standalone program, the Microsoft J++ compiler has created this additional file for support.

```
import java.awt.*;

class Dialog3Frame extends Frame
```

```
{
  public Dialog3Frame(String str)
  {
    super (str);
  }

  public boolean handleEvent(Event evt)
  {
    switch (evt.id)
    {
      case Event.WINDOW_DESTROY:
        dispose();
        System.exit(0);
        return true;

      default:
        return super.handleEvent(evt);
    }
  }
}
```

The first job is, of course, to design a properly laid out dialog box capable of accepting the two integer values. This is done in a manner similar to the previous example, because the integer values are entered as strings in a text field. You can see this in the following portion of code.

```
Panel firstpanel = new Panel();
firstpanel.setLayout(new GridLayout(2, 2, 5, 5));
firstpanel.add(new Label("Integer #1:", Label.CENTER));
NewNum1 = new TextField(20);
firstpanel.add(NewNum1);
firstpanel.add(new Label("Integer #2:", Label.CENTER));
NewNum2 = new TextField(20);
firstpanel.add(NewNum2);
add("Center", firstpanel);

Panel secondpanel = new Panel();
secondpanel.add(new Button("Okay"));
secondpanel.add(new Button("Cancel"));
add("South", secondpanel);
```

```
    .
    .
```

When the Okay button is clicked, the string information is returned to *mystring1* and *mystring2*. Remember, this is how modal dialog box information is processed.

```
    .
    .
    .
// retrieve data from dialog box
MyFrame.mystring1 = NewNum1.getText();
MyFrame.mystring2 = NewNum2.getText();
    .
    .
    .
```

Before the graphics are drawn on the canvas, the string must be converted to actual integer data. This is fairly easy to do, as you can see in the following portion of code:

```
int intx, inty;

intx = Integer.parseInt(MyFrame.mystring1);
inty = Integer.parseInt(MyFrame.mystring2);
g.drawOval(50, 50, intx, inty);
```

Figure 14.11 shows this dialog box along with a corresponding graphics shape on the screen.

As dialog boxes become more complicated, Microsoft J++ programmers can turn to the Resource Toolkit, which allows dialog box design and control layout in a graphical editor. This important tool is covered in the following section.

Using the Java Resource Wizard

Designing a dialog box is no simple task. Windows programmers have been able to design dialog boxes graphically with the help of the Resource Toolkit provided in Microsoft C++ and Visual Basic products. Controls are then simply dragged from a menu bar and placed in the dialog box under design.

Microsoft J++ allows a similar design through a two-step process. First, the dialog box is designed with the use of the Resource Toolkit, and saved as a compiled resource file (a .res file extension). Next, that

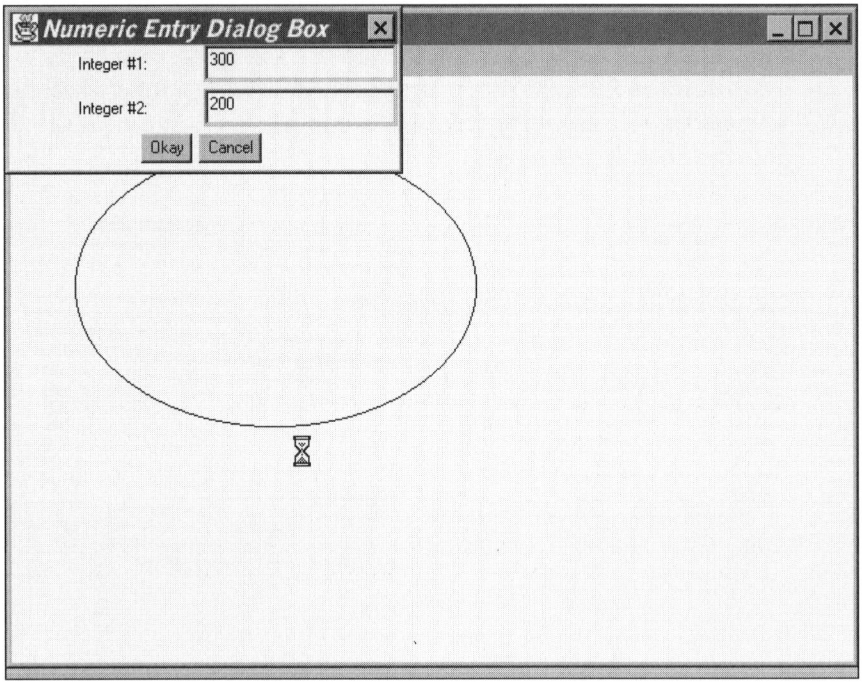

Figure 14.11: The Numeric Entry Dialog box for the Dialog3 example.

file is converted with the Java Resource Wizard supplied with the Microsoft J++ compiler. When converted, the Microsoft J++ compiler creates a new file with a .java file extension specifying the dialog box resource in text format.

The following example, Dialog4, illustrates how this is done. The basic code from the previous example is used, except that this time the dialog box is designed in the Resource Toolkit.

The Java Resource Wizard The Microsoft Developer Studio provides a graphical Resource Toolkit for Windows programmers. Menus and dialog boxes, for example, can be designed in a graphical environment in which controls are selected from a toolbox and then graphically dragged to the proper location. The alternative to dialog box design, described in the previous section, is to specify a particular layout design and manually place controls.

To graphically design a dialog box, select Insert | Resource from the main Developer Studio menu and select Dialog Box as the resource to create.

Microsoft J++ contains a Java Resource Wizard that is capable of converting a resource file created with the Resource Toolkit and saved with an .res file extension into Java code. This Java code can then be incorporated into your Java project.

The only hitch to this marvel of engineering is that because Java code is highly portable, the Java Resource Wizard cannot always convert every graphical dialog box design into perfect Java code. For example, not every font available under Windows is acceptable under Java. The Java Resource Wizard will do its best, sometimes making decisions as to what is best for a particular conversion.

Designing a Resource The following discussion assumes that you have had some experience using the graphical editors in the Resource Toolkit. Additional information on the Resource Toolkit can be obtained with the compiler's built-in Help facility or in books dealing with Windows programming.

From the main Developer Studio menu, select Insert | Resource and click on the Dialog item in the list. You will see a default dialog box design, similar to the one shown in Figure 14.12.

Select and drag label and button controls to produce an **About** dialog box similar to that shown in Figure 14.13.

You should also design a menu for this application at this time. When the menu and dialog box have been designed, save the completed file as both a Script4.rc and Script4.res file. The .res file is needed by the Java Resource Wizard.

From the main Developer Studio menu, select Tools | Java Resource Wizard..., in order to convert the file from a compiled .res file to a Java text file. When the Resource Wizard requests a file name, use Script4.res for this example.

Note: The Java Resource Wizard dialog box warns that controls that are not supported by the AWT will be ignored. That includes controls, fonts, and so on.

If the conversion process is successful, you should have two new files: Menu1.java and Dlg1.java. These files are the text equivalent of the graphical menu and dialog box designs. Both of these files are used in the Dialog4 example.

The Menu1.java File Chapter 13 covers how to incorporate menu resources into Java applications. Here is the file created by the Java Resource Wizard for this application's menu.

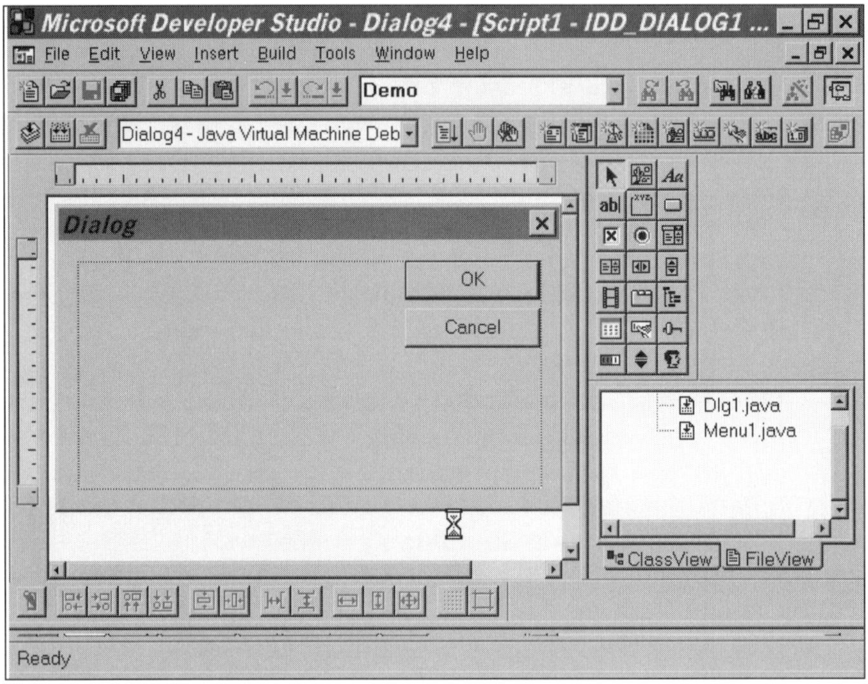

Figure 14.12: The default dialog box provided by the Resource Toolkit editor.

```
//------------------------------------------------------------
// Menu1.java:
//      Implementation for menu creation class Menu1
//
//------------------------------------------------------------
import java.awt.*;

public class Menu1
{
  Frame    m_Frame         = null;
  boolean m_fInitialized = false;

  // MenuBar definitions
  //------------------------------------------------------------
  MenuBar mb;

  // Menu and Menu item definitions
  //------------------------------------------------------------
```

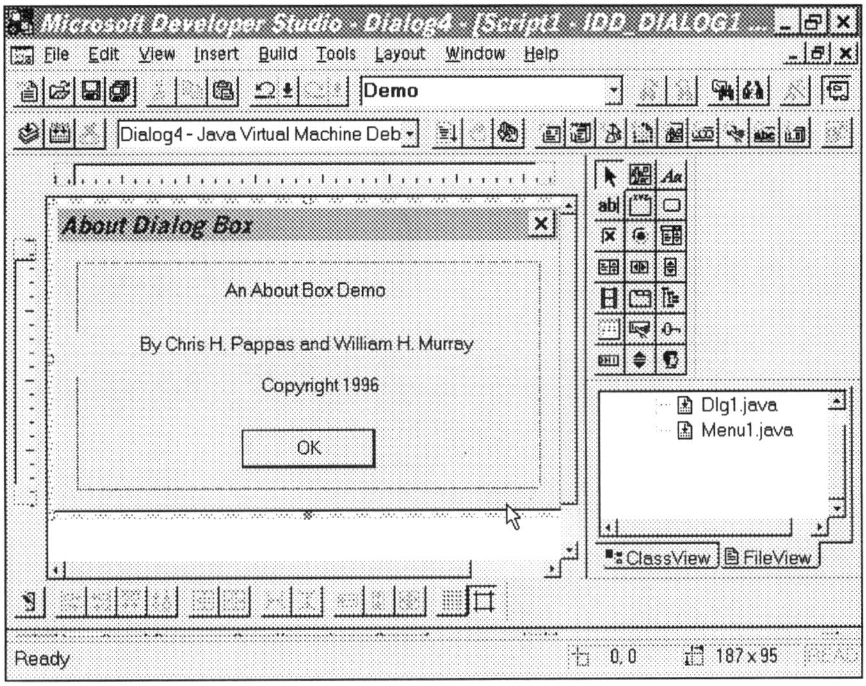

Figure 14.13: The About dialog box design for the Dialog4 application.

```
Menu m1;  // Information
MenuItem m2;  // About...
MenuItem m3;  // Separator
MenuItem m4;  // Exit

// Constructor
//-------------------------------------------------------------
public Menu1 (Frame frame)
{
  m_Frame = frame;
}

// Initialization.
//-------------------------------------------------------------
public boolean CreateMenu()
{
   // Can only init controls once
   //-----------------------------------------------------------
```

```
    if (m_fInitialized || m_Frame == null)
      return false;

    // Create menubar and attach to the frame
    //-------------------------------------------------------------
    mb = new MenuBar();
    m_Frame.setMenuBar(mb);

    // Create menu and menu items and assign to menubar
    //-------------------------------------------------------------
    m1 = new Menu("Information");
    mb.add(m1);
      m2 = new MenuItem("About...");
      m1.add(m2);
      m3 = new MenuItem("-");
      m1.add(m3);
      m4 = new MenuItem("Exit");
      m1.add(m4);

    m_fInitialized = true;
    return true;
  }
}
```

The bolded portions of code indicate that this application will have a menu with two menu items: **About** and **Exit**. The **About** menu item will create a simple **About** dialog box on the screen. The **Exit** option will let you terminate the application.

The Dlg1.java File The Dlg1.java file describes, in text, the appearance of the graphical dialog box. When you use this file, the class must be passed the name of the parent. To actually create the dialog box and place controls, the **CreateControls()** member function is used.

```
//-------------------------------------------------------------
// Dlg1.java:
// Implementation for container control init class Dlg1
//
//-------------------------------------------------------------
import java.awt.*;
import DialogLayout;
```

```
public class Dlg1
{
  Container    m_Parent       = null;
  boolean      m_fInitialized = false;
  DialogLayout m_Layout;

  // Control definitions
  //--------------------------------------------------------
  Button       Btn1;
  Label        Lbl1;
  Label        Lbl2;
  Label        Lbl3;


  // Constructor
  //--------------------------------------------------------
  public Dlg1 (Container parent)
  {
    m_Parent = parent;
  }

  // Initialization.
  //--------------------------------------------------------
  public boolean CreateControls()
  {
    // Can only init controls once
    //------------------------------------------------------
    if (m_fInitialized || m_Parent == null)
      return false;

    // Parent must be a derivation of the Container class
    //------------------------------------------------------
    if (!(m_Parent instanceof Container))
      return false;

    // Since there is no way to know if a given font is
    // supported from platform to platform, we only change
    // the size of the font, and not type face name.  And,
    // we only change the font if the dialog resource
    // specified a font.
```

```
//----------------------------------------------------------
if (true)
{
  Font OldFnt = m_Parent.getFont();
  Font NewFnt = new Font(OldFnt.getName(),
                         OldFnt.getStyle(), 16);

  m_Parent.setFont(NewFnt);
}

// All position and sizes are in Dialog Units, so, we
// use the DialogLayout manager.
//------------------------------------------------------------
m_Layout = new DialogLayout(m_Parent, 196, 108);
m_Parent.setLayout(m_Layout);
m_Parent.addNotify();

Dimension size   = m_Layout.getDialogSize();
Insets    insets = m_Parent.insets();

m_Parent.resize(insets.left + size.width  + insets.right,
                insets.top  + size.height + insets.bottom);

// Control creation
//-----------------------------------------------------------
Btn1 = new Button ("OK");
m_Parent.add(Btn1);
m_Layout.setShape(Btn1, 70, 75, 50, 14);

Lbl1 = new Label ("An About Box Demo ");
m_Parent.add(Lbl1);
m_Layout.setShape(Lbl1, 7, 10, 182, 16);

Lbl2 = new Label ("by Chris Pappas and William Murray
");
m_Parent.add(Lbl2);
m_Layout.setShape(Lbl2, 7, 30, 182, 18);

Lbl3 = new Label ("Copyright 1996 ");
m_Parent.add(Lbl3);
m_Layout.setShape(Lbl3, 7, 50, 182, 19);
```

```
    m_fInitialized = true;
    return true;
  }
}
```

When the dialog box was designed in the graphical environment, a new font size was requested. You can see how that request was translated in a bolded portion of the previously listed code.

You should also be able to find where the OK button and three labels are included. You'll learn how to access this code in the Dialog4 example.

Dialog4 This Java application produces an **About** dialog box, similar to that produced by the Dialog1 example. However, in this case both the menu resource and dialog box resource were designed graphically and then converted with the Java Resource Wizard. All four files—Dialog4.java, Dialog4Frame.java, Menu1.java, and Dlg1.java—are listed in this section. First is the Dialog4.java file:

```
import java.applet.*;
import java.awt.*;
import Dialog4Frame;
import Dlg1;
import Menu1;

public class Dialog4 extends Applet
{
  // STANDALONE APPLICATION SUPPORT:
  //    m_fStandAlone will be set to true if applet is run
  //    standalone
  //--------------------------------------------------------------
  boolean m_fStandAlone = false;

  public static void main(String args[])
  {
    Dialog4Frame frame = new Dialog4Frame("Dialog4");

    // Must show Frame before we size it so insets() will
    // return valid values
    //----------------------------------------------------------
    //frame.show();
    frame.resize(frame.insets().left+frame.insets().right+640,
```

```
            frame.insets().top  + frame.insets().bottom + 480);

    Dialog4 applet_Dialog4 = new Dialog4();

    frame.add("Center", applet_Dialog4);
    applet_Dialog4.m_fStandAlone = true;
    applet_Dialog4.init();
    applet_Dialog4.start();
  }

  public Dialog4()
  {
  }

  public String getAppletInfo()
  {
    return "Name: Dialog4\r\n" +
           "Author: Chris H. Pappas and  William H. Murray\r\n"+
           "Created with Microsoft Visual J++";
  }

  public void init()
  {
    resize(640, 480);
    new MyFrame("");
  }

  public void destroy()
  {
  }

  public void paint(Graphics g)
  {
  }

  public void start()
  {
  }

  public void stop()
  {
```

```
  }

}

class MyFrame extends Frame
{
  NewCanvas newcanvas;

  MyFrame(String title) {
    // Add a menu bar
    super("Menu Bar");
    add("Center", newcanvas = new NewCanvas());
    reshape(0, 0, 639, 479);

    // allows new menu bar & menu items
    // from resource file to be displayed
    Menu1 myMenu = new Menu1(this);
    myMenu.CreateMenu();

    show();
  }

  public boolean action(Event event, Object object) {
    String label = (String)object;
    if (event.target instanceof MenuItem) {
      if(label.equals("About...")) {
        AboutDialog ab = new AboutDialog(this);
        ab.show();
      }
      if(label.equals("Exit")) {
        System.exit(0);
      }
      return true;
    }
    else
      return false;
  }
}

class AboutDialog extends Dialog {
```

```
    public AboutDialog(Frame parent) {
      super(parent, "About Dialog Box", true);

      // Draw dialog box converted by Resource Wizard
      Dlg1 mydlg = new Dlg1(this);
      mydlg.CreateControls();
    }

    public boolean action(Event event, Object object) {
      String label = (String)object;
      if (event.target instanceof Button) {
        if(label.equals("OK")) {
          dispose();
        }
        return true;
      } else
      return false;
    }
  }

  // draw on the new canvas
  class NewCanvas extends Canvas {
    public void paint(Graphics g) {
      g.fillRect(100, 100, 100, 100);
      g.drawString("This is an event!",
                   110, 30);
    }
  }
```

The Dialog4Frame.java file has been added by the Microsoft J++ compiler to support a standalone application:

```
import java.awt.*;

class Dialog4Frame extends Frame
{
  public Dialog4Frame(String str)
  {
    super (str);
  }

  public boolean handleEvent(Event evt)
  {
```

```
    switch (evt.id)
    {
      case Event.WINDOW_DESTROY:
        dispose();
        System.exit(0);
        return true;

      default:
        return super.handleEvent(evt);
    }
  }
}
```

You will notice in the Dialog4.java listing that two additional import statements are included:

```
import Dlg1;
import Menu1;
```

These allow access to both the Menu1.java and Dlg1.java files. Both of these files need to be added to the project list. This is done from the Microsoft Developer Studio's main menu by selecting Insert | Files Into Project. From the dialog box provided, double-click on each file to add it to the project list, as shown in Figure 14.14.

The menu for this application is created with the following portion of code.

```
// allows new menu bar & menu items
// from resource file to be displayed
Menu1 myMenu = new Menu1(this);
myMenu.CreateMenu();
```

The dialog box is created when the user selects the About... menu item. Here is the code for this event.

```
public boolean action(Event event, Object object) {
String label = (String)object;
if (event.target instanceof MenuItem) {
  if(label.equals("About...")) {
    AboutDialog ab = new AboutDialog(this);
    ab.show();
  }
```

The new dialog box resource is accessed via the AboutDialog class.

```
class AboutDialog extends Dialog {
```

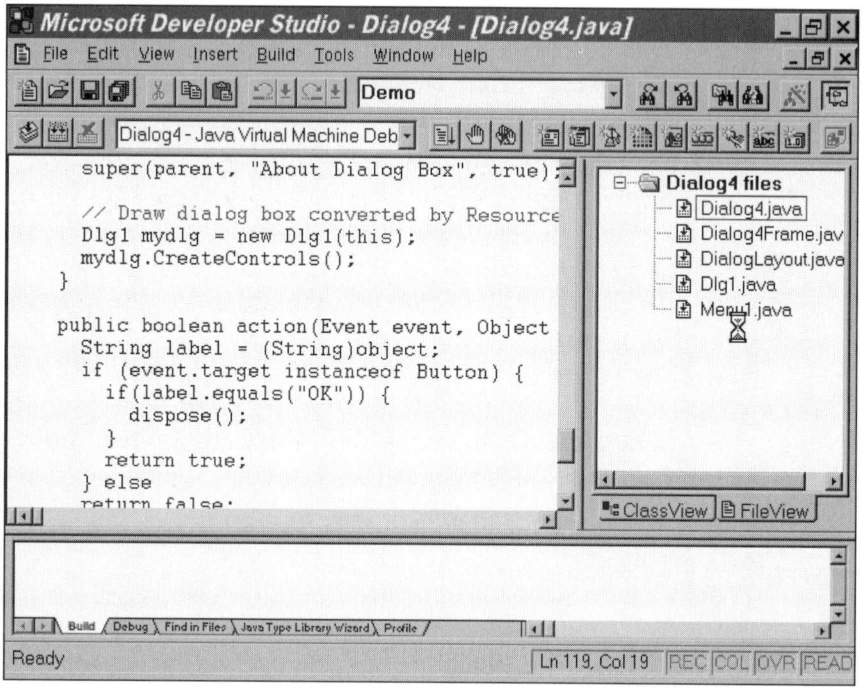

Figure 14.14: The Menu1 and Dlg1 files are added to the project file list.

```
public AboutDialog(Frame parent) {
  super(parent, "About Dialog Box", true);

  // Draw dialog box converted by Resource Wizard
  Dlg1 mydlg = new Dlg1(this);
  mydlg.CreateControls();
}
 .
 .
 .
```

You'll also see, at this point, how the controls are placed in the dialog box with a call to the **CreateControls()** member function.

```
public boolean action(Event event, Object object) {
String label = (String)object;
  if (event.target instanceof Button) {
    if(label.equals("OK")) {
      dispose();
```

```
    }
    .
    .
    .
```

These are basically the only differences between including the dialog box control directly within the Java source code and bringing it in from a file converted by the Java Resource Wizard. The application is built in the normal manner.

When the application is run, you should see a dialog box similar to that shown in Figure 14.15.

Compare Figure 14.15 to Figure 14.13. Any differences? Basically the only difference is that the labels were centered in the original dialog box designed in the Resource Toolkit. When the conversion took place, the labels ended up left-justified. This may be a problem that you have

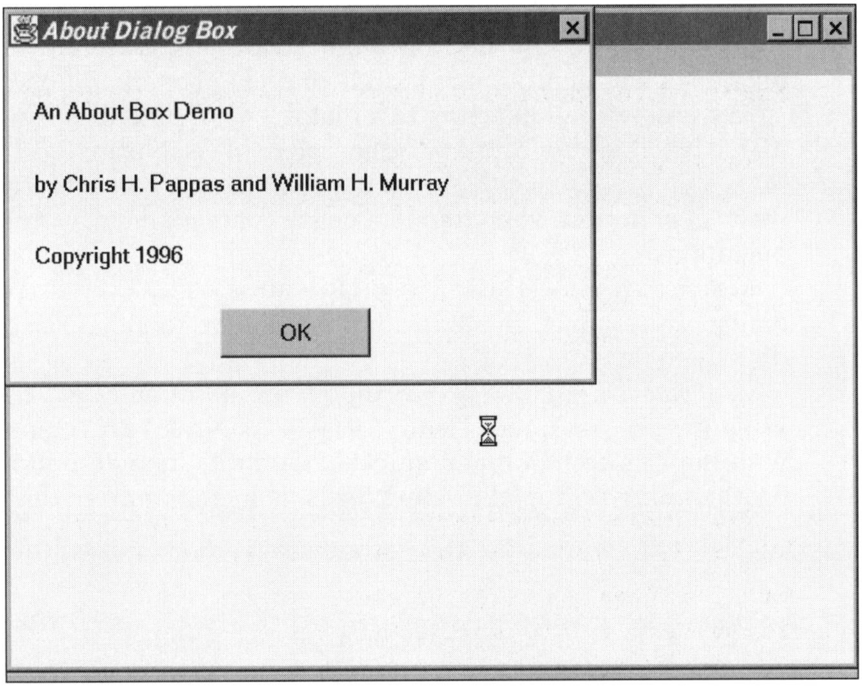

Figure 14.15: The Dialog5 dialog box provided by the Java Resource Wizard.

to live with, or one that will be repaired in the version of the Microsoft J++ compiler that you are using.

Remember, the Java Resource Wizard makes the best conversion possible, but not always a perfect conversion!

Chapter 15 includes additional examples of how the Resource Toolkit and the Java Resource Wizard can aid in dialog box implementation. That chapter explains how to return data from dialog boxes to the program.

COMING TO TERMS

About dialog box—A special dialog box used to inform the user about the application, developer, and any copyright information.

Dialog box—A dialog box lets your application or applet take on a Windows appearance and provide a familiar and consistent interface to the user. Dialog boxes can be a major form for data entry.

modal—When referring to a dialog box, this term means that the dialog box will capture the focus of the application. Normal screen operation will not be returned until the dialog box is closed. This is the most frequently encountered mode of dialog box operation.

modeless—When referring to a dialog box, this term means that the dialog box does not capture the complete focus. Normal screen operations can continue with the dialog box present on the screen. This mode is preferred when frequent changes are made to an applications operations.

Resource Wizard—The Microsoft Resource Wizard allows a graphical dialog box resource, created with the Resource Toolkit, to be converted directly to Java code.

UI component—These Java components are often called controls by Windows programmers. Using the term "controls" prevents confusion with the Abstract Component class. Controls include buttons, check boxes, radiobuttons, labels, text fields, text areas, and so on.

Chapter 15

DEVELOPING QUALITY GRAPHICS PROGRAMS

This chapter introduces two presentation graphics applications or applets that are the culmination of the graphical techniques explained across several past chapters. The bar chart and pie chart applications are robust examples that use the graphical, color, font, menu and dialog discussed in Chapters 8 through 14.

Chapter 14 outlined two methods of describing menu and dialog box resources. With the conventional method of coding, resource descriptions are entered in the Java program code directly, with controls placed manually by the programmer. The second technique uses the Microsoft Resource Toolkit and the Java Resource Wizard to convert graphical resource descriptions directly to Java code. The bar chart application uses the conventional technique for adding these resources, while the pie chart application makes use of the Java Resource Wizard.

This chapter explains how to use the power of the Java language to build applications that function like professionally developed graphics applications used by Windows 95 or NT.

A COMPLETE BAR CHART PROGRAM

Chapter 12 outlined the development of a simple bar chart program. That program generated a simple bar chart using fixed data. This was necessary because the inclusion of menu and dialog resources was not covered until Chapters 13 and 14. That simple bar chart application can now be expanded to include both menu and dialog resources.

You might want to take a minute to return to Chapter 12 to study the bar chart components of that simple program. This section concentrates on the efforts required to add the menu and dialog resources.

The base code for the bar chart application, BarCht, is created by the Microsoft J++ Java Applet Wizard. All other code is then added to complete the application. If you have written Windows programs with the Microsoft C++ compiler, you know that these applications usually contain separate header, resource, and C++ source code files. They are compiled and linked together to form a final executable. Java applications and applets, such as the following example, are usually written in several separate files. For example, this application uses a file named BarCht.java and BarChtFrame.java. If you are entering the following code from the book's text, take your time to do it carefully because the listings are very long. As you examine each listing, notice that several areas have been set in a bold font for later discussion.

```
import java.applet.*;
import java.awt.*;
import BarChtFrame;

public class BarCht extends Applet
{
  // STANDALONE APPLICATION SUPPORT:
  //   m_fStandAlone will be set to true if applet is run
  //   standalone
  //--------------------------------------------------------------------
  boolean m_fStandAlone = false;

  public static void main(String args[])
  {
    BarChtFrame frame = new BarChtFrame("BarCht");

    // Must show Frame before we size it so insets() will
    // return valid values
    //------------------------------------------------------------------
    frame.show();
    frame.hide();
    frame.resize(frame.insets().left+frame.insets().right+640,
           frame.insets().top  + frame.insets().bottom + 480);
```

```
    BarCht applet_BarCht = new BarCht();

    frame.add("Center", applet_BarCht);
    applet_BarCht.m_fStandAlone = true;
    applet_BarCht.init();
    applet_BarCht.start();
    // frame.show();
  }

  public BarCht()
  {
  }

  public String getAppletInfo()
  {
    return "Name: BarCht\r\n" +
           "Author: Chris H. Pappas and William H. Murray\r\n"+
           "Created with Microsoft Visual J++";
  }

  public void init()
  {
    resize(640, 480);
    new MyFrame("");
  }

  public void destroy()
  {
  }

  public void paint(Graphics g)
  {
  }

  public void start()
  {
  }

  public void stop()
```

```
    {
    }

}

class MyFrame extends Frame
{
  NewCanvas newcanvas;
  Dialog AboutDialog, LabelDialog,
         DataDialog, LegendDialog;
  static String charttitle = "Title";
  static String vertlabel = "vert. axis";
  static String horzlabel = "horz. axis";
  static String[] legend = {"red", "blue", "yellow", "green",
                            "cyan", "white", "magenta",
                            "orange", "pink", "gray",
                            "dark gray",  "black"};
  static String[] height = {"10", "20", "30", "40", "50",
                            "60", "70", "80", "60", "40",
                            "20", "5"};

  MyFrame(String title) {
    // Add menu bar
    super("Bar Chart");
    add("Center", newcanvas = new NewCanvas());
    reshape(0, 0, 639, 479);
    MenuBar menubar = new MenuBar();
    setMenuBar(menubar);

    // Information menu and menu items
    Menu chtinfo = new Menu("Information");
    chtinfo.add(new MenuItem("About..."));
    chtinfo.add(new MenuItem("-"));
    chtinfo.add(new MenuItem("Exit"));
    menubar.add(chtinfo);

    // Data menu and menu items
    Menu chtdata = new Menu("Data");
    chtdata.add(new MenuItem("Labels..."));
    chtdata.add(new MenuItem("Bar Heights..."));
    chtdata.add(new MenuItem("Legend..."));
```

```
      menubar.add(chtdata);

      show();
    }

    public boolean action(Event event, Object object) {
      String label = (String)object;
      if (event.target instanceof MenuItem) {
        if(label.equals("About...")) {
          Dialog AbDialog = new AboutDialog(this);
          AbDialog.show();
        } else
        if(label.equals("Labels...")) {
          Dialog LabDialog = new LabelDialog(this);
          LabDialog.show();
        } else
        if(label.equals("Bar Heights...")) {
          Dialog HtDialog = new HeightDialog(this);
          HtDialog.show();
        } else
        if(label.equals("Legend...")) {
          Dialog LegDialog = new LegendDialog(this);
          LegDialog.show();
        } else
        if(label.equals("Exit")) {
          System.exit(0);
        }
        return true;
      }
      else
        return false;
    }
  }

  // Information for About dialog box creation
  class AboutDialog extends Dialog {
    public AboutDialog(Frame parent) {
      super(parent, "About Dialog Box", true);

      // About dialog box
      Panel firstpanel = new Panel();
```

```
      firstpanel.setLayout(new GridLayout(3,1,5,5));
      firstpanel.add(new Label("Bar Chart Application",
                               Label.CENTER));
      firstpanel.add(new Label("C. Pappas and W. Murray",
                               Label.CENTER));
      firstpanel.add(new Label("Copyright (c) 1996",
                               Label.CENTER));
      add("Center", firstpanel);

      Panel secondpanel = new Panel();
      secondpanel.add(new Button("Okay"));
      add("South", secondpanel);

      reshape(200, 200, 300, 200);
    }

    // process dialog box button events
    public boolean action(Event event, Object object) {
      String label = (String)object;
      if (event.target instanceof Button) {
        if(label.equals("Okay")) {
          dispose();
        }
        return true;
      } else
      return false;
    }
  }

  // Information for Label dialog box creation
  class LabelDialog extends Dialog {
    public LabelDialog(Frame parent) {
      super(parent, "Label Dialog Box", true);

      // Label dialog box
      Panel firstpanel = new Panel();
      firstpanel.setLayout(new GridLayout(3,2,5,5));
      firstpanel.add(new Label("Title:", Label.RIGHT));
      TitleText = new TextField(15);
      firstpanel.add(TitleText);
      firstpanel.add(new Label("Vert Axis Label:",
```

```
                                    Label.RIGHT));
      VertText = new TextField(15);
      firstpanel.add(VertText);
      firstpanel.add(new Label("Horz Axis Label:",
                                    Label.RIGHT));
      HorzText = new TextField(15);
      firstpanel.add(HorzText);
      add("Center", firstpanel);

      Panel secondpanel = new Panel();
      secondpanel.add(new Button("Okay"));
      secondpanel.add(new Button("Cancel"));
      add("South", secondpanel);

      reshape(200, 200, 300, 175);
    }

    // process dialog box button events
    public boolean action(Event event, Object object) {
      String label = (String)object;
      if (event.target instanceof Button) {
        if(label.equals("Okay")) {
          // retrieve data from dialog box
          MyFrame.charttitle = TitleText.getText();
          MyFrame.vertlabel = VertText.getText();
          MyFrame.horzlabel = HorzText.getText();
          dispose();
        }
        else
          if (label.equals("Cancel")) {
            dispose();
        }
        return true;
      } else
      return false;
    }

  TextField TitleText, VertText, HorzText;
  }

  // Information for Height dialog box creation
```

```
class HeightDialog extends Dialog {
  public HeightDialog(Frame parent) {
    super(parent, "Height Dialog Box", true);

    // Heights dialog box
    Panel firstpanel = new Panel();
    firstpanel.setLayout(new GridLayout(13, 2, 5, 5));
    firstpanel.add(new Label("Height Bar #1:",
                             Label.RIGHT));
    Num1 = new TextField("0", 10);
    firstpanel.add(Num1);
    firstpanel.add(new Label("Height Bar #2:",
                             Label.RIGHT));
    Num2 = new TextField("0", 10);
    firstpanel.add(Num2);
    firstpanel.add(new Label("Height Bar #3:",
                             Label.RIGHT));
    Num3 = new TextField("0", 10);
    firstpanel.add(Num3);
    firstpanel.add(new Label("Height Bar #4:",
                             Label.RIGHT));
    Num4 = new TextField("0", 10);
    firstpanel.add(Num4);
    firstpanel.add(new Label("Height Bar #5:",
                             Label.RIGHT));
    Num5 = new TextField("0", 10);
    firstpanel.add(Num5);
    firstpanel.add(new Label("Height Bar #6:",
                             Label.RIGHT));
    Num6 = new TextField("0", 10);
    firstpanel.add(Num6);
    firstpanel.add(new Label("Height Bar #7:",
                             Label.RIGHT));
    Num7 = new TextField("0", 10);
    firstpanel.add(Num7);
    firstpanel.add(new Label("Height Bar #8:",
                             Label.RIGHT));
    Num8 = new TextField("0", 10);
    firstpanel.add(Num8);
    firstpanel.add(new Label("Height Bar #9:",
                             Label.RIGHT));
```

```
    Num9 = new TextField("0", 10);
    firstpanel.add(Num9);
    firstpanel.add(new Label("Height Bar #10:",
                            Label.RIGHT));
    Num10 = new TextField("0", 10);
    firstpanel.add(Num10);
    firstpanel.add(new Label("Height Bar #11:",
                            Label.RIGHT));
    Num11 = new TextField("0", 10);
    firstpanel.add(Num11);
    firstpanel.add(new Label("Height Bar #12:",
                            Label.RIGHT));
    Num12 = new TextField("0", 10);
    firstpanel.add(Num12);
    add("Center", firstpanel);

    Panel secondpanel = new Panel();
    secondpanel.add(new Button("Okay"));
    secondpanel.add(new Button("Cancel"));
    add("South", secondpanel);

    reshape(200, 50, 200, 400);
  }

  // process dialog box button events
  public boolean action(Event event, Object object) {
    String label = (String)object;
    if (event.target instanceof Button) {
      if(label.equals("Okay")) {
        // retrieve data from dialog box
        MyFrame.height[0] = Num1.getText();
        MyFrame.height[1] = Num2.getText();
        MyFrame.height[2] = Num3.getText();
        MyFrame.height[3] = Num4.getText();
        MyFrame.height[4] = Num5.getText();
        MyFrame.height[5] = Num6.getText();
        MyFrame.height[6] = Num7.getText();
        MyFrame.height[7] = Num8.getText();
        MyFrame.height[8] = Num9.getText();
        MyFrame.height[9] = Num10.getText();
        MyFrame.height[10] = Num11.getText();
```

```
          MyFrame.height[11] = Num12.getText();
          dispose();
        }
        else
          if (label.equals("Cancel")) {
            dispose();
        }
        return true;
      } else
      return false;
    }

TextField Num1, Num2, Num3, Num4,
          Num5, Num6, Num7, Num8,
          Num9, Num10, Num11, Num12;
}


// Information for Legend dialog box creation
class LegendDialog extends Dialog {
  public LegendDialog(Frame parent) {
    super(parent, "Legend Dialog Box", true);

    // Heights dialog box
    Panel firstpanel = new Panel();
    firstpanel.setLayout(new GridLayout(13, 2, 5, 5));
    firstpanel.add(new Label("Label Bar #1:",
                       Label.RIGHT));
    Leg1 = new TextField(10);
    firstpanel.add(Leg1);
    firstpanel.add(new Label("Label Bar #2:",
                       Label.RIGHT));
    Leg2 = new TextField(10);
    firstpanel.add(Leg2);
    firstpanel.add(new Label("Label Bar #3:",
                       Label.RIGHT));
    Leg3 = new TextField(10);
    firstpanel.add(Leg3);
    firstpanel.add(new Label("Label Bar #4:",
                       Label.RIGHT));
    Leg4 = new TextField(10);
```

```
firstpanel.add(Leg4);
firstpanel.add(new Label("Label Bar #5:",
                         Label.RIGHT));
Leg5 = new TextField(10);
firstpanel.add(Leg5);
firstpanel.add(new Label("Label Bar #6:",
                         Label.RIGHT));
Leg6 = new TextField(10);
firstpanel.add(Leg6);
firstpanel.add(new Label("Label Bar #7:",
                         Label.RIGHT));
Leg7 = new TextField(10);
firstpanel.add(Leg7);
firstpanel.add(new Label("Label Bar #8:",
                         Label.RIGHT));
Leg8 = new TextField(10);
firstpanel.add(Leg8);
firstpanel.add(new Label("Label Bar #9:",
                         Label.RIGHT));
Leg9 = new TextField(10);
firstpanel.add(Leg9);
firstpanel.add(new Label("Label Bar #10:",
                         Label.RIGHT));
Leg10 = new TextField(10);
firstpanel.add(Leg10);
firstpanel.add(new Label("Label Bar #11:",
                         Label.RIGHT));
Leg11 = new TextField(10);
firstpanel.add(Leg11);
firstpanel.add(new Label("Label Bar #12:",
                         Label.RIGHT));
Leg12 = new TextField(10);
firstpanel.add(Leg12);
add("Center", firstpanel);

Panel secondpanel = new Panel();
secondpanel.add(new Button("Okay"));
secondpanel.add(new Button("Cancel"));
add("South", secondpanel);

reshape(200, 50, 200, 400);
```

```
  }

  // process dialog box button events
  public boolean action(Event event, Object object) {
    String label = (String)object;
    if (event.target instanceof Button) {
      if(label.equals("Okay")) {
        // retrieve data from dialog box
        MyFrame.legend[0] = Leg1.getText();
        MyFrame.legend[1] = Leg2.getText();
        MyFrame.legend[2] = Leg3.getText();
        MyFrame.legend[3] = Leg4.getText();
        MyFrame.legend[4] = Leg5.getText();
        MyFrame.legend[5] = Leg6.getText();
        MyFrame.legend[6] = Leg7.getText();
        MyFrame.legend[7] = Leg8.getText();
        MyFrame.legend[8] = Leg9.getText();
        MyFrame.legend[9] = Leg10.getText();
        MyFrame.legend[10] = Leg11.getText();
        MyFrame.legend[11] = Leg12.getText();
        dispose();
      }
      else
        if (label.equals("Cancel")) {
          dispose();
      }
      return true;
    } else
    return false;
  }

TextField Leg1, Leg2, Leg3, Leg4, Leg5, Leg6,
          Leg7, Leg8, Leg9, Leg10, Leg11, Leg12;
}

class NewCanvas extends Canvas {

  Font titlefont, labelfont, legendfont;
  FontMetrics fm;
```

```
public void paint(Graphics g) {

  Color barColor[] = {Color.red,     // bar colors
                      Color.blue,
                      Color.yellow,
                      Color.green,
                      Color.cyan,
                      Color.white,
                      Color.magenta,
                      Color.orange,
                      Color.pink,
                      Color.gray,
                      Color.darkGray,
                      Color.black};
  int iBarMax;
  int oldBar[] = new int[12];
  int newBar[] = new int[12];
  int numBars = 0;
  int maxBars = 12;
  int newstart = 2;                    // start position

  // convert string to integer find # of bars
  for(int i = 0; i < maxBars; i++) {
    oldBar[i] = Integer.parseInt(MyFrame.height[i]);
    if(oldBar[i] > 0) numBars++;
  }

  int width = 300 / numBars;          // width of a bar

  // Find bar with highest value
  iBarMax = oldBar[0];
  for(int i = 0; i < numBars; i++)
    if (iBarMax < oldBar[i]) iBarMax = oldBar[i];

  // Scale data values
  for (int i = 0; i < numBars; i++)
    newBar[i] = oldBar[i] * 270 / iBarMax;

  // create fonts
```

```
titlefont = new Font("TimesRoman", Font.BOLD, 36);
labelfont = new Font("TimesRoman", Font.PLAIN, 14);
legendfont = new Font("TimesRoman", Font.ITALIC, 10);

// draw coordinate axes
g.translate(99, 379);        // move origin
g.drawLine(0, -329, 0, 0);  // vert. axis
g.drawLine(0, 0, 329, 0);   // horz. axis

// draw and center chart title
g.setFont(titlefont);
fm = getFontMetrics(titlefont);
g.drawString(MyFrame.charttitle,
             165 -
             (fm.stringWidth(MyFrame.charttitle)/2),
             -340);

// draw vertical label and center horizontal label
g.setFont(labelfont);
fm = getFontMetrics(labelfont);
g.drawString(MyFrame.vertlabel,
             -10 -
             fm.stringWidth(MyFrame.vertlabel),
             -150);
g.drawString(MyFrame.horzlabel,
             165 -
             (fm.stringWidth(MyFrame.horzlabel)/2),
             40);

// draw and fill bars
for (int i = 0; i < numBars; i++) {
  g.setColor(barColor[i]);  // set fill color
  g.fillRect(newstart,      // draw a bar
             -newBar[i],
             width,
             newBar[i] - 1);
  newstart += 2 + width;           // set new position
}

// draw, fill and label chart legend
```

```
      g.setFont(legendfont);
      for (int i = 0; i < numBars; i++) {
        g.setColor(barColor[i]);  // set fill color
        g.fillRect(360, -330 + (i * 30), 15, 15);

        // bar labels
        g.setColor(Color.black);  // set font color
        g.drawString(MyFrame.legend[i], 380,
                     -320 + (i * 30));
      }
    }
}
```

Because this program can run as a standalone application, the Microsoft J++ Applet Wizard also creates a BarChtFrame.java file.

```
import java.awt.*;

class BarChtFrame extends Frame
{
  public BarChtFrame(String str)
  {
    super (str);
  }

  public boolean handleEvent(Event evt)
  {
    switch (evt.id)
    {
      case Event.WINDOW_DESTROY:
        dispose();
        System.exit(0);
        return true;

      default:
        return super.handleEvent(evt);
    }
  }
}
```

The following sections discuss the key aspects of this application's code and then examine several sample executions.

Bar Chart Menus and Dialog Boxes

The conventional techniques used to build the menu and dialog boxes for this application are the same as those discussed in Chapters 13 and 14. Let's look as several sections of the program code, each proceeded by a comment.

// **Add menu bar**—The code under this comment is responsible for adding a new menu bar. Recall, from Chapter 13, that a new frame is created and that drawing will take place on a new canvas created on this frame. Two menus will be added to the menu bar. The first menu is the Information menu and the second is the Data menu.

// **Information menu and menu items**—The code under this comment adds a pop-up menu with two menu items and a separator bar. The user will use this menu to bring up an **About** dialog box or exit the application. Figure 15.1 shows the **Information** menu.

// **Data menu and menu items**—This code allows access to several dialog boxes used for data entry: **Labels**, **Bar Heights**, and **Legend**. Figure 15.2 shows this pop-up menu.

// **Information for About dialog box creation**—This code describes the look and layout of the **About** dialog box. This code is patterned after the **About** dialog box code discussed in Chapter 14. The **About** dialog box uses a single Okay button. Figure 15.3 shows the **About** dialog box for this example.

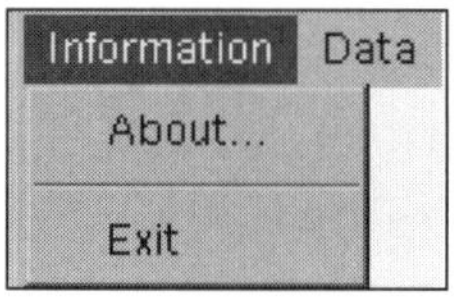

Figure 15.1: The Information menu lets the user view an About dialog box or exit the application.

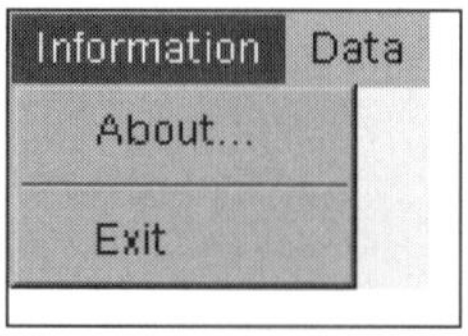

Figure 15.2: The Data menu lets the user select any of three data entry dialog boxes.

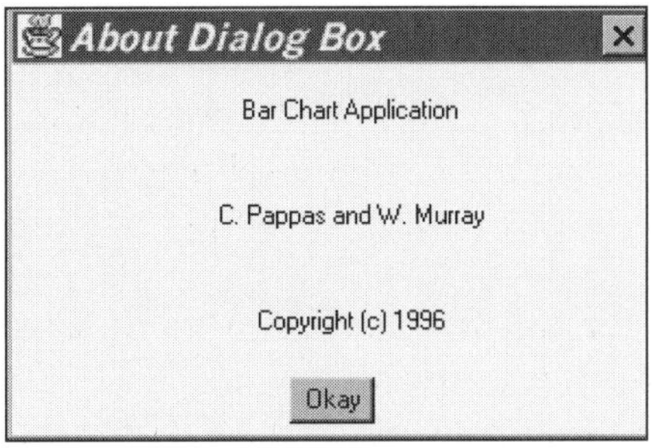

Figure 15.3: The About dialog box for the bar chart application.

Also included in this portion of code is the event handler for processing the push of the Okay dialog box button.

// **Information for Label dialog box creation**—This code is used to generate three labels and three text fields for various bar chart labels. Figure 15.4 shows the label data entry dialog box for this example.

Notice that this data entry dialog box uses both an Okay and Cancel button. The event handler processes button events from either the Okay or Cancel buttons.

// **Information for Height dialog box creation**—This code produces a data entry dialog box that allows the user to enter the height of each bar on the bar chart. Figure 15.5 shows an example of this dialog box.

Twelve bars are permitted on this bar chart, so twelve text fields and twelve labels are used in the dialog box's layout. The text information entered in the text entry controls of this dialog box will eventually be converted to integer values for plotting.

// **Information for the Legend dialog box creation**—This code produces a data entry dialog box that allows the user to enter twelve

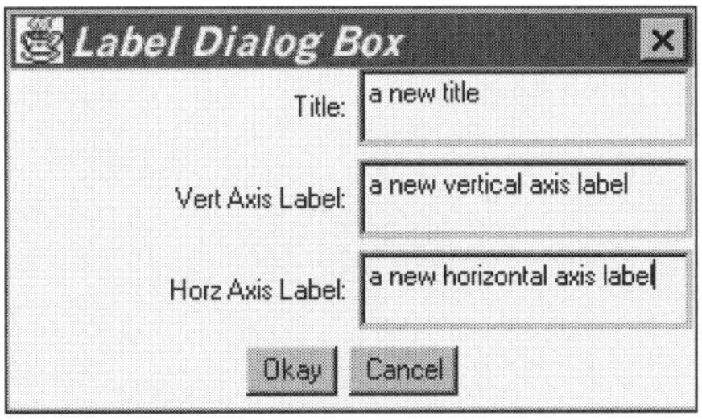

Figure 15.4: The label dialog box allows a chart title and axes labels to be entered by the user.

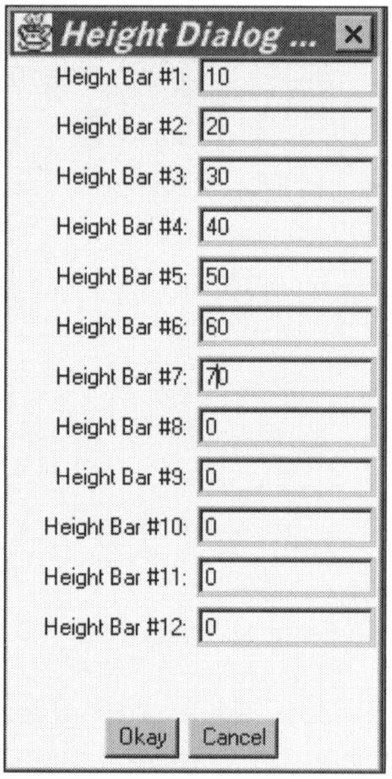

Figure 15.5: The Bar Data dialog box lets the user enter each bar's relative height for the bar chart.

legend values. These legend values are then used to identify each bar on the bar chart. Figure 15.6 shows an example of this dialog box.

As you studied the code in the original listing, you may have noticed that the techniques from Chapters 13 and 14 have been used without much modification. The main difference here is that this application uses two pop-up menus and four dialog boxes. As the number of menus and dialog boxes grows, so does the size and complexity of the listing. That, in itself, might be a good reason for making use of the Java Resource Wizard, as you'll see in the pie chart example!

If you view each new addition as a building block, you will not become overwhelmed with the increased code size.

Bar Chart Action Events

All of the dialog boxes are modal dialog boxes whose information is processed when a button control event occurs. In this example, an Okay button is used to intercept new information from any of the dialog boxes. Here is a small portion of the code used in the application.

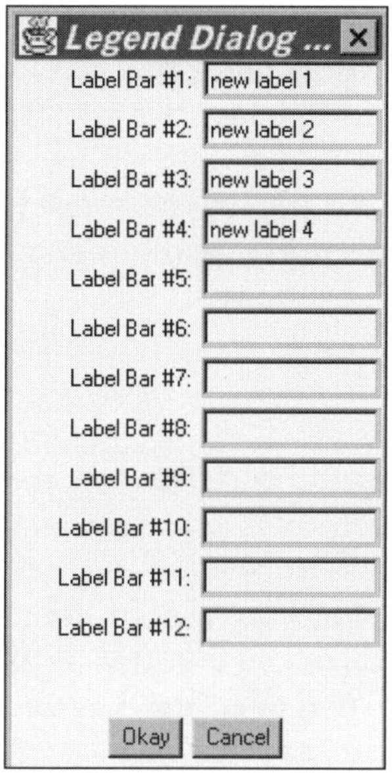

Figure 15.6: Twelve legend labels can be entered using the Legend dialog box.

```
        .
        .
        .
if (event.target instanceof Button) {
        if(label.equals("Okay")) {
          // retrieve data from dialog box
          MyFrame.legend[0] = Leg1.getText();
          MyFrame.legend[1] = Leg2.getText();
          MyFrame.legend[2] = Leg3.getText();
              .
              .
              .
          dispose();
        .
        .
        .
```

This code uses the **getText()** member function to return chart labels, up to twelve data values for bar heights, and up to twelve legend descriptions. The important thing to notice is that all of this information is returned in essentially the same manner. Once the information has been collected, the dialog boxes are disposed of (**dispose()**) and the application awaits any further changes requested by the user.

Again, this code is built on the models developed in Chapters 13 and 14 for handling and processing menu and dialog box information. The code is just more extensive.

Bar Chart Code

This section discusses the code responsible for creating the bar graph itself. Recall that much of this code has already been developed and discussed in Chapters 10 and 12. This section focuses on blocks of important code preceded by a comment. All comments refer to the complete listing shown earlier in this section.

// **convert string to integer find number of bars**—This converts the information returned to the *height[]* array as a string to integer information stored in the *oldBar[]* array. A parser, **Integer.parseInt()**, is used to make the conversion. Up to twelve bars can be used on the bar chart, but the actual number is determined by scanning each entry looking for the first "0" value. The first zero value marks the end of the bar data. And, yes, that means for this example that there can be no bar heights of zero! Each time a non-zero entry is found, the counter, *numBars*, is incremented.

Bar widths are determined by taking the horizontal drawing area used for bars and dividing it by the number of bars.

// **Find bar with highest value**—Bar data is scaled to fit the parameters of the charting surface. The bar with the largest value will always be drawn to the maximum drawing height. All other bars are adjusted proportionally to this height. So the first job is to find the bar, in the array, with the greatest height. This is done with a simple **for** loop and **if** statement.

// **Scale data values**—This section of code takes the maximum bar value, just found, scales it to 270 pixels, and adjusts all other values proportionally. Again, a **for** loop is used.

Next, the chart's fonts are created. Then the coordinate axes are drawn along with the chart title and axis labels. See Chapter 12 for more details on the creation and use of fonts.

// **draw and fill bars**—This section of code selects a bar color from the *barColor[]* array and then draws the bar using the **fillRect()** member function. Values in the *newBar[]* array are used to denote the new horizontal positions and widths for each bar.

// **draw, fill and label chart legend**—This code is used to draw a small rectangular icon, of the same color as the present bar, and then plot a bar legend label to the right of the icon. In this manner, each bar on the chart can be identified.

Applications that reach this size are best developed incrementally. This process is also at work in Chapters 10, 12, and 15. While the code has grown quite large, it has not become conceptually more difficult.

Running the Bar Chart Application

Let's look at a few examples generated by this application. Figure 15.7 shows the default bar chart, with the default labels, bars, and legend.

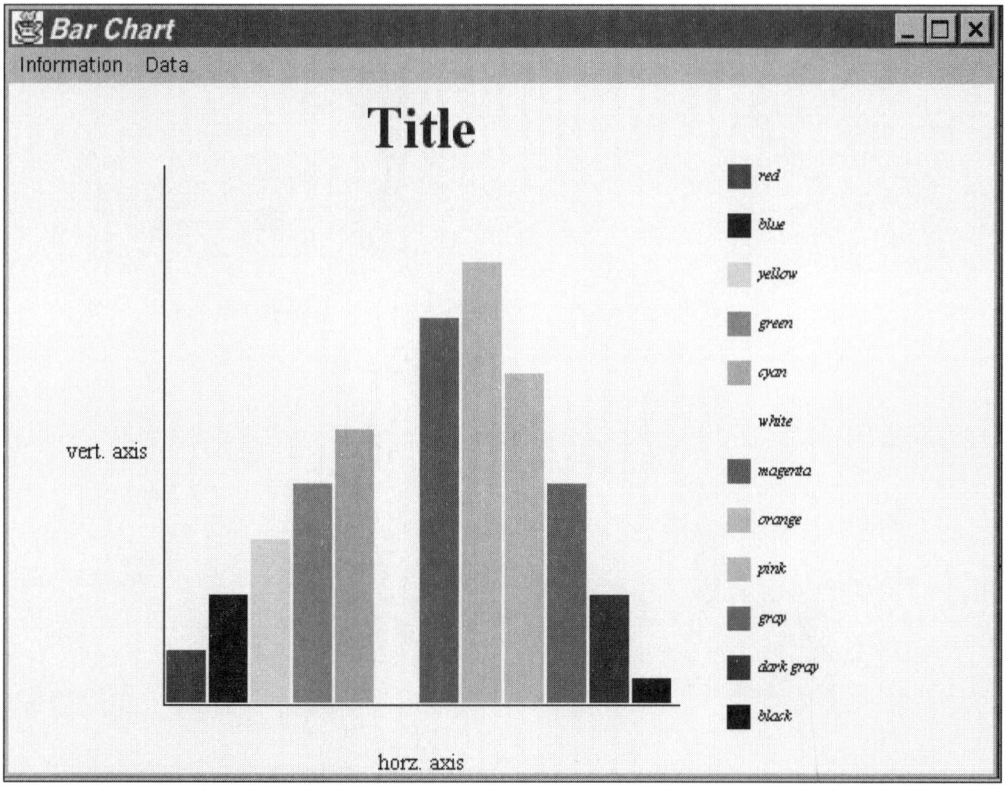

Figure 15.7: The default bar chart produced by the BarCht application.

Next, try experimenting by changing the bar chart labels, number of bars, and writing meaningful legend labels. As you can see in Figure 15.8, remember that everything you read might not necessarily be true.

A COMPLETE PIE CHART PROGRAM

Chapter 12 examined the development of a simple pie chart program. That application can now be expanded to include both menu and dialog resources. This section focuses on the efforts required to add the menu and dialog resources to the base code developed in Chapter 12. In this application, the menu and dialog box resources are created with the Microsoft Resource Editor, converted with the Java Resource Wizard, and included in the Java code as separate files. While this will make the pie chart listing considerably shorter than the bar chart

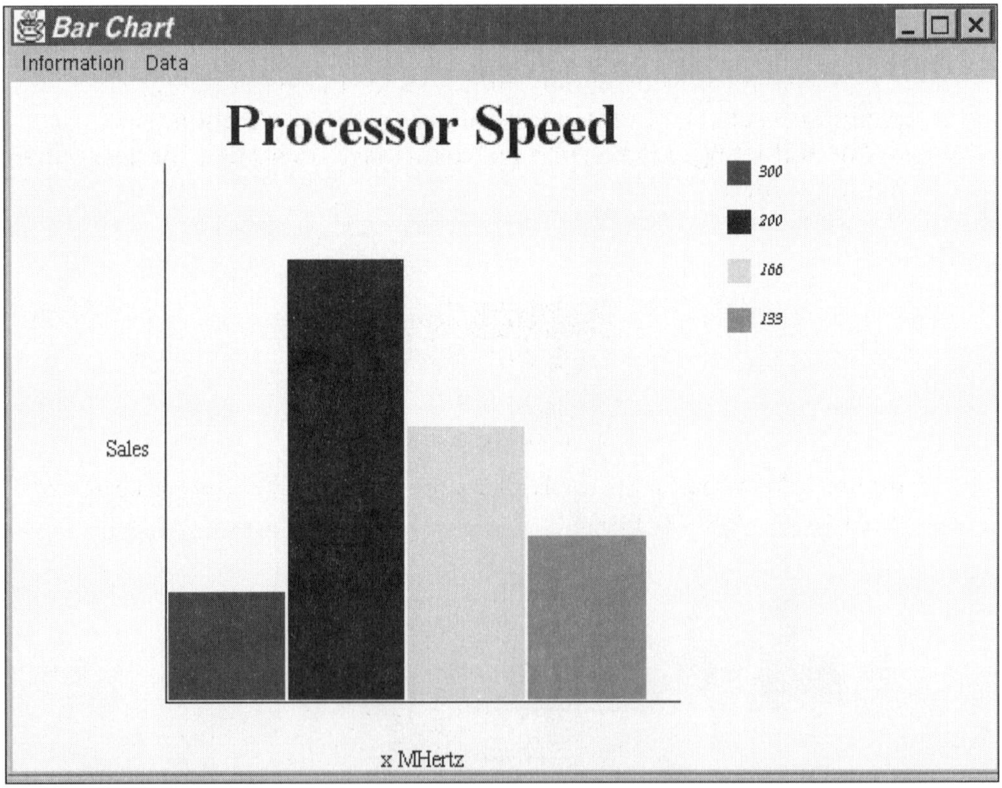

Figure 15.8: A unique bar chart demonstrates the range of values that can be used when plotting bar chart data.

application covered in this chapter, the number of separate files for the project does increase.

The next sections look at each of these files separately.

Resource Files

The resource files for this project include the menu and four dialog boxes. Each were designed with the Microsoft Resource Editor and converted with the Java Resource Wizard. The listings in the following sections are for the converted resource files. If you saved this resource information while in Resource Editor, the original files would be named Script1.rc and Script1.res. Once converted, the files are separated and named Menu1.java, Dlg1.java, Dlg2.java, Dlg3.java, and Dlg4.java,

The Menu1 Menu Resource The menu for this application consists of two menu bar items with multiple menu items. Figure 15.9 shows the first pop-up menu and menu items.

The second pop-up menu is shown in Figure 15.10.

The second pop-up menu allows users to access dialog boxes for entering labels, data, or legend values for the application.

The following code, saved as Menu1.java, describes the converted menu resource.

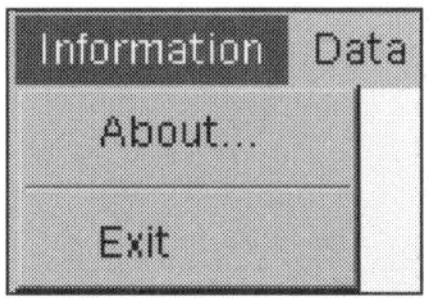

Figure 15.9: The PieCht application's first pop-up menu provides access to an About box and Exit option.

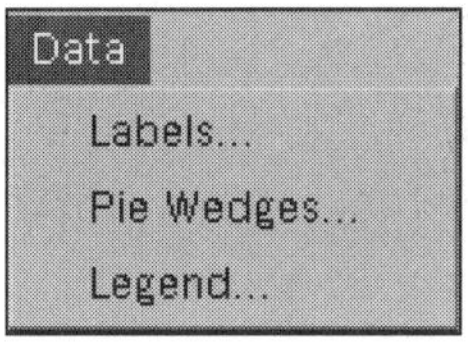

Figure 15.10: The second pop-up menu provides access to three data entry dialog boxes.

```
// ------------------------------------------------------------
// Menu1.java:
//     Implementation for menu creation class Menu1
//
//-----------------------------------------------------------
import java.awt.*;

public class Menu1
{
  Frame    m_Frame          = null;
  boolean m_fInitialized = false;

  // MenuBar definitions
  //----------------------------------------------------------
  MenuBar mb;

  // Menu and Menu item definitions
  //----------------------------------------------------------
  Menu m1;  // Information
  MenuItem m2;  // About...
  MenuItem m3;  // Separator
  MenuItem m4;  // Exit
  Menu m5;  // Data
  MenuItem m6;  // Labels...
  MenuItem m7;  // Pie Wedges...
  MenuItem m8;  // Legend...

  // Constructor
  //----------------------------------------------------------
  public Menu1 (Frame frame)
  {
    m_Frame = frame;
  }

  // Initialization.
  //----------------------------------------------------------
  public boolean CreateMenu()
  {
    // Can only init controls once
```

```
    //--------------------------------------------------------------
    if (m_fInitialized || m_Frame == null)
      return false;

    // Create menubar and attach to the frame
    //--------------------------------------------------------------
    mb = new MenuBar();
    m_Frame.setMenuBar(mb);

    // Create menu and menu items and assign to menubar
    //--------------------------------------------------------------
    m1 = new Menu("Information");
    mb.add(m1);
      m2 = new MenuItem("About...");
      m1.add(m2);
      m3 = new MenuItem("-");
      m1.add(m3);
      m4 = new MenuItem("Exit");
      m1.add(m4);
    m5 = new Menu("Data");
    mb.add(m5);
      m6 = new MenuItem("Labels...");
      m5.add(m6);
      m7 = new MenuItem("Pie Wedges...");
      m5.add(m7);
      m8 = new MenuItem("Legend...");
      m5.add(m8);

    m_fInitialized = true;
    return true;
  }
}
```

The main program listing will show how the Menu1.java resource file is accessed.

The Dlg1 About Dialog Box Resource The Dlg1.java file contains the description for the **About** dialog box resource used in this application. Figure 15.11 shows this **About** dialog box.

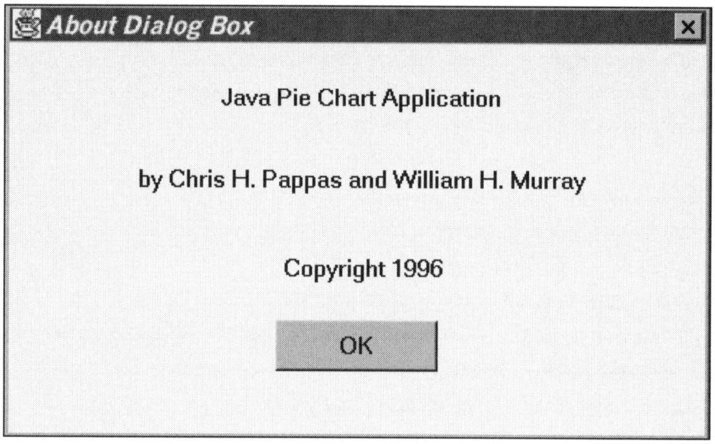

Figure 15.11: The About box resource used by the PieCht application.

About box resources and designs were first described in Chapter 14. The following code, saved as Dlg1.java, describes the converted **About** box resource.

```
//-----------------------------------------------------------------
// Dlg1.java:
//     Implementation of "control creator" class Dlg1
//-----------------------------------------------------------------

import java.awt.*;
import DialogLayout;

public class Dlg1
{
  Container     m_Parent        = null;
  boolean       m_fInitialized = false;
  DialogLayout m_Layout;

  // Control definitions
  //--------------------------------------------------------------
  Button        Btn1;
  Label         Lbl1;
  Label         Lbl2;
  Label         Lbl3;
```

```
// Constructor
//-------------------------------------------------------------
public Dlg1 (Container parent)
{
  m_Parent = parent;
}

// Initialization.
//-------------------------------------------------------------
public boolean CreateControls()
{
  // CreateControls should be called only once
  //-----------------------------------------------------------
  if (m_fInitialized || m_Parent == null)
    return false;

  // m_Parent must be extended from the Container class
  //-----------------------------------------------------------
  if (!(m_Parent instanceof Container))
    return false;

  // Since a given font may not be supported across all
  // platforms, it is safe to modify only the size of the
  // font, not the typeface.
  //-----------------------------------------------------------
    Font OldFnt = m_Parent.getFont();
    if (OldFnt != null)
    {
    Font NewFnt = new Font(OldFnt.getName(),
                           OldFnt.getStyle(), 16);

      m_Parent.setFont(NewFnt);
    }

  // All position and sizes are in dialog logical units,
  // so we use a DialogLayout as our layout manager.
  //-----------------------------------------------------------
  m_Layout = new DialogLayout(m_Parent, 218, 120);
  m_Parent.setLayout(m_Layout);
```

```
        m_Parent.addNotify();

        Dimension size    = m_Layout.getDialogSize();
        Insets    insets = m_Parent.insets();

        m_Parent.resize(insets.left + size.width  +
                        insets.right, insets.top  +
                        size.height + insets.bottom);

        // Control creation
        //----------------------------------------------------
        Btn1 = new Button ("OK");
        m_Parent.add(Btn1);
        m_Layout.setShape(Btn1, 83, 76, 50, 14);

        Lbl1 = new Label ("Java Pie Chart Application ",
                          Label.CENTER);
        m_Parent.add(Lbl1);
        m_Layout.setShape(Lbl1, 7, 7, 204, 16);

        Lbl2 = new Label ("by Chris Pappas and William Murray ",
                          Label.CENTER);
        m_Parent.add(Lbl2);
        m_Layout.setShape(Lbl2, 7, 29, 204, 17);

        Lbl3 = new Label ("Copyright 1996", Label.CENTER);
        m_Parent.add(Lbl3);
        m_Layout.setShape(Lbl3, 7, 53, 204, 18);

        m_fInitialized = true;
        return true;
    }
}
```

The main program listing will clarify how the Dlg1.java resource file is accessed.

The Dlg2 Label Dialog Box Resource The Dlg2.java file contains the description for the Label dialog box resource used in this application. Figure 15.12 shows this Label dialog box.

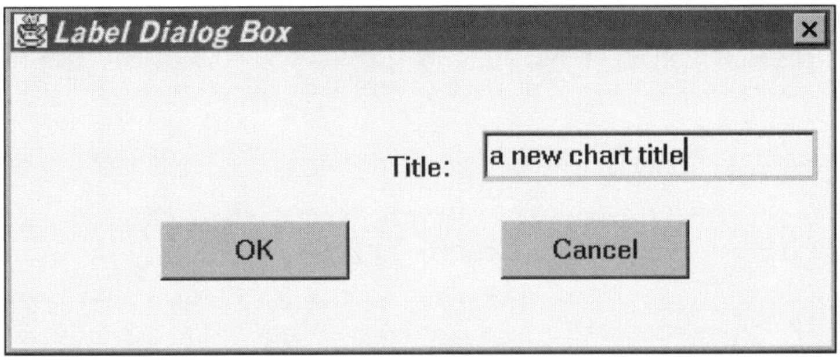

Figure 15.12: The Label dialog box resource used by the PieCht application.

The **Label** dialog box will be used to obtain a label, entered by the user, for the pie chart. The design of this dialog box is very similar to designing an **About** dialog box. However, there is one difference: the dialog box returns information to the application! The following code, saved as Dlg2.java, describes the converted **Label** dialog box resource.

```
//------------------------------------------------------------------
// Dlg2.java:
//    Implementation of "control creator" class Dlg2
//------------------------------------------------------------------
import java.awt.*;
import DialogLayout;

public class Dlg2
{
  Container    m_Parent       = null;
  boolean      m_fInitialized = false;
  DialogLayout m_Layout;

  // Control definitions
  //-----------------------------------------------------------------
  Button        Btn1;
  Button        Btn2;
  Label         Lbl1;
  static TextField Txt1;

  // Constructor
  //-----------------------------------------------------------------
  public Dlg2 (Container parent)
```

```
{
  m_Parent = parent;
}

// Initialization.
//--------------------------------------------------------------
public boolean CreateControls()
{
  // CreateControls should be called only once
  //--------------------------------------------------------------
  if (m_fInitialized || m_Parent == null)
    return false;

  // m_Parent must be extended from the Container class
  //--------------------------------------------------------------
  if (!(m_Parent instanceof Container))
    return false;

  // Since a given font may not be supported across all
  // platforms, it is safe to modify only the size of the
  // font, not the typeface.
  //--------------------------------------------------------------
    Font OldFnt = m_Parent.getFont();
    if (OldFnt != null)
    {
    Font NewFnt = new Font(OldFnt.getName(),
                           OldFnt.getStyle(), 16);

      m_Parent.setFont(NewFnt);
    }

  // All position and sizes are in dialog logical units,
  // so we use a DialogLayout as our layout manager.
  //--------------------------------------------------------------
  m_Layout = new DialogLayout(m_Parent, 221, 83);
  m_Parent.setLayout(m_Layout);
  m_Parent.addNotify();

  Dimension size   = m_Layout.getDialogSize();
  Insets    insets = m_Parent.insets();
```

```
        m_Parent.resize(insets.left + size.width  +
                        insets.right, insets.top  +
                        size.height + insets.bottom);

        // Control creation
        //-----------------------------------------------------
        Btn1 = new Button ("OK");
        m_Parent.add(Btn1);
        m_Layout.setShape(Btn1, 40, 40, 50, 14);

        Btn2 = new Button ("Cancel");
        m_Parent.add(Btn2);
        m_Layout.setShape(Btn2, 130, 40, 50, 14);

        Lbl1 = new Label ("Title:", Label.RIGHT);
        m_Parent.add(Lbl1);
        m_Layout.setShape(Lbl1, 7, 20, 110, 15);

        Txt1 = new TextField ("");
        m_Parent.add(Txt1);
        m_Layout.setShape(Txt1, 125, 19, 89, 12);

        m_fInitialized = true;
        return true;
    }
}
```

The discussion of the main program listing explains how to access the Dlg2.java resource file.

The Dlg3 Wedge Dialog Box Resource The Dlg3.java file contains the description for the **Wedge** dialog box resource used in this application. Figure 15.13 shows this **Wedge** dialog box.

The **Wedge** dialog box will be used to obtain all of the wedge sizes for the pie chart. The design of this dialog box is similar to the **Label** dialog box created in the previous section. The main difference is in the number of values to be entered by the user. In Figure 15.13, notice that all of the initial wedge sizes are set to zero. The reason for this is outlined in the discussion of the main program listing.

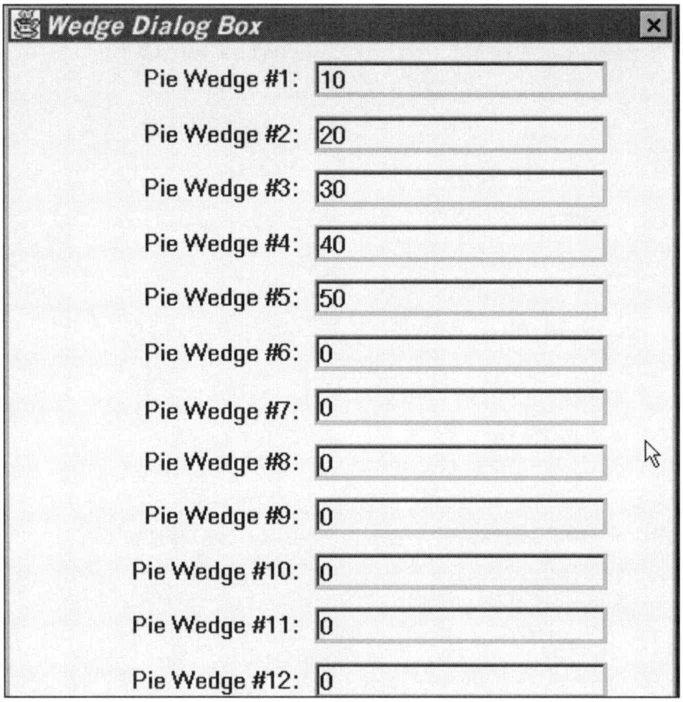

Figure 15.13: The Wedge dialog box resource used by the PieCht application.

The following code, saved as Dlg3.java, describes the converted **Wedge** dialog box resource.

```
//-----------------------------------------------------------------------
// Dlg3.java:
//     Implementation of "control creator" class Dlg3
//-----------------------------------------------------------------------
import java.awt.*;
import DialogLayout;

public class Dlg3
{
  Container     m_Parent        = null;
  boolean       m_fInitialized = false;
  DialogLayout m_Layout;

  // Control definitions
```

```
//--------------------------------------------------------------
Button        Btn1;
Button        Btn2;
Label         Lbl1;
Label         Lbl2;
Label         Lbl3;
Label         Lbl4;
Label         Lbl5;
Label         Lbl6;
Label         Lbl7;
Label         Lbl8;
Label         Lbl9;
Label         Lbl10;
Label         Lbl11;
Label         Lbl12;
static TextField Txt1;
static TextField Txt2;
static TextField Txt3;
static TextField Txt4;
static TextField Txt5;
static TextField Txt6;
static TextField Txt7;
static TextField Txt8;
static TextField Txt9;
static TextField Txt10;
static TextField Txt11;
static TextField Txt12;

// Constructor
//--------------------------------------------------------------
public Dlg3 (Container parent)
{
  m_Parent = parent;
}

// Initialization.
//--------------------------------------------------------------
public boolean CreateControls()
{
  // CreateControls should be called only once
```

```
//--------------------------------------------------------------
if (m_fInitialized || m_Parent == null)
  return false;

// m_Parent must be extended from the Container class
//--------------------------------------------------------------
if (!(m_Parent instanceof Container))
  return false;

// Since a given font may not be supported across all
// platforms, it is safe to modify only the size of the
// font, not the typeface.
//--------------------------------------------------------------
  Font OldFnt = m_Parent.getFont();
  if (OldFnt != null)
  {
  Font NewFnt = new Font(OldFnt.getName(),
                         OldFnt.getStyle(), 16);

    m_Parent.setFont(NewFnt);
  }

// All position and sizes are in dialog logical units,
// so we use a DialogLayout as our layout manager.
//--------------------------------------------------------------
m_Layout = new DialogLayout(m_Parent, 208, 228);
m_Parent.setLayout(m_Layout);
m_Parent.addNotify();

Dimension size   = m_Layout.getDialogSize();
Insets    insets = m_Parent.insets();

m_Parent.resize(insets.left + size.width  +
                insets.right, insets.top  +
                size.height + insets.bottom);

// Control creation
//--------------------------------------------------------------
Btn1 = new Button ("OK");
m_Parent.add(Btn1);
```

```
m_Layout.setShape(Btn1, 30, 185, 50, 14);

Btn2 = new Button ("Cancel");
m_Parent.add(Btn2);
m_Layout.setShape(Btn2, 95, 185, 50, 14);

Lbl1 = new Label ("Pie Wedge #1:", Label.RIGHT);
m_Parent.add(Lbl1);
m_Layout.setShape(Lbl1, 5, 5, 85, 10);

Lbl2 = new Label ("Pie Wedge #2:", Label.RIGHT);
m_Parent.add(Lbl2);
m_Layout.setShape(Lbl2, 5, 20, 85, 10);

Lbl3 = new Label ("Pie Wedge #3:", Label.RIGHT);
m_Parent.add(Lbl3);
m_Layout.setShape(Lbl3, 5, 35, 85, 10);

Lbl4 = new Label ("Pie Wedge #4:", Label.RIGHT);
m_Parent.add(Lbl4);
m_Layout.setShape(Lbl4, 5, 50, 85, 10);

Lbl5 = new Label ("Pie Wedge #5:", Label.RIGHT);
m_Parent.add(Lbl5);
m_Layout.setShape(Lbl5, 5, 65, 85, 10);

Lbl6 = new Label ("Pie Wedge #6:", Label.RIGHT);
m_Parent.add(Lbl6);
m_Layout.setShape(Lbl6, 5, 80, 85, 10);

Lbl7 = new Label ("Pie Wedge #7:", Label.RIGHT);
m_Parent.add(Lbl7);
m_Layout.setShape(Lbl7, 5, 96, 85, 10);

Lbl8 = new Label ("Pie Wedge #8:", Label.RIGHT);
m_Parent.add(Lbl8);
m_Layout.setShape(Lbl8, 5, 110, 85, 10);

Lbl9 = new Label ("Pie Wedge #9:", Label.RIGHT);
m_Parent.add(Lbl9);
```

```
m_Layout.setShape(Lbl9, 5, 125, 85, 10);

Lbl10 = new Label ("Pie Wedge #10:", Label.RIGHT);
m_Parent.add(Lbl10);
m_Layout.setShape(Lbl10, 5, 140, 85, 10);

Lbl11 = new Label ("Pie Wedge #11:", Label.RIGHT);
m_Parent.add(Lbl11);
m_Layout.setShape(Lbl11, 5, 155, 85, 10);

Lbl12 = new Label ("Pie Wedge #12:", Label.RIGHT);
m_Parent.add(Lbl12);
m_Layout.setShape(Lbl12, 5, 170, 85, 10);

Txt1 = new TextField ("0");
m_Parent.add(Txt1);
m_Layout.setShape(Txt1, 95, 5, 90, 10);

Txt2 = new TextField ("0");
m_Parent.add(Txt2);
m_Layout.setShape(Txt2, 95, 20, 90, 10);

Txt3 = new TextField ("0");
m_Parent.add(Txt3);
m_Layout.setShape(Txt3, 95, 35, 90, 10);

Txt4 = new TextField ("0");
m_Parent.add(Txt4);
m_Layout.setShape(Txt4, 95, 50, 90, 10);

Txt5 = new TextField ("0");
m_Parent.add(Txt5);
m_Layout.setShape(Txt5, 95, 65, 90, 10);

Txt6 = new TextField ("0");
m_Parent.add(Txt6);
m_Layout.setShape(Txt6, 95, 80, 90, 10);

Txt7 = new TextField ("0");
m_Parent.add(Txt7);
```

```
        m_Layout.setShape(Txt7, 95, 95, 90, 10);

        Txt8 = new TextField ("0");
        m_Parent.add(Txt8);
        m_Layout.setShape(Txt8, 95, 110, 90, 10);

        Txt9 = new TextField ("0");
        m_Parent.add(Txt9);
        m_Layout.setShape(Txt9, 95, 125, 90, 10);

        Txt10 = new TextField ("0");
        m_Parent.add(Txt10);
        m_Layout.setShape(Txt10, 95, 140, 90, 10);

        Txt11 = new TextField ("0");
        m_Parent.add(Txt11);
        m_Layout.setShape(Txt11, 95, 155, 90, 10);

        Txt12 = new TextField ("0");
        m_Parent.add(Txt12);
        m_Layout.setShape(Txt12, 95, 170, 90, 10);

        m_fInitialized = true;
        return true;
    }
}
```

There was only one modification made to this file. In the section, set in a bolded font, the static modifier is added to allow access to these variables from the PieCht.java file.

The discussion of the main program listing explains how to access the Dlg3.java resource file.

The Dlg4 Legend Dialog Box Resource The Dlg4.java file contains the description for the Legend dialog box resource used in this application. Figure 15.14 shows this Legend dialog box.

The **Legend** dialog box will be used to obtain all of the wedge legend labels for the pie chart. This dialog box is almost a carbon copy of the **Wedge** dialog box described in the previous section.

The following code, saved as Dlg4.java, describes the converted **Legend** dialog box resource.

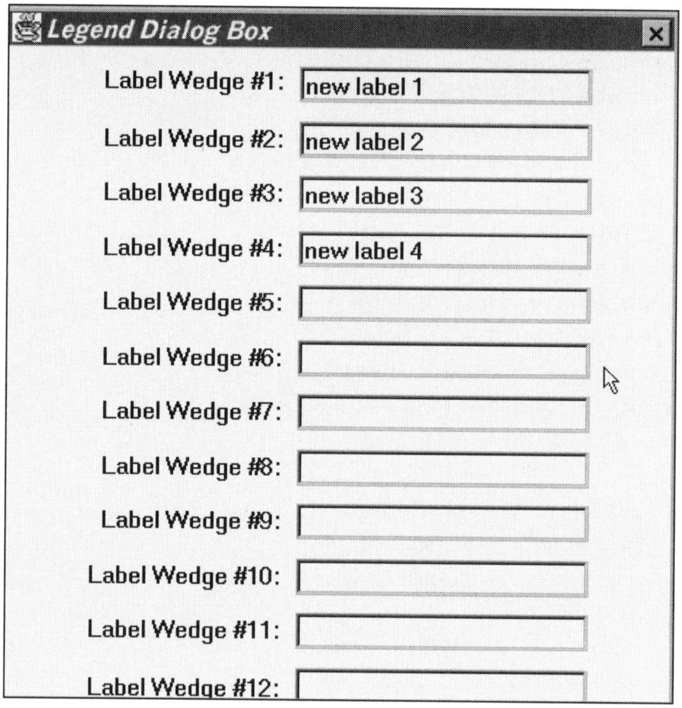

Figure 15.14: The Legend dialog box resource used by the PieCht application.

```
//------------------------------------------------------------------
// Dlg4.java:
//     Implementation of "control creator" class Dlg4
//------------------------------------------------------------------
import java.awt.*;
import DialogLayout;

public class Dlg4
{
  Container    m_Parent        = null;
  boolean      m_fInitialized  = false;
  DialogLayout m_Layout;

  // Control definitions
  //----------------------------------------------------------------
  Button         Btn1;
  Button         Btn2;
```

```
static TextField Txt1;
static TextField Txt2;
static TextField Txt3;
static TextField Txt4;
static TextField Txt5;
static TextField Txt6;
static TextField Txt7;
static TextField Txt8;
static TextField Txt9;
static TextField Txt10;
static TextField Txt11;
static TextField Txt12;
Label          Lbl1;
Label          Lbl2;
Label          Lbl3;
Label          Lbl4;
Label          Lbl5;
Label          Lbl6;
Label          Lbl7;
Label          Lbl8;
Label          Lbl9;
Label          Lbl10;
Label          Lbl11;
Label          Lbl12;


// Constructor
//-----------------------------------------------------------
public Dlg4 (Container parent)
{
  m_Parent = parent;
}

// Initialization.
//-----------------------------------------------------------
public boolean CreateControls()
{
  // CreateControls should be called only once
  //---------------------------------------------------------
  if (m_fInitialized || m_Parent == null)
```

```
    return false;

  // m_Parent must be extended from the Container class
  //-----------------------------------------------------------
  if (!(m_Parent instanceof Container))
    return false;

  // Since a given font may not be supported across all
  // platforms, it is safe to modify only the size of the
  // font, not the typeface.
  //-----------------------------------------------------------
    Font OldFnt = m_Parent.getFont();
    if (OldFnt != null)
    {
    Font NewFnt = new Font(OldFnt.getName(),
                           OldFnt.getStyle(), 16);

      m_Parent.setFont(NewFnt);
    }

  // All position and sizes are in dialog logical units,
  // so we use a DialogLayout as our layout manager.
  //-----------------------------------------------------------
  m_Layout = new DialogLayout(m_Parent, 208, 228);
  m_Parent.setLayout(m_Layout);
  m_Parent.addNotify();

  Dimension size   = m_Layout.getDialogSize();
  Insets    insets = m_Parent.insets();

  m_Parent.resize(insets.left + size.width  +
                  insets.right, insets.top  +
                  size.height + insets.bottom);

  // Control creation
  //-----------------------------------------------------------
  Btn1 = new Button ("OK");
  m_Parent.add(Btn1);
  m_Layout.setShape(Btn1, 30, 190, 50, 14);
```

```
Btn2 = new Button ("Cancel");
m_Parent.add(Btn2);
m_Layout.setShape(Btn2, 105, 190, 50, 14);

Txt1 = new TextField ("");
m_Parent.add(Txt1);
m_Layout.setShape(Txt1, 90, 5, 90, 10);

Txt2 = new TextField ("");
m_Parent.add(Txt2);
m_Layout.setShape(Txt2, 90, 20, 90, 10);

Txt3 = new TextField ("");
m_Parent.add(Txt3);
m_Layout.setShape(Txt3, 90, 35, 90, 10);

Txt4 = new TextField ("");
m_Parent.add(Txt4);
m_Layout.setShape(Txt4, 90, 50, 90, 10);

Txt5 = new TextField ("");
m_Parent.add(Txt5);
m_Layout.setShape(Txt5, 90, 65, 90, 10);

Txt6 = new TextField ("");
m_Parent.add(Txt6);
m_Layout.setShape(Txt6, 90, 80, 90, 10);

Txt7 = new TextField ("");
m_Parent.add(Txt7);
m_Layout.setShape(Txt7, 90, 95, 90, 10);

Txt8 = new TextField ("");
m_Parent.add(Txt8);
m_Layout.setShape(Txt8, 90, 110, 90, 10);

Txt9 = new TextField ("");
m_Parent.add(Txt9);
m_Layout.setShape(Txt9, 90, 125, 90, 10);
```

```
Txt10 = new TextField ("");
m_Parent.add(Txt10);
m_Layout.setShape(Txt10, 90, 140, 90, 10);

Txt11 = new TextField ("");
m_Parent.add(Txt11);
m_Layout.setShape(Txt11, 90, 155, 90, 10);

Txt12 = new TextField ("");
m_Parent.add(Txt12);
m_Layout.setShape(Txt12, 90, 170, 90, 10);

Lbl1 = new Label ("Label Wedge #1:", Label.RIGHT);
m_Parent.add(Lbl1);
m_Layout.setShape(Lbl1, 5, 5, 80, 8);

Lbl2 = new Label ("Label Wedge #2:", Label.RIGHT);
m_Parent.add(Lbl2);
m_Layout.setShape(Lbl2, 5, 20, 80, 10);

Lbl3 = new Label ("Label Wedge #3:", Label.RIGHT);
m_Parent.add(Lbl3);
m_Layout.setShape(Lbl3, 5, 35, 80, 10);

Lbl4 = new Label ("Label Wedge #4:", Label.RIGHT);
m_Parent.add(Lbl4);
m_Layout.setShape(Lbl4, 5, 50, 80, 10);

Lbl5 = new Label ("Label Wedge #5:", Label.RIGHT);
m_Parent.add(Lbl5);
m_Layout.setShape(Lbl5, 5, 65, 80, 10);

Lbl6 = new Label ("Label Wedge #6:", Label.RIGHT);
m_Parent.add(Lbl6);
m_Layout.setShape(Lbl6, 5, 80, 80, 10);

Lbl7 = new Label ("Label Wedge #7:", Label.RIGHT);
m_Parent.add(Lbl7);
m_Layout.setShape(Lbl7, 5, 95, 80, 10);
```

```
        Lbl8 = new Label ("Label Wedge #8:", Label.RIGHT);
        m_Parent.add(Lbl8);
        m_Layout.setShape(Lbl8, 5, 110, 80, 10);

        Lbl9 = new Label ("Label Wedge #9:", Label.RIGHT);
        m_Parent.add(Lbl9);
        m_Layout.setShape(Lbl9, 5, 125, 80, 10);

        Lbl10 = new Label ("Label Wedge #10:", Label.RIGHT);
        m_Parent.add(Lbl10);
        m_Layout.setShape(Lbl10, 5, 140, 80, 10);

        Lbl11 = new Label ("Label Wedge #11:", Label.RIGHT);
        m_Parent.add(Lbl11);
        m_Layout.setShape(Lbl11, 5, 155, 80, 10);

        Lbl12 = new Label ("Label Wedge #12:", Label.RIGHT);
        m_Parent.add(Lbl12);
        m_Layout.setShape(Lbl12, 5, 171, 80, 10);

        m_fInitialized = true;
        return true;
    }
}
```

Notice in this listing, in the portion set in a bolded font, that a static modifier has been added to allow access to these variables from the PieCht.java file.

The discussion of the main program listing explains how to access the Dlg4.java resource file.

The PieCht.java and PieChtFrame.java Files

The base code for the pie chart application, PieCht, is created by the Microsoft J++ Java Applet Wizard. If you are entering the pie chart application from the following listing, take your time to do it carefully. Here is the complete listing for the PieCht example. As you examine the listing, notice that several areas have been set in a bold font for later discussion, as was done with the bar chart example.

```
import java.applet.*;
import java.awt.*;
import PieChtFrame;

public class PieCht extends Applet
{
  // STANDALONE APPLICATION SUPPORT:
  //    m_fStandAlone will be set to true if applet is run
  // standalone
  //-----------------------------------------------------------
  boolean m_fStandAlone = false;

  public static void main(String args[])
  {
    PieChtFrame frame = new PieChtFrame("PieCht");

    // Must show Frame before we size it so insets() will
    // return valid values
    //---------------------------------------------------------
    frame.show();
    frame.hide();
    frame.resize(frame.insets().left+frame.insets().right+640,
           frame.insets().top  + frame.insets().bottom + 480);

    PieCht applet_PieCht = new PieCht();

    frame.add("Center", applet_PieCht);
    applet_PieCht.m_fStandAlone = true;
    applet_PieCht.init();
    applet_PieCht.start();
    // frame.show();
  }

  public PieCht()
  {
  }

  public String getAppletInfo()
  {
    return "Name: PieCht\r\n" +
```

```
            "Author: Chris H. Pappas and William H.
Murray\r\n"+
            "Created with Microsoft Visual J++";
  }

  public void init()
  {
    resize(640, 480);
    new MyFrame("");
  }

  public void destroy()
  {
  }

  public void paint(Graphics g)
  {
  }

  public void start()
  {
  }

  public void stop()
  {
  }

}

class MyFrame extends Frame
{
  NewCanvas newcanvas;
  static String charttitle = "Title";
  static String[] legend = {"red", "blue", "yellow", "green",
                            "cyan", "white", "magenta",
                            "orange", "pink", "gray",
                            "dark gray",  "black"};
  static String[] wedge = {"10", "20", "30", "40", "50",
                           "60", "70", "80", "60", "40",
                           "20", "5"};
```

```
MyFrame(String title) {
  // Add menu bar
  super("Pie Chart");
  add("Center", newcanvas = new NewCanvas());
  reshape(0, 0, 639, 479);

  // allows new menu bar and menu items
  // to be included from external menu1.java
  Menu1 extmenu = new Menu1(this);
  extmenu.CreateMenu();

  show();
}

public boolean action(Event event, Object object) {
  String label = (String)object;
  if (event.target instanceof MenuItem) {
    if(label.equals("About...")) {
      Dialog AbDialog = new AboutDialog(this);
      AbDialog.show();
    } else
    if(label.equals("Labels...")) {
      Dialog LabDialog = new LabelDialog(this);
      LabDialog.show();
    } else
    if(label.equals("Pie Wedges...")) {
      Dialog WgDialog = new WedgeDialog(this);
      WgDialog.show();
    } else
    if(label.equals("Legend...")) {
      Dialog LegDialog = new LegendDialog(this);
      LegDialog.show();
    } else
    if(label.equals("Exit")) {
      System.exit(0);
    }
    return true;
  }
  else
```

```
      return false;
    }

    public boolean handleEvent(Event event) {
      if(event.id == Event.WINDOW_DESTROY
        && event.target == this)
        System.exit(0);
      else return super.handleEvent(event);
      return true;
    }
}

// Information for About dialog box creation
class AboutDialog extends Dialog {
  public AboutDialog(Frame parent) {
    super(parent, "About Dialog Box", true);
    // Allows the About dialog box created
    // by the Java Resource Wizard to be used
    Dlg1 abdlg = new Dlg1(this);
    abdlg.CreateControls();
  }

  // process dialog box button events
  public boolean action(Event event, Object object) {
    String label = (String)object;
    if (event.target instanceof Button) {
      if(label.equals("OK")) {
        dispose();
      }
      return true;
    } else
    return false;
  }

  public boolean handleEvent(Event event) {
    if(event.id==Event.WINDOW_DESTROY)
      dispose();
    else return super.handleEvent(event);
    return true;
  }
```

```
}

// Information for Label dialog box creation
class LabelDialog extends Dialog {
  public LabelDialog(Frame parent) {
    super(parent, "Label Dialog Box", true);
    // Allows the Label dialog box created
    // by the Java Resource Wizard to be used
    Dlg2 lbdlg = new Dlg2(this);
    lbdlg.CreateControls();
  }

  // process dialog box button events
  public boolean action(Event event, Object object) {
    String label = (String)object;
    if (event.target instanceof Button) {
      if(label.equals("OK")) {
        dispose();
        // return data from dialog box
        MyFrame.charttitle = Dlg2.Txt1.getText();
      }
      else
        if (label.equals("Cancel")) {
          dispose();
      }
      return true;
    } else
    return super.action(event, object);
  }

  public boolean handleEvent(Event event) {
    if(event.id==Event.WINDOW_DESTROY)
      dispose();
    else return super.handleEvent(event);
    return true;
  }
}

// Information for Wedge dialog box creation
class WedgeDialog extends Dialog {
```

```
public WedgeDialog(Frame parent) {
  super(parent, "Wedge Dialog Box", true);
  // Allows the Wedge dialog box created
  // by the Java Resource Wizard to be used
  Dlg3 weddlg = new Dlg3(this);
  weddlg.CreateControls();
}

// process dialog box button events
public boolean action(Event event, Object object) {
  String label = (String)object;
  if (event.target instanceof Button) {
    if(label.equals("OK")) {
      // return data from dialog box
      MyFrame.wedge[0] = Dlg3.Txt1.getText();
      MyFrame.wedge[1] = Dlg3.Txt2.getText();
      MyFrame.wedge[2] = Dlg3.Txt3.getText();
      MyFrame.wedge[3] = Dlg3.Txt4.getText();
      MyFrame.wedge[4] = Dlg3.Txt5.getText();
      MyFrame.wedge[5] = Dlg3.Txt6.getText();
      MyFrame.wedge[6] = Dlg3.Txt7.getText();
      MyFrame.wedge[7] = Dlg3.Txt8.getText();
      MyFrame.wedge[8] = Dlg3.Txt9.getText();
      MyFrame.wedge[9] = Dlg3.Txt10.getText();
      MyFrame.wedge[10] = Dlg3.Txt11.getText();
      MyFrame.wedge[11] = Dlg3.Txt12.getText();
      dispose();
    }
    else
      if (label.equals("Cancel")) {
        dispose();
    }
    return true;
  } else
  return super.action(event, object);
}

public boolean handleEvent(Event event) {
  if(event.id==Event.WINDOW_DESTROY)
    dispose();
```

```
      else return super.handleEvent(event);
      return true;
    }
  }

  // Information for Legend dialog box creation
  class LegendDialog extends Dialog {
    public LegendDialog(Frame parent) {
      super(parent, "Legend Dialog Box", true);
      // Allows the Legend dialog box created
      // by the Java Resource Wizard to be used
      Dlg4 leddlg = new Dlg4(this);
      leddlg.CreateControls();
    }

    // process dialog box button events
    public boolean action(Event event, Object object) {
      String label = (String)object;
      if (event.target instanceof Button) {
        if(label.equals("OK")) {
          // return data from dialog box
          MyFrame.legend[0] = Dlg4.Txt1.getText();
          MyFrame.legend[1] = Dlg4.Txt2.getText();
          MyFrame.legend[2] = Dlg4.Txt3.getText();
          MyFrame.legend[3] = Dlg4.Txt4.getText();
          MyFrame.legend[4] = Dlg4.Txt5.getText();
          MyFrame.legend[5] = Dlg4.Txt6.getText();
          MyFrame.legend[6] = Dlg4.Txt7.getText();
          MyFrame.legend[7] = Dlg4.Txt8.getText();
          MyFrame.legend[8] = Dlg4.Txt9.getText();
          MyFrame.legend[9] = Dlg4.Txt10.getText();
          MyFrame.legend[10] = Dlg4.Txt11.getText();
          MyFrame.legend[11] = Dlg4.Txt12.getText();
          dispose();
        }
        else
          if (label.equals("Cancel")) {
            dispose();
        }
        return true;
```

```
    } else
    return super.action(event, object);
  }

  public boolean handleEvent(Event event) {
    if(event.id==Event.WINDOW_DESTROY)
      dispose();
    else return super.handleEvent(event);
    return true;
  }
}

class NewCanvas extends Canvas {
  Font titlefont, legendfont;
  FontMetrics fm;

  public void paint(Graphics g) {
    Color sliceColor[] = {Color.red,    // pie colors
                          Color.blue,
                          Color.yellow,
                          Color.green,
                          Color.cyan,
                          Color.white,
                          Color.magenta,
                          Color.orange,
                          Color.pink,
                          Color.gray,
                          Color.darkGray,
                          Color.black};
    int numWedges = 0;
    int oWeg[] = new int[12];
    int nWeg[] = new int[13];

    int maxWedge = 12;
    int tWeg = 0;
    int startAngle = 0;
    int sweepAngle = 0;

    g.translate(100, 90);          // move origin
```

```
// convert string to integer find # of wedges
for(int i = 0; i < maxWedge; i++) {
  oWeg[i] = Integer.parseInt(MyFrame.wedge[i]);
  if (oWeg[i] > 0) numWedges++;
}

for (int i = 0; i < numWedges; i++)
  tWeg += oWeg[i];

for (int i = 0; i < numWedges; i++)
  nWeg[i] =
(int)Math.round((double)(oWeg[i]*360)/tWeg);

sweepAngle = nWeg[0];

// create fonts
titlefont = new Font("TimesRoman", Font.BOLD, 36);
legendfont = new Font("TimesRoman", Font.ITALIC, 10);

// draw and center chart title
g.setFont(titlefont);
fm = getFontMetrics(titlefont);

g.drawString(MyFrame.charttitle,
            165 -
            (fm.stringWidth(MyFrame.charttitle)/2),
            -25);

// draw and fill pie slices
for (int i = 0; i < numWedges; ++i) {
  g.setColor(sliceColor[i]); // set fill color
  g.fillArc(0, 0, 300, 300,
            startAngle, sweepAngle);
  startAngle += nWeg[i];
  sweepAngle = nWeg[i+1];
}

// draw, fill and label chart legend
g.setFont(legendfont);
for (int i = 0; i < numWedges; i++) {
```

```
        g.setColor(sliceColor[i]); // set fill color
        g.fillRect(360, -20 + (i * 30), 15, 15);

        // wedge labels
        g.setColor(Color.black);   // set font color
        g.drawString(MyFrame.legend[i], 380,
                     -10 + (i * 30));
      }
    }
  }
```

Because this project is designed to run as a standalone application, a PieChtFrame.java file has also been created.

```
import java.awt.*;

class PieChtFrame extends Frame
{
  public PieChtFrame(String str)
  {
    super (str);
  }

  public boolean handleEvent(Event evt)
  {
    switch (evt.id)
    {
      case Event.WINDOW_DESTROY:
        dispose();
        System.exit(0);
        return true;

      default:
        return super.handleEvent(evt);
    }
  }
}
```

The following sections discuss the key aspects of this application's code and then examine several sample executions. You also discover that much of the work done in the previous bar chart example can be used again in the pie chart application.

Returning Dialog Box Data To access a dialog box, the user clicks on an appropriate menu item. Here is a small portion of code that shows how the menu item Pie Wedges... will allow access to the **Wedge** dialog box.

```
    .
    .
    .
if(label.equals("Pie Wedges...")) {
        Dialog WgDialog = new WedgeDialog(this);
        WgDialog.show();
    .
    .
    .
```

This code merely sends you to the WedgeDialog class listed later in the application. Here is a portion of the WedgeDialog class code:

```
// Information for Wedge dialog box creation
class WedgeDialog extends Dialog {
  public WedgeDialog(Frame parent) {
    super(parent, "Wedge Dialog Box", true);
    // Allows the Wedge dialog box created
    // by the Java Resource Wizard to be used
    Dlg3 weddlg = new Dlg3(this);
    weddlg.CreateControls();
  }
    .
    .
    .
```

This first portion of code, *weddlg,* uses the Dlg3 class to allow access to the external dialog box resource, Dlg3.java. The parent is identified with the **this** pointer. The **CreateControls()** member function draws the dialog box.

Next, an event handler is created to respond to various button actions. This dialog box uses two buttons, OK and Cancel.

```
    .
    .
    .
  // process dialog box button events
  public boolean action(Event event, Object object) {
    String label = (String)object;
```

```
    if (event.target instanceof Button) {
      if(label.equals("OK")) {
        // return data from dialog box
        MyFrame.wedge[0] = Dlg3.Txt1.getText();
        MyFrame.wedge[1] = Dlg3.Txt2.getText();
            .
            .
            .
        MyFrame.wedge[11] = Dlg3.Txt12.getText();
        dispose();
      }
      else
        if (label.equals("Cancel")) {
          dispose();
      }
      return true;
    } else
    return super.action(event, object);
  }
```

Returned dialog box information is processed when the user clicks the OK dialog box button. The idea is to return up to twelve pie wedge values to the application. The following code accesses the first Dlg3 data member.

```
MyFrame.wedge[0] = Dlg3.Txt1.getText();
```

Here, the dialog resource is identified (Dlg3), followed by the data member (*Txt1*) followed by the member function (**getText()**) used to obtain the text field value. The information is returned to the appropriate *wedge[0]* array value. The remaining eleven data values are obtained in a similar fashion. As noted shortly, these array values are converted to integer data.

If the user selects the Cancel button, the dialog box is disposed of without returning any new data.

All three data dialog boxes for this application return information in a similar manner.

Additional Action Events Handlers As you studied each dialog class description, in the main program listing, did you notice the addition of other event handlers? Each dialog box class also contains the following portion of code.

```
    public boolean handleEvent(Event event) {
      if(event.id==Event.WINDOW_DESTROY)
        dispose();
      else return super.handleEvent(event);
      return true;
    }
}
```

This code is required in order to allow the system menu and Close button in the dialog box frame to function properly. You might have noticed in the **About** dialog box example in Chapter 14 that these were nonfunctional!

By now, you have probably noticed that a similar problem occurs with the main frame window. In order to make those same frame items functional, the following code is added to the frame class code.

```
public boolean handleEvent(Event event) {
      if(event.id == Event.WINDOW_DESTROY
        && event.target == this)
        System.exit(0);
      else return super.handleEvent(event);
      return true;
  }
```

Pie Chart Code This section outlines the code for generating the pie chart itself. The pie graph discussed here has been under construction since Chapter 10. Much of the programming details have already been explained. This discussion is focused on blocks of important code that are preceded by a comment. All comments refer to the complete listing for the pie chart code shown earlier.

// **convert string to integer find # of wedges**—Converts the information returned to the *wedge[]* array as a string to integer information stored in the *oWeg[]* array. A parser, **Integer.parseInt()**, is used to make the conversion. Up to twelve pie wedges can be used on the pie chart, but the actual number is determined by scanning each entry looking for the first "0" value. The first zero value marks the end of the pie data. Each time a non-zero entry is found, the counter, *numWedges*, is incremented. That's why the dialog box initialized all initial entries to "0". The user changes values in order from first to last, the first unchanged value of "0" triggers the end of the wedge count!

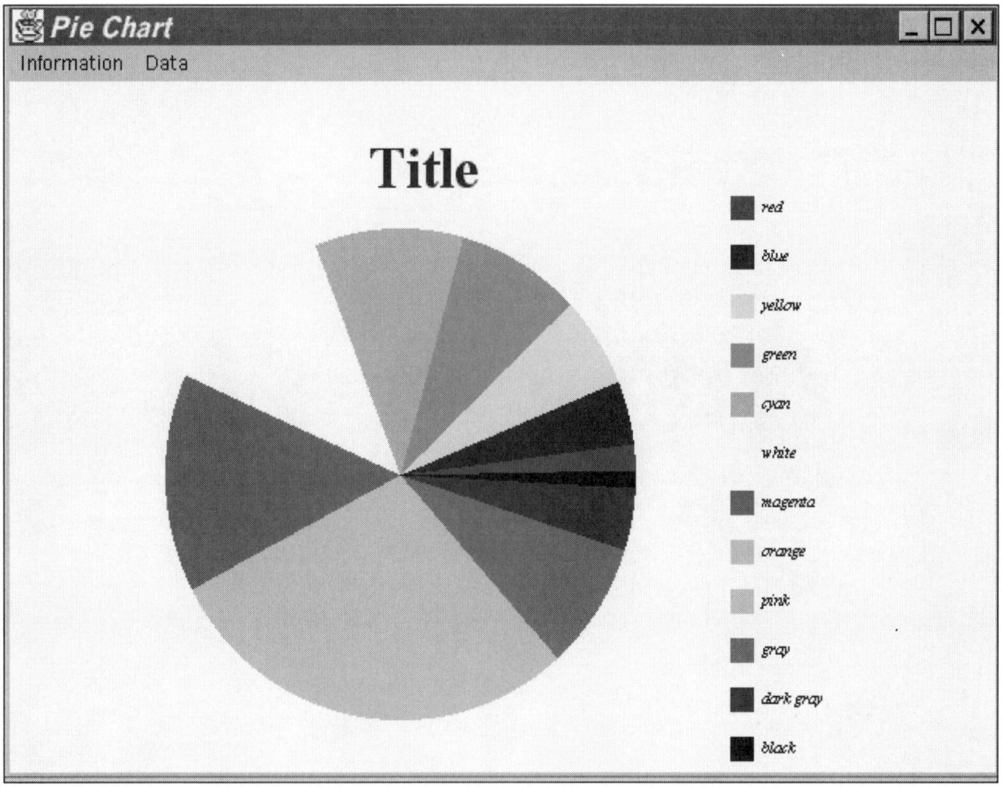

Figure 15.15: The default pie chart produced by the Piecht application.

Pie wedge widths are determined by first calculating the total number of individual wedge width values, then dividing each slice by the number to form a proportional slice value. This is done with the use of two separate **for** loops, as you can see by examining the code.

Next, the chart's fonts are created, and then the chart title is drawn.

// **draw and fill pie slices**—This section of code selects a wedge color from the *sliceColor[]* array then draws the wedge using the **fillArc()** member function. Values in the *startAngle* and *sweepAngle* variables are used to denote the new starting positions and ending positions for each slice or wedge.

// **draw, fill and label chart legend**—This code is used to draw a small rectangular icon, of the same color as the present pie slice. A legend label is drawn to the right of the icon. In this manner, each pie wedge on the chart can be identified.

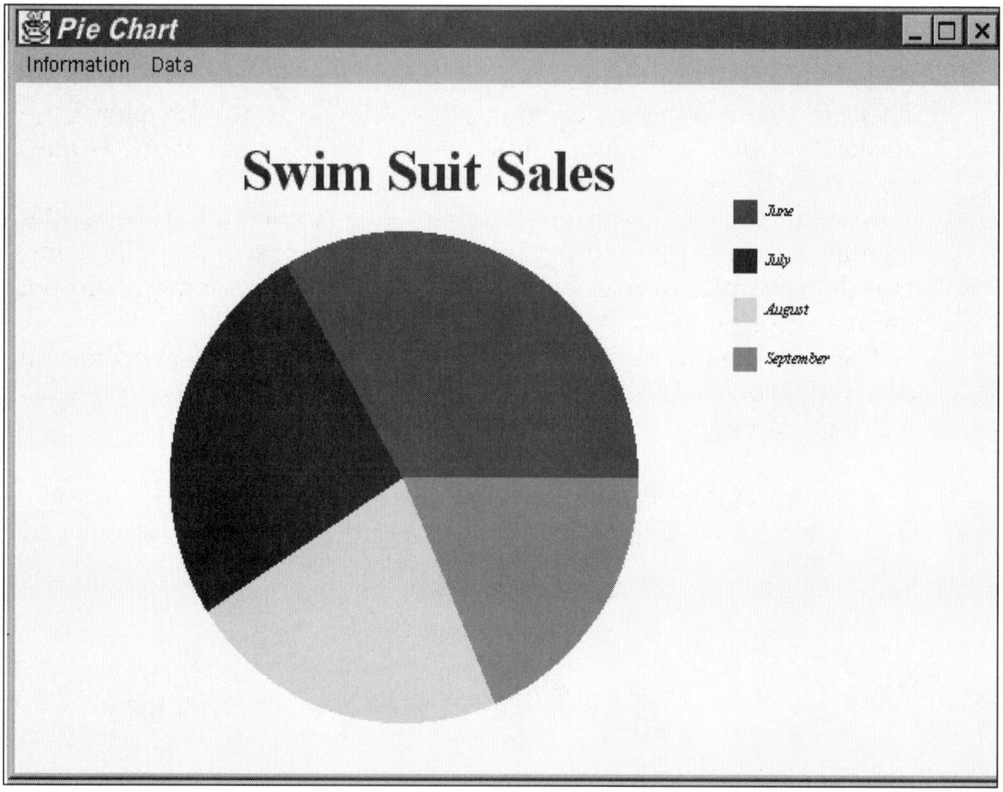

Figure 15.16: A unique pie chart demonstrates the unique values that can be used when plotting pie chart data.

RUNNING THE PIE CHART APPLICATION

Let's look at a few examples generated by this application. Figure 15.15 shows the default pie chart, with the default labels, pie wedges, and legend.

Next, you'll experiment by changing the pie chart title, changing the number of wedges, and writing new legend labels.

As you view Figure 15.16, remember that everything you read might not necessarily be true.

WHAT'S NEXT

First, notice that this chapter doesn't have a Coming To Terms section! There are no new terms or concepts presented in this chapter. Each application that you have studied, even though quite large, is built upon the concepts presented in earlier chapters.

So, what's next? It's up to you. You have studied all of the fundamental tools necessary to write robust Java applets and applications. Use the examples in this chapter as a guide for developing your own unique projects.

There is only one topic left—animation. If your applet or application demands motion during execution, you'll want to study the animation techniques presented in the next chapter.

Chapter 16

INVESTIGATING THREADS AND ANIMATION

This chapter builds on information from earlier chapters, adding just a few new programming concepts. It covers how to build multi-threaded applets and applets with animation. Chapter 4 explains the concepts relating to single and multiple-threaded programs. Chapter 10 covers techniques for retrieving graphics files and then drawing those objects in an applet. Chapter 11 explains how to incorporate sound resource files into your project. These key concepts and a little programming knowledge are used in this chapter to draw a few different images on the screen, and then move them about with a timing method. Instant animation!

The animation example uses four images of a flying saucer with a little creature inside. As the saucer bounces off each edge of the screen, the creature emits a sound (after all, it hurts). Four images are used to give the saucer and creature movement, within the larger context of moving the saucer about on the screen. All saucer movement is done with classical animation code for this type of action. If you are a C or C++ programmer, you might already be familiar with the type of coding that checks positions, movements, and boundary collisions.

WHY THREADS?

As noted in Chapter 4, threads can be used to allow multiple applets to run independently on the same screen. Thread support is used in the animation example that follows, too. Threads are easy to add with Microsoft's Java Applet Wizard. If thread support is requested during the applet specification process, the Applet Wizard adds all necessary code.

Here is the Microsoft Java Applet Wizard's template code, named NewThread, with thread support requested. The portion of the listing that deals directly with threads and that was added by the Applet Wizard is bolded.

```
import java.applet.*;
import java.awt.*;

public class NewThread extends Applet implements Runnable
{
  Thread    m_NewThread = null;


  public NewThread()
  {
  }

  public void finalize()
  {
  }

  public String getAppletInfo()
  {
    return "Name: NewThread\r\n" +
           "Author: Chris H. Pappas and William H. Murray\r\n"+
           "Created with Microsoft Visual J++";
  }

  public void init()
  {
    resize(640, 480);
  }

  public void destroy()
  {
  }
```

```
public void paint(Graphics g)
{
  g.drawString("Running: " + Math.random(), 10, 20);
}

public void start()
{
  if (m_NewThread == null)
  {
    m_NewThread = new Thread(this);
    m_NewThread.start();
  }
}

public void stop()
{
  if (m_NewThread != null)
  {
    m_NewThread.stop();
    m_NewThread = null;
  }
}

public void run()
{
  while (true)
  {
    try
    {
      repaint();
      Thread.sleep(50);
    }
    catch (InterruptedException e)
    {
      stop();
    }
  }
}
```

```
}
```

The Microsoft J++ compiler also provides an HTML file for applets.

```
<html>
<head>
<title>NewThread</title>
</head>
<body>
<hr>
<applet
    code=NewThread.class
    width=640
    height=480 >
</applet>
<hr>
<a href="NewThread.java">The source.</a>
</body>
</html>
```

This applet contains the necessary code and methods for starting (**start()**) and stopping (**stop()**) a thread. As you examine the previous listing, you'll also notice a **try/catch** block of code. This code is used to set a timer interval between each move of the saucer. When **Thread.sleep()** throws an exception, the exception will be caught by the **catch** portion of the code. In this case, an effective timer is created for each thread.

The previous portion really doesn't do much. However, if this base code is now integrated into an animation example, you'll be able to run multiple instances of the same applet independently of one another.

A SIMPLE ANIMATION EXAMPLE

This applet uses code that builds on the last example. Examine the following listing carefully. The animation portion of code has been set in a bold font.

```
import java.applet.*;
import java.awt.*;
import java.applet.AudioClip;
import SaucerFrame;
```

```
public class Saucer extends Applet implements Runnable
{
  Thread m_Saucer = null;

  Image saucer1, saucer2, saucer3, saucer4;
  AudioClip soundclip;
  static int xPosInit, yPosInit, xStep, yStep;
  static int xPos, yPos;

  // STANDALONE APPLICATION SUPPORT:
  //   m_fStandAlone will be set to true if applet is run
  //   standalone
  //--------------------------------------------------------------
  boolean m_fStandAlone = false;

  public static void main(String args[])
  {
    SaucerFrame frame = new SaucerFrame("Saucer");

    // Must show Frame before we size it so insets() will
    // return valid values
    //------------------------------------------------------------
    frame.show();
    frame.resize(frame.insets().left+frame.insets().right+640,
           frame.insets().top  + frame.insets().bottom + 480);

    Saucer applet_Saucer = new Saucer();

    frame.add("Center", applet_Saucer);
    applet_Saucer.m_fStandAlone = true;
    applet_Saucer.init();
    applet_Saucer.start();
  }

  public Saucer()
  {
  }

  public String getAppletInfo()
  {
```

```
  return "Name: Saucer\r\n" +
         "Author: Chris H. Pappas and William H. Murray\r\n"+
         "Created with Microsoft Visual J++";
}

public void init()
{
  resize(640, 480);

  saucer1 = getImage(getCodeBase(), "images/BMP1.gif");
  saucer2 = getImage(getCodeBase(), "images/BMP2.gif");
  saucer3 = getImage(getCodeBase(), "images/BMP3.gif");
  saucer4 = getImage(getCodeBase(), "images/BMP4.gif");
  soundclip = getAudioClip(getCodeBase(),
                           "audio/sound.au");

  int xPosInit = 100;
  int yPosInit = 100;
  xStep = 2;
  yStep = 2;
  xPos = xPosInit;
  yPos = yPosInit;
}

public void destroy()
{
}

public void paint(Graphics g)
{
  xPos+=xStep;
  yPos+=yStep;

  // draw image 1
  int objwidth = saucer1.getWidth(this);
  int objheight = saucer1.getHeight(this);
  g.drawImage(saucer1, xPos, yPos, this);
  timedelay(50);
```

```
    // draw image 2
    objwidth = saucer2.getWidth(this);
    objheight = saucer2.getHeight(this);
    g.drawImage(saucer2, xPos, yPos, this);
    timedelay(50);

    // draw image 3
    objwidth = saucer3.getWidth(this);
    objheight = saucer3.getHeight(this);
    g.drawImage(saucer3, xPos, yPos, this);
    timedelay(50);

    // draw image 4
    objwidth = saucer4.getWidth(this);
    objheight = saucer4.getHeight(this);
    g.drawImage(saucer4, xPos, yPos, this);
    timedelay(50);

    // check left and right window edges
    if((xPos+objwidth > 640) ||
        (xPos < 0)) {
         xStep=-xStep;
         soundclip.play();
    }

    // check top and bottom window edges
    if((yPos+objheight > 480) ||
        (yPos < 0)) {
         yStep=-yStep;
         soundclip.play();
    }
}

void timedelay(int time) {
    try
      Thread.sleep(time);
    catch (InterruptedException e) {};
}

public void start()
```

```
{
  if (m_Saucer == null)
  {
    m_Saucer = new Thread(this);
    m_Saucer.start();
  }
}

public void stop()
{
  if (m_Saucer != null)
  {
    m_Saucer.stop();
    m_Saucer = null;
  }
}

public void run()
{
  setBackground(Color.white);

  for (;;) {
    repaint();
    timedelay(100);
    xPos+=xStep;
    yPos+=yStep;
  }
}

public boolean mouseDown(Event evt, int x, int y)
{
  System.exit(0);
  return true;
}

// Key pressed
public boolean keyDown(Event event, int key)
{
  System.exit(0);
  return true;
```

```
    }

}
```

In the **init()** method, several graphical resources and a sound resource are brought into the thread. Additionally, several variables are initialized for starting the saucer's movement.

The **mouseDown()** and **keyDown()** member functions are added to allow the user to terminate the applet by pressing a key or clicking a mouse button.

The real programming action takes place under the **paint()** method, starting with the following portion of code.

```
xPos+=xStep;
yPos+=yStep;

// draw image 1
int objwidth = saucer1.getWidth(this);
int objheight = saucer1.getHeight(this);
graphic.drawImage(saucer1, xPos, yPos, this);
timedelay(50);
```

Each time the saucer is moved to a new screen location, a series of four saucer images are drawn with a 50-millisecond delay between images. Each of the four images moves an arm and changes a saucer light color. This gives the illusion that the creature within the saucer is having a panic attack at the thought of another collision with a screen edge. As you examine the listing, you'll notice four similar portions of code.

After the four images have been properly displayed, the xPos and yPos are checked against the screen boundaries. In this example, the dimensions of a VGA screen are hardwired into the code. You can change these values to a smaller number, or determine them automatically for the screen size you are currently using. Hardwiring the values keeps the coding much simpler.

You need to make two checks: one for the top and bottom collisions and one for the right and left collisions. Here is the portion of code that accomplishes that task.

```
// check left and right window edges
    if((xPos+objwidth > 640) ||
       (xPos < 0)) {
        xStep=-xStep;
```

```
        soundclip.play();
    }

    // check top and bottom window edges
    if((yPos+objheight > 480) ||
        (yPos < 0)) {
        yStep=-yStep;
        soundclip.play();
    }
```

The strategy is to simply change the direction of movement once a boundary is hit. The sound clip is played when any boundary is hit, making the user aware that the little creature has just suffered another rough encounter.

Each movement of the saucer requires that the old image be erased. In the following portion of code, this is done with **repaint()** without too much flicker on the screen. The time delay for the saucer movement, in addition to the delay inserted by drawing four different objects, is 100 milliseconds. The endless **for()** loop ensures that the saucer will continue to fly until the user terminates the application.

```
setBackground(Color.white);

for (;;) {
  repaint();
  timedelay(100);
  xPos+=xStep;
  yPos+=yStep;
}
```

The background color must be set to white in order to match the background color of each small graphic image.

A small HTML file is generated by the Microsoft J++ compiler because this is going to be run as an applet. Here is that HTML code.

```
<html>
<head>
<title>Saucer</title>
</head>
<body>
<hr>
<applet
    code=Saucer.class
```

```
    width=640
    height=480 >
</applet>
<hr>
<a href="Saucer.java">The source.</a>
</body>
</html>
```

The *width* and *height* values have been changed to match the dimensions of a VGA screen.

Figure 16.1 shows the helpless creature flying about on the screen.

The previous example can be modified to move other images about the screen, though it is not intended as a generic animation example. Microsoft, however, has provided generic code for that purpose. All you have to do is request animation support when you use the

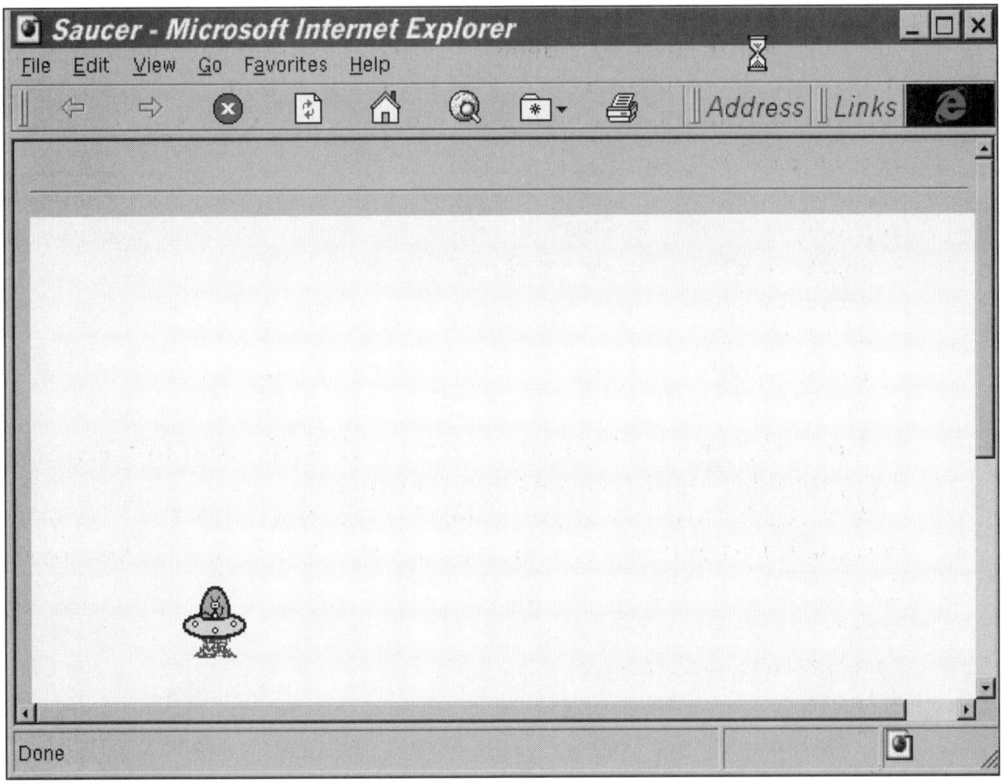

Figure 16.1: The creature and saucer moving about in a classical animation example written in Java.

Microsoft J++ Java Applet Wizard. You'll see how this is done in the next example.

A ROBUST ANIMATION EXAMPLE

You can include animation code in an application or applet when designing code with the Java Applet Wizard. The base animation code will load eighteen images of the world and then generate a rotating globe on the screen.

If you change the images, you can customize the animation base code to suit your needs. Here is the code for Animation.java.

```
import java.applet.*;
import java.awt.*;
import AnimationFrame;

public class Animation extends Applet implements Runnable
{
  Thread    m_Animation = null;

  private Graphics m_Graphics;
  private Image    m_Images[];
  private int      m_nCurrImage;
  private int      m_nImgWidth  = 0;
  private int      m_nImgHeight = 0;
  private boolean  m_fAllLoaded = false;
  private final int NUM_IMAGES = 18;

  // STANDALONE APPLICATION SUPPORT:
  //   m_fStandAlone will be set to true if applet is run
  //   standalone
  //----------------------------------------------------------
  boolean m_fStandAlone = false;

  public static void main(String args[])
  {
    AnimationFrame frame = new AnimationFrame("Animation");

    // Must show Frame before we size it so insets() will
    // return valid values
```

```
  //---------------------------------------------------------
  frame.show();
  frame.resize(frame.insets().left+frame.insets().right+640,
         frame.insets().top  + frame.insets().bottom + 480);

  Animation applet_Animation = new Animation();

  frame.add("Center", applet_Animation);
  applet_Animation.m_fStandAlone = true;
  applet_Animation.init();
  applet_Animation.start();
}

public Animation()
{
}

public String getAppletInfo()
{
  return "Name: Animation\r\n" +
         "Author: Chris H. Pappas and William H. Murray\r\n"+
         "Created with Microsoft Visual J++";
}

public void init()
{
  resize(640, 480);
}

public void destroy()
{
}

public boolean imageUpdate(Image img, int flags, int x,
                           int y, int w, int h)
{
  if (m_fAllLoaded)
    return false;
```

```
    if ((flags & ALLBITS) == 0)
      return true;

    if (++m_nCurrImage == NUM_IMAGES)
    {
      m_nCurrImage = 0;
      m_fAllLoaded = true;
    }

    return false;
  }

  private void displayImage(Graphics g)
  {
    if (!m_fAllLoaded)
      return;

    g.drawImage(m_Images[m_nCurrImage],
            (size().width - m_nImgWidth)   / 2,
            (size().height - m_nImgHeight) / 2, null);
  }

  public void paint(Graphics g)
  {
    // ANIMATION SUPPORT:
    //     The following code displays a status message until
    //     all the images are loaded. Then it calls
    //     displayImage to display the current image.
    //----------------------------------------------------------
    if (m_fAllLoaded)
    {
      Rectangle r = g.getClipRect();

      g.clearRect(r.x, r.y, r.width, r.height);
      displayImage(g);
    }
    else
      g.drawString("Loading images...", 10, 20);
  }
```

```
public void start()
{
  if (m_Animation == null)
  {
    m_Animation = new Thread(this);
    m_Animation.start();
  }
}

public void stop()
{
  if (m_Animation != null)
  {
    m_Animation.stop();
    m_Animation = null;
  }
}

public void run()
{
  repaint();

  m_Graphics = getGraphics();
  m_nCurrImage   = 0;
  m_Images    = new Image[NUM_IMAGES];

  String strImage;

  // For each image in the animation, this method first
  // constructs a string containing the path to the image
  // file; then it begins loading the image into the
  // m_Images array.  Note that the call to getImage
  // will return before the image is completely loaded.
  //-----------------------------------------------------------
  for (int i = 1; i <= NUM_IMAGES; i++)
  {
    strImage = "Image\img00"+((i < 10)?"0":"")+i+".gif";
    if (m_fStandAlone)
      m_Images[i-
1]=Toolkit.getDefaultToolkit().getImage(strImage);
```

```
    else
      m_Images[i-1]=getImage(getDocumentBase(), strImage);
    if (m_nImgWidth == 0)
    {
      try
      {
        // The getWidth() and getHeight() methods of the
        // Image class return -1 if the dimensions are not
        // yet known. The following code keeps calling
        // getWidth() and getHeight() until they return
        // actual values.
        // NOTE: This is only executed once in this loop,
        //       since we are assuming all images are the
        //       same width and height.  However, since we
        //       do not want to duplicate the above image
        //       load code, the code resides in the loop.
        //-----------------------------------------------
        while ((m_nImgWidth=m_Images[i-1].getWidth(null))<0)
          Thread.sleep(1);

        while ((m_nImgHeight=m_Images[i-1].getHeight(null))<0)
          Thread.sleep(1);
      }
      catch (InterruptedException e)
      {
      }
    }
    m_Graphics.drawImage(m_Images[i-1], -1000, -1000, this);
  }

  while (!m_fAllLoaded)
  {
    try
    {
      Thread.sleep(10);
    }
    catch (InterruptedException e)
    {
    }
```

```
      }

      repaint();

      while (true)
      {
        try
        {
          displayImage(m_Graphics);
          m_nCurrImage++;
          if (m_nCurrImage == NUM_IMAGES)
            m_nCurrImage = 0;

          Thread.sleep(50);
        }
        catch (InterruptedException e)
        {
          stop();
        }
      }
    }

}
```

The code that supports a standalone application is contained in the AnimationFrame.java file.

```
import java.awt.*;

class AnimationFrame extends Frame
{
  public AnimationFrame(String str)
  {
    super (str);
  }

  public boolean handleEvent(Event evt)
  {
    switch (evt.id)
    {
      case Event.WINDOW_DESTROY:
```

```
          dispose();
          System.exit(0);
          return true;

        default:
          return super.handleEvent(evt);
      }
    }
}
```

To run this example as an applet, use the following HTML file, generated by the Microsoft J++ Java Applet Wizard.

```
<html>
<head>
<title>Animation</title>
</head>
<body>
<hr>
<applet
    code=Animation.class
    width=640
    height=480 >
</applet>
<hr>
<a href="Animation.java">The source.</a>
</body>
</html>
```

Animation Code Highlights

If you examine the Animation.java code, you will notice three basic areas of interest: a portion of code that creates multiple threads, a portion of code responsible for locating and loading the various graphics images, and a portion of code responsible for displaying the images in sequence. What's new? Nothing! You have worked with similar code and you have expanded your programming skills throughout the book. Microsoft has just saved you from reinventing the wheel each time you want to add a portion of animation code.

With the base animation code, you can change the number of images, the images themselves, and even position them on a different portion of the screen.

Figure 16.2 shows a screen shot of the rotating globe example.

WHAT'S NEXT

You are now ready to launch your creative efforts to build standalone applications or applets to use on your own home page. The potential for programs is limitless. Animation catches user's attention and makes your programming efforts all the more professional in appearance.

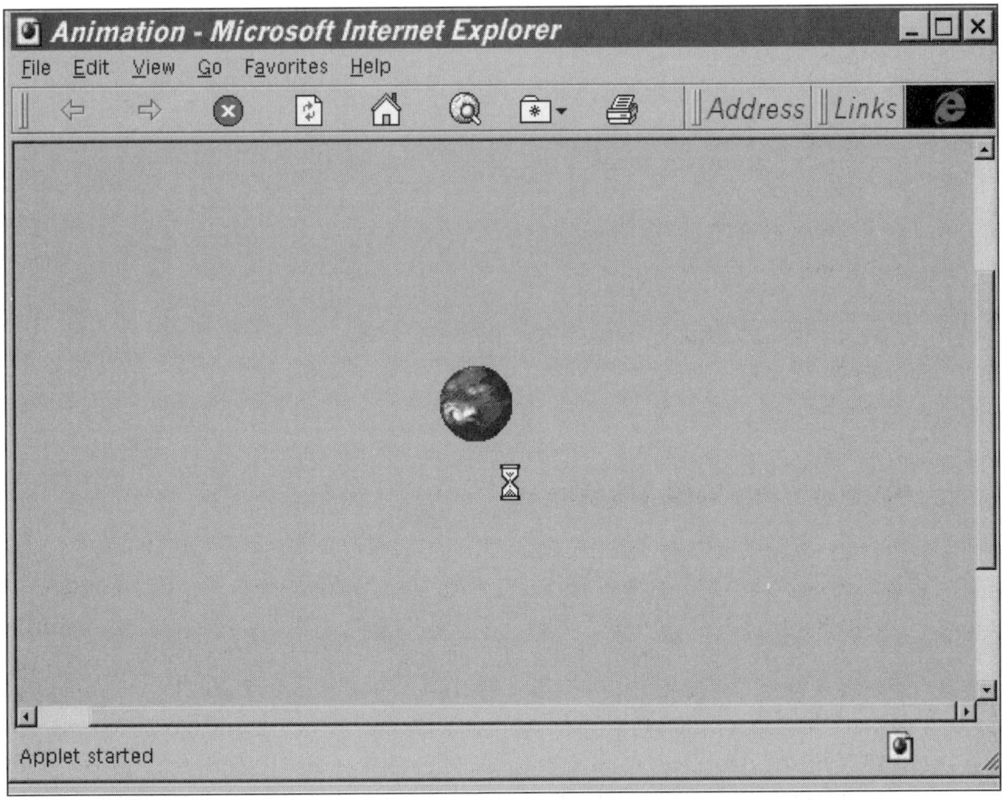

Figure 16.2: Microsoft's base code for animation generated a rotating globe.

Index

A

D

G

H

I

J

K

L

M

P

Q

R

S

T

U

V

W

Y

A 3.5-INCH HIGH-DENSITY DISK OFFER

A 3.5-inch high-density floppy disk is available containing all of the program listings in this book. To use the disk, you need a computer capable of using a 3.5-inch high-density (1.44MB) disk, with Windows properly installed and running. You must also be using the latest version of the Microsoft J++ compiler.

To order the disk, send a bank check, money order, or personal check for $20.00 in U.S. currency to the address below. Please allow three weeks for personal checks to clear. No purchase orders can be accepted. For all foreign orders, outside North America, please include a check drawn on a U.S. bank (U.S. currency) for $25.00. Foreign orders will be sent via Air Mail.

Please send me the program listings for this Microsoft J++ Java programming book by Pappas and Murray. Enclosed is a money order, bank check, or personal check for $20.00 ($25.00 for foreign orders) in U.S. funds, which covers the cost of the disk and all handling and postage. Sorry, no purchase orders can be accepted! This coupon may be copied. Note: Only 3.5-inch high-density (1.44MB) disks are available.

Mail to: Nineveh National Research
Microsoft J++ Disk Offer
P.O. Box 2943
Binghamton, NY 13902

Name: ____

Address: ____

City: ____

State:_____ ZIP: ____________

Country: ______________________

This is solely the offer of the authors. Academic-Press takes no responsibility for the fulfillment of this offer.